Interconnecting Cisco Network Devices

Steve McQuerry, Editor

Cisco Press

Cisco Press
201 West 103rd Street
Indianapolis, IN 46290 USA

Interconnecting Cisco Network Devices

Steve McQuerry, Editor

Copyright© 2000 Cisco Systems, Inc.

Published by:
Cisco Press
201 West 103rd Street
Indianapolis, IN 46290 USA

Printed in the United States of America   8 9 0

Eighth Printing September 2001

Library of Congress Cataloging-in-Publication Number: 98-86493

ISBN: 1-57870-111-2

Warning and Disclaimer

This book is designed to provide information about interconnecting Cisco network devices. Every effort has been made to make this book as complete and as accurate as possible, but no warranty or fitness is implied.

The information is provided on an "as is" basis. The author, Cisco Press, and Cisco Systems, Inc., shall have neither liability nor responsibility to any person or entity with respect to any loss or damages arising from the information contained in this book or from the use of the discs or programs that may accompany it.

The opinions expressed in this book belong to the author and are not necessarily those of Cisco Systems, Inc.

Trademark Acknowledgments

All terms mentioned in this book that are known to be trademarks or service marks have been appropriately capitalized. Cisco Press or Cisco Systems, Inc., cannot attest to the accuracy of this information. Use of a term in this book should not be regarded as affecting the validity of any trademark or service mark.

Feedback Information

At Cisco Press, our goal is to create in-depth technical books of the highest quality and value. Each book is crafted with care and precision, undergoing rigorous development that involves the unique expertise of members of the professional technical community.

Reader feedback is a natural continuation of this process. If you have any comments regarding how we could improve the quality of this book, or otherwise alter it to better suit your needs, you can contact us through e-mail at feedback@ciscopress.com. Please make sure to include the book title and ISBN in your message.

We greatly appreciate your assistance.

Publisher	John Wait
Editor-in-Chief	John Kane
Cisco Systems Management	Michael Hakkert
	Tom Geitner
	William Warren
Managing Editor	Patrick Kanouse
Senior Acquisitions Editor	Brett Bartow
Development Editor	Christopher Cleveland
Project Editor	Sheri Replin
Copy Editor	Gayle Johnson
Technical Editors	Elan Beer, Shawn Coville, David Hucaby, Stephen Wisniewski
Course Developers	Keith Serrao, Ilona Serrao, Pat Lao, Joe Bagg, Gary Hauser, Diane Teare
Team Coordinator	Amy Lewis
Book Designer	Gina Rexrode
Cover Designer	Louisa Klucznik
Compositor	Steve Gifford
Indexer	Christopher Cleveland
Proofreader	Bob LaRoche

CISCO SYSTEMS

Corporate Headquarters
Cisco Systems, Inc.
170 West Tasman Drive
San Jose, CA 95134-1706
USA
http://www.cisco.com
Tel: 408 526-4000
    800 553-NETS (6387)
Fax: 408 526-4100

European Headquarters
Cisco Systems Europe s.a.r.l.
Parc Evolic, Batiment L1/L2
16 Avenue du Quebec
Villebon, BP 706
91961 Courtaboeuf Cedex
France
http://www-europe.cisco.com
Tel: 33 1 69 18 61 00
Fax: 33 1 69 28 83 26

Americas Headquarters
Cisco Systems, Inc.
170 West Tasman Drive
San Jose, CA 95134-1706
USA
http://www.cisco.com
Tel: 408 526-7660
Fax: 408 527-0883

Asia Headquarters
Nihon Cisco Systems K.K.
Fuji Building, 9th Floor
3-2-3 Marunouchi
Chiyoda-ku, Tokyo 100
Japan
http://www.cisco.com
Tel: 81 3 5219 6250
Fax: 81 3 5219 6001

Cisco Systems has more than 200 offices in the following countries. Addresses, phone numbers, and fax numbers are listed on the Cisco Connection Online Web site at http://www.cisco.com/offices.

Argentina • Australia • Austria • Belgium • Brazil • Canada • Chile • China • Colombia • Costa Rica • Croatia • Czech Republic • Denmark • Dubai, UAE Finland • France • Germany • Greece • Hong Kong • Hungary • India • Indonesia • Ireland • Israel • Italy • Japan • Korea • Luxembourg • Malaysia Mexico • The Netherlands • New Zealand • Norway • Peru • Philippines • Poland • Portugal • Puerto Rico • Romania • Russia • Saudi Arabia • Singapore Slovakia • Slovenia • South Africa • Spain • Sweden • Switzerland • Taiwan • Thailand • Turkey • Ukraine • United Kingdom • United States • Venezuela

About the Editor

Steve McQuerry is a Certified Cisco Systems Instructor (CCSI) who works as a contract instructor and consultant throughout the U.S., teaching networking professionals how to configure and integrate Cisco equipment into their networks. Steve also holds CNE, MCSE, MCT, CCNP, and CCNA certifications. He has worked in the networking industry for over 10 years and has experience with multiple protocols in small and large networks, including TCP/IP and IPX. Steve currently teaches the Cisco courses ICND, ACRC, CIT, and CLSC with Global Knowledge.

About the Technical Reviewers

Elan Beer, CCIE# 1837. As president and founder of Synaptic Solutions Inc., for the past 14 years, Elan has held several key positions within the telecommunications industry, including Senior Telecommunications Consultant, Project Manager, and Telecommunications Instructor, as well as Canadian Training Manager with GeoTrain Corporation, a multinational training and consulting organization. Through his global consulting and training engagements, Elan is recognized internationally as a telecommunications industry expert. Elan's strong technical skills have enabled him to attain several top-level industry certifications, including Cisco Systems' top-level certification, the Cisco Certified Internetworking Expert (CCIE).

As one of the first product-based public Certified Cisco Instructors in the world, Elan has utilized his expertise in multiprotocol internetworking, LAN, WAN, and MAN technology, network management, and software engineering to provide training and consulting services to many of Canada's top companies. As a senior trainer and course developer, Elan has designed and presented intensive public and implementation-specific technical courses for clients in North America, Europe, Australia, Africa, Asia, and Scandinavia.

Shawn Coville, a double CCIE (#4432) in Routing and Switching and ISP-Dial, is a consultant and instructor for Chesapeake Computer Consultants, where he regularly teaches several Cisco router courses, including ICND, ACRC, BCRAN, and MCNS, as well as Check Point Firewall courses. In his consulting position, Shawn has gained extensive, practical experience in the installation and configuration of Cisco routers, PIX Firewall, and Cisco AS5200 access servers. Before joining Chesapeake, Shawn worked as a Senior Computer Specialist for the US Information Agency, where he was responsible for a worldwide Lotus Notes deployment and local-area network support, as well as Internet access installation.

David Hucaby, CCIE #4594, is a Senior Network Consultant for The Information Connection, where he provides consulting and troubleshooting services for a variety of clientele. He has extensive design, implementation, and management experience with switched and routed enterprise networks using Cisco Catalyst switches, routers, firewalls, VPNs, and IP telephony products. He has implemented network operations center services for multiple clients. Prior to his current position, David designed, implemented, and maintained networks for the University of Kentucky Hospital using Cisco routers and switches and IBM devices. David has a B.S. and M.S. in Electrical Engineering from the University of Kentucky.

Stephen Wisniewski has a master's degree in telecommunications management from Stevens Institute of Technology. His numerous network certifications include Microsoft MCSE, Novell CNE, Cisco CCNA, and Cisco CCNP. Stephen teaches telecommunications part-time at Devry Institute in North Brunswick, New Jersey, and he travels the world installing Cisco WAN networking implementations for Net2Phone Inc. Stephen resides in East Brunswick, New Jersey, with his wife, Ellen.

Dedications

I would like to dedicate this work to Becky, Katie, Logan, and Cameron, for the love, support, and understanding that only a family could offer.

Acknowledgments

I would like to acknowledge all of those who have been instrumental in making this book possible:

Cisco WWT and the course developers: Keith Serrao, Ilona Serrao, Pat Lao, Joe Bagg, Gary Hauser, and Diane Teare.

Everyone at Cisco Press, especially Amy Lewis, Brett Bartow, and Chris Cleveland, for all the patience they showed and guidance they offered during this process.

The technical editors—Elan Beer, Shawn Coville, Dave Hucaby, and Steve Wisniewski—for all their comments and suggestions. Their expertise and sharp eyes have been critical in providing a "sanity check" for me during the editing of this book.

All the students and instructors I have had the pleasure of teaching and working with over the past few years. Your questions, comments, and challenges offered many of the tips, cautions, and questions for this book.

My family, for their patience and understanding during this project and all of my projects.

God, for giving me the skills, talents, and opportunity to work in such a challenging and exciting profession.

Contents at a Glance

Contents

Foreword

In April 1998, Cisco Systems, Inc., announced a new professional development initiative called the Cisco Career Certifications. These certifications address the growing worldwide demand for more (and better) trained computer networking experts. Building upon our highly successful Cisco Certified Internetwork Expert (CCIE) program—the industry's most respected networking certification vehicle—Cisco Career Certifications enable you to be certified at various technical proficiency levels.

Interconnecting Cisco Network Devices presents, in book format, all the topics covered in the challenging instructor-led and e-learning certification preparation courses of the same name. The ICND courses are the latest iteration of the CCNA recommended training material previously covered in Introduction to Cisco Router Configuration (ICRC 11.3) and Cisco Routers and LAN Switches (CRLS 3.0), as well as a portion of Cisco LAN Switch Configuration (CLSC). Whether you are studying to become CCNA certified or you just need a better understanding of the concepts, commands, and practices required to configure Cisco switches and routers in multiprotocol networks, you will benefit from the information presented in this book.

Cisco and Cisco Press present this material in text-based format to provide another learning vehicle for our customers and the broader user community in general. Although a publication does not duplicate the instructor-led or e-learning environments, we acknowledge that not everyone responds in the same way to the same delivery mechanism. It is our intent that presenting this material via a Cisco Press publication will enhance the transfer of knowledge to a broad audience of networking professionals.

This is the seventh in a series of course supplements planned for Cisco Press, following *Introduction to Cisco Router Configuration, Advanced Cisco Router Configuration, Building Cisco Remote Access Networks, Cisco Internetwork Troubleshooting, Designing Cisco Networks,* and *Cisco Internetwork Design.* Cisco will present existing and future courses through these coursebooks to help achieve Cisco Worldwide Training's principal objectives: to educate the Cisco community of networking professionals and to enable that community to build and maintain reliable, scalable networks. The Cisco Career Certifications and classes that support these certifications are directed at meeting these objectives through a disciplined approach to progressive learning. The books Cisco creates in partnership with Cisco Press will meet the same standards for content quality demanded of our courses and certifications. It is our intent that you will find this and subsequent Cisco Press certification and training publications of value as you build your networking knowledge base.

Thomas M. Kelly

Director, Worldwide Training

Cisco Systems, Inc.

December 1999

Figure Icons Used in This Book

Throughout this book, you will see the following icons used for networking devices:

Router

Bridge

Hub

DSU/CSU

Catalyst
Switch

Multilayer
Switch

ATM
Switch

ISDN/Frame Relay
Switch

Communication
Server

Gateway

Access
Server

The following icons are used for peripherals and other devices:

PC

PC with
Software

Sun
Workstation

Macintosh

Terminal

File
Server

Web
Server

Cisco Works
Workstation

Printer

Laptop

IBM
Mainframe

Front End
Processor

Cluster
Controller

The following icons are used for networks and network connections:

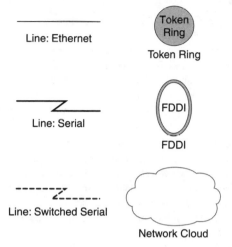

Line: Ethernet

Token Ring

Line: Serial

FDDI

Line: Switched Serial

Network Cloud

Introduction

Since the introduction of the personal computer in the early 1970s, businesses have found more uses and applications for technology in the workplace. With the introduction of local-area networks, file sharing, and print sharing in the 1980s, it became obvious that distributed computing was no longer a passing fad. By the 1990s, computers became less expensive, and innovations such as the Internet allowed everyone to connect to computer services worldwide. Computing was becoming big and distributed. The days of punch cards and greenbar paper are behind us, and a new generation of computing experts is being asked to keep this distributed technology operational. These experts are destined to have a new set of issues and problems to deal with, the most complex of them being connectivity and compatibility between differing systems and devices.

The primary challenge with data networking today is to link multiple devices' protocols and sites with maximum effectiveness and ease of use for the end users. Of course, this must all be accomplished in a cost-effective way. Cisco Systems offers a variety of products to give network managers and analysts the ability to face and solve the challenges of internetworking. As networking professionals begin working with this equipment to create solutions, they must understand how to use and configure these devices. Cisco Worldwide Training (WWT) develops courses to help networking professionals learn the fundamentals of configuring and installing Cisco products. This book is based on the Cisco WWT course Interconnecting Cisco Network Devices (ICND). ICND is a combination of and replaces two Cisco Courses: CRLS (Cisco Routers and LAN Switches) and ICRC (Introduction to Cisco Router Configuration). It also draws from CLSC (Cisco LAN Switch Configuration). ICND results in a single course that covers Cisco switches and routers in a realistic environment.

This book is based on the course materials. It presents the concepts, commands, and practices required to configure Cisco switches and routers in multiprotocol internetworks. You will find information that will help you identify and recommend the best Cisco solutions for small to medium-sized businesses. You will be introduced to all the basic configuration procedures required to build a multirouter, multigroup internetwork that uses LAN and WAN interfaces for the most commonly used routing and routed protocols. ICND provides the installation and configuration information that technical support people require to install and configure Cisco products.

This is an introductory-level book designed for people who have one to three years of internetworking experience, who are familiar with basic internetworking concepts, and who have some experience with the TCP/IP protocol. This book is useful for those who are pursuing the CCNA (Cisco Certified Networking Associate) certification. Also, network administrators responsible for implementing and managing small and medium-sized business networks might find the information in this book helpful. Network support staff who perform a help desk role in a medium- or enterprise-sized company will find this a valuable resource. Finally, Cisco customers or channel resellers and network technicians entering the internetworking industry who are new to Cisco products can benefit from the contents of this book.

Goals

Readers can expect to gain the knowledge needed to select, connect, and configure Cisco devices. You will learn the structure and terminology of the Cisco IOS (Internetwork Operating System). You will be introduced to the basic concepts of routing and Layer 2 switching, and you will learn how to select and configure Cisco devices to fill these roles in your data networks.

This book also helps you prepare for the CCNA certification, because it covers many of the topics associated with that test.

NOTE	Readers interested in the CCNA certification should consult the Cisco web site at http://www.cisco.com/warp/public/10/wwtraining/certprog/lan/programs/ccna.html for more information. To schedule a Cisco certification test, contact Sylvan Prometric at 800 204-EXAM or on the web at www.2test.com.

Chapter Organization

This book is broken up into five parts. This book is designed to be read in order, because many chapters build on content from a previous chapter.

Part I "Getting Started with Cisco Networks," includes chapters that contain an overview of networking and Cisco devices. Chapter 1, "Internetworking Concepts Overview," reviews some basic internetworking concepts. Chapter 2, "Assembling and Cabling Cisco Devices," explores the physical connections needed to assemble network devices. Chapter 3, "Operating and Configuring a Cisco IOS Device," explains the concepts and structure of the Cisco Internetwork Operating System. Chapter 4, "Managing Your Network Environment," discusses topics such as Telnet, configuration file management, and Cisco Discovery Protocol, which help you control and manage network devices.

Part II, "Interconnecting Catalyst Switches," explores the operation and configuration of the Catalyst 1900 switch. Chapter 5, "Catalyst 1900 Switch Operations," discusses basic switch theory, including IEEE 802.1 Spanning-Tree Protocol. This chapter also discusses basic switch configuration. Chapter 6, "Extending Switched Networks with Virtual LANs," explores the theory and operation of virtual LANs and interswitch VLAN configurations. This chapter includes discussions of Inter-Switch Link (ISL) trunking and the Virtual Trunking Protocol (VTP).

Part III, "Interconnecting Cisco Routers," looks at the interconnectivity between networks using Layer 3 protocols such as TCP/IP and IPX. Chapter 7, "Interconnecting Networks with TCP/IP," provides an overview of the TCP/IP protocol suite, including discussions of basic IP subnetting. This chapter also details how to configure IP addresses on your router interfaces. In Chapter 8, "Determining IP Routes," you learn how a router provides connectivity between the different networks in an internetwork. You also learn how routers exchange and maintain routing information using distance vector routing protocols such as the Routing Information Protocol (RIP) and Cisco's Interior Gateway Routing Protocol (IGRP). Chapter 9, "Basic IP Traffic Management with Access Lists," discusses the control of IP traffic. This chapter discusses the need to effectively manage IP traffic in the internetwork and shows you how access lists provide traffic management on Cisco routers. The final chapter in this part, Chapter 10, "Configuring Novell IPX," looks at the operation and configuration of Novell's Internetwork Packet Exchange (IPX) protocol. This chapter discusses IPX addressing, routing, and traffic control.

Part IV, "Extending the Network to WANs," looks beyond the local-area network (LAN) and discusses connecting devices across wide geographic locations. Chapter 11, "Establishing Serial Point-to-Point Connections," provides an overview of wide-area networking (WAN) connectivity. This chapter discusses methods of connecting to remote sites using leased lines with protocols such as PPP (Point-to-Point Protocol) and HDLC (High-Level Data Link Control). This chapter also discusses PPP options such as authentication. In Chapter 12, "Completing an ISDN BRI Call," you learn how to establish a dial-on-demand circuit to a remote site using Integrated Services Digital Network (ISDN) circuits. This chapter shows how this digital technology can be used to provide on-demand access to and from remote sites. Finally, in Chapter 13, "Establishing a Frame Relay PVC Connection," you learn how to connect remote sites through Frame Relay services. This chapter discusses the Frame Relay terminology, concepts, and parameters required to allow connectivity between remote locations.

Part V, "Appendixes," is the final part of this book. It begins with Appendix A, "Configuring AppleTalk," which discusses addressing, routing, and configuring routers connected to an AppleTalk network. Appendix B, "Establishing a HyperTerminal Session," walks you through the process of connecting your router to a PC or laptop for configuration purposes. Appendix C, "Cisco 700 Series Routers," examines the configuration and operation of the Cisco 700 series Small Office/Home Office (SOHO) router. In Appendix D, "Password Recovery," you learn how the configuration register is used to restore administrative control for a router. Finally, Appendix E, "Answers to Review Questions," provides answers to the review questions at the end of each chapter.

Features

This book features actual router and switch output to aid in the discussion of the configuration of these devices. There are also many notes, tips, and cautions spread throughout the text. In addition, you will find many references to standards, documents, books, and web sites that will help you understand networking concepts. At the end of each chapter, your comprehension and knowledge are tested by review questions prepared by a Cisco Certified Systems Instructor.

NOTE   The operating systems used in this book are Cisco IOS Version 12.0 for the routers and Cisco Catalyst 1900/2820 Enterprise Edition Software Version V8.01.01 for the switch.

Getting Started with Cisco Networks

Upon completion of this chapter, you will be able to perform the following tasks:

- Describe the process in which data is transferred from an application across a network.

- Given a network topology, identify the roles and functions of each network device and determine where each device best fits into the network.

- Given a network that combines switching, routing, and remote access, select the appropriate Cisco equipment.

CHAPTER 1

Internetworking Concepts Overview

The purpose of this chapter is to review basic internetworking concepts. These concepts are used throughout this book and are fundamental in understanding the functions of Cisco network devices.

Defining Network Components

The purpose of a data network is to help an organization increase productivity by linking all the computers and computer networks so that people have access to the information regardless of differences in time, location, or type of computer equipment.

Data networks have changed how we view our companies and employees. It is no longer necessary to have everyone in the same location in order to access the information needed to do the job. Because of this, many companies have changed their business strategy to utilize these networks in the way they do business. It is now typical for a company to organize the corporate internetwork in a way that allows it to optimize its resources. Figure 1-1 shows that the network is defined based on grouping employees (users) in the following ways:

- The main office is where everyone is connected to a LAN and where the majority of the corporate information is located. A main office could have hundreds or thousands of users who depend on the network to do their jobs. The main office might be a building with many local-area networks (LANs) or might be a campus of such buildings. Because everyone needs access to central resources and information, it is common to see a high-speed backbone LAN as well as a centralized data center with mainframe computers and application servers.

- The other connections are a variety of remote access locations that need to connect to the resources at the main offices and/or each other, including the following:

    - **Branch offices**—These are remote locations where smaller groups of people work. These users connect to each other via a LAN. In order to access the main office, these users access wide-area network (WAN) services. Although some information might be stored at the branch office, it is likely that users will have to access much of the data from the main office. How often the main office network is accessed determines whether the WAN connection will be a permanent or dialup connection.

— **Telecommuters**—These are employees who work out of their homes. These users typically require an on-demand connection to the main office and/or the branch office in order to access network resources.

— **Mobile users**—These individuals work from various locations and rely on different services to connect to the network. While at the main or branch offices, these users connect to the LAN. When they are out of the office, these users usually rely on dialup services to connect to the corporate network.

Figure 1-1 *Corporate Networking Strategy*

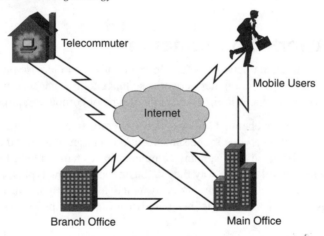

In order to understand what types of equipment and services to deploy in your network and when, it is important to understand business and user needs. You can then subdivide the network into a hierarchical model that spans from the end user's machine to the core (backbone) of the network. Figure 1-2 shows how the different employee groups interconnect.

To subdivide an internetwork into smaller components, Cisco uses a three-layer hierarchical model, as described in the following section.

Figure 1-2 *Group Interconnection*

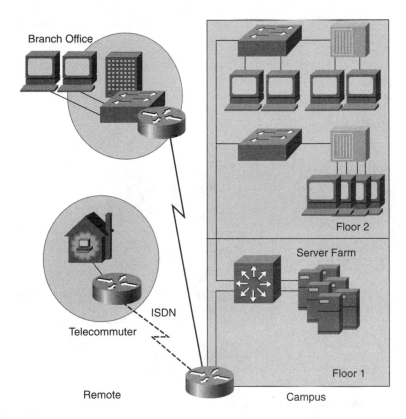

Mapping Business Needs to a Hierarchical Model

To simplify network designs, implementation, and management, Cisco uses a hierarchical model to describe the network. Although using this model is typically associated with designing a network, it is important to understand the model in order to know what equipment and features are needed in your network.

Campus networks have traditionally placed basic network-level intelligence and services at the center of the network and shared bandwidth at the user level. As businesses continue to place more emphasis on the network as a productivity tool, distributed network services and switching will continue to migrate to the desktop level.

User demands and network applications have forced networking professionals to use the traffic patterns in the network as the criteria for building an internetwork. Networks cannot be divided into subnetworks based only on the number of users. The emergence of servers that run global applications also has a direct impact on the load across the network. A higher traffic load across the entire network results in the need for more efficient routing and switching techniques.

Traffic patterns now dictate the type of services needed by end users in networks. To properly build an internetwork that can effectively address a user's needs, a three-layer hierarchical model is used to organize traffic flow (see Figure 1-3).

Figure 1-3   *Three-Layer Hierarchical Network Model*

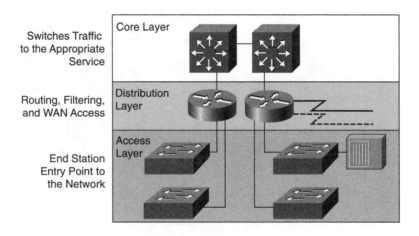

The model consists of three layers:

- Access
- Distribution
- Core

Each of these layers serves a function in delivering network services, as described in the following sections.

Access Layer

The access layer of the network is the point at which end users are connected to the network. This is why the access layer is sometimes referred to as the desktop layer. Users, and the resources they need to access most, are locally available. Traffic to and from local resources is confined between the resources, switches, and end users. Multiple groups of users and their resources exist at the access layer.

In many networks, it is not possible to provide users with local access to all services, such as database files, centralized storage, or dial-out access to the web. In these cases, user traffic for these services is directed to the next layer in the model, the distribution layer.

Distribution Layer

The distribution layer of the network (also referred to as the workgroup layer) marks the point between the access layer and the core services of the network. It is the primary function of this layer to perform functions such as routing, filtering, and WAN access. In a campus environment, the distribution layer represents a multitude of functions, including the following:

- Serving as an aggregation point for access layer devices
- Routing traffic to provide departmental or workgroup access
- Segmenting the network into multiple broadcast/multicast domains
- Translating between different media types, such as Token Ring and Ethernet
- Providing security and filtering services

The distribution layer can be summarized as the layer that provides policy-based connectivity, because it determines if and how packets can access the core services of the network. The distribution layer determines the fastest way for a user request (such as file server access) to be forwarded to the server. After the distribution layer chooses the path, it forwards the request to the core layer. The core layer then quickly transports the request to the appropriate service.

Core Layer

The core layer (also called the backbone layer) switches traffic as fast as possible to the appropriate service. Typically, the traffic being transported is to and from services common to all users. These services are referred to as global or enterprise services. Examples of these services are e-mail, Internet access, and videoconferencing.

When a user needs access to enterprise services, the request is processed at the distribution layer. The distribution layer device then forwards the user's request to the backbone. The backbone simply provides quick transport to the desired enterprise service. The distribution layer device provides controlled access to the core.

To properly build a network, you must first understand how your internetwork is used, your business needs, and your user needs. Those needs can then be mapped into a model that can be used to build your internetwork.

One of the best ways to understand how to build an internetwork is to first understand the way in which traffic is passed across the network. This is done through a conceptual network framework, the most popular of which is the OSI reference model. It is described in the following sections.

OSI Reference Model Overview

The OSI reference model serves several functions for the internetworking community:

- It provides a way to understand how an internetwork operates.

- It serves as a guideline or framework for creating and implementing network standards, devices, and internetworking schemes.

Here are some of the advantages of using a layered model:

- Breaks down the complex operation of networking into simple elements.

- Enables engineers to specialize design and development efforts on modular functions.

- Provides the capability to define standard interfaces for "plug-and-play" compatibility and multivendor integration.

As shown in Figure 1-4, the OSI reference model has seven layers. The four lower layers define ways for end stations to establish connections to each other in order to exchange data. The three upper layers define how the applications within the end stations will communicate with each other and with the users.

Figure 1-4   *OSI Reference Model*

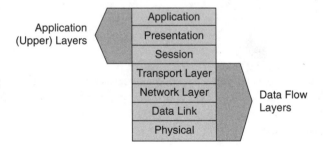

The following sections break down the layers and look at how they function to provide network connectivity.

Upper Layers

The three upper layers of the OSI reference model are often referred to as the *application* layers. These layers deal with the user interface, data formatting, and application access. Figure 1-5 shows the upper layers and provides information on their functionality with some examples.

Figure 1-5   *Upper Layers*

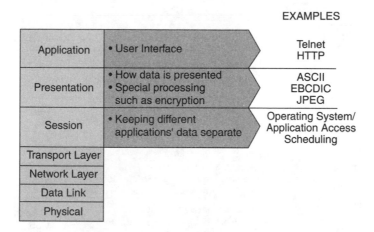

- **Application layer**—This is the highest layer of the model. It is the point where the user or application interfaces with the protocols to gain access to the network. For example, a word processor is serviced by file transfer services at this layer.

- **Presentation layer**—The presentation layer provides a variety of coding and conversion functions that are applied to application layer data. These functions ensure that data sent from the application layer of one system can be read by the application layer of another system. An example of coding functions is the encryption of data after it leaves an application. Another example is the jpeg and gif formats of images displayed on web pages. This formatting ensures that all web browsers, regardless of operating system, can display the images.

- **Session layer**—The session layer is responsible for establishing, managing, and terminating communications sessions between presentation layer entities. Communication at this layer consists of service requests and responses that occur between applications located in different devices. An example of this type of coordination would be between a database server and a database client.

Lower Layers

The four lower layers of the OSI reference model are responsible for defining how data is transferred across a physical wire, through internetwork devices, to the desired end station, and finally to the application on the other side. The focus of this book is Cisco's implementation of these layers. Figure 1-6 summarizes the basic functions of these four layers. We will discuss each layer in greater detail later in this chapter.

Figure 1-6   *Lower Layers*

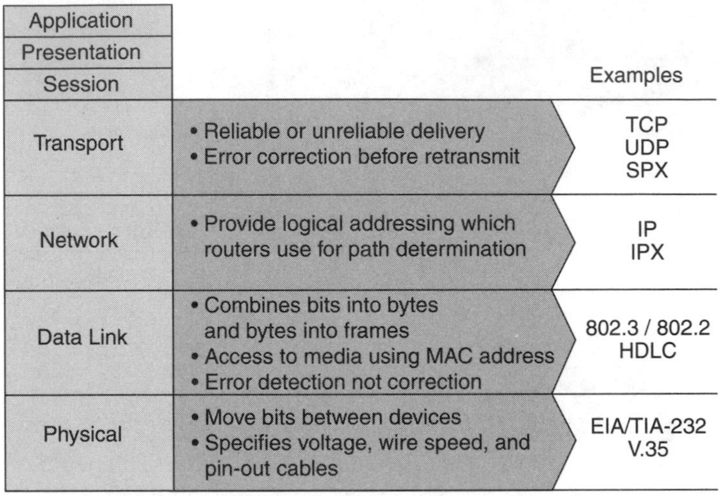

		Examples
Application		
Presentation		
Session		
Transport	• Reliable or unreliable delivery • Error correction before retransmit	TCP UDP SPX
Network	• Provide logical addressing which routers use for path determination	IP IPX
Data Link	• Combines bits into bytes and bytes into frames • Access to media using MAC address • Error detection not correction	802.3 / 802.2 HDLC
Physical	• Move bits between devices • Specifies voltage, wire speed, and pin-out cables	EIA/TIA-232 V.35

Communicating Between OSI Reference Model Layers

It is the responsibility of the protocol stack to provide communications between network devices. A protocol stack is the set of rules that define how information travels across the network. An example of this would be TCP/IP. The OSI reference model provides the basic framework common to most protocol stacks.

Each layer of the model allows data to pass across the network. These layers exchange information to provide communications between the network devices. The layers communicate with one another using protocol data units (PDUs). These PDUs control information that is added to the user data. The control information resides in fields called *headers* and *trailers*. In Figure 1-7, the Media Access Control (MAC) header and frame check sequence (FCS) at the data link layer represent a header and trailer.

Figure 1-7   *Data Encapsulation*

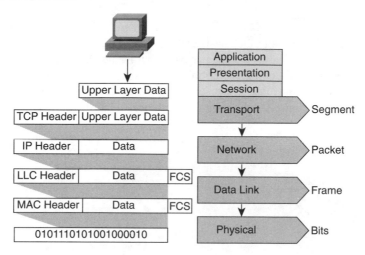

Because a PDU includes different information as it goes up or down the layers, it is given a name according to the information it is carrying. For example, in a TCP/IP stack (see Figure 1-7), after a transport layer TCP header has been added to the upper-layer data, that unit is called a *segment*. The segment is then passed down to the network layer, where an IP header is added, and it becomes a *packet*. The packet is packaged into a Layer 2 header, which becomes a *frame*. Finally, the frame is converted into bits, and the electrical signals are transmitted across the network media.

This method of passing data down the stack and adding headers and trailers is called *encapsulation*. After the data is encapsulated and passed across the network, the receiving device removes the information added, using the messages in the header as directions on how to pass the data up the stack to the appropriate application.

Data encapsulation is an important concept to networks. It is the function of like layers on each device, called *peer* layers, to communicate critical parameters such as addressing and control information.

Although encapsulation seems like an abstract concept, it is actually quite simple. Imagine that you want to send a coffee mug to a friend in another city. How will the mug get there? Basically, it will be transported on the road or through the air. You can't go outside and set the mug on the road or throw it up in the air and expect it to get there. You need a service to pick it up and deliver it. So, you call your favorite parcel carrier and give them the mug. But, that's not all. You need to give the carrier some information as to where the mug is going. So you provide the parcel carrier with an address and send the mug on its way. But first, the mug needs to be packaged. Here's the complete process:

Step 1   Pack the mug in a box.

Step 2   Place an address label on the box.

Step 3 Give the box to a parcel carrier.

Step 4 The carrier drives it down the road.

This process is similar to the encapsulation method that protocol stacks use to send data across networks. After the package arrives, your friend has to reverse the process. He takes the package from the carrier, reads the label to see who it's from, and finally opens the box and removes the mug. The reverse of the encapsulation process is known as de-encapsulation. Figure 1-8 represents the de-encapsulation process up a protocol stack.

Figure 1-8 *De-Encapsulation*

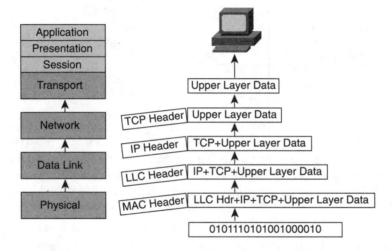

As networking professionals, it is our responsibility to implement networks that support the transport of user data. In order to implement and configure devices to do this, we must understand the processes of the lower layers of the OSI model. Understanding these processes makes configuring and troubleshooting network devices less troublesome.

Physical Layer Functions

To fully understand the network process, we must first closely examine each of the lower layers. Starting with the physical layer, shown in Figure 1-9, we will examine the function of each layer.

Figure 1-9   *Physical Layer*

The physical layer defines the media type, connector type, and signaling type. It specifies the electrical, mechanical, procedural, and functional requirements for activating, maintaining, and deactivating the physical link between end systems. The physical layer also specifies characteristics such as voltage levels, data rates, maximum transmission distances, and physical connectors. In the analogy used earlier, the physical layer is the road on which the mug is carried. The roadway is a physical connection between different cities that allows us to go from one place to another. Different roads have different rules, such as speed limits or weight limits, just as different network media have different bandwidths or maximum transmission units (MTUs).

Physical Media and Connectors

The physical media and the connectors used to connect devices into the media are defined by standards at the physical layer. In this book, the primary focus is on the standards that are associated with Ethernet implementations.

The Ethernet and IEEE 802.3 (CSMA/CD) standards define a bus topology LAN that operates at a baseband signaling rate of 10 megabits per second (Mbps). Figure 1-10 shows three defined physical layer wiring standards, defined as follows:

- **10Base2**—Known as Thinnet. Allows network segments up to 185 meters on coaxial cable by interconnecting or chaining devices together.

- **10Base5**—Known as Thicknet. Allows network segments up to 500 meters on large coaxial cable with devices tapping into the cable to receive signals.

- **10BaseT**—Carries Ethernet signals up to 100 meters on inexpensive twisted-pair wiring back to a centralized concentrator called a *hub*.

Figure 1-10 *Defined Physical Layer 10Base Wiring Standards*

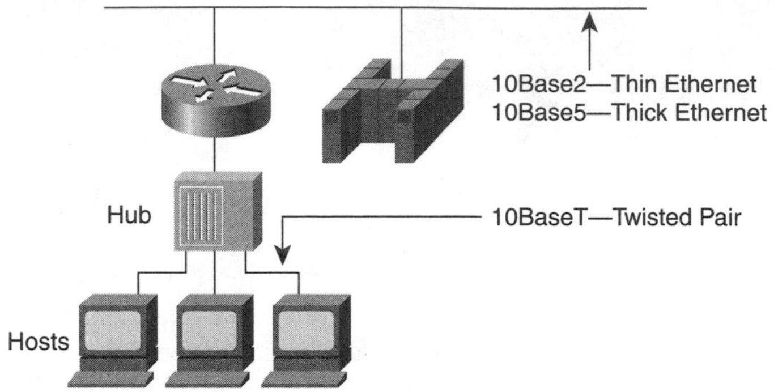

The 10Base5 and 10Base2 standards provide access for multiple stations on the same segment by physically connecting each device to a common Ethernet segment. 10Base5 cables attach to the bus using a cable and an attachment unit interface (AUI). 10Base2 networks chain devices together using coaxial cable and T connectors to connect the stations to the common bus.

Because the 10BaseT standard provides access for a single station at a time, each station must attach to a common bus structure to interconnect all the devices. The hub becomes the bus of the Ethernet devices and is analogous to the segment.

Collision/Broadcast Domains

Because all stations on an Ethernet segment are connected to the same physical media, signals sent out across that wire are received by all devices. This also means that if any two devices send out a signal at the same time, those signals will collide. The structure of Ethernet must therefore have rules that allow only one station to access the media at a time. There must also be a way to detect and correct errors known as *collisions* (when two or more stations try to transmit at the same time).

When discussing networks, it is critical to define two important concepts:

- **Collision domain**—A group of devices connected to the same physical media such that if two devices access the media at the same time, the result is a collision of the two signals

- **Broadcast domain**—A group of devices in the network that receive one another's broadcast messages

These terms help you understand the basic structure of traffic patterns and help define the needs for devices such as switches and routers.

Most Ethernet segments today are devices interconnected with hubs. Hubs allow the concentration of many Ethernet devices into a centralized device that connects all the devices to the same physical bus structure in the hub. This means that all the devices connected to the hub share the same media and, consequently, share the same collision domain, broadcast domain, and bandwidth. The resulting physical connection is that of a star topology as opposed to a linear topology. Figure 1-11 shows a common connection to the hub.

Figure 1-11 *Ethernet Hub*

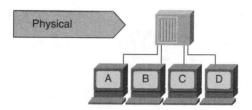

A hub does not manipulate or view the traffic that crosses that bus; it is used only to extend the physical media by repeating the signal it receives in one port out all the other ports. This means that a hub is a physical layer device. It is concerned only with propagation of the physical signaling, without any regard for upper-layer functions. This does not change the rules of Ethernet, however. Stations still share the bus of the hub, which means that contention still occurs.

Because all devices are connected to the same physical media, a hub is a single collision domain. If one station sends out a broadcast, the hub propagates it to all other stations, so it is also a single broadcast domain.

The Ethernet technology used in this instance is known as carrier sense multiple access collision detection (CSMA/CD). This means that multiple stations have access to the media, and before one station can access that media, it must first "listen" (carrier sense) to make sure that no other station is using the same media. If the media is in use, the station must wait before sending out any data. If two stations both listen and hear no other traffic, and then they both try to transmit at the same time, the result is a collision.

For example, in Figure 1-12, both cars try to occupy the same road at the same time, and they collide. In a network, as with cars, the resulting collision causes damage. In fact, the damaged frames become error frames, which the stations detect as a collision, forcing both stations to retransmit their respective frames. A backoff algorithm determines when the stations retransmit in order to minimize the chance of another collision. The more stations that exist on an Ethernet segment, the greater the chance that collisions will occur. These excessive collisions are the reason that networks are segmented (broken up) into smaller collision domains using switches and bridges.

Figure 1-12 *Ethernet Collisions*

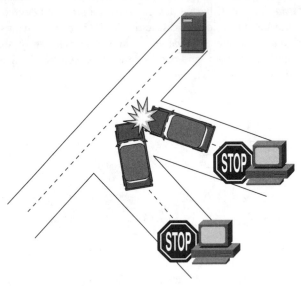

Data Link Layer Functions

Before traffic can be placed on the network, it must be given some details about where to go and what to do when it gets there. The data link layer provides this function. The data link layer is Layer 2 of the OSI reference model, and it differs depending on the topology. Figure 1-13 shows the various physical topologies and some corresponding data link encapsulation methods.

Figure 1-13 *Data Link Layer*

Physical	Data Link
Ethernet	
802.3	802.2
EIA/TIA-232	HDLC
V.35	Frame Relay

The purpose of this layer is to provide the communications between workstations at the first logical layer above the bits on the wire. Because of this, many functions are provided by the data link layer. The physical addressing of the end stations is done at the data link layer to help the network devices determine whether they should pass a message up the protocol stack. Fields also exist in this layer to tell the device which upper-layer stack to pass the data to (such as IP, IPX, AppleTalk, and so on). The data link layer provides support for connection-oriented and connectionless services and provides for sequencing and flow control.

To provide these functions, the IEEE data link layer is defined by two sublayers:

- **Media Access Control (MAC) Sublayer (802.3)**—The Media Access Control (MAC) sublayer is responsible for how the data is transported over the physical wire. This is the part of the data link layer that communicates downward to the physical layer. It defines such functions as physical addressing, network topology, line discipline, error notification, orderly delivery of frames, and optional flow control.

- **Logical Link Control (LLC) Sublayer (802.2)**—The Logical Link Control sublayer is responsible for logically identifying different protocol types and then encapsulating them in order to be transmitted across the network. A type code or service access point (SAP) identifier does the logical identification. The type of LLC frame used by an end station depends on what identifier the upper-layer protocol expects. Additional LLC options include support for connections between applications running on the LAN, flow control to the upper layer, and sequence control bits. For some protocols, LLC defines reliable or unreliable services for data transfer, instead of the transport layer. (Reliable and unreliable services are discussed further in the section, "Transport Layer Functions.")

MAC Sublayer Frames

Figure 1-14 illustrates the frame structure for the MAC sublayer IEEE 802.3 frames.

Figure 1-14 *MAC Sublayer Frame*

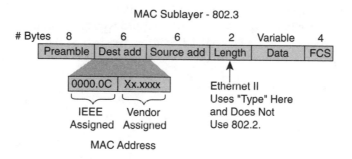

Figure 1-14 shows the standard frame structure to provide an example of how control information is used to transmit information at this layer. The definitions of the MAC sublayer fields are as follows:

- The IEEE 802.3 frame begins with an alternating pattern of 1s and 0s called a *preamble*. The preamble tells receiving stations that a frame is coming.

- Immediately following the preamble are the *destination* and *source physical address* fields. These addresses are referred to as *MAC layer addresses*. They are unique to each device in the internetwork. On most LAN interface cards, the MAC address is burned into ROM, thus explaining the term burned-in-address (BIA). When the network interface card initializes, this address is copied into RAM to identify the device on the network.

The MAC address is a 48-bit address expressed as 12 hexadecimal digits. The first 24 bits or 6 hexadecimal digits of the MAC address contain a manufacturer identification or vendor code. Another name for this part of the address is the Organizationally Unique Identifier (OUI). To ensure vendor uniqueness, the IEEE administers OUIs. The last 24 bits or 6 hexadecimal digits are administered by each vendor and often represent the interface serial number.

The source address is always a unicast (single node) address, and the destination address might be unicast, multicast (group of nodes), or broadcast (all nodes).

- In IEEE 802.3 frames, the two-byte field following the source address is a *length* field, which indicates the number of bytes of data that follow this field and precede the frame check sequence (FCS) field.

- Following the length field is the *data* field, which includes the LLC control information, other upper-layer control information, and the user data.

- Finally, following the data field is a 4-byte *FCS* field containing a cyclic redundancy check (CRC) value. The CRC is created by the sending device and recalculated by the receiving device to check for damage that might have occurred to the frame in transit.

LLC Sublayer Frames

There are two LLC frame types: Service Access Point (SAP) and Subnetwork Access Protocol (SNAP). Which frame type your system uses depends on the applications that you have running on your system. Some applications define themselves by a SAP ID, and others define themselves using a type code. Figure 1-15 shows the format of the SAP and SNAP frame types.

Figure 1-15 *SAP and SNAP LLC Sublayer Frames*

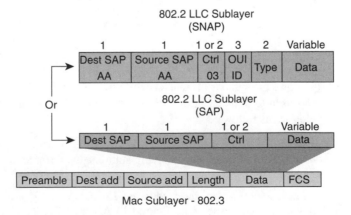

In the LLC header, the destination SAP (DSAP) and source SAP (SSAP) fields are 1 byte each and act as pointers to the upper-layer protocols in a station. For example, a frame with a SAP of 06 hex is destined for IP, and a frame with a SAP of E0 hex is destined for IPX. From the perspective of these lower MAC sublayers, the SAP process provides a convenient interface to the upper layers of the protocol stack. These SAP entries allow the physical and data link connections to provide services for many upper-layer protocols.

In order to specify that the frame uses SNAP, the SSAP and DSAP addresses are both set to AA hex, and the control field is set to 03 hex. In addition to the SAP fields, a SNAP header has a type code field that allows for the inclusion of the EtherType. The EtherType defines which upper-layer protocol receives the data.

In a SNAP frame, the first three bytes of the SNAP header after the control field are the OUI vendor code. Following the OUI vendor code is a two-byte field containing the EtherType for the frame. Here is where the backward compatibility with Ethernet Version II is implemented. As with the 802.3 frame, a 4-byte FCS field follows the data field and contains a CRC value.

Data Link Layer Devices

Bridges and Layer 2 switches are devices that function at the data link layer of the protocol stack. Figure 1-16 shows the devices typically encountered at Layer 2. Layer 2 switching is hardware-based bridging. In a switch, frame forwarding is handled by specialized hardware called application-specific integrated circuits (ASICs). ASIC technology allows a silicon chip to be programmed to perform a specific function as it is built. This technology allows functions to be performed at much higher rates of speed than that of a chip that is programmed by software. Because of ASIC technology, switches provide scalability to gigabit speeds with low latency.

Figure 1-16 *Data Link Devices*

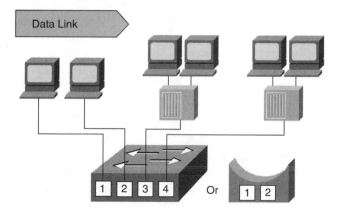

NOTE   Although there are Layer 3 and Layer 4 switches that perform routing, this book uses the term *switch* to refer to a Layer 2 device.

When a bridge or switch receives a frame, it uses the data link information to process the frame. In a transparent bridge environment, the bridge processes the frame by determining whether it needs to be copied to other connected segments. A transparent bridge hears every frame that crosses a segment and views each frame and source address field to determine on what segment the source station resides. The transparent bridge stores this information in memory in what is known as a *forwarding table*. The forwarding table lists each end station (from which the bridge has heard a frame within a particular time period) and the segment on which it resides. When a bridge hears a frame on the network, it views the destination address and compares it to the forwarding table to determine whether to filter, flood, or copy the frame onto another segment.

This decision process occurs as follows:

- If the destination device is on the same segment as the frame, the bridge blocks the frame from going on to other segments. This process is known as *filtering*.
- If the destination device is on a different segment, the bridge forwards the frame to the appropriate segment.
- If the destination address is unknown to the bridge, the bridge forwards the frame to all segments except the one on which it was received. This process is known as *flooding*.

Because a bridge learns all the station destinations by listening to source addresses, it will never learn the broadcast address. Therefore, all broadcasts will always be flooded to all the segments on the bridge or switch. All segments in a bridged or switched environment are therefore considered to be in the same broadcast domain.

NOTE   This book focuses on transparent bridging because this is the function performed by the Catalyst 1900 series of switches. This is also the most common form of bridging/switching in Ethernet environments. It should also be noted that there are other types of bridges, such as source-route bridging, in which the source determines the route to be taken through the network, and translational bridging, which allows the frame to move from a source route to a transparent environment between Ethernet and Token Ring.

A bridged/switched network provides excellent traffic management. The purpose of the Layer 2 device is to reduce collisions, which waste bandwidth and prevent packets from reaching their destinations. Part A of Figure 1-17 shows how a switch reduces collisions by giving each segment its own collision domain. Part B of Figure 1-17 shows that when two or more packets need to get onto a segment, they are stored in memory until the segment is available for use.

Figure 1-17 *Bridging Reduces Collisions*

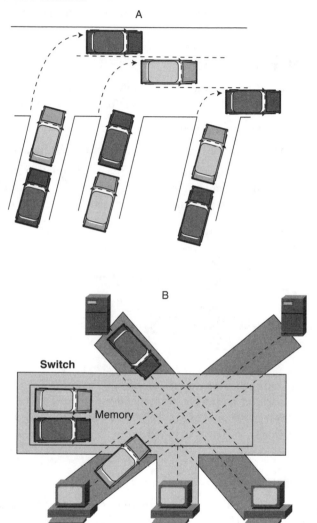

Bridged/switched networks have the following characteristics:

- Each segment is its own collision domain.

- All devices connected to the same bridge or switch are part of the same broadcast domain.

- All segments must use the same data link layer implementation, such as all Ethernet or all Token Ring. If an end station must communicate with another end station on different media, then some device, such as a router or translational bridge, must translate between the different media types.

- In a switched environment, there can be one device per segment, and each device can send frames at the same time, thus allowing the primary pathway to be shared.

Network Layer Functions

The network layer defines how to transport traffic between devices that are not locally attached in the same broadcast domain. Two pieces of information are required to achieve this:

- A logical address associated with the source and destination stations.

- A path through the network to reach the desired destination.

Figure 1-18 shows the location of the network layer in relation to the data link layer. The network layer is independent of the data link and can therefore be used to connect devices residing on different physical media. The logical addressing structure is used to provide this connectivity.

Figure 1-18 *Location of the Network Layer in the Protocol Model*

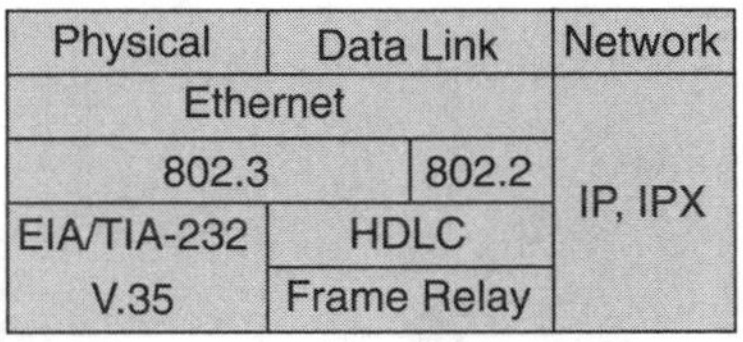

Physical	Data Link	Network
Ethernet		
802.3	802.2	IP, IPX
EIA/TIA-232	HDLC	
V.35	Frame Relay	

Logical addressing schemes are used to identify networks in an internetwork and the location of the devices within the context of those networks. These schemes vary based on the network layer protocol in use. This book discusses the network layer operation for the TCP/IP and IPX (Novell) protocol stacks.

Network Layer Addresses

Network layer addresses (also called *virtual* or *logical addresses*) exist at Layer 3 of the OSI reference model. Unlike data link layer addresses, which usually exist within a flat address space, network layer addresses are usually hierarchical in that they define networks first and then devices or nodes on each of those networks. In other words, network layer addresses are like postal addresses, which describe a person's location by providing a ZIP code and a street address. The ZIP code defines the city and state, and the street address is a particular location in that city. This is in contrast to the MAC layer address, which is flat in nature. A good example of a flat address space is the U.S. Social Security numbering system, in which each person has a single, unique Social Security number. Figure 1-19 shows a sample logical address as defined within a network layer packet.

Figure 1-19 *Network Layer Logical Addressing*

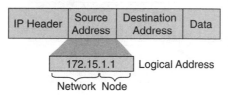

The logical network address consists of two portions. One part uniquely identifies each network within the internetwork, and the other part uniquely identifies the hosts on each of those networks. Combining both portions results in a unique network address for each device. This unique network address has two functions:

- The network portion identifies each network in the internetwork structure, allowing the routers to identify paths through the network cloud. The router uses this address to determine where to send network packets, in the same manner that the ZIP code on a letter determines the state and city that a package should be delivered to.

- The host portion identifies a particular device or a device's port on the network in the same manner that a street address on a letter identifies a location within that city.

There are many network layer protocols, and they all share the function of identifying networks and hosts throughout the internetwork structure. Most of these protocols have different schemes for accomplishing this task. TCP/IP is a common protocol that is used in routed networks. An IP address has the following components to identify networks and hosts:

- A 32-bit address, divided into four 8-bit sections called *octets*. This address identifies a specific network and a specific host on that network by subdividing the bits into network and host portions.

- A 32-bit subnet mask that is also divided into four 8-bit octets. The subnet mask is used to determine which bits represent the network and which represent the host. The bit pattern for a subnet mask is a string of recursive 1s followed by the remaining bits, which are 0. Figure 1-20 shows that the boundary between the 1s and the 0s marks the boundary for the network and host portions of the address, the two components necessary to define an IP address on an end device.

Figure 1-20 *IP Address Components*

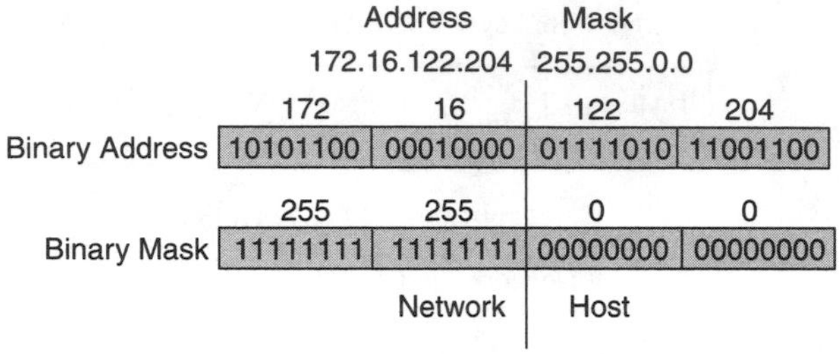

                              Address   Mask
                         172.16.122.204   255.255.0.0

                          172   16   122   204
    Binary Address | 10101100 | 00010000 | 01111010 | 11001100 |

                          255   255   0   0
    Binary Mask | 11111111 | 11111111 | 00000000 | 00000000 |

                              Network | Host

NOTE   IP addresses are represented by taking the 8-bit octets and converting them to decimal and then separating the octets with dots or periods. This format is known as *dotted decimal* and is done to simplify addressing for those of us who count in Base10.

Router Operation at the Network Layer

Routers operate at the network layer by tracking and recording the different networks and choosing the best path to those networks. The routers place this information in a routing table, which includes the following items (see Figure 1-21):

- **Network addresses**—Represent known networks to the router. A network address is protocol-specific. If a router supports more than one protocol, it will have a unique table for each protocol.

- **Interface**—Refers to the interface used by the router to reach a given network. This is the interface that will be used to forward packets destined for the listed network.

- **Metric**—Refers to the cost or distance to the target network. This is a value that helps the router choose the best path to a given network. This metric changes depending on how the router chooses paths. Common metrics include the number of networks that must be crossed to get to a destination (also known as *hops*), the time it takes to cross all the interfaces to a given network (also known as *delay*), or a value associated with the speed of a link (also known as *bandwidth*).

Figure 1-21 *Routing Tables*

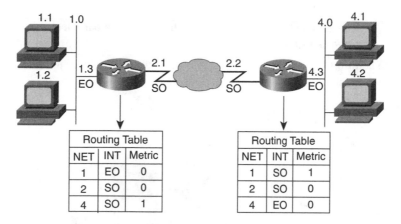

Because routers function at the network layer of the OSI model, they are used to separate segments into unique collision and broadcast domains. Each segment is referred to as a *network* and must be identified by a network address to be reached by end stations. In addition to identifying each segment as a network, each station on that network must also be uniquely identified by the logical address. This addressing structure allows for hierarchical network configuration (that is, a station is not known merely by a host identifier) but is defined by the network it is on as well as a host identifier. In order for routers to operate on a network, it is required that each interface be configured on the unique network it represents. The router must also have a host address on that network. The router uses the interface's configuration information to determine the network portion of the address to build a routing table.

In addition to identifying networks and providing connectivity, routers also provide other functions:

- Routers do not forward Layer 2 broadcast or multicast frames.

- Routers attempt to determine the optimal path through a routed network based on routing algorithms.

- Routers strip Layer 2 frames and forward packets based on Layer 3 destination addresses.

- Routers map a single Layer 3 logical address to a single network device; therefore, routers can limit or secure network traffic based on identifiable attributes within each packet. These options, controlled via access lists, can be applied to inbound or outbound packets.

- Routers can be configured to perform both bridging and routing functions.

- Routers provide connectivity between different virtual LANs (VLANs) in a switched environment.

- Routers can be used to deploy quality of service parameters for specified types of network traffic.

In addition to the benefits in the campus, routers can be used to connect remote locations to the main office using WAN services, as illustrated in Figure 1-22.

Figure 1-22 *Routers Connect Remote Locations to the Main Office*

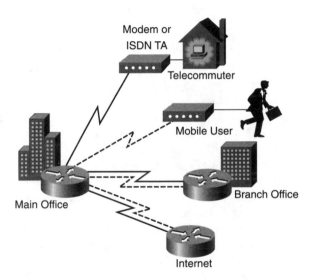

Routers support a variety of physical layer connectivity standards that allow you to build WANs. In addition, they can provide the security and access controls that are needed when interconnecting remote locations.

Transport Layer Functions

In order to connect two devices in the fabric of the network, a connection or session must be established. The transport layer defines the end-to-end station establishment guidelines between two end stations. A session constitutes a logical connection between the peer transport layers in source and destination end stations. Figure 1-23 shows the relationship of some transport layer protocols to their respective network layer protocols. Different transport layer functions are provided by these protocols.

Figure 1-23 *Transport Layer Protocols*

Network	Transport
IP	TCP
	UDP
IPX	SPX

Specifically, the transport layer defines the following functions:

- Allows end stations to assemble and disassemble multiple upper-layer segments into the same transport layer data stream. This is accomplished by assigning upper-layer application identifiers. Within the TCP/IP protocol suite, these identifiers are known as *port numbers*. The OSI reference model refers to these identifiers as Service Access Points (SAPs). The transport layer uses these port numbers to identify application layer entities such as FTP and Telnet. An example of a port number is 23, which identifies the Telnet application. Data with a transport port number of 23 would be destined for the Telnet application.

- Allows applications to request reliable data transport between communicating end systems. Reliable transport uses a connection-oriented relationship between the communicating end systems to accomplish the following:

  — Ensure that segments delivered will be acknowledged back to the sender.

  — Provide for retransmission of any segments that are not acknowledged.

  — Put segments back into their correct sequence order at the receiving station.

  — Provide congestion avoidance and control.

At the transport layer, data can be transmitted reliably or unreliably. For IP, the TCP protocol is reliable or connection-oriented, and UDP is unreliable or connectionless. A good analogy to connection-oriented versus connectionless is a phone call versus a post card. With a phone call, you establish a dialogue that lets you know how well you are communicating. A post card offers no real-time feedback.

In order for a connection-oriented transport layer protocol to provide these functions reliably, a connection must be established between the end stations, data is transmitted, and then the session is disconnected.

Like a phone call, in order to communicate with a connection-oriented service, you must first establish the connection. To do this within the TCP/IP protocol suite, the sending and receiving stations perform an operation known as a three-way handshake (see Figure 1-24). A three-way handshake is accomplished by the sending and receiving of synchronization and acknowledgment packets. With a phone call, this would be like each party saying "hello" to indicate that they were ready to talk.

Figure 1-24 *The Three-Way Handshake*

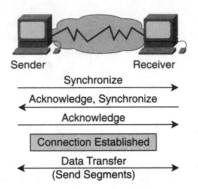

After the synchronization has occurred, the transfer of information begins. During the transfer, the two end stations continue to communicate with their network layer PDUs (headers) to verify that the data is received correctly. If the receiving station does not acknowledge a packet within a predefined amount of time, the sender retransmits the package. This ensures reliable delivery of all traffic. After the data transfer is complete, the session is disconnected, like saying "good-bye" during a telephone conversation.

OSI Lower Layer Review

Now that we have defined and discussed the lower four layers of the OSI model and defined the concepts of collision and broadcast domains, let's review what we have learned.

Each device shown in Figure 1-25 operates at a different layer of the OSI model:

- At Layer 1 (the physical layer) is the hub. The hub retransmits our packets and acts as a concentration device for our other network devices. The hub forms a single segment, providing one collision domain and one broadcast domain.

- The switch and the bridge are Layer 2 devices. These devices divide our network into separate segments, providing fewer users per segment. Each segment is a single collision domain, so in the figure, the bridge and switch each support four collision domains. Broadcast traffic, however, propagates across all segments, so only one broadcast domain is associated with each device.

- At Layer 3 (the network layer), the router provides paths to all the networks throughout the internetwork. The router segments the network into separate collision domains and broadcast domains. In Figure 1-25, we see that there are four collision domains and four broadcast domains.

Figure 1-25 *Network Device Functions*

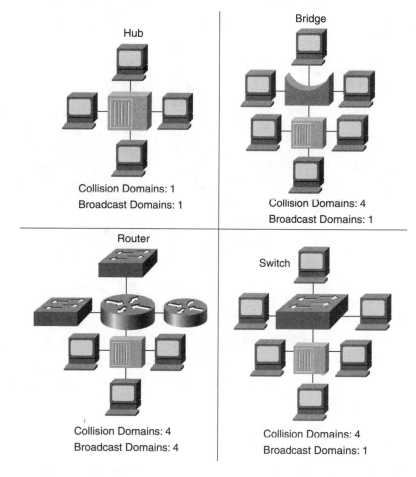

Hub

Collision Domains: 1
Broadcast Domains: 1

Bridge

Collision Domains: 4
Broadcast Domains: 1

Router

Collision Domains: 4
Broadcast Domains: 4

Switch

Collision Domains: 4
Broadcast Domains: 1

Selecting Cisco Products

Earlier in this chapter, we discussed the hierarchical model used to design and implement networks. Figure 1-26 reviews the structure of this model, shown earlier in Figure 1-3. Given a particular function of networking and what we have discussed about the service performed at each layer, you should be able to match Cisco products to your internetworking needs.

Figure 1-26 *The Three-Layer Hierarchical Network Model*

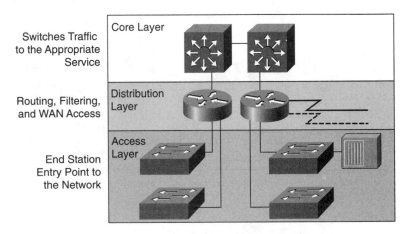

The following list summarizes the factors for selecting networking devices:

- Device provides desired functionality and features
- Device has required capacity and performance
- Device is easy to install and offers centralized management
- Device provides network resiliency
- Device provides investment protection in existing infrastructure
- Device provides migration path for change and growth

The most important task is to understand the needs and then identify the device functions and features that meet those needs. In order to accomplish this, obtain information about where in the internetworking hierarchy the device needs to operate, and then consider factors such as ease of installation, capacity requirements, and so forth.

Other factors, such as remote access, also play a role in product selection. When supporting remote access requirements, you must first determine the kind of WAN services that meet your needs. Then, you will be able to select the appropriate device.

The type and number of required WAN connections will significantly affect your choice of devices. The most important factor in choosing WAN services is the availability of the service. It is also important to know what your bandwidth requirements are and how much the service will cost. Figure 1-27 shows a graph relating cost to usage for some common WAN services. As you can see, depending on the usage, it might be more cost-effective to get a service that provides a fixed rate.

Figure 1-27 *WAN Cost Versus Usage*

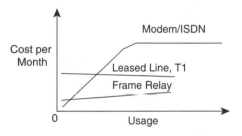

It is also important to choose a service that can be supported by your product.

When determining WAN service bandwidth requirements, you must look at the type of traffic that needs to cross the WAN service. Figure 1-28 gives you an idea of WAN technology as it maps to a given application.

Figure 1-28 *Application Bandwidth Requirements*

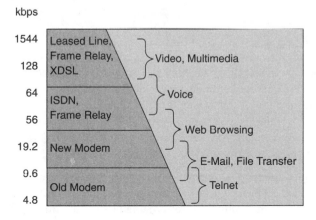

After you have chosen the type of network device you need, you can select a particular product. Cisco Systems offers a large variety of networking products, including hubs, switches, and routers.

Cisco Hub Products

Figure 1-29 shows the selection issues for hubs, along with a sampling of the Cisco hub product line. This figure represents the low-end to high-end line. The cost of these products also increases along this line.

Figure 1-29 *Cisco Hub Product Line*

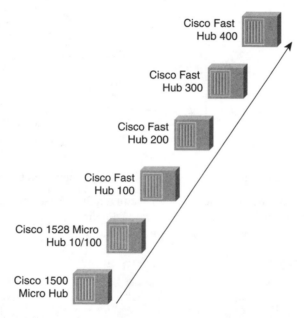

Criteria used in selecting hubs includes the media speed needed, the number of ports needed, ease of installation, and the need for remote management. The Micro Hub series represents the low-end hub with low-speed fixed-port densities. FastHub 100 and 200 represent the mid-level solution, offering higher-speed connectivity and some management. The FastHub 300 and 400 series offer the most flexibility with modular ports and manageability; however, they are 100 Mbps-only devices.

Before implementing hubs, assess which workstations need 10 Mbps and which higher-end stations need 100 Mbps. Lower-end hubs offer only 10 Mbps, whereas mid-range hubs offer both. The mid-range devices provide growth and migration potential.

The scope of consolidated connections refers to the issue of how many hub ports your users will require. Hubs allow for a variety of port densities, and you can stack hubs to get multiples of the hub densities.

Most hubs are simple to plug in and operate. For most hubs, there is no management or console port. If you want to be able to manage the hub, select from the higher-end hub series.

Catalyst Switch Products

Figure 1-30 shows a sampling of the Cisco switch product line. The figure represents the low-end to high-end selection of some of the switch products and shows where in the network these products can be used.

Figure 1-30 *Cisco Switch Product Line*

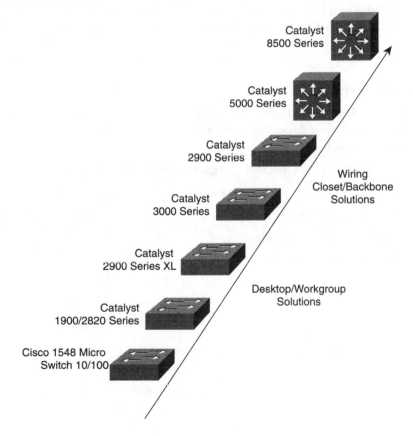

Here are the key selection issues when selecting switch products:

- Media speed requirements
- The need for interswitch communication (trunking)
- The need for broadcast segmentation (VLANs)
- Port density needs
- The need for configuration interface consistency

Because one of the major advantages of switches is the variety of link speeds that are offered, one of the key issues to consider is whether 10 or 100 Mbps access is required.

Other consideration factors for switches are the number of ports, the need for further segmentation using VLANs, and different media and topology connections and enterprise functionality, such as interswitched links for trunking. Many of these functions are discussed later in this book. Finally, you might want all the network devices to have a consistent user configuration interface. Cisco switch products have a variety of user interfaces, including command line, menu, and web. These interfaces could play a role in product selection.

Cisco Router Products

Figure 1-31 shows a sampling of the Cisco router product line. The figure represents the low-end to high-end selection of some of the router products and shows where in the network these products may be used.

Here are the key selection issues when selecting router products:

- Scale of the routing features needed
- Port density/variety requirements
- Capacity and performance
- Common user interface

Figure 1-31   *Cisco Router Product Line*

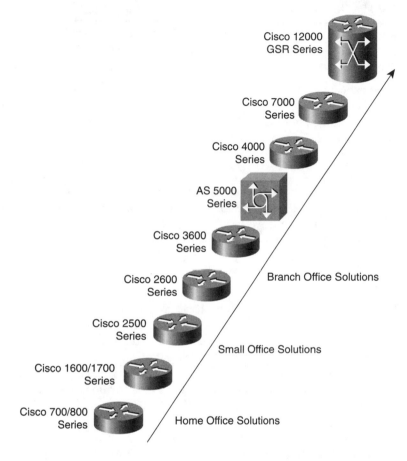

A key criterion in router selection is knowing what router service features are needed. Different routers in the Cisco product line incorporate different feature sets. You will learn about many advanced router features later in this book.

Port densities and interface speeds generally increase as you move to the upper end of the various Cisco router families. For example, the 12000 series is the first in a product class of gigabit switch routers (GSRs). The 12000 GSR initially supports an IP backbone link at OC-12 (622 Mbps) and can scale to handle links at OC-48 (2.4 Gbps). In contrast, the 800 series router is designed to handle 10 Mbps Ethernet connections to the SOHO network and 128 kbps ISDN services to the Internet or corporate office.

If your network requires WAN links, the router selection issues involve which router provides the necessary type and number of links in a cost-effective manner. A typical production network will have several LAN switches interconnected to the WAN by a router.

Please note that the products listed in these sections reflect a snapshot of Cisco's offerings. Cisco's product lines are continuously evolving in response to customer needs and other technology migration issues. For the current Cisco offerings, consult Cisco Connection Online (www.cisco.com) or your dealer/distributor.

NOTE   Cisco offers a product selection tool at the web site http://www.cisco.com/pcgi-bin/front.x/corona/prodtool/select.pl. This tool is categorized into three groups—hubs, routers, and switches. It is an interactive JavaScript application used to help you select Cisco products.

Summary

In this chapter, we introduced some basic concepts of internetworking. These concepts include the ability to describe (using the OSI reference model) the process in which data is transferred from an application across the network. You learned the roles of each network device that will be discussed in this book and saw how each fits into the hierarchy of network design. You learned at which layer of the OSI model each of these devices functions. Finally, you learned how to use this information to select products based on the needs of your network.

Review Questions

1   Which three functions are defined by the Cisco hierarchical model?

2   What is one advantage of the OSI reference model?

3   Describe the data encapsulation process.

4   Define a collision domain, and give an example of a device that combines all devices in a single collision domain.

5   Define a broadcast domain, and give an example of a device that separates each segment into different broadcast domains and provides connectivity between the segments.

6   At which layer of the OSI model does a bridge or switch operate?

7 How many broadcast domains are associated with a bridge or switch (assuming no VLANs)?

8 Which OSI layer defines an address that consists of a network portion and a node portion?

9 Which OSI layer defines a flat address space?

10 Which process establishes a connection between two end stations using a reliable TCP/IP transport layer protocol?

Upon completion of this chapter, you will be able to perform the following tasks:

- Identify and connect the necessary components to provide connectivity between switches and routers.

- Determine what components are necessary to enable WAN connectivity over serial or ISDN BRI connections for a Cisco router.

- Set up console connectivity to Cisco routers and switches to provide configuration and monitoring of these devices.

- Determine the need for differing cable types and topologies in a network environment.

CHAPTER 2

Assembling and Cabling Cisco Devices

The focus of this book is on the installation and configuration of Cisco devices. Although many configuration parameters and services are common across most Cisco products, this book focuses on lower-end products such as the 1600, 2600, 4000, and 3600 series of products and the 1900 and 2820 series of switches. In this chapter, you learn how to cable your Cisco devices to provide connectivity for devices in your network and how to configure your Cisco device.

Cabling the LAN

Interconnection of network devices takes place through the structured cabling of the local-area network (LAN) and wide-area network (WAN). Figure 2-1 illustrates the interconnection of devices via the structured cabling of the network.

Figure 2-1 *Network Cabling*

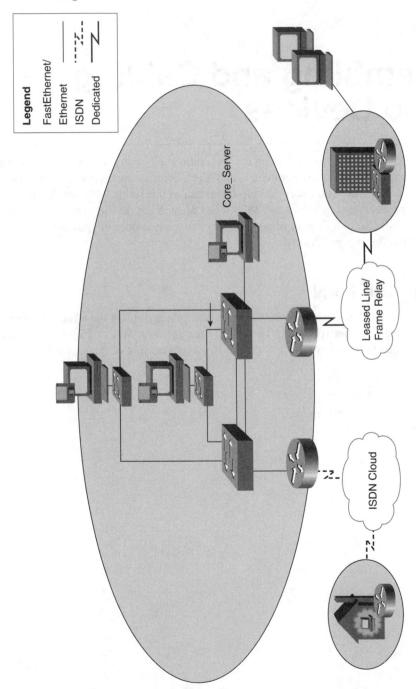

The following sections examine these aspects of cabling the LAN:

- LAN physical layer implementations
- Positioning Ethernet in the campus
- Comparing Ethernet media requirements
- Differentiating between connectors
- UTP implementation
- Cabling the campus

LAN Physical Layer Implementations

The cabling aspect of the LAN exists at Layer 1 of the OSI reference model. Many topologies support LANs and many different physical media. This book focuses on Ethernet as the physical and data link connections for many of the LAN connections; thus, much of this section deals with the physical aspects of that topology. Figure 2-2 shows a subset of physical layer implementations that can be deployed to support Ethernet.

Figure 2-2 *Ethernet: LAN Implementations*

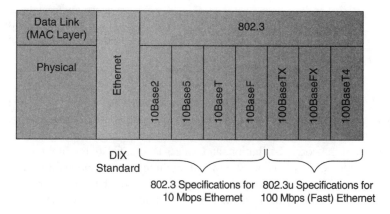

The term *Ethernet* refers to a family of LAN implementations. Physical layer implementations vary, and all support various media types, as shown in Figure 2-2. The following list documents the three principal categories:

- **Ethernet (DIX) and IEEE 802.3**—LAN specifications that operate at 10 Mbps over coaxial cable, UTP, or fiber.

- **100 Mbps Ethernet (IEEE 802.3u)**—LAN specification known as Fast Ethernet that operates over UTP or fiber.

- **1000 Mbps Ethernet**—LAN specification known as Gigabit Ethernet that operates at 1000 Mbps over fiber. This technology is beyond the scope of this book.

Positioning Ethernet in the Campus

Given the variety of Ethernet speeds that can be deployed in the campus, you need to determine when, if, and where you want to upgrade to one or more of the Fast Ethernet implementations. Technology is currently in place to support the implementation of 10 Mbps or 100 Mbps Ethernet throughout the LAN, provided that you have the correct hardware and cabling infrastructure.

Where and what type of connectivity you use can be mapped back to the networking hierarchy of core, distribution, and access discussed in Chapter 1. Table 2-1 documents suggested Ethernet connectivity specifications according to the three-layer hierarchical model.

Table 2-1 *Ethernet Connectivity Recommendations in a Hierarchical Network Model*

	Ethernet 10BaseT Position	**Fast Ethernet Position**
Access Layer	Provides connectivity between the end-user device and the access switch.	Gives high-performance PCs and workstations 100-Mbps access to the server.
Distribution Layer	Not typically used at this layer.	Provides connectivity between the access and distribution layers. Provides connectivity from the distribution layer to the core layer. Provides connectivity from the server block to the core layer.
Core Layer	Not typically used at this layer.	Provides inter-switch connectivity.

As noted in Table 2-1, 10 Mbps Ethernet is typically implemented at the access layer to connect to desktops, and faster technologies are used to interconnect network devices, such as routers and switches. However, many designers are considering the use of Gigabit Ethernet at the core, distribution, and access layers. Costs for cabling and adapters can make implementing Gigabit Ethernet at all three layers unappealing. Before making any decision, you must consider your networking needs and any future requirements you have that might potentially overwhelm a network running on slower media.

In general, Fast Ethernet technology can be used in a campus network in several different ways:

- Fast Ethernet is used as the link between the access and distribution layer devices, supporting the aggregate traffic from each Ethernet segment on the access link.

- Many client/server networks suffer from too many clients trying to access the same server, creating a bottleneck where the server attaches to the LAN. To enhance client/server performance across the campus network, enterprise servers are connected by Fast Ethernet links to ensure the avoidance of bottlenecks at the server. Fast Ethernet, in combination with switched Ethernet, creates an effective solution for avoiding slow networks.

- Fast Ethernet links can also be used to provide the connection between the distribution layer and the core. Because the campus network model supports dual links between each distribution layer router and core switch, the combined traffic from multiple access switches can be load-balanced across these links.

Comparing Ethernet Media Requirements

In addition to considering network needs, before selecting an Ethernet implementation, you must consider the media and connector requirements for each implementation.

The cables and connector specifications used to support Ethernet are derived from the Electronic Industries Association and the newer Telecommunications Industry Association (EIA/TIA) standards body. The categories of cabling defined for Ethernet are derived from the EIA/TIA-568 (SP-2840) Commercial Building Telecommunications Wiring Standards. The EIA/TIA specifies a RJ-45 connector for unshielded twisted-pair (UTP) cable. The letters "RJ" stand for registered jack, and the number 45 refers to a specific wiring sequence.

Table 2-2 compares the cable and connector specifications for the most popular Ethernet implementations. The important difference to note is the media used for 10 Mbps Ethernet and 100 Mbps Ethernet. In today's networks, where you will see a mix of 10 Mbps and 100 Mbps needs, you must be aware of the need to change over to UTP category 5 to support Fast Ethernet.

Table 2-2   *Ethernet Cabling and Connector Specifications*

	10Base5	**10BaseT**	**100BaseTX**	**100BaseFX**
Media	50-ohm coax (thick)	EIA/TIA Category 3, 4, 5 UTP, 2 pair	EIA/TIA Category 5 UTP, 2 pair	62.5/125 micron multimode fiber
Maximum Segment Length	500 meters	100 meters	100 meters	400 meters
Topology	Bus	Star	Star	Point-to-point
Connector	AUI	ISO 8877 (RJ-45)	ISO 8877 (RJ-45)	Duplex media interface connector (MIC) ST

As the acronym UTP implies, this cable consists of paired wires twisted together and wrapped in an unshielded outer jacket. These wires are unshielded because UTP derives all of its protection from the cancellation effect of the twisted pairs. The mutual cancellation effect of the wire twists minimizes the absorption of radiation of electrical energy from the surrounding environment. This helps reduce the problems in transmitting the signal, such as crosstalk (interference measured on a wire that is located near the wire sending the signal) and the effects of nearby electrical fields (noise).

Differentiating Between Connections

Figure 2-3 illustrates the different connection types used by each physical layer implementation. Of the three examples shown, the RJ-45 connector and jack are the most common.

Figure 2-3 *Connector Types for Ethernet Cabling*

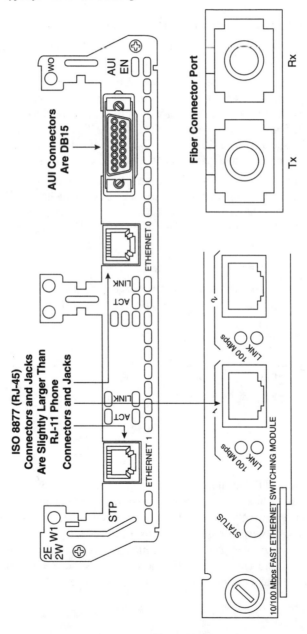

UTP Implementation

If you look at an RJ-45 transparent end connector, you can see eight colored wires. These wires are twisted into four pairs within the outer jacket. Four of the wires are tip conductors (T1 through T4), and the other four are the ring conductors (R1 through R4). Tip and ring are terms that originated in the early days of the telephone. Today, these terms refer to the positive wire (tip) and the negative wire (ring) in the pair. The wires in the first port in a cable or connector are designated as T1 and R1, the second pair is T2 and R2, and so on. Table 2-3 and Table 2-4 detail two common UTP wiring standards.

Table 2-3 *UTP EIA/TIA 568A Wiring Standard*

Pin 1	Pair 2	White/Green	Tx + (Tip)
Pin 2	Pair 2	Green	Tx – (Ring)
Pin 3	Pair 3	White/Orange	Rx + (Tip)
Pin 4	Pair 1	Blue	Not used in 10BaseT or 100BaseT
Pin 5	Pair 1	White/Blue	Not used in 10BaseT or 100BaseT
Pin 6	Pair 3	Orange	Rx – (Ring)
Pin 7	Pair 4	White/Brown	Not used in 10BaseT or 100BaseT
Pin 8	Pair 4	Brown	Not used in 10BaseT or 100BaseT

Table 2-4 *UTP EIA/TIA 568B Wiring Standard*

Pin 1	Pair 2	White/Orange	Tx + (Tip)
Pin 2	Pair 2	Orange	Tx – (Ring)
Pin 3	Pair 3	White/Green	Rx + (Tip)
Pin 4	Pair 1	Blue	Not used in 10BaseT or 100BaseT
Pin 5	Pair 1	White/Blue	Not used in 10BaseT or 100BaseT
Pin 6	Pair 3	Green	Rx – (Ring)
Pin 7	Pair 4	White/Brown	Not used in 10BaseT or 100BaseT
Pin 8	Pair 4	Brown	Not used in 10BaseT or 100BaseT

An RJ-45 connector is the male component crimped on the end of the cable. As you look at the male connector from the front with the clip on the top, the pin locations are numbered 1 on the left down to 8 on the right, as shown in Figure 2-4.

Figure 2-4   *RJ-45 Connector*

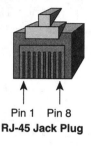

Pin 1   Pin 8
RJ-45 Jack Plug

Pin	Wire Pair T is Tip, R is Ring
1	Pair 2 T2
2	Pair 2 R2
3	Pair 3 T3
4	Pair 1 R1
5	Pair 1 T1
6	Pair 3 R3
7	Pair 4 T4
8	Pair 4 R4

The jack is the female component in a network device, wall or cubicle partition outlet, or patch panel. As you look at the device port, the corresponding female plug locations are 1 on the left and 8 on the right.

In order for electricity to run between the connector and the jack, the order of the wires must follow the EIA/TIA 568A and 568B standards, listed in Table 2-3 and Table 2-4. In addition to identifying the correct EIA/TIA category of cable to use for connecting a device, you will need to determine whether to use either a straight-through cable or a crossover cable.

Straight-Through Cable

A straight-through cable maintains the pin connection all the way through the cable. Thus, the wire connected to pin 1 is the same on both ends of the cable.

Figure 2-5 illustrates that the RJ-45 connectors on both ends show all of the wires in the same order. If you hold the two RJ-45 ends of a cable side by side in the same orientation, you'll see the colored wires (or strips or pins) at each connector end. If the order of the colored wires is the same at both ends, the cable is straight-through.

Figure 2-5   *Straight-Through Cable Connections*

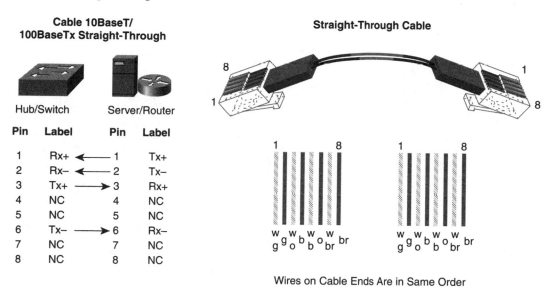

Wires on Cable Ends Are in Same Order

Use a straight-through cable to connect devices such as PCs or routers to devices such as hubs or switches. Figure 2-6 shows the connection guidelines when using straight-through cable.

Figure 2-6 *Determining When to Use Straight-Through Cable*

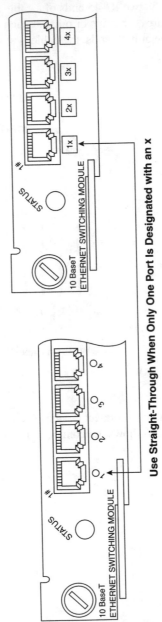

Crossover Cable

A crossover cable crosses the critical pairs in order to properly align, transmit, and receive signals on devices with like connectors.

Figure 2-7 shows that the RJ-45 connectors on both ends have some of the wires on one side of the cable crossed to a different pin on the other side of the cable. Specifically for Ethernet, pin 1 on one side should be connected to pin 3 at the other end. Also, pin 2 on one end should be connected to pin 6 on the other end.

Figure 2-7   *Crossover Cable Connections*

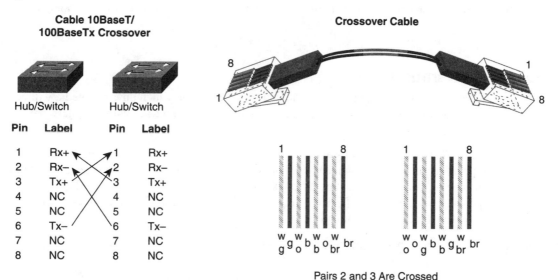

A crossover cable is used for connecting similar devices—for example, switch to switch, switch to hub, hub to hub, router to router, or PC to PC. Figure 2-8 shows some guidelines for using crossover cables.

Figure 2-8   *Determining When to Use Crossover Cable*

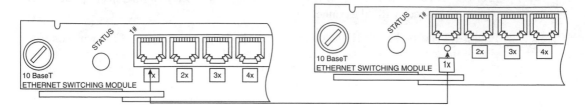

Use a Crossover Cable When BOTH Ports Are Designated with an x or Neither Port Is Designated with an x

Cabling the Campus

In order to cable the campus location, you must determine which physical media will be used and what type of connectors and cables you need to interface with your network devices.

Figure 2-9 illustrates how a variety of cable types may be required in a given network. The type of cabling required will be based on the type of Ethernet you choose to implement. In general, you must determine the physical media used—10 Mbps or 100 Mbps. This indicates what category of cable is required. Finally, locate the interface and determine if you need a crossover or straight-through cable.

Figure 2-9   *Networks Might Require a Variety of Cable Types*

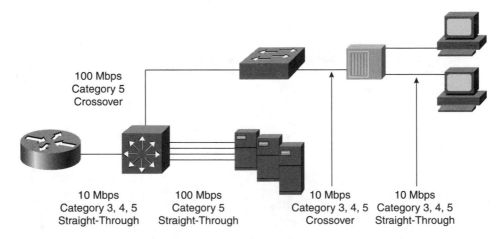

TIP	Category 5 wiring is an ideal medium for cabling a building or campus, because it supports data rates of 10 Mbps as well as 100 Mbps. Should the need arise to migrate from one to the other, it would not be necessary to rewire the facility.

Cabling the WAN

In order to connect our networks to other remote networks, it is sometimes necessary to utilize WAN services. WAN services provide different connection methods, and the cabling standards differ from those of LANs. It is therefore important to understand the types of cabling needed to connect to these services. Figure 2-10 illustrates the cabling in a typical WAN.

This section discusses the following topics:

- WAN physical layer implementations
- Differentiating between WAN serial connectors
- Cabling routers for serial connections
- Cabling routers for ISDN BRI connections

Figure 2-10 *WAN Cabling*

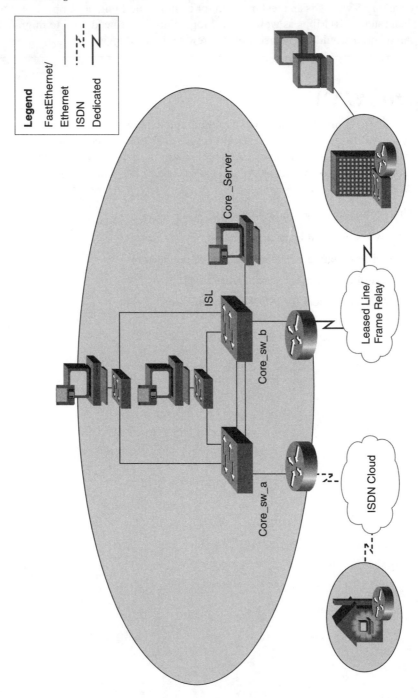

WAN Physical Layer Implementations

Many physical implementations carry traffic across the WAN. Needs vary, depending on the distance of the equipment from the services, the speed, and the actual service itself. Figure 2-11 lists a subset of the physical implementations that support some of the more common WAN solutions today. The type of physical layer you will choose depends on the distance, speed, and what type of interface in which you need to connect.

Figure 2-11 *WAN Physical Layer Implementations*

HDLC	PPP	Frame Relay	ISDN BRI (with PPP)
EIA/TIA-232 EIA/TIA-449 X.21 V.24 V.35 HSSI			RJ-45 NOTE: Pinouts Are Different Than RJ-45 Used in Campus

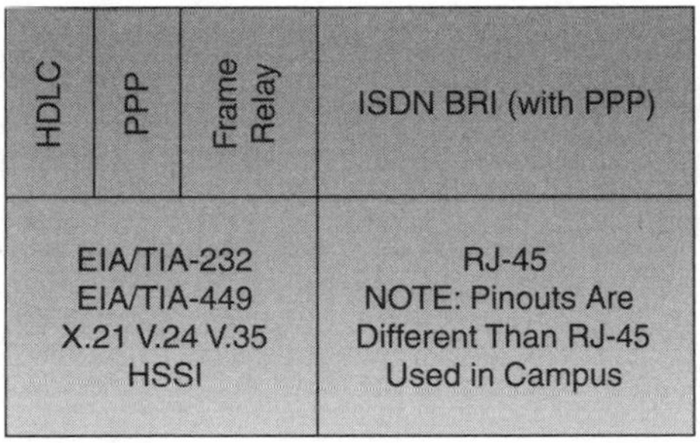

Serial connections are used to support WAN services such as dedicated leased lines running Point-to-Point Protocol (PPP), High-Level Data Link Control (HDLC), or Frame Relay encapsulations at Layer 2. The speeds of the connections typically range from 56 Kbps to T1/E1 (1.544/2.048 Mbps). Other WAN services, such as ISDN, offer dial-on-demand connections or dial backup services. An ISDN BRI (Basic Rate Interface) is composed of two 64 Kbps Bearer channels for data, and one Delta channel at 16 Kbps used for signaling and other link-management tasks. PPP is typically used to carry data over the B channels. You will learn more about the data link operation, ISDN, and Frame Relay in Chapters 11, 12, and 13.

Differentiating Between WAN Serial Connections

Serial transmission is a method of data transmission in which bits of data are transmitted over a single channel. This one-at-a-time transmission contrasts with parallel data transmission, which passes several bits at a time. For long-distance communication, WANs use serial transmission. To carry the energy represented in bits, serial channels use a specific electromagnetic or optical frequency range.

Frequencies, described in terms of their cycles per second (or Hertz), function as a band or spectrum for communications—for example, the signals transmitted over voice-grade telephone lines up to 3 kHz (kilo, or thousand, Hertz). The size of this frequency is called *bandwidth*.

Several types of physical connections allow us to connect to serial WAN services. Depending on the physical implementation you choose, or the physical implementation imposed by your provider, you will need to select the correct serial cable type to use with your router. Figure 2-12 shows the different serial connector options available. Note that serial ports on most Cisco routers use a proprietary 60-pin connector. Therefore, the router-ends of most port adapter cables use a male 60-pin connector, while the network ends of the adapter cable must match the specific WAN service hardware.

Figure 2-12 *WAN Serial Connection Options*

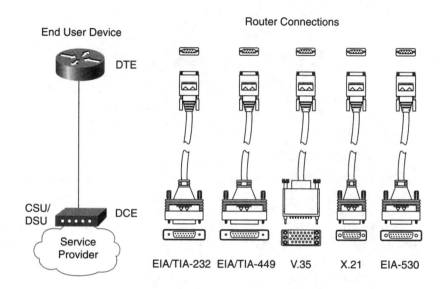

Another way to express bandwidth is to specify the amount of data in bits per second (bps) that can be carried using two of the physical layer implementations shown in Figure 2-12. Table 2-5 compares the physical standards for WAN serial connection options.

Table 2-5   *Comparison of Physical Standards*

Data in bps	Distance (Meters) EIA/TIA-232	Distance (Meters) EIA/TIA-449
2400	60	1,250
4800	30	625
9600	15	312
19,200	15	156
38,400	15	78
115,200	3.7	N/A
T1 (1,544,000 bps)	N/A	15

Cabling Routers for Serial Connections

In addition to determining cable type, you will need to determine if you need data terminal equipment (DTE) or data circuit-terminating equipment (DCE) connectors for your equipment. The DTE is the endpoint of the user's device on the WAN link. The DCE is typically the point where responsibility for delivering data passes into the hands of the service provider.

As shown in Figure 2-13, if you are connecting directly to a service provider, or to a device that will perform signal clocking, the router is a DTE and needs a DTE serial cable. This is typically the case for routers.

Figure 2-13 *DTE/DCE Connections*

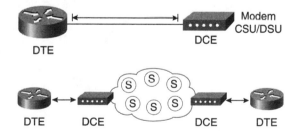

There are cases, however, where the router will need to be the DCE. For example, if you are performing a back-to-back router scenario in a test environment, one of the routers will be a DTE, and the other will be a DCE.

When you're cabling routers for serial connectivity, the routers will have either a fixed or modular port. The type of port being used will affect the syntax you use later to configure each interface.

Figure 2-14 shows an example of a router with fixed serial ports (interfaces). Each port is given a label of port type and port number, such as "serial 0." To configure a fixed interface, you specify the interface using this convention.

Figure 2-14 *Fixed Serial Ports on a 2500 Router*

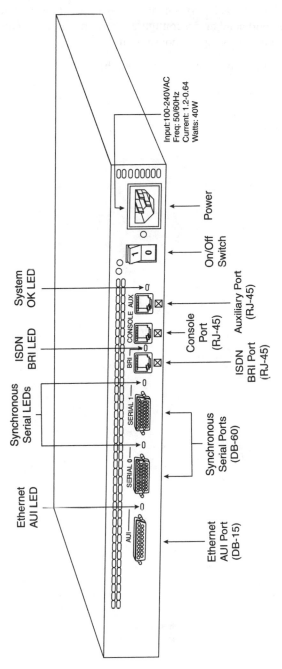

Other routers have modular ports. Figure 2-15 shows examples of routers with modular serial ports. Usually each port is given a label of port type, slot number (the location of the module), and port number. To configure a port on a modular card, you will be asked to specify the interface using this convention:

<port type> <slot number>/<port number>

An example would be serial 1/0.

Figure 2-15 *Modular Serial Ports on a 1603 Router and a 3640 Router*

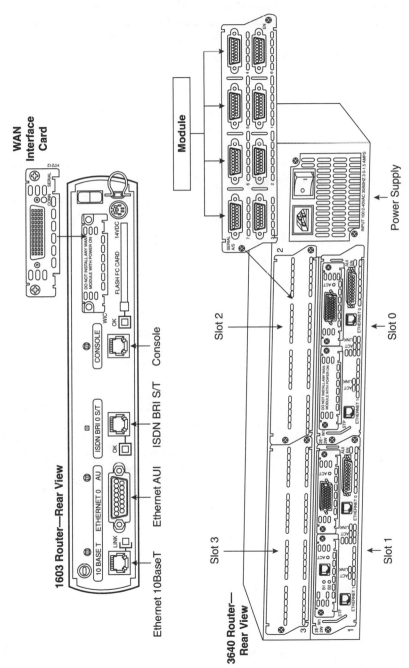

NOTE   Depending on the type of router you have, port designation convention might change. For example, some high-end routers such as a 7500 series device can have a virtual interface processor. Designation of these ports would also include the VIP slot:

<port type> <slot number>/<port adapter number>/<port number>

An example would be serial 1/0/0.

NOTE   The 1603 router shown in Figure 2-15 has both fixed and modular serial interfaces. Even though the serial port shown is a modular interface, you configure it as though it were fixed, using a label of port type and port number, such as serial 0.

Cabling Routers for ISDN BRI Connections

With BRI, there are two types of interfaces that you can use—BRI S/T and BRI U. To determine which interface type you need, you must determine whether you or the service provider will provide an NT1 device.

An NT1 device is an intermediate device between the router and the service provider's ISDN switch (the cloud) that is used to connect four-wire subscriber wiring to the conventional two-wire local loop. NT1 refers to a network termination type 1 device. In North America, the NT1 is typically provided by the customer, while in the rest of the world, the service provider provides the NT1 device.

If you need to provide the NT1 device, you can use an ISDN BRI with a U interface; a U interface indicates that the NT1 device is built in. If you are using an external NT1 device, or if your service provider uses an NT1 device, the router needs an ISDN BRI S/T interface. Because routers can have multiple ISDN interface types, you need to determine which interface you need when you purchase the router. You can determine which type of ISDN connector the router has by looking at the port label. Figure 2-16 shows the different port types for the ISDN interface.

Figure 2-16 *ISDN Port Types*

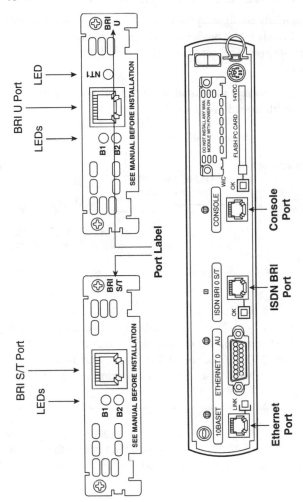

To interconnect the ISDN BRI port to the service provider device, you will use a UTP category 5 straight-through cable.

CAUTION It is important to insert a cable running from an ISDN BRI port only to an ISDN jack or an ISDN switch. ISDN BRI uses voltages that can seriously damage non-ISDN devices.

Setting Up Console Connections to Cisco Devices

In order to initially configure your Cisco device, you will need to provide a management connection directly to the device. For Cisco equipment, this management attachment is called a *console port*. The console port allows you to monitor and configure a Cisco hub, switch, or router.

The cable used between a terminal and a console port is a rollover cable with RJ-45 connectors, as illustrated in Figure 2-17.

Figure 2-17 *Connecting a Device with a Console Cable*

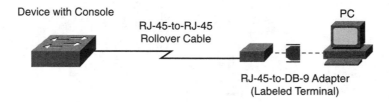

NOTE   Not all Cisco devices use a rollover cable to connect a console port to a PC. The rollover cable is the most common and is used for the routers and switches that this book focuses on (that is, 1600, 2500, 2600, and 3600 series routers and 1900 and 2820 switches). If you have a different device, please check your documentation for console connectivity requirements.

A rollover cable has a different pinout than the straight-through or crossover RJ-45 cables used with Ethernet or ISDN BRI. The pinout for a rollover is as follows:

1—8
2—7
3—6
4—5
5—4
6—3
7—2
8—1

To set up the connection between your terminal and the Cisco console port, you must do the following:

Step 1 Cable the device using a rollover cable. You may need an RJ-45-to-DB-9 or an RJ-45-to-DB-25 adapter for your PC or terminal.

Step 2 Configure terminal emulation application with the following COM port settings: 9600 bps, 8 data bits, no parity, 1 stop bit, and no flow control. This provides out-of-band console access.

NOTE The AUX port provided on some devices can be used to provide out-of-band management via a modem. The AUX port must be configured using the console port before it can be used. The AUX port also uses the settings of 9600 bps, 8 data bits, no parity, and 1 stop bit. The speed of this port can be set as high as 15,200 bps on some devices. The AUX port can be used for various other functions, including data transfer for dial-on-demand-routing.

Summary

In this chapter, you learned about the physical layer support needed to interconnect Cisco devices. For the LAN, there are different media types and different connectors. Straight-through and crossover cables are used to interconnect different network devices. For WAN services, serial cables are used to connect to leased lines, and for ISDN, routers need the appropriate interface to connect to the service provider cloud. Finally, you learned the process for connecting a Cisco device to a terminal in order to perform configuration and monitoring.

Review Questions

  1 What are the three Ethernet bandwidths?

  2 Which category of cable can be used for 10 Mbps and 100 Mbps Ethernet?

  3 What type of connection cable has a pinout that is identical on both ends when compared to one another?

  4 Name one instance when you would use a crossover cable.

  5 Name three types of serial connectors.

  6 Which type of ISDN connector has an integrated NT1?

  7 What type of cable is needed to connect to a console port?

Upon completion of this chapter, you will be able to perform the following tasks:

- Start the Cisco switch and router and describe and recognize a normal boot sequence.

- Provide an initial configuration for the switch and apply a basic initial configuration to the router using the setup facility.

- Describe and use the command modes to interact with the Cisco IOS software.

- Use the online help facilities associated with the command-line interface to modify the configuration of a device.

- Use the Cisco switch and router **show** commands to determine fundamental operational characteristics of the switch.

CHAPTER 3

Operating and Configuring a Cisco IOS Device

In this chapter, you will learn the process of starting and configuring a Cisco switch and router. You will also learn to perform tasks using the Cisco IOS software user interface. In order to install Cisco devices in your network, you need to understand the startup of the Cisco switch and router and describe and recognize a normal boot sequence. It will also be important to provide an initial configuration for the switch and apply a basic initial configuration to the router using the setup facility.

After you have established an initial setup, you will need to describe and use the command modes to interact with the Cisco IOS software. Learn to use the online help facilities associated with the command-line interface to modify the configuration of a device. Finally, you will need to use the Cisco switch and router **show** commands to determine fundamental operational characteristics of the switch.

Basic Operation of Cisco IOS Software

Cisco's internetwork operating system (IOS) software platform is implemented on the varied hardware discussed in this book. IOS software delivers network services and enables networked applications. It is the embedded software architecture in all of the Cisco routers, and it is also the operating system of the Catalyst 1900 enterprise series switches.

Cisco IOS enables network services in these products, including the following:

- Features to carry the chosen network protocols and functions
- Connectivity to provide high-speed traffic between devices
- Security to control access and discourage unauthorized network use
- Scalability to add interfaces and capability as the need for networking grows
- Reliability to ensure dependable access to networked resources

A Cisco IOS command-line interface (CLI) can be accessed through a console connection, modem connection, or Telnet session. Regardless of which connection method is used, access to the IOS command-line interface is generally referred to as an *EXEC session*.

You will learn to use the Cisco IOS software to communicate the configuration details for the switches and routers discussed in this book. The purpose here is to help facilitate the knowledge transfer for configuring Cisco devices. Back on the job, you can use this knowledge to support a configuration that will reflect the policy of functions and authorizations that are required by your organization.

Protocol addresses and parameters will be guided by the objectives of this book and will be structured to help you understand internetworking. Back on the job, address and related parameters will reflect legal addressing and the protocol requirements of your company.

When you start the Catalyst switch for the first time, it uses an initial configuration with default settings.

When you start the Cisco router for the first time, it does not have an initial configuration. The router software will prompt you for a minimum of details using an optional dialog called Setup.

You will learn to set up a minimum device configuration for the router and the switch in this chapter. Changes to these minimum or default configurations constitute much of your network administrator tasks. Most of these configuration changes will occur later in this book.

Operations upon Router/Switch Startup

When the Catalyst switch or Cisco router starts up, three main operations are performed on the networking device:

Step 1 The device finds the hardware and performs hardware-checking routines. A term often used to describe this initial set of routines is power-on self test (POST).

Step 2 After the hardware has been shown to be in good working order, the devices perform system startup routines. These routines initiate the switch or router by locating and loading the operating system software.

Step 3 After the operating system is loaded, the devices try to find and apply software configuration settings that establish the details needed for network operation.

There is typically a sequence of fallback routines that provide software startup alternatives if needed.

In the next several pages of this chapter, you will learn about and practice using these three main operations. You will start up the switch first, and then the router.

Router/Switch Configuration Locations

The switch and the router can be configured from many locations:

- Upon initial installation, the network administrator typically configures the networking devices from the console terminal, which is connected via the console port.

- If the administrator is supporting remote devices, a local modem connection at the device's auxiliary port permits the administrator to configure the network devices.

- For selected routers and switches, a CD-ROM can provide a rapid configuration application, such as Cisco Fast Step, to make the most simple configuration tasks easier to accomplish.

After initial startup, there are additional external sources for software that connect to device interfaces:

- Devices with established IP addresses can allow Telnet connections for configuration work.

- Download a configuration file from a Trivial File Transfer Protocol (TFTP) server.

- Configure the device via a Hypertext Transfer Protocol (HTTP) browser.

NOTE   All three of the methods just mentioned assume an active IP configuration and network connectivity to the device.

IOS Command Modes

Cisco IOS software uses a command-line interface as its traditional console environment. Although Cisco IOS software is a core technology that extends across many products, Cisco IOS operation details vary on different internetworking devices.

To enter commands into the user interface, you type your entries within one of several console command modes. Each command mode is indicated by a distinctive prompt.

Cisco IOS software uses a hierarchy of commands in its command-mode structure. Each command mode supports specific Cisco IOS commands related to a type of operation on the device.

As a security feature, Cisco IOS separates EXEC sessions into two different default access levels: user EXEC level and privileged EXEC level.

User EXEC level lets you access only a limited number of basic monitoring commands.

Privileged EXEC level lets you access all router commands (for example, configuration and management). It can be password-protected to allow only authorized users to configure or maintain the router.

The Enter key instructs the device to parse and execute the command.

For example, when an EXEC session is started, the router will display a **hostname>** prompt. The right arrow (>) in the prompt indicates that the router is at the user EXEC level.

The user EXEC level does not contain any commands that might allow the user to control the operation of the router (for example, reload or configure).

To list the commands available at the user EXEC level, type a question mark (**?**) at the **hostname>** prompt. (This feature is referred to as *context-sensitive help*.)

Critical commands (for example, configuration, management, and debugging) require that the user be at the privileged EXEC level. Privileged EXEC mode provides the user with a detailed examination of a switch or router.

To change to the privileged EXEC level, type **enable** at the **hostname>** prompt. If an **enable** password or **enable secret** password is configured, the switch or router will then prompt you for that password.

When the correct **enable** password is entered, the switch or router prompt will change to **hostname#**, indicating that the user is now at the privileged EXEC level.

Typing a question mark (**?**) at the privileged EXEC level will reveal many more command options than those available at the user EXEC level. To return to the user EXEC level, type **disable** at the **hostname#** prompt.

What Happens When You Start a Switch

Initial startup of the switch includes the following steps:

Step 1   Before you start the switch, verify the following:

— All network cable connections are secure

— Your terminal is connected to the console port

— Your console terminal application is selected

Step 2   Attach the power cable plug to the switch power supply socket and power on if there is an off/on switch. Note that not all devices have a switch. Those that don't have a switch start as soon as they are plugged in.

Step 3   Observe the boot sequence:

— Look at the light-emitting diodes (LEDs) on the switch chassis. Figure 3-1 shows an example of these Catalyst switch LEDs.

— Observe the Cisco IOS software output text on the console.

NOTE   This book discusses the 1900 enterprise switch only. Switch information and configuration commands are specific to the 1900 series product line. Your switch might differ.

Catalyst Switch Status LEDs

The Catalyst switches have several status LEDs (as illustrated in Figure 3-1) that are generally green when the switch is functioning normally but turn amber when there is a malfunction.

Figure 3-1   *LEDs on a Catalyst 1900 Series Switch*

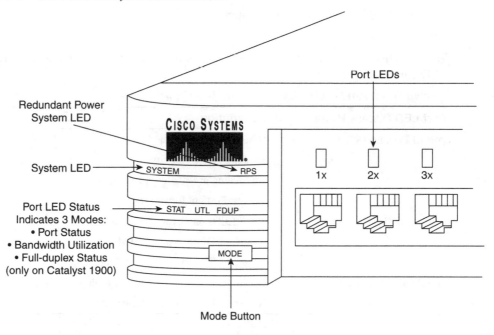

Table 3-1 explains the functions of the System and redundant power supply (RPS) LEDs on a Catalyst switch based on the light status.

Table 3-1   *Catalyst Switch System and RPS LED Status Descriptions*

Switch LED	Description
System LED	Green: System is powered and operational
	Amber: System malfunction
Redundant power supply	Green: RPS is operational
	Amber: RPS is installed but not operational
	Flashing green: Both the RPS and internal power supply are on, and the internal supply is powering the switch

Catalyst switch port LEDs have several modes of operation. As you will see later, the initial startup routines use LEDs to display power-on self test (POST) status.

If the switch is up and running, when you press the MODE button (shown in Figure 3-1), you toggle through other LED display modes. These three modes indicate

- Port status
- Bandwidth utilization for the switch
- Full-duplex support

Table 3-2 lists the port LED display modes and what they indicate based on the various LED colors or lighting.

Table 3-2 *Catalyst Switch Port LED Display Mode Status Descriptions*

Port LED Display Mode	Description
Port LED status (STAT)	Green: Link present
	Flashing green: Activity
	Alternating green/amber: Link fault
	Amber: Port not forwarding
Utilization (UTL)	1 to 8 LEDs on: 0.1 to < 6 Mbps
	9 to 16 LEDs on: 6 to < 120 Mbps
	17 to 24 LEDs on: 120 to 280 Mbps
Full duplex (FDUP)	Green: Ports are configured in full-duplex mode
	No green: Ports are half-duplex

The utilization values shown are for the 24-port switch. Here are the values for the 12-port switch:

1 to 4: 0.1 to < 1.5 Mbps

5 to 8: 1.5 to 20 Mpbs

9 to 12: 20 to 120 Mbps

The Catalyst POST is executed only when the switch is powered up. The POST uses the switch's port LEDs to indicate the test progress and status. Initially, all port LEDs light with green. This condition indicates the start of POST and that the LEDs are functioning properly. Each of the first 16 port LEDs (1x through 16x) is associated with one of the POST tests, as shown in Table 3-3.

Table 3-3   *Port LED/POST Test Associations*

LED	Component Tested	Failure Type
LED 16x	ECU DRAM	Fatal
LED 15x	Not used	
LED 14x	Not used	
LED 13x	Not used	
LED 12x	Forwarding engine	Fatal
LED 11x	Forwarding engine SRAM	Fatal
LED 10x	Packet DRAM	Fatal
LED 9x	ISLT ASIC	Fatal
LED 8x	Port control/status	Fatal
LED 7x	System timer interrupt	Fatal
LED 6x	Content-addressable (CAM) SRAM	Fatal
LED 5x	Real-time clock	Non-fatal: If this test failed, the switch forwards packets. However, if the switch unexpectedly shuts down, it cannot restart itself automatically.
LED 4x	Console port	Non-fatal: If this test failed, you cannot access the management console through the console port. You can still Telnet to the management console.
LED 3x	CAM	Fatal
LED 2x	Burned in address	Non-fatal: If this test failed, the switch uses its default Ethernet and begins forwarding packets.
LED 1x	Port loopback	Non-fatal: If this test failed, some functionality to one or more ports is lost. The switch disables any ports that failed this test, and the failure message on the Menu Console Logon Screen indicates which port(s) did not pass the test. Use only ports that passed the test.

On a Catalyst 1912, the Ax LED is used instead of port 16x to indicate the ECU DRAM test.

After each POST test, the LED for that test indicates test results:

- If the test completes without failure, the LED for that test turns off.
- If the test turns up a failure, the LED for that test turns amber; the system LED also turns amber.

On successful POST completion with no failures, the LEDs blink and then turn off.

If there are fatal failures as indicated in Table 3-3, the switch is not operational. The switch is still operational with non-fatal failures, but it might have limited functionality.

Logging On to a 1900 Switch After Startup

If POST test failures are detected during initial startup, they will be reported to the console. If POST completes successfully, the first display shown is that of the Menu Console Logon Screen, as shown in Example 3-1.

Example 3-1 *Menu Console Logon Screen*

```
Catalyst 1900 Management Console
Copyright (c) Cisco Systems, Inc.  1993-1998
All rights reserved.
Enterprise Edition Software
Ethernet Address:        00-50-BD-73-E2-C0

PCA Number:              73-3121-01
PCA Serial Number:       FAA0252A0QX
Model Number:            WS-C1924-EN
System Serial Number:    FAA0304S0U3
Power Supply S/N:        PHI025101F3
-------------------------------------------------

1 user(s) now active on Management Console.

        User Interface Menu

     [M] Menus
     [K] Command Line
     [I] IP Configuration

Enter Selection:
```

From the logon screen, you initially have three choices:

- Type **M** to enter menu mode.
- Type **K** to enter command-line mode.
- Type **I** to enter IP configuration mode.

M mode is menu mode. This mode can be used to set all switch settings. Menu mode provides descriptions and prompts you for configuration parameters. This can be a useful mode if you are unfamiliar with the parameters you want to set. This is the only mode available on a standard 1900 switch.

When you configure the switch from the user interface that runs on a console or remote terminal, Cisco IOS software provides a command-line interface (CLI), option K, called EXEC mode. The EXEC process interprets the commands you enter and carries out the corresponding operations. In order to access this mode, you must first log in to the device.

As mentioned earlier, for security purposes, the EXEC process has two levels of access to the commands: user mode and privileged mode.

- **User mode**—Typical tasks include those that check the switch status (look-only mode).
- **Privileged mode**—Typical tasks include those that change the switch's configuration.

Example 3-2 illustrates the process of moving between the EXEC levels, where the > prompt indicates user mode and the # prompt indicates privileged mode.

Example 3-2 *Navigating Between User and Privileged EXEC Levels*

```
>
> enable
Enter password:
#
# disable
> exit
```

NOTE   For security reasons, the network device will not echo the password that is entered. However, if you are configuring a network device over a modem link or using Telnet, the password is sent in clear text. Telnet does not offer a method to secure packets.

Keyboard Help in Switch Command-Line Interface

The Catalyst switch uses Cisco IOS software with several command-line input help facilities, including the following:

- **Context-sensitive help**—Provides a list of commands and the arguments associated with a specific command.
- **Console error messages**—Identify problems with switch commands entered incorrectly so that you can alter or correct them.
- **Command history buffer**—Allows the recall of long or complex commands or entries for re-entry, review, or correction.

Context-Sensitive Help for Switches

A question mark (**?**) during the EXEC session will always provide help. Two types of context-sensitive help are available: word help and command syntax help.

You can use **?** to get a list of commands that begin with a particular sequence of characters. To do this, type the character(s) followed immediately by **?**. Do not include a space before the question mark. The switch will then display a list of commands that start with the characters that were entered. For example, **s?** might provide the output shown in Example 3-3.

Example 3-3   *Example of Command Help Feature*

```
cisco 1900#s?
session  show
cisco 1900#s
```

You can use **?** to get command syntax help so that you can see how to complete a command. Enter **?** in place of a keyword or argument that you are unsure of. Remember to include a space before **?**. The network device will then display a list of available command options, with **<cr>** standing for carriage return (this does not occur in Example 3-3). Example 3-4 shows the output you would see when entering **show ?** after the prompt.

Example 3-4   *show ? Output*

```
cisco 1900#show ?
  bridge-group        Display port grouping using bridge groups
  cdp                 cdp information
  cgmp                Cgmp information
  history             Display the session command history
  interfaces          Interface status and configuration
  ip                  Display IP configuration
  line                Display console/RS-232 port configuration
  mac-address-table   MAC forwarding table
  port                Display port information
  running-config      Show current operating configuration
  snmp                Display snmp related information
  spantree            Spanning tree subsystem
  spantree-option     Show STP port option parameter
  spantree-template   Show STP bridge template parameters
  storm-control       Show broadcast storm control configuration
  tacacs              Shows tacacs+ server configuration
  terminal            Display console/RS-232 port configuration
  tftp                TFTP configuration and status
  trunk               Display trunk information
  uplink-fast         Uplink Fast
  usage               Display usage summaries
  version             System hardware and software status
  vlan                Show VLAN information
  vlan-membership     Show VLAN membership information
  vtp                 VLAN trunk protocol
```

TIP	You can abbreviate commands in the Cisco IOS by entering enough of the command to be unique. For example, instead of typing the command **show interface**, you could type **sh int**.

Console Error Messages for Switches

Console error messages on the Catalyst switch help you identify problems with incorrect command entries. Interpreting the message will help you figure out how to alter your command-line entry to correct the problem.

Table 3-4 lists and describes some common CLI errors and shows you how to get help.

Table 3-4   *Common CLI Error Messages*

Error Message	Meaning	How to Get Help
% Ambiguous command: "show con"	You did not enter enough characters for your switch to recognize the command.	Reenter the command followed by a question mark (**?**) with no space between the command and the question mark.
		The possible keywords that you can enter with the command are displayed.
% Incomplete command.	You did not enter all the keywords or values required by this command.	Reenter the command followed by a question mark (**?**) with a space between the command and the question mark.
% Invalid input detected at '^' marker.	You entered the command incorrectly. The caret (**^**) marks the point of the error.	Enter a question mark (**?**) to display all the commands that are available in this command mode.

Command History Buffer for Switches

Reviewing the command history provides you with a list of the contents of the switch's substitution buffer. This is a list of commands that you have most recently entered. To see these commands, you enter the Cisco IOS software command **history**:

```
Switch#history
```

Then, when you see the list of your command history, you can recall a command in the list without having to retype it.

To redisplay a command you previously entered, press the up-arrow key. You can continue to press the up-arrow key for more commands. Some keyboards might not have an up-arrow key, or the application might not support these keys. An alternative to the up-arrow key is the **Ctrl-p** key sequence. If you pass a command going up the history list, you can move back down the list using the down-arrow or **Ctrl-n** key sequence. After you reach the top or bottom of the list, no more commands will be displayed; the list does not wrap. Table 3-5 describes the functions of the command history feature.

Table 3-5   *Navigating the Command History*

Key Sequence or Command	Functionality
Ctrl-p or up-arrow key	Last (previous) command recall
Ctrl-n or down-arrow key	More recent command recall
Switch> **show history**	Shows command buffer contents

Commands to Get Basic Switch Information

Certain CLI commands provide information about the configuration and status of the switch. These commands are typically **show** commands that instruct the switch to display information at the command prompt. Many **show** commands can be entered in both user EXEC mode and privileged EXEC mode. Some commands are limited to privileged EXEC mode. Switch status commands are described in the following sections.

show version Command

The **show version** command displays information about the system hardware, the software version, the names and sources of configuration files, and the boot images, as shown in Example 3-5.

Example 3-5   *show version Output from a Catalyst Switch*

```
wg_sw_c#show version

Cisco Catalyst 1900/2820 Enterprise Edition Software
Version V8.01.01     written from 171.068.229.225
Copyright (c) Cisco Systems, Inc.  1993-1998
wg_sw_c uptime is 15day(s) 21hour(s) 53minute(s) 11second(s)
cisco Catalyst 1900 (486sxl) processor with 2048K/1024K bytes of memory
Hardware board revision is 5
Upgrade Status: No upgrade currently in progress.
Config File Status: No configuration upload/download is in progress
27 Fixed Ethernet/IEEE 802.3 interface(s)
Base Ethernet Address: 00-50-BD-73-E2-C0
```

show version lets you determine the switch's current operating system. This information can be useful in determining a switch's capabilities and can also aid in troubleshooting. Table 3-6 shows key output fields from this command.

Table 3-6 *Key Fields from **show version** Output*

Output	Description
Software version	Information identifying the software by name and version number, including the date and time it was compiled. Always specify the complete version number when reporting a possible software problem.
Switch uptime	The number of days, hours, minutes, and seconds since the system was last booted.
Cisco...	The remaining output shows hardware information and any nonstandard software options.

NOTE   The 1900 series switch supports two versions of software: standard and enterprise. The enterprise version is the one discussed in this book because of its enhanced functions. Standard software does not support the command-line interface option for configuration. Some 1900 series switches can be upgraded to the enterprise version of software, but not all models support this. Please consult Cisco Connection Online (www.cisco.com) for upgrade information.

show running-configuration Command

show running-configuration is a privileged command that displays the switch's active configuration file, including passwords, the system name, and the settings for interfaces and the console and auxiliary ports. Example 3-6 displays the output when you execute the **show running-configuration** command on a Catalyst 1924 and then on a Catalyst 1912.

Example 3-6 *show running-configuration on Catalyst 1924 and Catalyst 1912*

```
wg_sw_c#show run

Building configuration...
Current configuration:
!
hostname "wg_sw_c"
!
ip address 10.1.1.33 255.255.255.0
ip default-gateway 10.3.3.3
!
interface Ethernet 0/1
```

continues

Example 3-6   *show running-configuration* on Catalyst 1924 and Catalyst 1912 (Continued)

```
<text omitted>
interface Ethernet 0/24
!
Interface Ethernet 0/25
!
interface FastEthernet 0/26
!
interface FastEthernet 0/27

wg_sw_c#show run

Building configuration...
Current configuration:
!
hostname "wg_sw_c"
!
ip address 10.1.1.33 255.255.255.0
ip default-gateway 10.3.3.3
!
interface Ethernet 0/1
<text omitted>
interface Ethernet 0/12
!
Interface Ethernet 0/25
!
interface FastEthernet 0/26
!
interface FastEthernet 0/27
```

NOTE   Cisco IOS configuration files typically show nondefault configuration information. For example, you can't tell that the Spanning-Tree Protocol is enabled by looking at this file, but as a default setting it is actually enabled.

show interfaces Command

The **show interfaces** command displays statistics for all interfaces configured on the switch. Both the switch trunks and the switch line ports are considered interfaces. The resulting output varies, depending on the network for which an interface has been configured. Usually, you enter this command with the options *type* and *slot/number*, where *type* allows values such as Ethernet and FastEthernet, and *slot/number* indicates the slot and port number on the selected interface. For 1900 series switches, the slot is always 0. Example 3-7 displays some sample output from running the **show interfaces** command.

Example 3-7 *show interfaces Output*

```
wg_sw_c#show interfaces ethernet 0/1

Ethernet 0/1 is Enabled
Hardware is Built-in 10Base-T
Address is 0050.BD73.E2C1
MTU 1500 bytes, BW 10000 Kbits
802.1d STP State:  Forwarding      Forward Transitions:  1
Port monitoring: Disabled
Unknown unicast flooding: Enabled
Unregistered multicast flooding: Enabled
Description:
Duplex setting: Half duplex
Back pressure: Disabled
--More--
```

The **show interfaces** command is a very useful command when configuring and troubleshooting the switch. Table 3-7 details the meaning of some of the significant fields in this output.

Table 3-7 *Key Fields from the show interfaces Output*

Output	Description
Ethernet 0/1 is Enabled	Indicates the current status of the interface hardware. Enabled indicates an active interface.
Hardware is ... 10BaseT	Shows the physical characteristics of the switch port.
Address is 0050.BD73.E2C1	The Media Access Control (MAC) address that identifies this switch port on the LAN segment.
MTU 1500 bytes	The size of the maximum transmission unit for the interface.
802.1d STP State: Forwarding	Indicates Spanning-Tree Protocol status. In this case, Spanning Tree is allowing this port to forward frames.

Note that two layers of the OSI model are represented in this output: **Hardware is 10BaseT** (physical) and **Address is 0050.BD73.E2C1** (data link). You should recall from Chapter 1 that switches operate at Layer 2 of the OSI model.

show ip Command

The **show ip** command displays the switch's current IP configuration. Example 3-8 displays some sample output from running the **show ip** command.

Example 3-8   *show ip Output*

```
wg_sw_a#show ip
IP Address: 10.5.5.11
Subnet Mask: 255.255.255.0
Default Gateway: 10.5.5.3
Management VLAN:  1
Domain name:
Name server 1: 0.0.0.0
Name server 2: 0.0.0.0
HTTP server : Enabled
HTTP port :  80
RIP : Enabled
wg_sw_a#
```

Output from the **show ip** command shows the IP address, subnet mask, gateway address, and other configurable IP parameters. The switch's IP configuration allows for in-band management of the switch.

Configuring the Switch from the Command Line

Most switch functions are built into the device's firmware to improve performance. Because of this and the fact that the switch operates independently of any Layer 3 protocol information, the switch can be implemented with minimal configuration. However, many of the switch's parameters can be modified to customize the switch to your networking needs. In order to configure a switch, you need to move into a command-line mode that allows you to change configuration parameters. The mode on the switch that allows you to do this is configuration mode. Many configuration modes are available to configure different switch parameters. To configure parameters on the switch, we will move from privileged EXEC mode to various configuration modes.

The following syntax demonstrates global configuration mode:

```
wg_sw_a# conf term
wg_sw_a(config)#
```

Interface configuration mode looks like this:

```
wg_sw_a(config)# interface e0/1
wg_sw_a(config-if)#
```

Note the change in the prompt when moving to different modes. As always, help is provided at this level of the CLI by the question mark (**?**). It is important to mention that configuration changes to the switch are immediate. As soon as you press Return in any configuration mode, the parameter has been changed, and the action executes in running memory.

One of the first things you should configure on your switch is a system name. Naming your switch helps you better manage your network by being able to uniquely identify each switch within the network. The name of the switch is considered to be the host name and is the name displayed at the system prompt. The following statement demonstrates the process of naming the switch (note that the change is immediate):

```
(config)#hostname wg_sw_c
wg_sw_c(config)#
```

Another parameter that you want to configure on the switch is an IP address. The IP address is a global parameter set on the switch and is required to Telnet to and from the switch. In addition, the IP address is used if you will use SNMP to manage the switch. The statement to configure the IP address (for the switch named **wg_sw_a**) would be **wg_sw_a(config)# ip address** *ip address mask*.

For example, you might have the following IP address assignment:

```
wg_sw_a(config)#ip address 10.5.5.11 255.255.255.0
```

NOTE   Simple Network Management Protocol (SNMP) can be used to manage and configure a network device. SNMP configuration is beyond the scope of this book.

What Happens When You Start a Router

Now that you have learned the startup procedure for a switch, let's take a look at the router. The system startup routines initiate router software. If needed, the router falls back to startup alternatives (as discussed later in this section). For router startup, you should adhere to the following guidelines:

Step 1   Before you start the router, verify the power, cabling, and console connection.

Step 2   Push the power switch to On.

Step 3   Observe the boot sequence (the Cisco IOS software output text appears on the console).

The startup routines for Cisco IOS software have the goal of starting router operations. To do this, the startup routines must do the following:

- Ensure that the router comes up with tested hardware (POST).
- Find and load the Cisco IOS software that the router uses for its operating system.

- Find and apply the configuration statements about router-specific attributes, protocol functions, and interface addresses.

The router will make sure that it has tested hardware. When a Cisco router powers up, it performs a power-on self test (POST). During this self-test, the router executes diagnostics to verify the basic operation of the CPU, memory, and interface circuitry.

After verifying the hardware functions, the router proceeds with software initialization. Example 3-9 shows setup mode. This is the mode that an unconfigured router would enter upon boot. Example 3-10 shows the user mode prompt. This would be the mode a router would enter if it were already configured, assuming that no console password was set.

Example 3-9 *Setup Mode for Router Initialization*

```
      --- System Configuration Dialog ---

Continue with configuration dialog? [yes/no]:yes

At any point you may enter a question mark '?' for help.
Use ctrl-c to abort configuration dialog at any prompt.
Default settings are in square brackets '[ ]'.
```

Example 3-10 *User Mode Prompt for Configured Router*

```
wg_ro_c con0 is now available

Press RETURN to get started.

wg_ro_c>
```

Some startup routines act as fallback operations that can perform the router startup should other routines be unable to do so. One example of this behavior is Boot ROM mode. This is the mode that the router falls into if there is no viable copy of IOS software in router memory. These options are discussed in later sections of this chapter. This flexibility allows Cisco IOS software to start up in a variety of initial situations.

Initial Router Configuration

Router configurations are stored in a special type of memory on the router called nonvolatile random-access memory (NVRAM). If no configuration file exists in NVRAM, the operating system executes a question-driven initial configuration routine referred to as the *system configuration dialog*. This special mode is also called the *setup dialog*.

Setup is not intended as the mode for entering complex protocol features in the router. You use setup to create a minimal configuration. Instead of setup, network administrators use various configuration-mode commands for most router configuration tasks.

The primary purpose of setup mode is to rapidly bring up a minimal-feature configuration for any router that cannot find its configuration from some other source.

Many of the prompts in the dialog of the setup command facility have default answers in square brackets ([ ]) following the question. Pressing the Return key allows you to use the defaults.

When the setup dialog begins, you can choose not to continue with the system configuration by entering **No** at the prompt. To begin the initial configuration process, enter **Yes**.

You can press **Ctrl-c** to terminate the process at any time. **Ctrl-c** returns you to the user EXEC prompt (**Router>**) without making any configuration changes. If you want to start the dialog again, type the **setup** command at the privileged EXEC prompt (**Router# setup**).

Normally, you will answer no to the **basic management setup** question illustrated in Example 3-11 so that you can enter extended setup and be able to configure the system interfaces.

Example 3-11 *System Configuration Dialog*

```
Router#setup


        --- System Configuration Dialog ---

Continue with configuration dialog? [yes/no]: y

At any point you may enter a question mark '?' for help.
Use ctrl-c to abort configuration dialog at any prompt.
Default settings are in square brackets '[]'.


Basic management setup configures only enough connectivity
for management of the system, extended setup will ask you
to configure each interface on the system

Would you like to enter basic management setup? [yes/no]: n
```

During setup, you are prompted for global parameters at the console. You use the configuration values you have determined for your router to enter the global parameters at the prompts. Example 3-12 shows the screen that prompts you for the initial global parameters.

Example 3-12 *Router Configuration: Initial Global Parameters*

```
Configuring global parameters:

  Enter host name [Router]:wg_ro_c

  The enable secret is a password used to protect access to
    privileged EXEC and configuration modes. This password, after
```

continues

Example 3-12   *Router Configuration: Initial Global Parameters (Continued)*

```
entered, becomes encrypted in the configuration.
Enter enable secret: cisco

The enable password is used when you do not specify an
enable secret password, with some older software versions, and
some boot images.
Enter enable password: sanfran

The virtual terminal password is used to protect
access to the router over a network interface.
Enter virtual terminal password: sanjose
Configure SNMP Network Management? [no]:
```

The first global parameter allows you to set the router host name. This host name will precede the Cisco IOS prompt in all configuration modes. At the factory, the router name default is shown between the square brackets as **[Router]**.

Use the next global parameters shown to set the various passwords used on the router.

You must enter an enable secret password. When you enter a string of password characters at the **Enter enable secret** prompt, the characters are processed by an MD5-based encryption algorithm, which can enhance the security of the password string. Whenever anyone lists the contents of the router configuration file, this **enable secret** password appears as a meaningless string of characters. The differences in these passwords are discussed later in this chapter.

TIP   Setup recommends, but does not require, that the enable password be different from the enable secret password. If you choose the same password, this password will be listed in plain text in the configuration file and could easily tip off anyone who might see this file.

NOTE   MD5 stands for Message Digest 5 and is defined by RFC 1321. MD5 is a one-way cryptographic algorithm used for encoding data.

As you continue through the setup dialog, you are prompted for additional global parameters at the console, as illustrated in Example 3-13. You use the configuration values you have determined for your router to enter the global parameters at the prompts.

Example 3-13 *Router Configuration: Initial Protocol Configurations*

```
Configure LAT? [yes]: n
  Configure AppleTalk? [no]:
  Configure DECnet? [no]:
  Configure IP? [yes]:
    Configure IGRP routing? [yes]: n
    Configure RIP routing? [no]:
  Configure CLNS? [no]:
  Configure IPX? [no]:
  Configure Vines? [no]:
  Configure XNS? [no]:
  Configure Apollo? [no]:
```

When you answer yes to a prompt, additional subordinate questions about that protocol might appear, as shown in Example 3-14.

Example 3-14 *Router Configuration: Additional Protocol Configurations*

```
BRI interface needs isdn switch-type to be configured
  Valid switch types are :
               [0]   none.........Only if you don't want to configure BRI.
               [1]   basic-1tr6....1TR6 switch type for Germany
               [2]   basic-5ess....AT&T 5ESS switch type for the US/Canada
               [3]   basic-dms100..Northern DMS-100 switch type for US/Canada
               [4]   basic-net3....NET3 switch type for UK and Europe
               [5]   basic-ni......National ISDN switch type
               [6]   basic-ts013...TS013 switch type for Australia
               [7]   ntt..........NTT switch type for Japan
               [8]   vn3..........VN3 and VN4 switch types for France
  Choose ISDN BRI Switch Type [2]:

Configuring interface parameters:

Do you want to configure BRI0 (BRI d-channel) interface? [no]:

Do you want to configure Ethernet0  interface? [no]: y
  Configure IP on this interface? [no]: y
    IP address for this interface: 10.1.1.33
    Subnet mask for this interface [255.0.0.0] : 255.255.255.0
    Class A network is 10.0.0.0, 24 subnet bits; mask is /24

Do you want to configure Serial0  interface? [no]:
```

You are prompted for parameters for each installed interface. Use the configuration values you have determined for your router interfaces to enter the interface-specific parameters at the prompts.

When you complete the configuration process for all installed interfaces on your router, the setup command presents the configuration command script that was created. Example 3-15 shows one example.

Example 3-15   *Router Configuration Command Script*

```
The following configuration command script was created:

hostname Router
enable secret 5 $1$/CCk$4r7zDwDNeqkxFO.kJxC3G0
enable password sanfran
line vty 0 4
password sanjose
no snmp-server
!
no appletalk routing
no decnet routing
ip routing
no clns routing
no ipx routing
no vines routing
no xns routing
no apollo routing
isdn switch-type  basic-5ess
interface BRI0
shutdown
no ip address
!
interface Ethernet0
no shutdown
ip address 10.1.1.31 255.255.255.0
no mop enabled
!
interface Serial0
shutdown
no ip address
<text omitted>
end

[0] Go to the IOS command prompt without saving this config.
[1] Return back to the setup without saving this config.
[2] Save this configuration to nvram and exit.

Enter your selection [2]:
```

At this point, the router has not yet been configured, but you are presented with three options:

- **[0]**—Go to the EXEC prompt without saving or using the created configuration.
- **[1]**—Go back to the beginning of setup without saving the created configuration.
- **[2]**—Accept and use the created configuration, save it to NVRAM, and exit to privileged EXEC mode.

If you select option **[2]**, the router is configured with this script and the script is saved to NVRAM, allowing this script to be used the next time the router is restarted. After you have made this choice, your system is ready for use.

Modifying Router Configuration

If you want to modify the configuration you have created, you will have to do so manually by entering configuration mode. The setup script only allows you to turn features on; it does not have any support for advanced routing features. Therefore, it should not be used to modify an existing configuration—only to create an initial one.

This configuration can be modified either from the console or by using remote access.

Cisco router IOS software provides a command interpreter called EXEC. EXEC interprets the commands you type and carries out the corresponding operations. This is the same as the modes discussed in the switch section of this chapter. You must log in to the router before you can enter an EXEC command.

For security purposes, the EXEC has two default levels of access to commands—user mode and privileged mode:

- **User mode**—Typical tasks include those that check the router status.
- **Privileged mode**—Typical tasks include those that change the router configuration.

When you first log in to the router, you will see a user mode prompt. EXEC commands available at this user level are a subset of the EXEC commands available at the privileged level. For the most part, these commands allow you to display information without changing router configuration settings.

To access the full set of commands, you must first enable privileged mode; by default, your EXEC prompt shows as a pound sign (#) while you are in this mode. From the privileged level, you can also access global configuration mode and the other specific configuration modes. These modes include interface, subinterface, line, router, route-map, and several others. Use the **disable** command to return to user EXEC mode from privileged EXEC mode, as demonstrated in Example 3-16.

Example 3-16 *Navigating Between User and Privileged EXEC Mode*

```
wg_ro_c con0 is now available
Press RETURN to get started.

wg_ro_c>
wg_ro_c>enable
wg_ro_c#
wg_ro_c#disable
wg_ro_c>
wg_ro_c>logout
```

Typing a question mark (**?**) at the user EXEC mode prompt or the privileged EXEC mode prompt displays a handy list of commonly used commands, as shown in Example 3-17.

Example 3-17 *Getting Help on User EXEC Mode Commands*

```
wg_ro_c>?
Exec commands:
  access-enable    Create a temporary Access-List entry
  atmsig           Execute Atm Signalling Commands
  cd               Change current device
  clear            Reset functions
  connect          Open a terminal connection
  dir              List files on given device
  disable          Turn off privileged commands
  disconnect       Disconnect an existing network connection
  enable           Turn on privileged commands
  exit             Exit from the EXEC
  help             Description of the interactive help system
  lat              Open a lat connection
  lock             Lock the terminal
  login            Log in as a particular user
  logout           Exit from the EXEC
-- More --
```

Notice the **-- More --** at the bottom of Example 3-17. It indicates that multiple screens are available as output and that more commands follow. Whenever the **More** prompt appears, you can proceed as follows:

- Resume output of the next available screen by pressing the space bar.

- Display the next line by pressing the Return key (or, on some keyboards, the Enter key).

- Press any other key to return to the EXEC prompt.

NOTE	Screen output will vary with Cisco IOS software level and router configuration.

Type **enable** to enter privileged mode. If the router is so configured, you might be prompted for a password.

Typing a question mark (**?**) at the user prompt or the privileged prompt displays a much longer list of EXEC commands, as illustrated in Example 3-18.

Example 3-18 *Getting Help with Privileged EXEC Mode Commands*

```
wg_ro_c#?
Exec commands:
  access-enable    Create a temporary Access-List entry
  access-profile   Apply user-profile to interface
  access-template  Create a temporary Access-List entry
  bfe              For manual emergency modes setting
  cd               Change current directory
  clear            Reset functions
  clock            Manage the system clock
  configure        Enter configuration mode
  connect          Open a terminal connection
  copy             Copy from one file to another
  debug            Debugging functions (see also 'undebug')
  delete           Delete a file
  dir              List files on a filesystem
  disable          Turn off privileged commands
  disconnect       Disconnect an existing network connection
  enable           Turn on privileged commands
  erase            Erase a filesystem
  exit             Exit from the EXEC
  help             Description of the interactive help system
 -- More --
```

NOTE	You can complete a command string by typing the unique character string and then pressing the Tab key. Screen output varies with Cisco IOS software level and router configuration.

Keyboard Help in Router Command-Line Interface

The Cisco router uses Cisco IOS software with extensive command-line input help facilities, including the following:

- **Context-sensitive help**—Provides a list of commands and the arguments associated with a specific command.

- **Console error messages**—Identify problems with router commands entered incorrectly so that you can alter or correct them.
- **Command history buffer**—Allows recall of long or complex commands or entries for re-entry, review, or correction.

Context-Sensitive Help for Routers

Like the help for Catalyst 1900 switches, Cisco IOS CLI on Cisco routers offers context-sensitive word help and command syntax help.

- For word help, use the question mark (**?**) following one or more characters. This provides a list of commands that begin with a particular character sequence.
- For command syntax help, use the **?** in the place of a keyword or argument. Include a space before the **?**.

NOTE   As mentioned in the switch section, the routers and the Catalyst 1900 switches have similar command-line help facilities. All the help facilities mentioned in this section for routers also apply to the Catalyst 1900 switches unless otherwise stated.

Special control and escape character combinations reduce the need to retype entire command strings. The Cisco IOS software on Cisco routers also provides several commands and characters to recall or complete command entries from a history buffer that keeps the last several commands that you entered. You can reuse rather than retype these commands if appropriate.

TIP   You can abbreviate commands in the Cisco IOS by entering enough of the command to be unique. For example, instead of typing the command **show interface**, you could type **sh int**.

Console Error Messages for Routers

Console error messages on the router help you identify problems with incorrect command entries. Interpreting the message will help you figure out how to alter your command-line entry to correct the problem.

Table 3-8 lists some of the error messages you might encounter while using the command-line interface on the router.

Table 3-8   *Common CLI Error Messages*

Error Message	Meaning	How to Get Help
% Ambiguous command: "show con"	You did not enter enough characters for your switch to recognize the command.	Reenter the command followed by a question mark (**?**) with no space between the command and the question mark. The possible keywords that you can enter with the command are displayed.
% Incomplete command.	You did not enter all the keywords or values required by this command.	Reenter the command followed by a question mark (**?**) with a space between the command and the question mark.
% Invalid input detected at '^' marker.	You entered the command incorrectly. The caret (**^**) marks the point of the error.	Enter a question mark (**?**) to display all the commands that are available in this command mode.

Command History Buffer for Routers

Reviewing the command history allows you to see a list of the contents of the device's command buffer. This is a list of commands that you have most recently entered. To see these commands, you enter the IOS software command **show history**.

This feature is particularly useful for recalling long or complex commands or entries. With the command history feature, you can complete the following tasks:

- Set the command history buffer size
- Recall commands
- Disable the command history feature

By default, command history is enabled, and the system records ten command lines in its history buffer. To change the number of command lines the system will record during the current terminal session, use the **terminal history size** or **history size** command. The maximum number of commands is 256.

NOTE The **terminal history size** and **history size** commands are not available on the Catalyst 1900 switches, but the history functionality is present.

TIP Although it is possible to store the last 256 commands you entered, it is unwise to do so. These commands waste valuable memory resources and are flushed at the end of each console connection.

To recall commands in the history buffer beginning with the most recent command, press **Ctrl-p** or the up-arrow key (on some terminal settings). Repeat the key sequence to recall successively older commands.

To return to more recent commands in the history buffer after recalling commands, use **Ctrl-n** or the down-arrow key. Repeat the key sequence to recall successively more recent commands.

Table 3-9 contains a brief summary of the command history controls.

Table 3-9 *Navigating the Router Command History*

Key Sequence or Command	Functionality
Ctrl-p or up-arrow	Last (previous) command recall
Ctrl-n or down-arrow	More recent command recall
Router> **show history**	Shows command buffer contents
Router> **terminal history size** *lines*	Sets session command buffer size

Using CLI Help Features Example

Suppose you want to set the router clock. If you do not know the command, use context-sensitive help to check the syntax for setting the clock. If you intend to type the word **clock**, but mistype it as **clok**, the system performs a symbolic translation of the mistyped command as parsed by the Cisco IOS software. IOS attempts to resolve an unknown command to a computer name in order to establish a Telnet session. If no command or computer name matches what you typed, an error message is returned.

You can use context-sensitive help to give you the command by typing just the first part, **cl**, and a **?** without a space (in other words, **cl?**). The router will then return the commands that start with the letters **cl**.

If you now type the correct command, **clock**, and press Return, the router gives you another error, **% Incomplete command**, meaning that you need to give the router more information. If you do not know what this information is, type a space and a **?** after the command (for example, **clock ?**). Help tells you that you need the keyword **set**.

After entering this, you will see that the router requires more information, such as the time in hh:mm:ss format. You can use the **?** character as an argument after any command string to see what options or requirements the router has for this string.

Example 3-19 documents the process of finding the correct **clock** command as described in the preceding paragraphs.

Example 3-19   *Using Router CLI Help to Resolve Command Problems*

```
Router# clok
Translating "CLOK"
% Unknown command or computer name, or unable to find computer address

Router# cl?
clear   clock

Router# clock
% Incomplete command.

Router# clock ?
set     set the time and date

Router# clock set
% Incomplete command.

Router# <Ctrl-P>clock set ?
hh:mm:ss Current Time
```

You can use last-command recall to retrieve the portion of the command you typed previously, so that you won't have to retype the command. Last-command recall occurs when you press **Ctrl-p** or use the up-arrow (if supported by the terminal emulation program). This automatically repeats the previous command entry. Example 3-19 shows that after last-command recall, the administrator adds a space and a **?** to reveal the additional arguments.

Example 3-20 illustrates the command structure needed for setting the clock, continued from Example 3-19.

Example 3-20   *Setting the Router Clock*

```
Router# clock set 19:56:00
% Incomplete command.

Router# clock set 19:56:00 ?
<1-31>      Day of the month
MONTH    Month of the year

Router# clock set 19:56:00 04 8
                            ^
% Invalid input detected at the '^' marker

Router# clock set 19:56:00  04  August
% Incomplete command

Router# clock set 19:56:00 04 August ?
<1993-2035>    Year
```

Command prompting works as follows: When you see the Cisco IOS software prompter indicating that the command entered is incomplete, enter the year using the correct syntax and press the Return key to execute the command.

Syntax checking uses the caret symbol (^) as an error location indicator. The caret symbol character appears at the point in the command string where you have entered an incorrect command, keyword, or argument. The error location indicator and interactive help system allow you to find and correct syntax errors easily.

Enhanced Editing Mode: Editing Key Functions

The user interface includes an enhanced editing mode that provides a set of editing key functions. Although enhanced editing mode is automatically enabled with the current software release, you can disable it and revert to the editing mode of previous software releases. You might also want to disable enhanced editing if you have written scripts that do not interact well when enhanced editing is enabled. Use the **no terminal editing** command at the privileged EXEC prompt to disable advanced editing features. To re-enable these features, use the **terminal editing** command.

NOTE   The **terminal editing** command is not available on the Catalyst 1900 switches, but these editing features are available.

The editing command set provides a horizontal scrolling feature for commands that extend beyond a single line on the screen. When the cursor reaches the right margin—69 characters by default—the command line shifts ten spaces to the left. You cannot see the first 10 characters of the line, but you can scroll back and check the syntax at the beginning of the command.

Look at the following command entry:

```
Router>$ value for customers, employees, and partners.
```

This command entry extends beyond one line. The dollar sign ($) indicates that the line has been scrolled to the left. Each time the cursor reaches the end of the line, the line is again shifted ten spaces to the left. To scroll back, press **Ctrl-b** or the left-arrow key repeatedly until you are at the beginning of the command entry, or press **Ctrl-a** to return directly to the beginning of the line.

The key sequences listed in Table 3-10 are shortcuts or hot keys provided by the CLI to navigate the command line. The Ctrl and Esc key sequences are based on the key sequences used by the Emacs editor in the UNIX operating system. Use these features to move the cursor around on the command line for corrections and changes.

Table 3-10   *CLI Editing Key Sequences*

Command Line Editing Key Sequence	Description
Ctrl-a	Moves the cursor to the beginning of the line.
Ctrl-e	Moves the cursor to the end of the line.
Ctrl-f	Moves the cursor forward one character.
Ctrl-b	Moves the cursor backward one character.
Esc-f	Moves the cursor forward one word.
Esc-b	Moves the cursor backward one word.
Ctrl-d	Deletes a single character.
Ctrl-k	Deletes everything to the right of the cursor.
Ctrl-x	Deletes everything to the left of the cursor.
Ctrl-w	Deletes a word.
Ctrl-u	Deletes a line.
Ctrl-r	Refreshes the command line and everything typed up to this point.
Backspace	Removes one character to the left of the cursor.
Tab	Completes a partially entered command if enough characters have been entered to make it unambiguous.

NOTE   The Esc (escape) key is not functional on all terminals.

Commands to Get Basic Router Information

In order to get information about the router's configuration and status, you will enter commands at the CLI. These commands are typically **show** commands that instruct the router to display information at the command prompt. Router status commands are described in the following sections.

show version Command

The **show version** command displays the configuration of the system hardware, the software version, the names and sources of configuration files, and the boot images. Example 3-21 displays the output when you execute the **show version** command on a Cisco router.

Example 3-21   *show version Output from a Cisco Router*

```
wg_ro_a#show version
Cisco Internetwork Operating System Software
IOS (tm) 2500 Software (C2500-JS-L), Version 12.0(3), RELEASE SOFTWARE (fc1)
Copyright (c) 1986-1999 by cisco Systems, Inc.
Compiled Mon 08-Feb-99 18:18 by phanguye
Image text-base: 0x03050C84, data-base: 0x00001000

ROM: System Bootstrap, Version 11.0(10c), SOFTWARE
BOOTFLASH: 3000 Bootstrap Software (IGS-BOOT-R), Version 11.0(10c),
  RELEASE SOFTWARE(fc1)

wg_ro_a uptime is 20 minutes
System restarted by reload
System image file is "flash:c2500-js-l_120-3.bin"
(output omitted)
--More--

Configuration register is 0x2102
```

show running-configuration and show startup-configuration Commands

Often, when you're configuring or troubleshooting routers, it is important to view the configuration files. There are two configuration files for Cisco routers—one that is active and volatile (stored in RAM), and one that the router uses to get configuration parameters during startup (stored in nonvolatile RAM [NVRAM]). These files are viewed with the **show running-configuration** or **show startup-configuration** command.

The **show running-configuration** command (**write term** on Cisco IOS software Release 10.3 or earlier) displays the active configuration file currently running in RAM and used by the IOS. Note that Example 3-22 indicates that this is the **Current configuration:**.

Example 3-22 *show running-configuration Displays the Current Router Configuration*

```
wg_ro_c#show running-config
Building configuration...

Current configuration:
!
version 12.0
!
      -- More --
```

The **show startup-configuration** command (**show config** on Cisco IOS software Release 10.3 or earlier) displays the backup configuration file found in NVRAM, which is used to configure the router during startup. Note that Example 3-23 shows that this file is **Using 1359 out of 32762 bytes**, indicating that it is stored.

Example 3-23 *Displaying the Saved Router Configuration with show startup-configuration*

```
wg_ro_c#show startup-config
Using 1359 out of 32762 bytes
!
version 12.0
!
      -- More --
```

NOTE   The commands **write term** and **show config** used with Cisco IOS software Release 10.3 and earlier have been replaced by new commands. These commands continue to perform their normal functions in the current release but are no longer documented. Support for these commands may cease in a future release.

Configuring a Router from the Command Line

The first method of router configuration presented was the setup utility. Setup allows a basic initial configuration to be created. For more complex and specific configurations, you can use the command-line interface to enter terminal configuration mode.

Recall that there are two variations of EXEC mode: user EXEC mode and privileged EXEC mode. From privileged EXEC mode you can enter global configuration mode with the

configure terminal command. From global configuration mode, you have access to specific configuration modes, which include the following:

- **Interface**—Supports commands that configure operations on a per-interface basis. The prompt for this configuration mode is as follows:

  ```
  Router(config-if)#
  ```

- **Subinterface**—Supports commands that configure multiple virtual (logical) interfaces on a single physical interface. The prompt for this configuration mode is as follows:

  ```
  Router(config-subif)#
  ```

- **Controller**—Supports commands that configure controllers (for example, E1 and T1 controllers). The prompt for this configuration mode is as follows:

  ```
  Router(config-controller)#
  ```

- **Line**—Supports commands that configure the operation of a terminal line. The prompt for this configuration mode is as follows:

  ```
  Router(config-line)#
  ```

- **Router**—Supports commands that configure an IP routing protocol. The prompt for this configuration mode is as follows:

  ```
  Router(config-router)#
  ```

- **IPX-router**—Supports commands that configure the Novell network layer protocol. The prompt for this configuration mode is as follows:

  ```
  Router(config-ipx-router)#
  ```

This is an abbreviated list of configuration modes. For a complete list of router configuration modes, refer to "Understanding the User Interface" on the Cisco Documentation CD-ROM.

If you type **exit** in any router mode, the router will back out one level, eventually allowing you to log out. In general, typing **exit** from one of the specific configuration modes will return you to global configuration mode. Pressing the **Ctrl-z** key sequence or typing **end** causes you to leave configuration mode completely and returns you to the privileged EXEC prompt.

In terminal configuration mode, you invoke an incremental compiler. Each configuration command entered is parsed as soon as you press the Return key. This means that if the command is in proper form, it is executed, is stored in running configuration, and is immediately effective.

Commands that affect the entire router are called *global commands*. The **hostname** and **enable password** commands are examples of global commands.

Commands that point to or indicate a process or interface that will be configured are called *major commands*. When entered, major commands cause the CLI to enter a specific configuration mode. Major commands have no effect unless they are immediately followed by a subcommand that supplies the configuration entry. For example, the major command **interface serial 0** has no effect unless it is followed by a subcommand that says what you want to do to that interface.

The following are examples of major commands and the subcommands that go with them:

```
Router(config)#interface serial 0 (major command)
Router(config-if)#shutdown (subcommand)

Router(config-if)#line console 0 (major command)
Router(config-line)#password cisco (subcommand)

Router(config-line)#router rip (major command)
Router(config-router)#network 10.0.0.0 (subcommand)
```

Notice that entering a major command will switch you from one configuration mode to another. However, you must know the syntax of the major command. The help function does not list major commands when in a subcommand configuration mode.

After you have made configuration changes, you must save the active configuration to NVRAM if you want the router to use these changes the next time it is restarted.

To save your configuration to NVRAM, you enter the command **copy running-configuration startup-configuration**. (Use **write memory** or **write** in pre-Release 10.3 software.) If you do not save your configuration changes, they will be lost if the router is powered off or reloaded. Example 3-24 shows how to copy the router's current configuration to NVRAM.

Example 3-24 *Copying the Router's Current Configuration to NVRAM*

```
wg_ro_c#
wg_ro_c#copy running-config startup-config
Destination filename [startup-config]?
Building configuration...

wg_ro_c#
```

One of the first things you want to configure on your router is a name. Naming your router helps you better manage your network by being able to uniquely identify each router within the network. The name of the router is considered to be the host name and is the name displayed at the system prompt. If no name is configured, the default router name is "Router." You assign the router name in global configuration mode. Example 3-25 demonstrates the process of naming the router.

Example 3-25 *Naming the Router*

```
Router(config)#hostname wg_ro_c
wg_ro_c(config)#
```

You can further identify your router by configuring a message-of-the-day banner to be displayed on all connected terminals. The banner is displayed at login and is useful for conveying security messages. When you enter the **banner motd** command, follow the command with one or more spaces and a delimiting character of your choice. In Example 3-26, the delimiting character is an ampersand sign (&). After you add the banner text, terminate the message with the same character and return to configuration mode. Press **Ctrl-c** to exit this mode without entering a message.

Example 3-26   *Configuring the Router's Message-of-the-Day Banner*

```
wg_ro_c(config)#banner motd  &
    Accounting Department
    You have entered a secured
    system. Authorized access
    only! &
```

You can also add a description of up to 80 characters in length to an interface to help you remember specific information about that interface, such as the network serviced by that interface's services. This description is meant solely as a comment to help identify how the interface is being used. The description will appear in the output when you display the configuration information that exists in router memory and in a **show interfaces** command display. Example 3-27 demonstrates how to configure a router interface description.

Example 3-27   *Configuring the Router's Interface Description*

```
wg_ro_c(config)#interface ethernet 0
wg_ro_c(config-if)#description Engineering LAN, Bldg. 18
```

You can secure your router by using passwords to restrict access. Passwords can be established both on individual lines and to privileged EXEC mode. Passwords are case-sensitive.

Example 3-28 uses the **line console 0** command followed by the **login** and then the **password** subcommands to establish a login password for the console terminal. The purpose here is to establish the need for a user to log in to the console before gaining access to the router. **console 0** designates the router's console connection, and **login** prompts a user for a password before allowing console connectivity.

Example 3-28   *Configuring the Router's Console Password*

```
Router(config)#line console 0
Router(config-line)#login
Router(config-line)#password cisco
```

As demonstrated in Example 3-29, the **line vty 0 4** command followed by the **password** subcommand establishes a login password on incoming Telnet sessions.

Example 3-29 *Configuring the Router's Virtual Terminal Password*

```
Router(config)#line vty 0 4

Router(config-line)#password sanjose
```

NOTE   You do not have to enter the **login** command on the vty lines, because it will already be there by default. This is why you cannot immediately Telnet to a router just by putting it on the network, assigning an IP address to the network interface, and enabling that interface. If you try to do so, you will get the following message:

```
Password required, but none set.
```

This message occurs because login processing is already enabled on all the vty lines.

The **enable password** global command restricts access to privileged EXEC mode. Example 3-30 demonstrates how to configure the enable password. You can also assign an encrypted form of the enable password called the enable secret password. Just enter the **enable secret** command with the desired password at the global configuration mode prompt, as demonstrated in Example 3-31. If you configure both of these passwords, the enable secret password will be used instead of the enable password.

Example 3-30 *Configuring the Router Enable Password*

```
Router(config)#enable password cisco
```

Example 3-31 *Configuring the Router Enable Secret Password*

```
Router(config)#enable secret sanfran
```

You can also add a further layer of security, which is particularly useful for passwords that are in configuration files stored on a TFTP server. Cisco provides a feature that allows you to use encrypted passwords. Passwords can be encrypted through the use of the **service password-encryption** command in global configuration mode. The encryption scheme used by this command is not as strong as the one used by the **enable secret** command.

To disable passwords, use the **no** form of the specific password command in global configuration mode, as shown in Example 3-32.

Example 3-32 *Disabling Passwords*

```
Router(config)#no enable secret sanfran
```

Additional Useful Console Commands

Other useful console commands include the **exec-timeout 0 0** command. This command sets the timeout for the EXEC session to zero minutes and zero seconds. The purpose of this is to prevent the session from timing out and disconnecting you. You could also type the command **no exec-timeout** to achieve the same purpose. Example 3-33 demonstrates how to enter this command.

Example 3-33 *Preventing Console Session Timeout*

```
Router(config)#line console 0
Router(config-line)#exec-timeout 0 0
```

Although the **exec-timeout 0 0** command is useful in a classroom or laboratory environment, it is not wise to do this on a production device. The end result would be leaving the console port open indefinitely, thereby bypassing all security you might have set on that port.

The **logging synchronous** console line command is useful whenever console messages are being displayed at the same time that you are attempting to input EXEC or configuration commands. Instead of the console messages being intermingled with your input, your input is redisplayed on a single line at the finish of each console message that "interrupts" your input. This makes reading your input and the message much easier. Example 3-34 demonstrates how to enter this command.

Example 3-34 *Redisplaying Interrupted Console Input*

```
Router(config)#line console 0
Router(config-line)#logging synchronous
```

Configuring Router Interfaces

A router's main function is to relay packets from one network device to another. In order to do that, you must define the characteristics of the interfaces through which the packets are received and sent. These characteristics include, but are not limited to, the address of the port, the data encapsulation method, media type, bandwidth, and direct memory access buffering parameters.

Many features are enabled on a per-interface basis. Interface configuration mode commands modify the operation of Ethernet, Token Ring, FDDI, serial, HSSI, loopback, dialer, null, async, ATM, BRI, and tunnel interface types. When you issue the **interface** *type number* command at the **Router(config)#** prompt, you must define both the interface *type* and *number*. The number is assigned to each interface at the factory or by the physical location of the interface hardware in the router and is used to identify each interface. This identification is critical when you have multiple interfaces of the same type in a single router. Here are some examples of an interface type and number:

```
Router(config)#interface serial 0
Router(config)#interface ethernet 1
```

You specify an interface in Cisco 2600, 3600, 4000, 7000, and 7200 series routers (modular routers) by the physical slot in the router and the port number on the module in that slot. Here's an example:

```
Router(config)#interface ethernet 1/0
```

You define an interface in the Cisco 7000 and 7500 series routers with VIP cards by slot, port adapter (a module on the VIP card), and the port number on the port adapter. Here's an example:

```
Router(config)#interface ethernet 1/0/0
```

To quit interface mode and return to global configuration mode, type **exit** at the **Router(config-if)#** prompt:

Step 1   Enter global configuration mode. As shown in the following command lines, you are configuring the interface from terminal mode:

```
Router#configure term
Router(config)#
```

Step 2   When in global configuration mode, you must identify the specific interface against which you will be issuing commands by entering the appropriate major command. As shown in the following command lines, the interface is serial 0.

```
Router(config)#interface serial 0
Router(config-if)#
```

Step 3   Enter the specified bandwidth for the interface. The **bandwidth** command overrides the default bandwidth that is displayed in the **show interfaces** command and is used by some routing protocols, such as IGRP. The default bandwidth for synchronous serial lines is T1 speed (1.544 Mbps). The bandwidth entered has no effect on the actual speed of the line. Instead, it is used to compute routing metrics and the load of the link. The following command lines show how to set the bandwidth for the router interface:

```
Router(config-if)#bandwidth 64
Router(config-if)#exit
Router(config)#exit
Router#
```

Step 4   In some environments (typically a laboratory), you might connect a data circuit-terminating equipment (DCE) cable to your router to simulate a carrier line. If a DCE cable is attached, issue the **clock rate** command with the desired speed. Be sure to type the complete clock speed. For example, a clock rate of 64,000 cannot be abbreviated as 64. To set the clock rate, you would issue the following command line:

```
Router(config-if)#clock rate 64000
Router(config-if)#
```

NOTE   Serial links have two sides. One side of the link is responsible for clocking and is called a
DCE. The other side of the link is called the DTE. The DCE cable has a female connector,
and the DTE has a male connector. In a production network, the DCE interface is provided
by the service provider and is typically a connection to a channel service unit/data service
unit (CSU/DSU). Routers are typically the data terminal equipment (DTE) side of the serial
interface. In environments where you want to simulate a serial connection, it is possible to
connect two routers back-to-back with a DTE and DCE cable. In order to simulate the
environment, one of these devices must provide clocking. Clocking is the function of the
router with the DCE cable. Clock rates that can be configured on serial interfaces are
typically 1,200, 2,400, 4,800, 9,600, 19,200, 38,400, 56,000, 64,000, 72,000, 125,000,
148,000, 500,000, 800,000, 1,000,000, 1,300,000, 2,000,000, and 4,000,000. However, this
can vary with the type of serial interface you have in your router.

After you configure the router, you will use **show** commands to verify the configuration
changes.

The **show interfaces serial 0** command shown in Example 3-35 shows the changes issued
in our initial serial interface configuration. Notice in the highlighted text that the interface
is up and that the bandwidth, shown here as BW, is set to 64 Kbps.

Example 3-35 *Verifying Router Interface Configuration Changes with* **show interface**

```
Router#show interface serial 0
Serial0 is up, line protocol is up
  Hardware is HD64570
  Internet address is 10.140.4.2/24
  MTU 1500 bytes, BW 64 Kbit, DLY 20000 usec, rely 255/255, load 1/255
  Encapsulation HDLC, loopback not set, keepalive set (10 sec)
  Last input 00:00:09, output 00:00:04, output hang never
  Last clearing of "show interface" counters never
  Input queue: 0/75/0 (size/max/drops); Total output drops: 0
  Queueing strategy: weighted fair
  Output queue: 0/1000/64/0 (size/max total/threshold/drops)
     Conversations  0/1/256 (active/max active/max total)
     Reserved Conversations 0/0 (allocated/max allocated)
  5 minute input rate 0 bits/sec, 0 packets/sec
  5 minute output rate 0 bits/sec, 0 packets/sec
(output omitted)
```

You might need to set the media type on an Ethernet interface. Ethernet interfaces have
different types of physical connections. For instance, you might have an AUI option and a
10BaseT connector, as in the case of a Cisco 4000 series router. This router series has both

of these physical connectors on a network interface module. The default connector is an AUI. Some routers might autosense the connection, but some might require that you select the connector in the configuration. Example 3-36 demonstrates how you would set the media type on an Ethernet interface.

Example 3-36   *Setting the Router's Ethernet Interface Media Type*

```
Router(config)#interface ethernet 2
Router(config-if)#media-type 10baset
```

There might be a need for you to disable an interface. This function is useful when you need to perform maintenance on a particular network segment. You may also choose to do this in order to isolate a network problem.

As shown in Example 3-37, the **shutdown** command administratively disables an interface. As demonstrated in Example 3-38, you use the **no shutdown** command in interface mode to reenable the interface.

Example 3-37   *Administratively Disabling a Router Interface*

```
Router#configure term
Router(config)#interface serial 0
Router(config-if)#shutdown
%LINK-5-CHANGED: Interface Serial0, changed state to administratively down
%LINEPROTO-5-UPDOWN: Line protocol on Interface Serial0, changed state to downd
```

Example 3-38   *Enabling a Router Interface That Is Administratively Shut Down*

```
Router#configure term
Router(config)#interface serial 0
Router(config-if)#no shutdown
%LINK-3-UPDOWN:  Interface Seria0, changed state to up
%LINEPROTO-5-UPDOWN:  Line Protocol on Interface Serial0, changed state to up
```

TIP   Whenever you first configure an interface, unless in setup mode, you must use the **no shutdown** command to administratively enable the interface before it can be used to transmit packets.

The **show interfaces** command displays statistics for the network interfaces on the router, as demonstrated in Example 3-39.

Example 3-39   *Displaying Statistics for Router Interfaces*

```
Router#show interfaces
Ethernet0 is up, line protocol is up
  Hardware is Lance, address is 00e0.1e5d.ae2f (bia 00e0.1e5d.ae2f)
  Internet address is 10.1.1.11/24
  MTU 1500 bytes, BW 10000 Kbit, DLY 1000 usec, rely 255/255, load 1/255
```

continues

Example 3-39   *Displaying Statistics for Router Interfaces (Continued)*

```
Encapsulation ARPA, loopback not set, keepalive set (10 sec)
ARP type: ARPA, ARP Timeout 04:00:00
Last input 00:00:07, output 00:00:08, output hang never
Last clearing of "show interface" counters never
Queueing strategy: fifo
Output queue 0/40, 0 drops; input queue 0/75, 0 drops
5 minute input rate 0 bits/sec, 0 packets/sec
5 minute output rate 0 bits/sec, 0 packets/sec
   81833 packets input, 27556491 bytes, 0 no buffer
   Received 42308 broadcasts, 0 runts, 0 giants, 0 throttles
   1 input errors, 0 CRC, 0 frame, 0 overrun, 1 ignored, 0 abort
   0 input packets with dribble condition detected
   55794 packets output, 3929696 bytes, 0 underruns
   0 output errors, 0 collisions, 1 interface resets
   0 babbles, 0 late collision, 4 deferred
   0 lost carrier, 0 no carrier
   0 output buffer failures, 0 output buffers swapped out
```

Table 3-11 describes the significant **show interfaces** output fields.

Table 3-11   *show interfaces Output Fields*

Output	Description
Ethernet ... is {up | down| administratively down}	Indicates whether the interface hardware is currently active and whether it has been taken down by an administrator.
line protocol is {up | down}	Indicates whether the software processes that handle the line protocol consider the interface usable (that is, whether keepalives are successful). If the interface misses three consecutive keepalives, the line protocol is marked as down.
Hardware	Hardware type (for example, MCI Ethernet, SCI, LANCE) and physical address.
Internet address	IP Protocol address followed by a subnet mask indicator.
MTU	Maximum Transmission Unit of the interface.
BW	Bandwidth of the interface in kilobits per second. The bandwidth parameter is used to compute routing metrics.
DLY	Delay of the interface in microseconds.
rely	Reliability of the interface as a fraction of 255 (255/255 is 100 percent reliability), calculated as an exponential average over 5 minutes.
load	Load on the interface as a fraction of 255 (255/255 is completely saturated), calculated as an exponential average over 5 minutes.
Encapsulation	Layer 2 encapsulation method assigned to the interface.
loopback	Indicates whether loopback is set on the interface.

Table 3-11 *show interfaces Output Fields (Continued)*

Output	Description
keepalive	Indicates whether keepalives are set.
ARP type	Type of Address Resolution Protocol assigned.
Last input	Number of hours, minutes, and seconds since the last packet was successfully received by an interface. Useful for knowing when a dead interface failed.
output	Number of hours, minutes, and seconds since the last packet was successfully transmitted by an interface. Useful for knowing when a dead interface failed.
Last clearing	Time at which the counters that measure cumulative statistics shown in this report (such as the number of bytes transmitted and received) were last reset to zero. Note that variables that might affect routing (for example, load and reliability) are not cleared when the counters are cleared. *** indicates that the elapsed time is too large to be displayed.
Output queue, input queue, drops	Number of packets in output and input queues. Each number is followed by a slash, the maximum size of the queue, and the number of packets dropped because of a full queue.
5 minute input rate, 5 minute output rate	Average number of bits and packets transmitted per second in the last 5 minutes. If the interface is not in promiscuous mode, it senses only network traffic it sends and receives (rather than all network traffic).
	The 5-minute input and output rates should be used only as an approximation of traffic per second during a given minute period. These rates are exponentially weighted averages with a time constant of 5 minutes. A period of four time constants must pass before the average will be within two percent of the instantaneous rate of a uniform stream of traffic over that period.
packets input	Total number of error-free packets received by the system.
bytes input	Total number of bytes, including data and MAC encapsulation, in the error-free packets received by the system.
no buffer	Number of received packets discarded because no buffer space was available for the interface. Compare this with "ignored" count. Broadcast storms on Ethernet are often responsible for no input buffer events.
Received... broadcasts	Total number of broadcast or multicast packets received by the interface. The number of broadcasts should be kept as low as practicable. An approximate threshold is less than 20 percent of the total number of input packets.

continues

Table 3-11   *show interfaces Output Fields (Continued)*

Output	Description
runts	Number of packets that are discarded because they are smaller than the minimum packet size. For example, any Ethernet packet that is less than 64 bytes is considered a runt. Runts are usually caused by collisions. More than one runt per million bytes received should be investigated.
giants	Number of packets that are discarded because they exceed the maximum packet size. For example, any Ethernet packet that is greater than 1518 bytes is considered a giant.

Summary

In this chapter, you explored the startup and initial configurations of Cisco Catalyst 1900 switches and Cisco routers. You learned how to maneuver through the EXEC mode of the switches and routers. You discovered help functions to aid in the use of the IOS. You also explored the other modes and the syntax of the Cisco Internetwork Operating System and learned how to get a base configuration on a router using setup. In later chapters, you will continue to use the basic functions and syntax learned here to perform advanced configurations on the routers and switches.

Review Questions

1 What is the name of the hardware test that a switch and router runs during power up?

2 What are the two default EXEC modes?

3 What command displays the commands in a given mode of the switch or router?

4 What is the command history, and how do you navigate it?

5 What Ctrl key sequence moves to the beginning of a line?

6 When does a router enter setup mode automatically?

7 What mode would you use to perform advanced configuration functions not available in setup mode?

8 Does the **bandwidth** statement affect the speed of a serial link? What is it used for?

9 How do you move back to global configuration mode from any of the specific configuration modes?

10 What command displays the configuration file in NVRAM? When is this file used by the router?

Upon completion of this chapter, you will be able to perform the following tasks:

- Determine names and addresses of neighboring devices, given a Cisco switch in an operational environment.

- Use CDP to obtain information remotely, given an operational switch and router.

- Use information gathered using CDP, Telnet, and IOS commands to create a simple network map of their environment, given operational Cisco network devices.

- Move configuration files between system components and network file servers, given an operational Cisco router.

CHAPTER 4

Managing Your Network Environment

This chapter extends the network perspective by looking beyond the standalone device. In this chapter, you will access and gather information about neighboring devices. You will also gather information about remote devices—devices beyond your immediate neighbor. To help understand the topology of your network, you will document the network, noting information you gathered using the Cisco-proprietary utility Cisco Discovery Protocol (CDP) and the IP utility Telnet.

In this chapter, you will learn the processes and the procedures to perform configuration management. You will learn where configuration files can reside, and you will apply the commands to save and restore configuration files. You will create and restore a backup software image using TFTP, Cisco IOS copy, and configurable boot-up options.

This chapter covers the management of a Cisco network device, including using CDP to build a network map, configuration file management, and IOS image management.

Getting Information About Neighboring Devices

This section contains an overview of Cisco Discovery Protocol (CDP). CDP is a protocol- and media-independent tool used to aid in the management of Cisco devices. Table 4-1 shows the lower three layers of the OSI model. Notice that CDP is a Layer 2 implementation and that it works with multiple media types and protocol types.

Table 4-1 *CDP Operates Across All Protocol Suites and SNAP-Supported Media Types*

Upper-Layer Entry Addresses	TCP/IP	Novell IPX	AppleTalk	Others
Cisco Proprietary Data Link Protocol	CDP discovers and shows information about directly connected Cisco devices.			
Media Supporting SNAP	LANs	Frame Relay	ATM	Others

Cisco Discovery Protocol is an information-gathering tool that enables network administrators to access a summary of protocol and address information about other Cisco devices (regardless of which protocol suite they are running) that are directly connected to the device initiating the command.

CDP runs over the data link layer, connecting the physical media to the upper-layer protocols. Because CDP operates at this level, two or more CDP devices that support different network layer protocols (for example, IP and Novell IPX) can learn about each other.

Physical media supporting the Subnetwork Access Protocol (SNAP) encapsulation connect CDP devices. These can include all LANs, Frame Relay and other WAN technologies, and ATM networks.

When a Cisco device boots up, CDP starts by default. Then, CDP can automatically discover neighboring Cisco devices running CDP, regardless of which protocol suite or suites are running.

NOTE   CDP runs on routers with Cisco IOS 10.3 or later and on Cisco switches and hubs.

Figure 4-1 is an example of how CDP exchanges information with its directly connected neighbors. The network administrator can display the results of this CDP information exchange on a console connected to a network device configured to run CDP on its interfaces.

Figure 4-1   *CDP Facilitates Information Exchange Between Neighboring Devices*

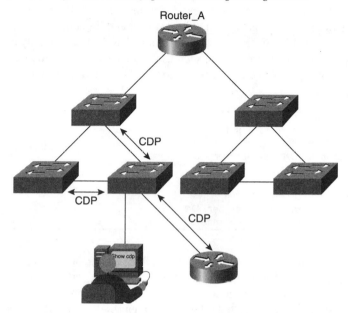

Displaying General Information About Neighboring Devices

The network administrator uses the **show cdp** command to display information about the devices and their associated networks directly connected to the switch. Packets formed by CDP provide the following information about each CDP neighbor device:

- **Device identifiers**—For example, the switch's configured name and domain name (if any).

- **Address list**—Up to one address for each protocol supported.

- **Port identifier**—The name of the local and remote port (in the form of an ASCII character string such as **ethernet0**).

- **Capabilities list**—Supported features. For example, the device acts as a source-route bridge and a router.

- **Platform**—The device's hardware platform—for example, Cisco 7000.

Displaying CDP Information About a Device

Notice that Router_A in Figure 4-1 is not connected directly to the switch of the administrator's console. To obtain CDP information about this device, the administrator would need to Telnet to a switch directly connected to this target device.

You can view the CDP output via the **show cdp** command. CDP itself has several keywords that enable you to get different types of information and different levels of detail, as demonstrated in Example 4-1. CDP is designed and implemented as a simple, low-overhead protocol. A CDP packet can be as small as 80 octets, mostly made up of the ASCII strings that represent information such as the device name, protocol addressing information, port connectivity information, and device operating system information.

Example 4-1   *show cdp Keyword Options*

```
RouterA#show cdp ?
  entry      Information for specific neighbor entry
  interface  CDP interface status and configuration
  neighbors  CDP neighbor entries
  traffic    CDP statistics
  <cr>
RouterA(config)#no cdp run
RouterA(config)#interface serial0
RouterA(config-if)#no cdp enable
```

CDP functionality is enabled by default on all interfaces, but it can be disabled at the device level. To prevent other non-CDP-capable devices from getting information about your device, use the global configuration command **no cdp run**. This will disable the CDP protocol for the entire device. Use the **no cdp enable** command to disable CDP on a given interface. This would be useful to conserve bandwidth when connecting to a non-Cisco device. To re-enable CDP on an interface, use the **cdp enable** interface configuration command.

Although CDP is a Layer 2 multicast, it is not forwarded by any Cisco switch. Two routers connected to a Cisco switch would show only the switch as a neighbor and not the other router. Disabling CDP on a switch would not allow it to forward packets from a router, only to stop sending and receiving CDP on that port.

NOTE   The **cdp run** command is not available on the 1900 switches; use the **cdp enable** and **no cdp enable** interface commands to enable or disable CDP per interface. This will prevent the switch from sending its CDP advertisements out each port, as well as ignore any CDP it received. You can do this on ports connected to hosts to conserve bandwidth.

Displaying CDP Information About Neighboring Devices

Figure 4-2 shows an example of a router named RouterA. This figure is the basis for the output demonstrated in Example 4-2 through Example 4-11.

Figure 4-2   *CDP Neighbors*

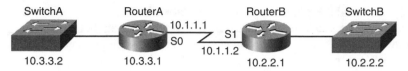

Running the **show cdp neighbors** command on RouterA will result in the output shown in Example 4-2.

Example 4-2   *show cdp neighbors Command Output for RouterA in Figure 4-2*

```
RouterA#show cdp neighbors
Capability Codes: R - Router, T - Trans Bridge, B - Source Route Bridge
                  S - Switch, H - Host, I - IGMP, r - Repeater

Device ID         Local Intrfce    Holdtme    Capability  Platform  Port ID
RouterB           Ser 0            148        R           2522      Ser 1
SwitchA0050BD855780 Eth 0          167        T S         1900      2
```

NOTE   Notice that SwitchA in Example 4-2 also provides its MAC address as part of the system name.

For each local port, the display (as demonstrated in Example 4-2) shows the following:

- Neighbor device ID
- Local interface
- The hold time value in seconds
- Neighbor device capability code
- Hardware platform of the neighbor
- Neighbor's remote port ID

The hold time value indicates how long the receiving device should hold the CDP packet before discarding it.

The format of the **show cdp neighbors** output varies between types, but the available information is generally consistent across devices.

The **show cdp neighbors** command can be used on the Catalyst switch to display the CDP updates received on the local interfaces. Note that on a switch, the local interface is referred to as the *local port*.

Displaying Detailed CDP Information About Neighboring Devices

If you append the **detail** argument to the **show cdp neighbors** command, the resulting output includes additional information concerning the neighbor device. The output from the **show cdp neighbors detail** command is identical to that produced from the **show cdp entry** * command.

Use the CDP command **show cdp entry** [*router-name*] to display detailed information about neighbor devices. This command displays information about a specific neighbor when the neighbor's name is included in the command string. The name entered here is case-sensitive and can be discovered using the **show cdp** command. Use the CDP entry command variable * to display information about all neighbors, as demonstrated in Example 4-3.

Example 4-3   *show cdp entry * Command Output for RouterA*

```
RouterA#sh cdp entry *
-------------------------
Device ID: RouterB
Entry address(es):
  IP address: 10.1.1.2
Platform: cisco 2522,  Capabilities: Router
Interface: Serial0,  Port ID (outgoing port): Serial1
Holdtime : 168 sec

Version :
Cisco Internetwork Operating System Software
IOS (tm) 2500 Software (C2500-JS-L), Version 12.0(3), RELEASE SOFTWARE (fci)
Copyright (c) 1986-1999 by Cisco Systems, Inc.
Compiled Mon 08-Feb-99 18:18 by phanguye
-------------------------
Device ID: SwitchA0030805AB240
Entry address(es):
  IP address: 10.3.3.2
Platform: cisco 1900,  Capabilities: Trans-Bridge Switch
Interface: Ethernet0,  Port ID (outgoing port): 9
Holdtime : 147 sec

Version :
V8.01
```

The output from the **show cdp entry** command displays the following information:

- Neighbor device ID
- Layer 3 protocol information (for example, IP addresses)
- The device's platform
- The device's capabilities
- The local interface type and outgoing remote port ID

- The hold time value in seconds
- IOS type and version

The output from the **show cdp entry** command includes all the Layer 3 addresses present in the neighbor router (up to one Layer 3 address per protocol).

NOTE   The output from the **show cdp neighbors detail** and the **show cdp entry** * commands displays the same information. On a router, either command can be used to display this information; only the **show cdp neighbors detail** command is available on the 1900 switches.

Displaying Information About Device Traffic

The **show cdp traffic** command displays information about interface traffic, as demonstrated in Example 4-4.

Example 4-4   *show cdp traffic Command Output for RouterA*

```
RouterA#sh cdp traffic
CDP counters :
        Packets output: 56, Input: 38
        Hdr syntax: 0, Chksum error: 0, Encaps failed: 3
        No memory: 0, Invalid packet: 0, Fragmented: 0
```

The **show cdp traffic** command shows the number of CDP packets sent and received, as well as the number of errors for the following error conditions:

- Syntax error
- Checksum error
- Failed encapsulations
- Out-of-memory conditions
- Invalid packets
- Fragmented packets

NOTE   The **show cdp traffic** command is not available on the 1900 switches.

Displaying Configuration Information and Interface Status for a Device

The **show cdp interface** command displays interface status and configuration information about the local device, as demonstrated in Example 4-5.

Example 4-5   *show cdp interface Command Output for RouterA*

```
RouterA#sh cdp interface
BRI0 is administratively down, line protocol is down
  Encapsulation HDLC
  Sending CDP packets every 60 seconds
  Holdtime is 180 seconds
```

The **show cdp interface** command displays the following status fields:

- Administrative and protocol condition of the interface
- Encapsulation type for the interface
- Frequency at which CDP packets are sent
- Number of seconds of hold time

CDP is limited to gathering information about immediate neighbors. Other tools are available for gathering information about remote devices, as described in the following section.

Getting Information About Remote Devices

This section contains an introduction to and overview of Telnet concepts.

The Cisco **cdp** command provides information about devices directly connected to the device initiating the **cdp** command. This helps you find out about local devices. To get information about remote devices—those not directly connected to the device initiating the command—we need to use a different tool.

Establishing a Telnet Session to a Remote Device

One way to learn about a remote network device is to connect to it using the Telnet application. Telnet is a virtual terminal protocol that is part of the TCP/IP protocol suite. Telnet allows connections and remote console sessions from one device to one or more other remote devices.

You will see slight variations when you use Telnet on Cisco routers compared to using it on most Catalyst switches.

With Cisco IOS software implementing TCP/IP on a router, you need not enter the **connect** or **telnet** command to establish your Telnet connection. If you prefer, you can just enter the

IP address or host name of the target device. To open a Telnet connection from a Catalyst switch, use the **telnet** command before the target IP address or host name. Example 4-6 demonstrates the use of the **telnet** command to establish a Telnet connection with a remote Catalyst switch.

Example 4-6   *telnet Command Establishes a Connection with a Remote Device*

```
RouterA#telnet 10.2.2.2
Trying 10.2.2.2 ... Open
------------------------------------------------
Catalyst 1900 Management Console
Copyright (c) Cisco Systems, Inc.  1993-1998
All rights reserved.
Enterprise Edition Software
Ethernet Address:       00-90-86-73-33-40
PCA Number:             73-2239-06
PCA Serial Number:      FAA02359H8K
Model Number:           WS-C1924-EN
System Serial Number:   FAA0237X0FQ
.
.
.
SwitchB>
```

NOTE   Some Cisco devices, such as the Catalyst 1900 switches, do not support the **telnet** command. In other words, you cannot initiate a Telnet session from them. However, the switch will respond to **telnet** commands initiated from remote devices.

Verifying and Displaying Active Telnet Sessions

For both router and switch targets, a successful Telnet connection is indicated by a prompt for console login. Use the console prompt as a way to make sure which device is active on your console.

To verify your Telnet connectivity, you should use the **show sessions** command, as demonstrated in Example 4-7.

Example 4-7   *The show sessions Command Verifies Telnet Connectivity*

```
RouterA#sh sessions
Conn Host               Address           Byte  Idle Conn Name
   1 10.2.2.2           10.2.2.2             0     1 10.2.2.2
*  2 10.3.3.2           10.3.3.2             0     0 10.3.3.2
```

The output of the **show sessions** command displays a list of hosts to which you have established Telnet connectivity. Information in the **show sessions** output displays the host name, the IP address, the byte count, the amount of time the device has been idle, and the connection name assigned to the session. If you have multiple sessions in progress, the asterisk (*) helps by indicating which was your last session and to which session you will return if you press the Enter key.

Use the **show user** command to show whether the console port is active, and to list all active Telnet sessions, with the IP address or IP alias of the originating host, on the local device, as demonstrated in Example 4-8.

Example 4-8 *The **show user** Command Lists Active Telnet Sessions and Verifies Console Port Activity*

```
RouterA#sh user
    Line       User      Host(s)              Idle Location
*   0 con 0              10.2.2.2             3
                         10.3.3.2             2
   11 vty 0              idle                 1 10.2.2.2
```

In the **show user** output, the line **con** represents the local console, and **vty** represents a remote connection. If there are multiple users, the asterisk (*) denotes the current terminal session user.

TIP   Although they aren't documented, some versions of Cisco IOS support the UNIX commands **who** and **where**. The **who** command is equivalent to the IOS **show users** command, and the **where** command is the equivalent of the IOS **show sessions** command.

Suspending, Re-Establishing, and Ending Active Telnet Sessions

Assume that you have an established Telnet session from RouterA to RouterB. To suspend a Telnet session and escape from the remote target system back to your local switch or router, press the keys **Ctrl-Shift-6** at the same time, release the key sequence, and then press the character **x**, as demonstrated in Example 4-9. The prompt of the local system indicates that our Telnet session has been suspended. A suspended Telnet session is one you have left open, but are not currently using. You would be able to return to this session later.

Example 4-9 *Suspending and Resuming an Active Telnet Session*

```
RouterB#<Ctrl-Shift-6>x
RouterA#sh session
Conn Host               Address          Byte  Idle Conn Name
   1 10.1.1.2           10.1.1.2            0     1 10.1.1.2
RouterA#resume 1
RouterB#
```

There are several ways to re-establish a suspended Telnet session:

- Press the **Enter** key twice to return to the previous device prompt.

- Type the **resume** command if there is only one session. (Typing **resume** without a *sessionnumber* will take you back to the last active session.)

- Use the **show sessions** command to find the session number, as demonstrated previously in Example 4-9.

- Use the **resume** *sessionnumber* command to reconnect to a specific Telnet session, as shown in Example 4-9.

Just as there is more than one way of resuming a connection, you can end a Telnet session on a Cisco device using one of the following methods:

- Enter the **exit** or **logout** EXEC command *while on the remote device*. This logs you out of the console session and returns your session to the local device. If you Telnet to a second device when you resuspend, you will return to the original device.

- Another way to end a Telnet session from the local device is to use the **disconnect** EXEC command *while on the local device,* as demonstrated in Example 4-10. If you have multiple sessions, you can disconnect from a single session using the **disconnect** [*sessionname*] [*sessionnumber*] command from the local device.

Example 4-10   *Using the **disconnect** Command to End a Telnet Session Opened by the Local Device*

```
RouterA#disconnect
Closing connection to 10.3.3.2 [confirm]
```

If you suspect a Telnet session from a remote user is causing bandwidth or other types of problems, ask the user to close the session. Alternatively, you can terminate the session from your console. To close a Telnet session from a foreign host, use the **clear line** command, as demonstrated in Example 4-11. At the other end of the connection, the user will get a notice that the connection was "closed by a foreign host." To determine which line to clear, use the **show users** command, illustrated in Example 4-8, to determine where the connection is coming from.

Example 4-11   *Using the **clear line** Command to End a Telnet Session Opened by a Remote Device*

```
RouterA#clear line 11
[confirm]
 [OK]
```

Documenting the Network with the ping and traceroute Commands

This section contains an overview of documenting the network.

Using CDP and Telnet helps you compile relevant device information about your immediate and remote networks. This information is useful to help you create and maintain a network topology map. Other tools that you can use to help understand your network topology include the **ping** command and the **traceroute** command.

The **ping** command (which is said to stand for packet Internet groper) verifies connectivity. The term actually originates from the practice in which Navy vessels send out sonar pings to locate or verify other vessels or obstructions. The **ping** command also tells you the minimum, average, and maximum times it takes for ping packets to find the specified system and return. This gives you an idea of the reliability of the path to the specified system. Example 4-12 shows output from a **ping** command.

Example 4-12 *Use the **ping** Command to Verify Device Connectivity to the Network*

```
Router##ping 10.1.1.10
Type escape sequence to abort.
Sending 5, 100-byte ICMP Echos to 10.1.1.10, timeout is 2 seconds:
!!!!!
Success rate is 100 percent (5/5), round-trip min/avg/max = 4/4/4 ms
```

Use the **trace** command to see the outgoing routes that packets take between devices, as shown in Example 4-13.

Example 4-13 *Use the **trace** Command to Display Packet Routes Between Devices*

```
Router#traceroute 10.1.1.10

Type escape sequence to abort.
Tracing the route to 10.1.1.10

  1 10.1.1.10 4 msec 4 msec 4 msec
Router#
```

For more information on the **ping** and **traceroute** commands, refer to the *Cisco Configuration Fundamentals Command Reference* and CCO (Cisco Connection Online) at www.cisco.com.

Router Booting Sequence and Verification Commands

This section covers in more detail the events that occur during router initialization. Included are commands to control and verify router operation.

Router Booting Sequence

The sequence of events that occurs during the power-up or the booting of a router is important to understand. Knowledge of this sequence can help you accomplish operational tasks and troubleshoot router problems.

When power is initially applied to a router, the following events occur in the order shown:

Step 1   **Power-on self test (POST)**—This event is a series of hardware tests to verify that all the router's components are functional. During this test, the router also determines what hardware is present. POST executes from microcode resident in the system ROM.

Step 2   **Load and run bootstrap code**—Bootstrap code is used to perform subsequent events, such as finding the IOS software, loading it, and then running it. After the IOS software is loaded and running, the bootstrap code is not used until the next time the router is reloaded or power-cycled.

Step 3   **Find the IOS software**—The bootstrap code determines where the IOS software to be run is located. The Flash memory is the normal place where the IOS image is found. The configuration register and configuration file in NVRAM help determine where the IOS images are and what image file should be used.

Step 4   **Load the IOS software**—After the bootstrap code has found the proper image, it then loads that image into RAM and starts the IOS running. Some routers (such as the 2500 series) do not load the IOS image into RAM, but execute it directly from Flash memory.

Step 5   **Find the configuration**—The default is to look in NVRAM for a valid configuration. A parameter can be set to have the router attempt to locate a configuration file from another location, such as a TFTP server.

Step 6   **Load the configuration**—The desired configuration for the router is loaded and executed. If no configuration exists or is being ignored, the router will enter the setup utility or attempt an Autoinstall. Autoinstall will be attempted if a router is connected to a functioning serial link and can resolve an address through a process of SLARP (Serial Line Address Resolution Protocol).

Step 7   **Run**—The router is now running the configured IOS.

Router Components

The following list describes the major components of a router (most are hardware):

- **RAM**—Random-access memory contains the software and data structures that allow the router to function. The principal software running in RAM is the Cisco IOS image and the running configuration. Some routers, such as the 2500 series, run IOS from Flash and not RAM.

- **ROM**—Read-only memory contains microcode for basic functions to start and maintain the router. RXBOOT is also contained in ROM.

- **Flash memory**—Flash is used primarily to contain the IOS software image. Some routers run the IOS image directly from Flash and do not need to transfer it to RAM.

- **NVRAM**—Nonvolatile random-access memory is used mainly to store the configuration. NVRAM uses a battery to maintain the data when power is removed from the router.

- **Configuration register**—The configuration register is used to control how the router boots up.

- **Interfaces**—The physical connections to the external world for the router. These interfaces include the following types:

  — Ethernet and Fast Ethernet

  — Asynchronous and synchronous serial

  — Token Ring

  — FDDI

  — ATM

  — Console and auxiliary ports

ROM Microcode

The four major areas of microcode that are contained in ROM are as follows:

- **Bootstrap code**—The bootstrap code is used to bring the router up during initialization. It reads the configuration register to determine how to boot and then, if instructed to do so, loads the IOS software.

- **Power-on self test code**—The microcode used to test the basic functionality of the router hardware and to determine what components are present.

- **ROM monitor**—A low-level operating system normally used for manufacturing testing and troubleshooting.

- **A "partial" IOS**—A subset of the IOS. This partial IOS can be used to load a new software image into Flash memory and to perform some other maintenance operations. It does not support IP routing and most other routing functions. Sometimes, this subset of the IOS is referred to as RXBOOT code or the bootloader.

The bootstrap code has the responsibility of locating the IOS software. Here is the sequence of events it follows to find the image:

Step 1   Check the boot field of the configuration register. The boot field is the lower four bits of the configuration register. It is used to specify how the router is to boot. These bits can point to Flash for the IOS image, and then the saved configuration (if one exists) will be searched for commands that tell the router how to boot. The field could indicate that the router should load the RXBOOT image, or it can specify that no IOS is to be loaded and to just start the ROM monitor image. The rest of the configuration register bits perform other functions as well, such as selecting console baud rate and choosing whether to use the configuration in NVRAM.

For example, a configuration register value of 0x2102 (the 0x indicates that the digits that follow are in hexadecimal notation) has a boot field value of 0x2. (The far-right digit in the register value is 2, and it represents the lower four bits of the register.)

Step 2   If the configuration register boot field value is from 0x2 to 0xF, the bootstrap code parses any configuration in NVRAM for **boot system** commands that specify the name and location of the IOS image to load. Several **boot system** commands can be in sequence to provide a fault-tolerant boot-up plan.

The **boot system** command is a global configuration command that allows you to specify the source of the IOS software image to load. Some of the syntax options available include the following:

— **boot system flash** [*filename*]

— **boot system rom**

— **boot system tftp** [*filename*][*server-address*]

Note   For the complete syntax of the **boot system** command, refer to documentation available on CD-ROM or from the CCO web site.

Step 3   If there are no **boot system** commands in the configuration, the router defaults to loading the first file in Flash memory and running it.

Step 4   If no valid file is found in Flash, the router attempts a **net boot** using the boot field value as a pointer for the name of the file to request to be downloaded.

Note   **net boot** is a seldom-used method of loading an IOS software image. Image pointer specifications for this method can be found in Appendix D, "Password Recovery."

Step 5   If **net boot** fails, and the configuration register is set to the default
settings, the router will boot the RXBOOT file from ROM.

Step 6   If there is no RXBOOT (mini-IOS) file, or if it is corrupted, the router
will boot the ROM monitor (ROMMON) from ROM.

The flowchart shown in Figure 4-3 displays the sequence of events that occur during router
boot.

Figure 4-3   *Router Boot Flowchart*

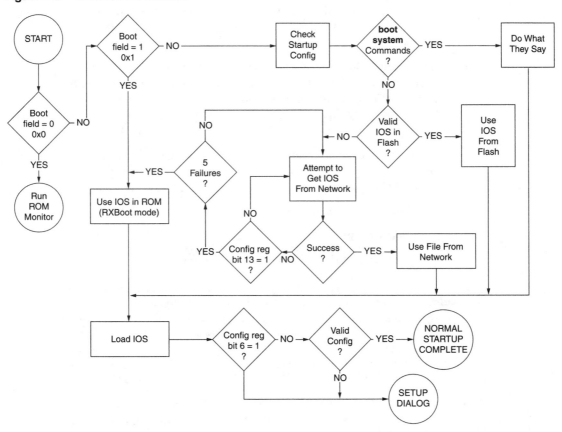

Before you alter the configuration register, you should determine how the router is currently
loading the software image. Use the **show version** command to obtain the current

configuration register value, as illustrated in Example 4-14. The last line of the display from the **show version** command contains the configuration register value.

Example 4-14 *Use **show version** to Display Current Router Configuration Register Value*

```
wg_ro_a#show version
Cisco Internetwork Operating System Software
IOS (tm) 2500 Software (C2500-JS-L), Version 12.0(3), RELEASE SOFTWARE (fc1)
Copyright (c) 1986-1999 by cisco Systems, Inc.
Compiled Mon 08-Feb-99 18:18 by phanguye
Image text-base: 0x03050C84, data-base: 0x00001000

ROM: System Bootstrap, Version 11.0(10c), SOFTWARE
BOOTFLASH: 3000 Bootstrap Software (IGS-BOOT-R), Version 11.0(10c),
  RELEASE SOFTWARE (fc1)

wg_ro_a uptime is 20 minutes
System restarted by reload
System image file is "flash:c2500-js-l_120-3.bin"

--More--

Configuration register is 0x2102
```

If you are in ROM monitor mode, use the **o** or the **config-register** command to list the configuration register setting. The command to use is processor- and platform-dependent. You can determine which command to use by using a **?** at the **rommon>** prompt.

You can change the default configuration register setting with the global configuration mode command **config-register**, as demonstrated in Example 4-15.

Example 4-15 *Use the **config-register** Command to Change the Router Default Configuration Register Setting*

```
Router#configure terminal
Router(config)#config-register 0x2102
[Ctrl-Z]
Router#reload
```

NOTE   Configuration parameters changed in configuration mode are dynamic and do not require a reload. This is not the case for the **config-register** command. This change alters a memory stack of the router and requires a reload before the value is set. Because this value is checked only during the boot process, it is not critical to reload the router immediately after changing the register.

The configuration register is a 16-bit register. The lowest four bits of the configuration register (bits 3, 2, 1, and 0) form the boot field. A hexadecimal number is used as the argument to set the value of the configuration register.

When changing the boot field, follow these guidelines:

- Set the boot field to **0** (0x0) to enter ROM monitor mode automatically upon next reboot. This value sets the boot field bits to **0-0-0-0**. The router displays the **>** or the **rommon>** prompt in this mode. You can boot manually using the **b** or **reset** command.

- Set the boot field to **1** (0x1) to configure the system to boot automatically from ROM. This value sets the boot field bits to **0-0-0-1**. The router displays the **Router(boot)>** prompt in this mode.

- Set the boot field to any value from **2** to **F** (0x2 to 0xF) to configure the system to use the **boot system** commands in NVRAM. This is the default. These values set the boot field bits to **0-0-1-0** through **1-1-1-1**. 0x2 is the default setting.

Use the **show version** command to verify your changes in the boot field setting, as demonstrated previously in Example 4-14.

CAUTION   When you use the **config-register** command, you set all 16 bits of the configuration register. Be careful to change only the bits that you are trying to change (the boot field, for example), and leave the other bits as they were. Remember that the other configuration register bits perform functions that include the selection of console baud rate and whether to use the configuration in NVRAM.

When the specified IOS image file is located, the image is normally loaded into RAM to run. Some routers, including the Cisco 2500 series, do not have an architecture that would accommodate the IOS image, system tables, and system buffers in RAM, and therefore run (execute the IOS software) directly from Flash memory.

If the image is to be loaded from Flash into RAM, it must first be decompressed. The files are compressed in Flash memory to save space. The IOS image file starts after it is decompressed into RAM. Figure 4-4 illustrates this process.

Figure 4-4   *IOS Image File Must Be Decompressed into RAM Before Starting*

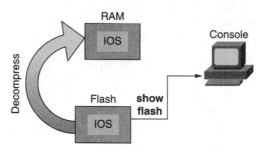

The **show flash** command displays the contents of Flash memory, which includes the image filenames and sizes, as shown in Example 4-16.

Example 4-16   *The **show flash** Command Displays Flash Memory Contents*

```
wg_ro_a#sh flash

System flash directory:
File  Length    Name/status
  1    10084696  c2500-js-l_120-3.bin
[10084760 bytes used, 6692456 available, 16777216 total]
16384K bytes of processor board System flash (Read ONLY)
```

Loading/Running the Router Configuration

After the IOS is loaded and started, the router must be configured to be useful. If there is an existing configuration in NVRAM, it is executed. If there is no configuration in NVRAM, the router will either commence Autoinstall or enter the setup utility. Figure 4-5 illustrates this process.

Figure 4-5   *Loading Configuration Parameters into RAM*

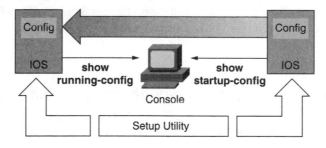

Autoinstall attempts to download a configuration from a TFTP server. Autoinstall requires a connection to the network and a previously configured TFTP server to respond to the download request.

Setup is a utility that prompts a user at the console for specific configuration information to create a basic initial configuration on the router that will be copied into both RAM (running configuration) and NVRAM (startup configuration) upon acceptance of the script created by the utility, as shown in Figure 4-5.

The **show running-config** and **show startup-config** commands are among the most-used Cisco IOS software EXEC commands because they allow an administrator to see the current running configuration in RAM on the router or the startup configuration commands in NVRAM that the router will use on the next restart. Example 4-17 and Example 4-18 demonstrate some sample output for the **show running-config** and **show startup-config** commands, respectively.

Example 4-17 *show running-config Displays the Current Router Configuration Running in RAM*

```
wg_ro_c#show running-config
Building configuration...

Current configuration:
!
version 12.0
!
      -- More --
```

Example 4-18 *show startup-config Displays the Router Configuration Saved in NVRAM*

```
wg_ro_c#show startup-config
Using 1359 out of 32762 bytes
!
version 12.0
!
      -- More --
```

You will know that you are looking at the active configuration file when you see the words **Current configuration** at the top of the display, as highlighted in Example 4-17.

You will know that you are looking at the backup configuration file when you see a message at the top telling you how much nonvolatile memory has been used, as highlighted in Example 4-18.

Managing Router Configurations with copy Commands

In addition to using either Autoinstall or the Setup utility to load or create a configuration, there are several other sources for configurations.

The IOS **copy** commands are used to move configurations from one component or device to another, as illustrated in Figure 4-6.

Figure 4-6   *IOS **copy** Commands Move Configurations Between Routers/Router Components*

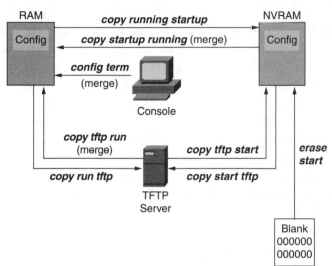

The syntax of the **copy** command requires that the first argument indicate the source (from where the configuration is to be copied) and then the destination (to where the configuration is to be copied). For example, in the command **copy running-configuration tftp** (**copy run tftp**), the running configuration in RAM is to be copied to a TFTP server.

You can copy a running configuration to NVRAM to be saved with the **copy running-configuration startup-configuration** (**copy running startup**) command. This command is used any time you make a configuration change and want to save it. Going the other way, you can copy the saved configuration in NVRAM back into RAM with **copy startup-configuration running-configuration** (**copy startup running**). Note that the commands can be abbreviated.

Analogous commands exist for copies between a TFTP server and either NVRAM or RAM.

NOTE   When a configuration is copied into RAM from any source, the configuration merges with, or overlays, any existing configuration in RAM rather than overwriting it. New configuration parameters will be added, and changes to existing parameters will overwrite the old parameters. RAM configuration commands for which there are no corresponding commands in NVRAM will be untouched.

Configurations are created interactively from the console (or remote terminal) with the **configure terminal** (**config term**) command.

Commands entered from configuration mode or files copied into a running configuration are merged with the existing information. If a file is copied into NVRAM, it is a complete overwrite. If you need to delete the NVRAM file, the **erase startup-configuration** command is used to write zeros into NVRAM and thereby delete the saved configuration.

TFTP servers can be used to store configurations in a central place. These devices must be set up and configured before the upload. The upload process allows centralized management and updating of configuration files.

The **copy running-config tftp** command allows you to upload and save your current configuration to a TFTP server. You are required to supply the TFTP server's address or name and to specify a filename for your uploaded configuration, as demonstrated in Example 4-19.

Example 4-19   *copy running-config tftp Uploads and Saves the Local Router Configuration to a TFTP Server*

```
wg_ro_a#copy running-config tftp
Address or name of remote host []? 10.1.1.1
Destination filename [running-config]? wgroa.cfg
.!!
1684 bytes copied in 13.300 secs (129 bytes/sec)
```

In the display, the series of exclamation marks is used to show the progress of the upload.

The **copy tftp running-config** command downloads a configuration file from the TFTP server to running memory. Again, you must specify the address or name of the TFTP server and the filename of the configuration you want to download. Remember that this is a merge process, not an overwrite. Example 4-20 demonstrates some sample output from the **copy tftp running-config** command.

Example 4-20   *copy tftp running-config Downloads a Configuration File from a TFTP Server to Active Router Configuration*

```
wg_ro_a#copy tftp running-config
Address or name of remote host []? 10.1.1.1
Source filename []? wgroa.cfg
Destination filename [running-config]?
Accessing tftp://10.1.1.1/wgroa.cfg...
Loading wgroa.cfg from 10.1.1.1 (via Ethernet0): !
[OK - 1684/3072 bytes]

1684 bytes copied in 17.692 secs (99 bytes/sec)
```

IOS File System

The Cisco IOS File System (IFS) feature provides a single interface to all the file systems that a router uses, including the following:

- Flash memory file systems
- Network file systems (TFTP, RCP, and FTP)
- Any other endpoint for reading or writing data (such as NVRAM, the running configuration, ROM, raw system memory, system bundled microcode, Xmodem, Flash load helper log, modems, and BRI MUX interfaces)

For a complete description of the IFS commands, refer to the "Cisco IOS File System Commands" chapter of the *Configuration Fundamentals Command Reference*. You can find it on your hardware documentation CD-ROM or at CCO (www.cisco.com).

One key feature of the IFS is the use of the Universal Resource Locator (URL) convention to specify files on network devices and the network. For example, on a Catalyst 1900 switch, the command to copy from NVRAM to a TFTP server would be as follows:

```
Switch#copy nvram: tftp://172.16.100.15/config.txt
```

172.16.100.15 is the IP address of the TFTP server, and **config.txt** is the name of the file to be saved.

Table 4-2 lists some commonly used URL prefixes for Cisco network devices.

Table 4-2   *Commonly Used IFS URL Prefixes*

Prefix	Description
bootflash:	Boot Flash memory.
flash:	Flash memory. This prefix is available on all platforms. For platforms that do not have a device named **flash:**, the **flash:** prefix is aliased to **slot0:**. Therefore, you can use the **flash:** prefix to refer to the main Flash memory storage area on all platforms.
flh:	Flash load helper log files.
ftp:	File Transfer Protocol (FTP) network server.
nvram:	NVRAM.
rcp:	Remote Copy Protocol (RCP) network server.
slot0:	First PCMCIA Flash memory card.
slot1:	Second PCMCIA Flash memory card.
system:	Contains the system memory, including the running configuration in RAM.
tftp:	Trivial File Transfer Protocol (TFTP) network server.

Moving/Managing Router Configuration Files

With Cisco IOS Release 12.0, commands used to copy and transfer configuration and system files have changed to conform to IFS specifications.

The old commands continue to perform their normal functions in the current release, but support for these commands may cease in a future release.

NOTE Commands presented in this book were the most commonly used formats at the time of publication.

Table 4-3 lists the old and new commands used for configuration file movement and management.

Table 4-3 *Configuration File Commands*

Old Commands	New Commands
configure network (pre-IOS release 10.3)	**copy ftp: system:running-config**
copy rcp running-config	**copy rcp: system:running-config**
copy tftp running-config	**copy tftp: system:running-config**
configure overwrite-network (pre-IOS release 10.3)	**copy ftp: nvram:startup-config**
	copy rcp: nvram:startup-config
copy rcp startup-config	**copy tftp: nvram:startup-config**
copy tftp startup-config	
show configuration (pre-IOS release 10.3)	**more nvram:startup-config**
show startup-config	
write erase (pre-IOS release 10.3)	**erase nvram:**
erase startup-config	
write memory (pre-IOS release 10.3)	**copy system:running-config nvram:startup-config**
copy running-config startup-config	
write network (pre-IOS release 10.3)	**copy system:running-config ftp:**
copy running-config rcp	**copy system:running-config rcp:**
copy running-config tftp	**copy system:running-config tftp:**
write terminal (pre-IOS release 10.3)	**more system:running-config**
show running-config	

Managing IOS Images

This section contains an introduction to and overview of managing IOS images.

As your network grows, there may come a time when you want to store your Cisco IOS software and configuration files on a central server. This would allow you to control the number and revision level of software images and configuration files you must maintain. In this section, we cover how to create and load a backup software image in case you lose the software image in the router.

Production internetworks usually span wide areas and contain multiple routers. For any network, it is always prudent to retain a backup copy of your Cisco IOS software image in case the system image in your router becomes corrupted.

Widely distributed routers need a source or backup location for software images. Using a network server allows image and configuration uploads and downloads over the network. The network server can be another router, a workstation, or a host system.

Before you copy software from Flash memory in the router to the network server, you should perform the following tasks:

Step 1   Check to make sure that you have access to the network server.

Step 2   Verify that the server has sufficient room to accommodate the Cisco IOS software image.

Step 3   Check the filename requirements.

Step 4   Create the destination file to receive the upload if required. This step is network server operating system-dependent.

The **show flash** command is an important tool for gathering information about your router memory and image file. With the **show flash** command, you can determine the following:

- Total amount of memory on your router

- Amount of memory available

- Name of the system image file used by the router

- Size of the system image file stored in Flash

Example 4-21 demonstrates how to use the **show flash** command to gather router memory and image file information to verify that you will have room on the server for the IOS image.

Example 4-21   *show flash Displays Router Memory and Image File Information*

```
wg_ro_a#show flash

System flash directory:
File  Length    Name/status
  1   10084696  c2500-js-l_120-3.bin

[10084760 bytes used, 6692456 available, 16777216 total]
16384K bytes of processor board System flash (Read ONLY)
```

The name of the Cisco IOS image file contains multiple parts, each with a specific meaning. For example, the filename **c2500-js-l_120-3.bin** (shown in Example 4-21) contains the following information:

- The first part of the image name identifies the platform on which the image runs. In this example, the platform is c2500.

- The second part of the name identifies the special capabilities of the image file. A letter or series of letters identifies the features supported in that image. In this example, the **j** indicates that this is an enterprise image, and the **s** indicates that it contains extended capabilities.

- The third part of the name specifies where the image runs and if the file is compressed. In this example, **l** indicates that the file can be relocated and is not compressed.

- The fourth part of the name indicates the version number. In this example, the version number is **120-3**.

- The final part of the name is the file extension. The **.bin** extension indicates that this file is a binary executable file.

The Cisco IOS software naming conventions, field meaning, image content, and other details are subject to change. Refer to your sales representative, distribution channel, or Cisco Connection Online (CCO) for updated details.

Backing Up Your IOS Image File

You create a software backup image file by copying the image file from a router to a network server. To copy the current system image file from the router to the network server, you would use the **copy flash tftp** command in privileged EXEC mode, as demonstrated in Example 4-22.

Example 4-22   *Using the copy flash tftp Command to Back Up Current Image Files Prior to Updating Flash*

```
wg_ro_a#copy flash tftp
Source filename []? c2500-js-l_120-3.bin
Address or name of remote host []? 10.1.1.1
Destination filename [c2500-js-l_120-3.bin]?
!!!!!!!!!!!!!!!!!!!!!!!!!!!!!!!!!!!!!!!!!!!!!!!!!!!!!!!!!!!!!!!!!!
<output omitted>
10084696 bytes copied in 709.228 secs (14223 bytes/sec)
wg_ro_a#
```

The **copy tftp flash** command requires you to enter the IP address of the remote host and the name of the source and destination system image file as demonstrated in Example 4-23.

Example 4-23 *The **copy tftp flash** Command Copies the IOS Image File to the Network Server*

```
wg_ro_a#copy tftp flash
Address or name of remote host [10.1.1.1]?
Source filename []? c2500-js-l_120-3.bin
Destination filename [c2500-js-l_120-3.bin]?
Accessing tftp://10.1.1.1/c2500-js-l_120-3.bin...
Erase flash: before copying? [confirm]
Erasing the flash filesystem will remove all files! Continue? [confirm]
Erasing device... eeeee (output omitted) ...erased
Erase of flash: complete
Loading c2500-js-l_120-3.bin from 10.1.1.1 (via Ethernet0): !!!!!!!!!!!!!!!!!!!!!!!
(output omitted)
[OK - 10084696/20168704 bytes]
Verifying checksum...  OK (0x9AA0)
10084696 bytes copied in 309.108 secs (32636 bytes/sec)
wg_ro_a#
```

Loading a New IOS Image File from the Network Server

You load a new system image file on your router if the existing image file has become damaged or if you are upgrading your system to a newer software version. You download the new image from the network server using the following command:

```
Router#copy tftp flash
```

The **copy tftp flash** command will prompt you for the IP address of the remote host and the name of the source and destination system image file. Enter the appropriate filename of the update image as it appears on the server.

After you confirm your entries, the procedure asks if you want to erase Flash. Erasing Flash makes room for the new image. You should perform this task if there is insufficient Flash memory for more than one Cisco IOS image.

If no free Flash memory space is available, or if the Flash memory has never been written to, the erase routine is required before new files can be copied. The system informs you of these conditions and prompts you for a response.

Each exclamation point (!) means that one User Datagram Protocol (UDP) segment has been successfully transferred. Example 4-24 shows the complete syntax for copying a new image from the tftp server into Flash memory. Note that the image file is erased from Flash memory before the new image is loaded. The output also displays a message that the image already exists.

Example 4-24 *The* **copy tftp flash** *Command Copies an IOS Image File from the Network Server to the Router*

```
wg_ro_a#copy tftp flash
Address or name of remote host [10.1.1.1]?
Source filename []? c2500-js-l_120-3.bin
Destination filename [c2500-js-l_120-3.bin]?
Accessing tftp://10.1.1.1/c2500-js-l_120-3.bin...
Erase flash: before copying? [confirm]
Erasing the flash filesystem will remove all files! Continue? [confirm]
Erasing device... eeeee (output omitted) ...erased
Erase of flash: complete
Loading c2500-js-l_120-3.bin from 10.1.1.1 (via Ethernet0): !!!!!!!!!!!!!!!!!!!!!!!
(output omitted)
[OK - 10084696/20168704 bytes]
Verifying checksum...  OK (0x9AA0)
10084696 bytes copied in 309.108 secs (32636 bytes/sec)
wg_ro_a#
```

Summary

In this chapter, you learned commands that help you determine names and addresses of neighboring devices. You also learned how to use CDP to obtain information remotely, given an operational switch and router. You also saw how to use information gathered using CDP, Telnet, and IOS commands to create a simple network map of their environment, given operational Cisco network devices. Finally, this chapter discussed how to move configuration files between system components and network file servers, given an operational Cisco router.

Review Questions

1 What is the proprietary Layer 2 protocol used by all Cisco devices that provides information about those devices?

2 What command allows you to disable CDP on a given interface?

3 After you have discovered an IP address of a directly connected router, how could you connect to the device to manage it?

4 How can you suspend an open Telnet session from a router?

5 Where is the configuration file used at startup stored in the router?

6 What are the last 4 bits of the configuration register known as? And what do they do?

7 What is the main purpose of Flash memory?

8 What command is used to save the current configuration to the one that will be used when the router is restarted?

9 What command is used to save the current configuration file to a TFTP server?

10 What commands in the startup configuration can change how the router boots?

PART II

Interconnecting Catalyst Switches

Upon completion of this chapter, you will be able to perform the following tasks:

- Describe Layer 2 switching (bridging) operations.
- Describe the Catalyst 1900 switch operations.
- Describe the Catalyst 1900 switch default configuration.
- Configure the Catalyst 1900 switch.
- Use **show** commands to verify Catalyst 1900 switch configuration and operations.

CHAPTER 5

Catalyst 1900 Switch Operations

This chapter introduces certain switch technology concepts, covers key operational components of a Catalyst switch, and introduces other functional aspects that influence the switch environment.

In addition, this chapter reviews OSI Layer 2 functions as they apply to Ethernet switching (bridging). This chapter also discusses the operations of Layer 2 switching and how a switch forwards frames to segments. You will also learn to configure the Catalyst 1900 family of Ethernet switches to implement these Layer 2 functions.

Basic Layer 2 Switching (Bridging) Technologies

In order to configure a switch to properly operate in a network environment, you must first understand how it functions. Ethernet switches operate at Layer 2 of the OSI model. Like bridges, they segment the network into multiple collision domains. Layer 2 switches have three major functions: address learning, packet forwarding/filtering, and loop avoidance.

The switching functions are similar to those provided by Ethernet bridges:

- An Ethernet switch learns the MAC addresses of devices attached to each of its ports. The address-to-port mappings are stored in a MAC database.

- When an Ethernet switch receives a frame, it consults the MAC database to determine which port can reach the station identified as the destination in the frame. If the address is found, the frame is retransmitted on only that port.

- When the switched network includes loops for redundancy, an Ethernet switch will prevent these loops from bringing down your network, but still allow backup paths to exist if Spanning Tree is configured.

Ethernet switching increases a network's available bandwidth, reducing the number of users per segment or even allowing dedicated segments and interconnecting these segments.

The Address Learning Function

An Ethernet switch learns addresses and operates like a transparent bridge. The switch maintains a MAC address table used to track the locations of devices connected to the switch. It then uses that table to decide which packets need to be forwarded to other segments. Figure 5-1 shows an initial MAC address table. Notice that upon initialization, the switch does not know on which interface a host resides.

Figure 5-1   *Address Learning: Initial MAC Address Table*

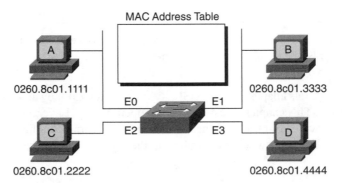

The goal of the switch is to segment the traffic so that packets destined for a host in a given collision domain do not propagate onto another segment. This is accomplished by the switch's "learning" where the hosts are located. The following items outline the major learning and forwarding process:

- When a switch is first initialized, the switch's MAC address table is empty, as shown in Figure 5-1.

- With an empty MAC address table, no source address-based filtering or forwarding decision is possible, so the switch must forward each frame to all connected ports other than that on which it arrived.

- Forwarding a frame to all connected ports is called "flooding" the frame.

- Flooding is the least-efficient way to transmit data across a switch because it wastes bandwidth by transmitting the frame onto a segment where it is not needed.

- Because switches handle traffic for multiple segments at the same time, switches implement buffering memory so that they can receive and transmit frames independently on each port or segment.

In order to understand the learning process, take a look at Figure 5-2, which illustrates a transaction between two workstations on different segments.

Figure 5-2   *Address Learning: Flooded Packet*

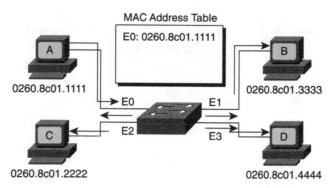

In Figure 5-2, Station A with MAC address 0260.8c01.1111 wants to send traffic to Station C with MAC address 0260.8c01.2222. The switch receives this frame and performs several actions:

Step 1   The frame is initially received from the physical Ethernet and stored in temporary buffer space.

Step 2   Because the switch does not yet know what interface connects it to the destination station, it is obligated to flood the frame through all other ports.

Step 3   While flooding the frame from Station A, the switch learns the source address and associates it with Port **E0** in a new MAC address table entry.

Step 4   A MAC table entry is cached. If the entry is not refreshed by a new frame transiting the switch within a time limit, the entry is discarded.

Switches and bridges become efficient because of the learning process. As stations continue to send frames to one another, the learning process continues, as illustrated in Figure 5-3.

Figure 5-3 *Address Learning: Station Response*

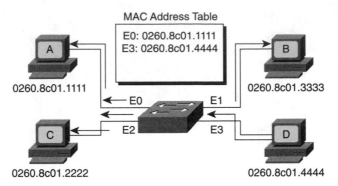

In Figure 5-3, Station D with MAC address 0260.8c01.4444 sends traffic to Station C with MAC address 0260.8c01.2222. The switch takes several actions:

Step 1 The source address, 0260.8c01.4444, is added to the MAC address table.

Step 2 The destination address from the transmitted frame, Station C, is compared to entries in the MAC address table.

Step 3 When the software determines that no port-to-MAC address mapping yet exists for this destination, the frame is flooded to all ports except the one on which it was received.

Step 4 When Station C sends a frame back to Station A, the switch can learn Station C's MAC address also, at Port E2.

Step 5 So long as all stations send data frames within the MAC address table entry lifetime, a complete MAC address table is built. These entries are then used to make intelligent forwarding and filtering decisions.

Forward/Filter Decision

When a frame arrives with a known destination address, it is forwarded only on the specific port connected to that station, not to all stations.

In Figure 5-4, Station A sends a frame to Station C. When the destination MAC address (Station C's MAC address) exists in the MAC address table, the switch retransmits the frame only on the port listed.

Figure 5-4   *Switch Filtering Decision*

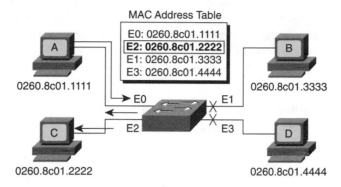

The sequence for Station A sending a frame to Station C is as follows:

Step 1   The destination MAC address from the transmitted frame, 0260.8c01.2222, is compared to entries in the MAC address table.

Step 2   When the switch determines that the destination MAC address can be reached through Port E2, it retransmits the frame to only this port.

Step 3   The switch does not retransmit the frame on Port E1 or Port E3 in order to preserve bandwidth on these links. This action is known as *frame filtering*.

If Station D in Figure 5-5 sends a broadcast or multicast frame, that frame is forwarded to all ports other than the originating port.

Figure 5-5   *Broadcast Frame*

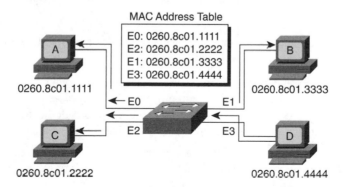

NOTE   Broadcast and multicast frames constitute a special case. Because broadcast and multicast frames might be of interest to all stations, the switch normally floods broadcast and multicast to all ports other than the originating port. A switch never learns a broadcast or multicast address because broadcast and multicast addresses never appear as the source address of a frame.

The fact that all stations receive the broadcast frame means that all of the segments in the switched network are in the same broadcast domain.

Loop Avoidance

The third function of the switch is loop avoidance. Bridged networks, including switched networks, are commonly designed with redundant links and devices. Such designs eliminate the possibility that a single point of failure will result in loss of function for the entire switched network. Figure 5-6 illustrates a switched network designed with redundancy between Segment 1 and Segment 2.

Figure 5-6   *Redundant Topology for a Switched Network*

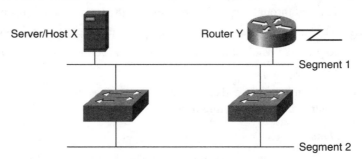

Although redundant designs might eliminate a single point of failure, they introduce several problems that must be considered:

- Without some loop avoidance service in operation, each switch will flood broadcasts endlessly. This situation is commonly called a *bridge loop*. The continual propagation of these broadcasts through the loop produces a broadcast storm, which results in wasted bandwidth and severely impacts network and host performance.

- Multiple copies of nonbroadcast frames may be delivered to destination stations. Many protocols expect to receive only a single copy of each transmission. Multiple copies of the same frame might cause unrecoverable errors.

- Instability in the MAC address table contents results from copies of the same frame being received on different ports of the switch. Data forwarding might be impaired when the switch consumes resources coping with address thrashing in the MAC address table.

The following sections address how loop avoidance can solve each problem.

Eliminating Broadcast Storms

Switches flood broadcast frames to all ports except the one on which the frame was received. Figure 5-7 illustrates the problem of broadcast storms, in which switches propagate broadcast traffic continuously.

Figure 5-7   *Broadcast Storms*

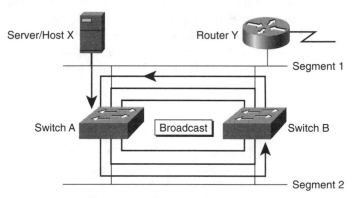

A broadcast storm is a condition of extreme congestion due to too many broadcasts on the network. This can be caused by a misbehaving NIC card, a poorly designed network, or a bridging/switching loop. The broadcast storm illustrated in Figure 5-7 is caused by the following sequence of events:

Step 1   When Host X sends a broadcast frame—for example, an ARP for resolving its default gateway at Router Y—the frame is received by Switch A.

Step 2   Switch A examines the destination address field in the frame and determines that the frame must be flooded onto the bottom Ethernet link, Segment 2.

Step 3   When this copy of the frame arrives at Switch B, the process repeats, and a copy of the frame is transmitted onto the top Ethernet, Segment 1.

Step 4 Because the original copy of the frame arrives at Switch B on Segment 1 sometime after the frame is received by Switch A, it would have also been forwarded by Switch B to Segment 2. These frames would therefore travel around the loop in both directions even after the destination station has received a copy of the frame.

A loop avoidance solution would eliminate this problem by preventing one of the four interfaces from transmitting or receiving frames during normal operation. You will see how Spanning Tree does this in the section, "How Spanning Tree Works."

Eliminating Duplicate Nonbroadcast Frame Transmissions

Most protocols are designed to neither recognize nor cope with duplicate transmissions. In general, protocols that make use of a sequence numbering mechanism assume that many transmissions have failed and that the sequence number has recycled. Other protocols attempt to hand the duplicate transmission to the appropriate upper-layer protocol—resulting in unpredictable results. Figure 5-8 illustrates how multiple transmissions occur within a switched network.

Figure 5-8 *Multiple Frame Copies*

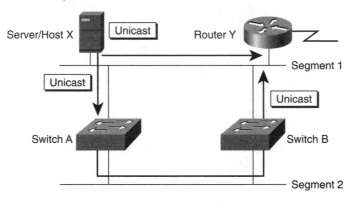

The following list documents how multiple transmissions can occur:

Step 1 When Host X sends a unicast frame to Router Y, one copy is received over the direct Ethernet connection, Segment 1. At more or less the same time, Switch A receives a copy and puts it into its buffers.

Step 2 If Switch A examines the destination address field in the frame and finds no entry in the MAC address table for router Y, Switch A floods the frame out on all ports except for the originating port.

Step 3   When Switch B receives a copy of the frame through Switch A on
Segment 2, Switch B also forwards a copy of the frame onto Segment 1
if there is no entry in the MAC address table for Router Y.

Step 4   Router Y receives a copy of the same frame for the second time.

A loop avoidance solution would eliminate this problem by preventing one of the four
interfaces from transmitting or receiving frames during normal operation. This is another
purpose of Spanning-Tree Protocol.

Eliminating Database Instability

Database instability results when multiple copies of a frame arrive on different ports of a
switch. In Figure 5-9, Switch B installs a mapping between Station X and the port to
Segment 1 when the first frame arrives. Sometime later, when the copy of the frame
transmitted through Switch A arrives, Switch B must remove the first entry and install one
that maps the MAC address of Station X to the port on Segment 2.

Figure 5-9   *Database Instability Resulting from Multiple Frames Received on Different Switch Ports*

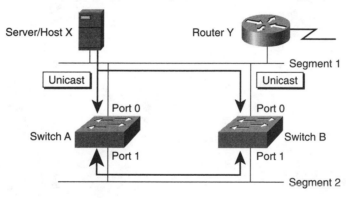

In Figure 5-9, the redundant path without Spanning Tree would create MAC database
instability. This is caused when the following steps occur:

Step 1   Host X sends a unicast frame to Router Y.

Step 2   The Router Y MAC address has not yet been learned by either switch.

Step 3   Switches A and B learn Host X's MAC address on Port 0.

Step 4   The frame to Router Y is flooded.

Step 5   Switches A and B incorrectly learn Host X's MAC address on Port 1.

Depending on the internal architecture of the switch in question, it might or might not cope well with rapid changes in its MAC database.

In this instance also, a loop avoidance solution would eliminate this problem by preventing one of the four interfaces from transmitting or receiving frames during normal operation. Preventing database instability is another function of the Spanning-Tree Protocol.

Multiple Loops in a Switched Network

A large complex switched or bridged network with multiple switches can cause multiple loops to occur in the switched network. As depicted in Figure 5-10, you can run into the following multiple-loop scenarios:

- A loop can exist within another loop.
- A broadcast storm of looping packets can quickly clog the network with unneeded traffic and prevent packet switching.

Figure 5-10 *Multiple Loops*

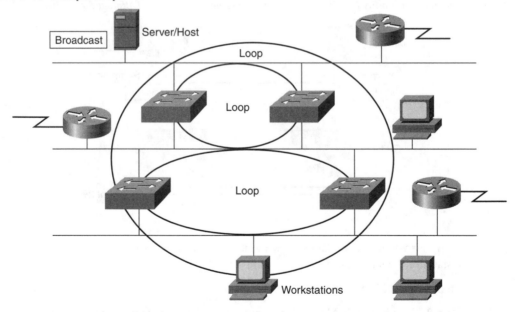

Layer 2 LAN protocols, such as Ethernet, lack a mechanism to recognize and eliminate endlessly looping packets. Some Layer 3 protocols, such as IP, implement a Time To Live (TTL) mechanism that limits the number of times a packet can be retransmitted by networking devices. Lacking such a mechanism, Layer 2 devices will continue to retransmit looping traffic indefinitely.

Therefore, there must be a mechanism to prevent loops in the bridged (or switched) network. This loop-avoidance mechanism is the main reason for the Spanning-Tree Protocol.

How Spanning Tree Works

Spanning-Tree Protocol is a bridge-to-bridge protocol developed by DEC. The DEC Spanning-Tree Algorithm was subsequently revised by the IEEE 802 committee and published in the IEEE 802.1d specification. The DEC and the IEEE 802.1d algorithm are not the same, nor are they compatible. The Catalyst 1900 switches use the IEEE 802.1d Spanning-Tree Protocol.

The purpose of the Spanning-Tree Protocol is to maintain a loop-free network. A loop-free path is accomplished when a device recognizes a loop in the topology and blocks one or more redundant ports. As illustrated in Figure 5-11, there is now only one active path from Segment 1 to Segment 2.

Figure 5-11 *Port Blocking*

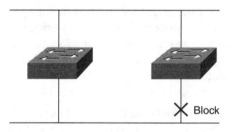

Spanning-Tree Protocol continually explores the network so that a failure or addition of a link, switch, or bridge is discovered quickly. When the network topology changes, Spanning-Tree Protocol reconfigures switch or bridge ports to avoid a total loss of connectivity or the creation of new loops.

NOTE   Spanning-Tree Protocol is enabled by default in Catalyst switches.

Figure 5-12 illustrates a loop-free network as created by the Spanning-Tree Protocol.

Figure 5-12 *Spanning-Tree Operation*

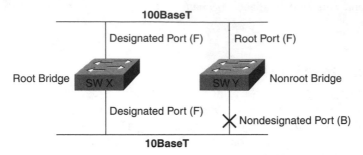

The Spanning-Tree Protocol provides a loop-free network topology by doing the following:

- **Electing a root bridge**—Only one bridge is designated as the root bridge in a given broadcast domain. All ports on the root bridge are in the forwarding state and are called designated ports. When in the forwarding state, a port can send and receive traffic. In Figure 5-12, Switch X is elected as the root bridge.

- **For each nonroot bridge, there will be one root port**—The root port is the lowest-cost path from the nonroot bridge to the root bridge. Root ports are in the forwarding state and provide connectivity back to the root bridge. Spanning Tree path cost is an accumulated cost based on bandwidth. In Figure 5-12, from Switch Y, the lowest-cost path to the root bridge is through the 100BaseT Fast Ethernet link. In the event that the cost is the same, the deciding factor would be the lowest port number.

- **On each segment, there is one designated port**—The designated port is selected on the bridge that has the lowest-cost path to the root bridge. Designated ports are in the forwarding state and are responsible for forwarding traffic for the segment. In Figure 5-12, the designated ports for both segments are on the root bridge because the root bridge is directly connected to both segments. The 10BaseT Ethernet port on Switch Y is a nondesignated port because there is only one designated port per segment. Nondesignated ports are normally in the blocking state to break the loop topology. When a port is in the blocking state, the port is not forwarding traffic. This does not mean that the port is disabled. It means that Spanning Tree is preventing it from forwarding traffic.

Bridge IDs and Port States

Switches (bridges) running the Spanning-Tree Algorithm exchange configuration messages with other switches (bridges) at regular intervals using a multicast frame called the Bridge Protocol Data Unit (BPDU). By default, the BPDU is sent every two seconds. One of the pieces of information included in the BPDU is the bridge ID.

Spanning Tree calls for each bridge to be assigned a unique identifier (bridge ID). Typically, the bridge ID is made up of a priority (2 bytes) plus the bridge MAC address (6 bytes). The (IEEE 802.1d) default priority is 32768, the midrange value. The root bridge is the bridge with the lowest bridge ID.

NOTE   Each switch selects one of its MAC addresses for use in the Spanning Tree bridge ID. A switch with multiple VLANs (discussed in the next chapter) uses an increment from this base MAC address for the Spanning Tree bridge ID for each VLAN.

In Figure 5-13, because both switches are using the same default priority, the one with the lower MAC address will be the root bridge. So in this example, Switch X is the root bridge with a bridge ID of 8000.0c00.1111.1111. The hexadecimal value 8000 is the bridge priority (decimal 32768). The 0c00.1111.1111 value is the device's MAC address.

Figure 5-13 *Bridge Communication*

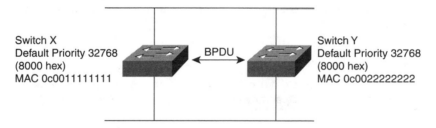

CAUTION   Spanning Tree root selection is automatic. Although this is convenient, it might not be acceptable, because it could cause your traffic to flow in a suboptimal path. It is always good practice to set the priority of the switch or bridge that needs to be designated as the root. In order to have a bridge become the root, you would want to lower the priority.

After the BPDUs have been exchanged, the port states on the switches would be in the states shown in Figure 5-14:

- The ports on Switch X, the root bridge, are designated ports (forwarding).
- The Fast Ethernet port on Switch Y is the root port (forwarding). It has a lower-cost path to the root bridge than the Ethernet port.

- The Ethernet port on switch Y is the nondesignated port (blocking). There is only one designated port per segment.

Figure 5-14 *Spanning Tree Port States*

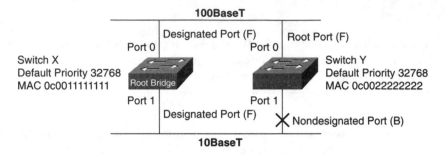

Spanning Tree Path Cost

Spanning Tree path cost is an accumulated total path cost based on the bandwidth of all the links in the path. Table 5-1 shows some of the path costs specified in the IEEE 802.1d specification.

Table 5-1 *Spanning Tree Path Cost*

Link Speed	Cost (Revised IEEE Specification)	Cost (Previous IEEE Specification)
10 Gbps	2	1
1 Gbps	4	1
100 Mbps	19	10
10 Mbps	100	100

The IEEE 802.1d specification was revised; in the older specification, the cost is calculated as 1000 M/bandwidth. The new specification adjusted the calculation to accommodate higher-speed interfaces, including 1 Gbps and 10 Gbps.

NOTE   The current version of the Catalyst 1900 software uses the older calculation for Spanning Tree costs. Other Catalyst switches, including the 2900XL, incorporate the revised calculations.

Look at Figure 5-15. Based on the setup of the switched network in this figure, try to determine the following (the subsequent list provides all the answers):

- What is the root bridge?
- What are the designated, nondesignated, and root ports?
- What are the forwarding and blocking ports?

Figure 5-15 *Spanning Tree Example*

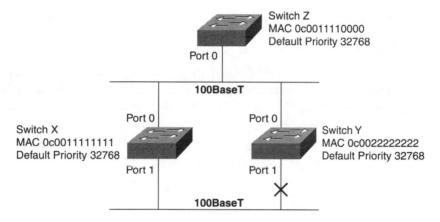

Using the Spanning-Tree Protocol, we can determine the following for the switched network in Figure 5-15:

- **Root bridge**—Switch Z, because it has the lowest bridge ID (priority and MAC address).
- **Root port**—Port 0s of Switches X and Y, because they are the path to the root.
- **Designated port**—Port 0 of Switch Z. All ports on the root are designated ports. Port 1 of Switch X is a designated port. Because both Switch X and Switch Y have the same path cost to the root bridge, the designated port is selected to be on Switch X because it has a lower bridge ID than Switch Y.
- **Blocking**—Port 1 of Switch Y. The nondesignated port on the segment.
- **Forwarding**—All designated ports and root ports are in the forwarding state.

Spanning Tree States

There are four Spanning Tree states:

- Blocking
- Listening

- Learning
- Forwarding

Spanning Tree transitions through these states to maintain a loop-free topology.

During normal operations, a port is in either the forwarding or blocking state. Forwarding ports provide the lowest-cost path to the root bridge. Two transitional states occur when a device recognizes a change in the network topology. During a topology change, a port temporarily implements the listening and learning states.

All ports start in the blocking state to prevent bridge loops. The port stays in a blocked state if the Spanning Tree determines that there is another path to the root bridge that has a better cost. Blocking ports can still receive BPDUs.

Ports transition from the blocked state to the listening state. When the port is in the transitional listening state, it can check for BPDUs. This state is really used to indicate that the port is getting ready to transmit but would like to listen for just a little longer to make sure it does not create a loop.

When the port is in learning state, it can populate its MAC address table with MAC addresses heard on its ports, but it does not forward frames.

In the forwarding state, the port can send and receive data.

The normal time it takes for a port to transition from the blocking state to the forwarding state is 50 seconds. Spanning Tree timers can be tuned to adjust the timing. Normally, these timers should be set to the default value. The default values are put in place to give the network enough time to gather all the correct information about the network topology. The time it takes for a port to transition from the listening state to the learning state or from the learning state to the forwarding state is called the *forward delay*. Spanning Tree timers are consistent throughout the bridge/switch topology, and their values are set by the root bridge. Table 5-2 lists the default values for Spanning Tree timers.

Table 5-2   *Spanning Tree Timers*

Timer	Primary Function	Default Setting
Hello Time	Time between sending of configuration BPDUs by the root bridge	2 seconds
Forward Delay	Duration of listening and learning states	30 seconds
Max Age	Time BPDU stored	20 seconds

Spanning Tree Recalculation

When there is a topology change due to a bridge or link failure, the Spanning-Tree Protocol readjusts the network topology to ensure connectivity by placing blocked ports to the forwarding states.

In Figure 5-16, if Switch X (the root bridge) fails, Switch Y will detect the missing BPDU from the root bridge. One of the Spanning Tree timers is called the Max Age timer. When the Max Age timer expires and a new BPDU has not been received from the neighbor, a new Spanning Tree recalculation is initiated. Port 1 moves to listening and then transitions to learning and finally to forwarding.

Figure 5-16 *Spanning Tree Recalculation*

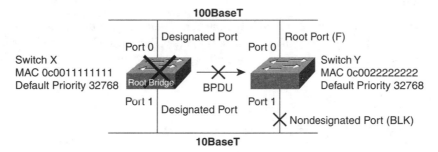

After the network is converged, Switch Y becomes the root bridge. It forwards traffic between the two segments when its ports transition to the forwarding state and become the designated ports.

How Devices Stay Informed About the Topology

Convergence is a necessity for normal network operations in a bridged/switched environment. For a switched or bridged network, a key issue is the amount of time required for convergence when network topology changes. Convergence in the Spanning-Tree Protocol means a state where all the switches and bridge ports have transitioned to either the forwarding or blocking state.

Fast convergence is a desirable network feature because it reduces the period of time that bridges and switches have ports in transitional states and are not sending traffic. Although the term *fast* is ambiguous at best, what is being stated here is that a topology change in the bridged/switched network will require time to reestablish full connectivity. It is important to remember this when designing bridged/switched networks.

NOTE During a topology change, affected devices will not be able to fully communicate until Spanning Tree has converged.

Catalyst Switch Technology

There are differences between a switch and a bridge. Although a switch essentially performs bridging, a switch is primarily hardware-based with ASICs and uses a high-capacity switching bus. Switches are faster than bridges.

Switches support multiple instances of Spanning Tree. This will be discussed in more detail in the next chapter.

Switches scale up their port density (number of ports) higher than bridges. Although bridges typically usually have 16 or fewer ports, a high-end Catalyst switch can have 100 or more ports. Table 5-3 sums up the differences between bridging and switching.

Table 5-3 *Bridging Versus Switching*

Bridging	Switching
Primarily software-based	Primarily hardware-based (ASIC)
One Spanning Tree instance per bridge	Many Spanning Tree instances per switch
Usually up to 16 ports per bridge	More ports on a switch

The following sections discuss how frames are transmitted on a switch and how a switch communicates with other network devices.

How Frames Are Transmitted

Three primary operating modes are used to handle frame switching:

- **Store-and-forward**—In store-and-forward mode, the switch must receive the complete frame before forwarding takes place. The destination and source addresses are read, the cyclic redundancy check (CRC) is performed, relevant filters are applied, and the frame is forwarded. If the CRC is bad, the frame is discarded. The latency (or delay) through the switch varies with frame length.

- **Cut-through**—In cut-through mode, the switch checks the destination address (DA) as soon as the header is received and immediately begins forwarding the frame. Depending on the network transport protocol being used (connectionless or connection-oriented), there is a significant decrease in latency from input port to output port. The delay in cut-through switching remains constant regardless of frame size, because this switching mode starts to forward the frame as soon as the switch reads the destination addresses. (In some switches, just the destination addresses are read.) The disadvantage of this process is that a switch would still forward a collision frame or a frame with a bad CRC value. Some switches continue to read the CRC and keep a count of errors. If the error rate is too high, the switch can be set—either manually or automatically—to use store-and-forward.

- **Fragment-free**—In fragment-free mode (also known as modified cut-through), the switch reads into the first 64 bytes before forwarding the frame. Usually, collisions happen within the first 64 bytes of a frame. By reading 64 bytes, the switch can filter out collision frames. Fragment-free switching is the default operating mode for the Catalyst 1900.

NOTE	*Latency* is defined as the delay through a network device. It is important to mention that in the switching methods described here, latency is measured as the first bit in the switch to the first bit out. This measurement gives a true representation of the time involved in switching a packet. However, when you read latency values for store-and-forward switching modes, note that latency is usually measured as last bit in to first bit out, because there is no other true way to measure latency because of variable frame sizes. The size of the frame doesn't matter in fragment-free or cut-through, because you are always dealing with a fixed amount of information.

How the Switch Talks to Other Devices

A network switch provides connectivity between devices in the network. One of the main reasons we place switches in the network is to improve this connectivity. As an intermediate device between end devices, the switch provides various modes of communication from the switch to the end device. The modes shown in Figure 5-17 that are used to communicate between the switch and the end device are half-duplex and full-duplex. These are configurable parameters that can affect how fast the device can send packets to the switch for transmission.

Figure 5-17 *Duplex Overview*

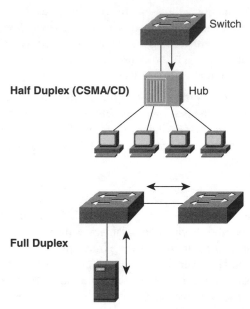

Half-duplex transmission mode implements Ethernet carrier sense multiple access collision detect (CSMA/CD). The traditional shared LAN operates in half-duplex mode and is susceptible to transmission collisions across the wire. Half-duplex is basically like a one-lane bridge across a stream. Only one car can cross the stream at a time.

Full-duplex Ethernet significantly improves network performance without the expense of installing new media. Full-duplex transmission between stations is achieved by using point-to-point Ethernet and Fast Ethernet connections. This arrangement is collision-free. Frames sent by the two connected end nodes cannot collide because they use two separate circuits in the twisted-pair cable. This is like a two-lane bridge crossing a stream. In short, this means that a given wire can accommodate twice the initial payload, effectively doubling the medium's bandwidth. Each full-duplex connection uses only one port.

Full-duplex port connections can use 10BaseT, 100BaseTX, and 100BaseFX media to provide point-to-point links between switches or end nodes, but not between shared hubs. Nodes directly attached to a dedicated switch port and with network interface cards that support full duplex should be connected to switch ports configured to operate in full-duplex mode. Most Ethernet and Fast Ethernet network interface cards sold today offer full-duplex capability. In full-duplex mode, the collision detect circuit is disabled.

Nodes attached to hubs, or nodes sharing their connection to a switch port, must operate in half-duplex mode because the end stations must be able to detect collisions.

Standard Ethernet configuration efficiency is typically rated at 50 to 60 percent of the 10 Mbps bandwidth. Full-duplex Ethernet offers 100 percent efficiency in both directions (10 Mbps transmit and 10 Mbps receive). Table 5-4 summarizes the differences between half-duplex and full-duplex connections.

Table 5-4   *Half Duplex Versus Full Duplex*

Half Duplex (CSMA/CD)	Full Duplex
Unidirectional data flow	Point-to-point only
Higher potential for collision	Collision-free
Hubs connectivity	Collision detect circuit disabled
	Attached to dedicated switched port
	Requires full-duplex support on both ends

Configuring the Catalyst 1900 Switch

This section contains an overview and concepts of configuring a switch. The Catalyst 1900 switch has three different configuration methods:

- Menu-driven interface from the console port
- Web-based Visual Switch Manager (VSM)
- Uses IOS command-line interface (CLI)

Each configuration method accomplishes the same tasks. Using VSM requires the switch to have an IP address configured and network connectivity to communicate with a web browser such as Netscape or Microsoft Internet Explorer. An IP address must also be assigned if you plan to connect to the switch through Telnet or if you plan to use SNMP to manage the switch.

This book focuses on using the CLI to configure the switch.

Default Configuration Settings for the Catalyst 1900 Switch

The Catalyst 1900 switch comes with factory default settings. For many parameters, the default configuration will suit your needs. However, you might want to change some of the default values to meet your specific network topology. The default values vary depending on the features of the switch. The following list provides some of the default settings for the Catalyst 1900 switch. Not all the defaults are listed.

- IP address: 0.0.0.0
- CDP: Enabled

- Switching mode: Fragment-free
- 100BaseT port: Autonegotiate duplex mode
- 10BaseT port: Half duplex
- Spanning Tree: Enabled
- Console password: None

Default Port Configurations for the Catalyst 1900 Switch

The 1912 and 1924 are two of the switches in the Catalyst 1900 switch family. Table 5-5 documents the ports found on the 1912 and 1924 switches.

Table 5-5   *Catalyst 1912 and 1924 Ports*

	Catalyst 1912	Catalyst 1924
10BaseT Ports	12 total (e0/1 to e0/12)	24 total (e0/1 to e0/24)
AUI Port	e0/25	e0/25
100BaseT Uplink Ports	fa0/26 (port A)	fa0/26 (port A)
	fa0/27 (port B)	fa0/27 (port B)

Ports on the Catalyst 1900 are referenced as either port or interface.

For example, for e0/1, the following points are true:

- The **show run** output (see Example 5-1) refers to e0/1 as interface Ethernet 0/1.
- The **show spantree** output (see Example 5-2) refers to e0/1 as Port Ethernet 0/1.
- The **show vlan-membership** output (see Example 5-3) refers to e0/1 as just Port 1.

Example 5-1   **show run** *Output Refers to Port e0/1 as Interface Ethernet 0/1*

```
wg_sw_d#sh run

Building configuration...
Current configuration:
!
!
interface Ethernet 0/1
!
interface Ethernet 0/2
```

Example 5-2 *show spantree Output Refers to Port e0/1 as Designated Port Ethernet 0/1*

```
wg_sw_d#sh spantree

Port Ethernet 0/1 of VLAN1 is Forwarding
    Port path cost 100, Port priority 128
    Designated root has priority 32768, address 0090.8673.3340
    Designated bridge has priority 32768, address 0090.8673.3340
    Designated port is Ethernet 0/1, path cost 0
    Timers: message age 20, forward delay 15, hold 1
```

Example 5-3 *show vlan-membership Output Refers to Port e0/1 as Port 1*

```
wg_sw_a#show vlan-membership

    Port  VLAN  Membership Type    Port  VLAN  Membership Type
    -----------------------------------------------------------------
    1     5          Static        13    1          Static
    2     1          Static        14    1          Static
    3     1          Static        15    1          Static
```

Configuration Modes for the Catalyst 1900 Switch

Similar to the router IOS, the Catalyst 1900 switch has various configuration modes. To configure global switch parameters such as the switch hostname or IP address, use the global configuration mode, the prompts for which are as follows:

```
wg_sw_a# conf term
wg_sw_a(config)#
```

To configure a particular port (interface), use the interface configuration mode, the prompts for which are as follows:

```
wg_sw_a(config)# interface e0/1
wg_sw_a(config-if)#
```

Configuring the IP Address, Subnet Mask, and Default Gateway on the Catalyst 1900 Switch

To configure an IP address and subnet mask on the switch, use the **ip address** global configuration command, which takes the following form:

```
wg_sw_a(config)#ip address address mask
```

For example, to configure a switch with IP address 10.5.5.11 and subnet mask 255.255.255.0, you would enter the following command:

```
wg_sw_a(config)#ip address 10.5.5.11 255.255.255.0
```

An IP address is required on the switch for management purposes. For example, using the VSM requires the switch to have an IP address configured and IP connectivity to communicate with a web browser such as Netscape or Microsoft Internet Explorer. An IP address must also be assigned if you plan to connect to the switch via Telnet, or if you plan to use SNMP to manage the switch. This address is assigned to the entire switch and is the management connection. Use the **no ip address** global configuration command to reset the IP address to the factory default of 0.0.0.0.

Use the **ip default-gateway** global configuration command to configure the default gateway. The **ip default-gateway** command takes the following form:

```
wg_sw_a(config)#ip default-gateway ip address
```

For example, to configure the default gateway with IP address 10.5.5.3 for a switch, you would enter the following command:

```
wg_sw_a(config)#ip default-gateway 10.5.5.3
```

The switch is assigned an IP address for management purposes. If the switch needs to send traffic to a different IP network than the one it is on, the switch sends the traffic to the default gateway, which is typically the router. A router is used to route traffic between different networks. Use the **no ip default-gateway** command to delete a configured default gateway, and set the gateway address to the default value of 0.0.0.0.

To verify the IP address, subnet mask, and default gateway settings, use the **show ip** command from the privileged EXEC mode, as demonstrated in Example 5-4.

Example 5-4 *show ip Command Verifies the IP Address, Subnet Mask, and Default Gateway Settings for a Catalyst 1900 Switch*

```
wg_sw_a#show ip
IP address: 10.5.5.11
Subnet mask: 255.255.255.0
Default gateway: 10.5.5.3
Management VLAN:  1
Domain name:
Name server 1: 0.0.0.0
Name server 2: 0.0.0.0
HTTP server: Enabled
HTTP port:  80
RIP: Enabled
wg_sw_a#
```

Configuring the Duplex Mode for a Catalyst 1900 Switch Interface

Use the **duplex** interface configuration command to change the duplex mode for an interface. The syntax for this command (on interface e0/1, for example) is as follows:

```
wg_sw_a(config)#interface e0/1
wg_sw_a(config-if)#duplex {auto | full | full-flow-control | half}
```

The options for the **duplex** interface configuration command include the following:

- **auto**—Sets the autonegotiation of duplex mode. **auto** is the default option for 100 Mbps TX ports.
- **full**—Sets full-duplex mode.
- **full-flow-control**—Sets full-duplex mode with flow control.
- **half**—Sets half-duplex mode. **half** is the default option for 10 Mbps TX ports.

For example, if you were to set half-duplex mode for interface e0/1 on Switch A, you would enter the following:

```
wg_sw_a(config)#interface e0/1
wg_sw_a(config-if)#duplex half
```

To verify the duplex settings on a given interface, use the **show interface** command. To display statistics for and the status of all or specified interfaces, use the **show interfaces** privileged EXEC command, as demonstrated in Example 5-5.

Example 5-5 *show interfaces Output Displays Statistics for and Status of All or Specified Switch Interfaces*

```
wg_sw_a#sh interfaces

Ethernet 0/1 is Enabled
Hardware is Built-in 10Base-T
Address is 0090.8673.3341
MTU 1500 bytes, BW 10000 Kbits
802.1d STP State:  Forwarding    Forward Transitions:  1
Port monitoring: Disabled
Unknown unicast flooding: Enabled
Unregistered multicast flooding:  Enabled
Description:
Duplex setting: Half duplex
Back pressure: Disabled

    Receive Statistics                    Transmit Statistics
-------------------------------      -------------------------------
Total good frames          44841     Total frames              404502
Total octets             4944550     Total octets            29591574
Broadcast/multicast frames 31011     Broadcast/multicast frames 390913
Broadcast/multicast octets 3865029   Broadcast/multicast octets 28470154
Good frames forwarded      44832     Deferrals                      0
Frames filtered                9     Single collisions              0
Runt frames                    0     Multiple collisions            0
No buffer discards             0     Excessive collisions           0
                                     Queue full discards            0
Errors:                              Errors:
  FCS errors                   0       Late collisions              0
  Alinment errors              0       Excessive deferrals          0
  Giant frames                 0       Jabber errors                0
  Address violations           0       Other transmit errors        0
```

As can be seen in the first highlighted line in Example 5-5, the duplex setting for any given interface can be determined by the **show interface** command.

Autonegotiation can, at times, produce unpredictable results. If an attached device does not support autonegotiation and is operating in full duplex, by default the Catalyst switch sets the corresponding switch port to half-duplex mode. This configuration—half duplex on one end and full duplex on the other—causes late collision errors at the full-duplex end. To avoid this situation, manually set the switch's duplex parameters to match the attached device.

If the switch port is in full-duplex mode, and the attached device is in half-duplex mode, check for frame check sequence (FCS) errors and late collisions on the switch full-duplex port.

Use the **show interfaces** command to check for FCS or late collision errors. A high number of late collisions often indicates a mismatch in duplex configuration. A mismatch will result in slow network response for the client. You can see late collision counters in the second highlighted line in Example 5-5.

MAC Addresses and Catalyst 1900 Switch Port Interfaces

Switches use the MAC address table to forward traffic between ports. The MAC table includes dynamic, permanent, and static addresses. Entering the **show mac-address-table** command displays the MAC address table and helps you determine how many dynamic, permanent, and static addresses are present and which type is used for each interface (see Example 5-6).

Example 5-6 *show mac-address-table Output Displays the MAC Address Table for the Port Interfaces on a Specified Switch*

```
wg_sw_a#sh mac-address-table
Number of permanent addresses : 0
Number of restricted static addresses : 0
Number of dynamic addresses : 6

Address            Dest Interface      Type       Source Interface List
------------------------------------------------------------------------
00E0.1E5D.AE2F     Ethernet 0/2        Dynamic    All
00D0.588F.B604     FastEthernet 0/26   Dynamic    All
00E0.1E5D.AE2B     FastEthernet 0/26   Dynamic    All
0090.273B.87A4     FastEthernet 0/26   Dynamic    All
00D0.588F.B600     FastEthernet 0/26   Dynamic    All
00D0.5892.38C4     FastEthernet 0/27   Dynamic    All
```

Dynamic MAC Addresses

Dynamic addresses are source Media Access Control (MAC) addresses that are learned by the switch and then dropped when they are not in use. The switch provides dynamic address learning by noting the source address of each packet it receives on each port and adding the address and its associated port number to the address table. As stations are added to or removed from the network, the switch updates the address table, adding new entries and aging out those that are currently not in use.

Permanent MAC Addresses

An administrator can specifically assign permanent addresses to certain ports using the **mac-address-table permanent** command, the syntax for which is as follows:

```
wg_sw_a(config)#mac-address-table permanent mac-address type module/port
```

Table 5-6 provides descriptions for the **mac-address-table permanent** command arguments.

Table 5-6   *mac-address-table permanent Command Arguments*

Command Argument	Meaning
mac-address	A MAC unicast address
type	The interface type: ethernet, fastethernet, fddi, atm, or port-channel
module/port	Module number: 0 for a Catalyst 1900 series
	Port number: 1-25 Ethernet
	26 and 27 Fast Ethernet
	28 Port-channel

Unlike dynamic addresses, permanent addresses are not aged out.

The Catalyst 1900 can store a maximum of 1024 MAC addresses in its MAC address table. When the MAC address table is full, it floods all new addresses until one of the existing entries gets aged out.

In order to ensure that an address will always be in the MAC table, you can use the **mac-address-table permanent** global configuration command to associate a permanent MAC address with a particular switched port interface (specified by type and module/port). Use the **no mac-address-table permanent** command to delete a permanent MAC address.

A permanent address in the MAC address table does not age out, and all interfaces can send traffic to this port, even if the device is moved.

For example, entering the following command:

```
wg_sw_a(config)#mac-address-table permanent 2222.2222.2222 ethernet 0/3
```

specifies that frames with the destination MAC address of 2222.2222.2222 should be forwarded out on the interface ethernet 0/3, and all interfaces can send traffic to 2222.2222.2222.

To verify that assigning the permanent MAC address was successful, enter the **show mac-address-table** command as demonstrated in Example 5-7.

Example 5-7 *show mac-address-table Output Verifies Permanent MAC Addresses*

```
wg_sw_a#sh mac-address-table
Number of permanent addresses : 1
Number of restricted static addresses : 0
Number of dynamic addresses : 4

Address          Dest Interface     Type        Source Interface List
----------------------------------------------------------------------
00E0.1E5D.AE2F   Ethernet 0/2       Dynamic     All
2222.2222.2222   Ethernet 0/3       Permanent   All
00D0.588F.B604   FastEthernet 0/26  Dynamic     All
00E0.1E5D.AE2B   FastEthernet 0/26  Dynamic     All
00D0.5892.38C4   FastEthernet 0/27  Dynamic     All
```

Static MAC Addresses

A static address allows you to restrict traffic to a particular MAC address from a specific source interface.

Use the **mac-address-table restricted static** global configuration command to associate a restricted static address with a particular switched port interface. The syntax for this command is as follows:

```
wg_sw_a(config)#mac-address-table restricted static mac-address
type module/port src-if-list
```

Table 5-7 describes the **mac-address-table restricted static** command arguments.

Table 5-7   *mac-address-table restricted static Command Arguments*

Command Argument	Meaning
mac-address	A MAC unicast address
type	The interface type: ethernet, fastethernet, fddi, atm, or port-channel
module/port	Module number: 0 for a Catalyst 1900 series
	Port number: 1-25 Ethernet
	26 and 27 Fast Ethernet
	28 Port-channel
src-if-list	List of acceptable interfaces separated by spaces

Use the **no mac-address-table restricted static** command to delete a restricted static address.

By entering the following command:

```
wg_sw_a(config)#mac-address-table restricted static 1111.1111.1111 e0/4 e0/1
```

the switch allows traffic to the restricted static address 1111.1111.1111 on e0/4 only from interface e0/1. To verify that assigning the restricted static MAC address was successful, enter the **show mac-address-table** command as demonstrated in Example 5-8.

Example 5-8   *show mac-address-table Output Verifies Restricted Static MAC Addresses*

```
wg_sw_a#sh mac-address-table
Number of permanent addresses : 1
Number of restricted static addresses : 1
Number of dynamic addresses : 4

Address           Dest Interface      Type        Source Interface List
--------------------------------------------------------------------------
1111.1111.1111    Ethernet 0/4        Static      Et0/1
00E0.1E5D.AE2F    Ethernet 0/2        Dynamic     All
2222.2222.2222    Ethernet 0/3        Permanent   All
00D0.588F.B604    FastEthernet 0/26   Dynamic     All
00E0.1E5D.AE2B    FastEthernet 0/26   Dynamic     All
00D0.5892.38C4    FastEthernet 0/27   Dynamic     All
```

Configuring Port Security on a Catalyst 1900 Switch

Another MAC-based restriction available as an option on the switch is port security. Port security has the following advantages:

- It configures an interface to be a secured port so that only certain devices are permitted to connect to a given switch port.

- It defines the maximum number of MAC addresses allowed in the address table for this port (ranging from 1 to 132, where 132 is the default).

Use the **port secure** interface configuration command to enable addressing security. The syntax for this command is as follows:

```
wg_sw_a(config-if)#port secure [max-mac-count count]
```

The *count* value entered for **max-mac-count** stipulates the maximum number of addresses allowed on the port. For example, to set to 1 the maximum number of addresses allowed to connect to interface e0/4, you would enter the following command:

```
wg_sw_a(config)#interface e0/4
wg_sw_a(config-if)#port secure max-mac-count 1
```

Use the **no port secure** command to disable addressing security, or set the maximum number of addresses allowed on the interface to the default value (132).

Secured ports restrict the use of a port to a user-defined group of stations. The number of devices on a secured port can range from 1 to 132. The MAC addresses for the devices on a secure port are statically assigned by an administrator or are *sticky-learned*. Sticky learning takes place when the address table for a secured port does not contain a full complement of static addresses. The port sticky-learns the source address of incoming frames and automatically assigns them as permanent addresses.

Use the **show mac-address-table security** privileged EXEC command to display and verify the port security configurations. Example 5-9 shows some sample output from the **show mac-address-table security** command.

Example 5-9   *show mac-address-table security Output Verifies Port Security Configurations*

```
wg_sw_a#show mac-address-table security
Action upon address violation : Suspend

Interface        Addressing Security    Address Table Size
----------------------------------------------------------
Ethernet 0/1     Disabled                    N/A
Ethernet 0/2     Disabled                    N/A
Ethernet 0/3     Disabled                    N/A
Ethernet 0/4     Enabled                     1
Ethernet 0/5     Disabled                    N/A
Ethernet 0/6     Disabled                    N/A
Ethernet 0/7     Disabled                    N/A
Ethernet 0/8     Disabled                    N/A
Ethernet 0/9     Disabled                    N/A
Ethernet 0/10    Disabled                    N/A
Ethernet 0/11    Disabled                    N/A
Ethernet 0/12    Disabled                    N/A
```

An address violation occurs when a secured port receives a source address that has been assigned to another secured port or when a port tries to learn an address that exceeds its address table size limit. When a security violation occurs, the options for action to be taken on a port include suspending, ignoring, or disabling the port. When a port is suspended, it is reenabled when a packet containing a valid address is received. When a port is disabled, it must be manually reenabled. If the action is ignored, the switch ignores the security violation and keeps the port enabled.

Use the **address-violation** global configuration command to specify the action for a port address violation. The syntax for this command is as follows:

```
wg_sw_a(config)#address-violation {suspend | disable | ignore}
```

Use the **no address-violation** command to set the switch to its default value (**suspend**).

Displaying Switch IOS Information

The IOS is the functional software that runs the switch's major operations and provides the management interface for configuration.

Use the **show version** user EXEC command to display basic information about hardware and the IOS software version, as demonstrated in Example 5-10.

Example 5-10 *show version Output Displays Switch Hardware and IOS Information*

```
wg_sw_a#show version

Cisco Catalyst 1900/2820 Enterprise Edition Software
Version V8.01.01
Copyright (c) Cisco Systems, Inc.   1993-1998
ROM:  System Bootstrap, Version 3.03
wg_sw_d uptime is 8day(s) 17hour(s) 53minute(s) 25second(s)
cisco Catalyst 1900 (486sx1) processor with 2048K/1024K bytes of memory
Hardware board revision is 1
Upgrade Status:  No upgrade currently in progress
Config File Status:  File wgswd.cfg downloaded from 10.1.1.1
27 Fixed Ethernet/IEEE 802.3 interface(s)
Base Ethernet Address:  00-90-86-73-33-40
wg_sw_a#
```

As shown in Example 5-10, the **show version** command contains valuable information about the operation of the switch software, including version number, memory information, and uptime.

Managing Switch Configuration Files

It is also important for you to be able to manage the configuration files on the switch. It is very useful to be able to copy these files to and from a TFTP server.

Use the **copy nvram tftp** privileged EXEC command to upload the running configuration to a TFTP server. The syntax for this command is as follows:

```
wg_sw_a#copy nvram tftp://host/dst_file
```

For example, to upload the running configuration file for Switch A to a targeted TFTP server with IP address 10.1.1.1, where the destination file is named wgswd.cfg, you would enter the following command:

```
wg_sw_a#copy nvram tftp://10.1.1.1/wgswd.cfg
Configuration upload is successfully completed
```

Use the **copy tftp nvram** privileged EXEC command to download a configuration file from the TFTP server. The syntax for this command is as follows:

```
wg_sw_a#copy tftp://host/src_file nvram
```

For example, to download a configuration file from a TFTP server with IP address 10.1.1.1 to Switch A's NVRAM, you would enter the following command:

```
wg_sw_a#copy tftp://10.1.1.1/wgswd.cfg nvram
TFTP successfully downloaded configuration file
```

NOTE	On the Catalyst 1900, the running configuration is automatically saved to NVRAM whenever a change is made to the running configuration.

If for some reason the device needs to be reset to the factory settings, you need to erase the switch's configuration by using the **delete nvram** privileged EXEC command. For example, to reset Switch D's configuration to the factory defaults, you would enter the following:

```
wg_sw_d#delete nvram
```

Catalyst 1900 Switch Command Summary

Table 5-8 lists some very useful commands discussed in this chapter.

Table 5-8   *Commands for Catalyst 1900 Switch Configuration*

Command	Description
ip address *address mask*	Sets the IP address for in-band management of the switch.
ip default-gateway	Sets the default gateway so that the management interface can be reached from a remote network.
show ip	Displays IP address configuration.
show interfaces	Displays interface information.
mac-address-table permanent *mac-address type module/port*	Sets a permanent MAC address.
mac-address-table restricted static *mac-address type module/port src-if-list*	Sets a restricted static MAC address.
port secure [**max-mac-count** *count*]	Sets port security.
show mac-address-table {**security**}	Displays the MAC address table. The **security** option displays information about the restricted or static settings.
address violation	Sets the action to be taken by the switch if there is a security address violation.
show version	Displays version information.
copy tftp://10.1.1.1/config.cfg nvram	Copies a configuration file from the TFTP server at IP address 10.1.1.1.

Table 5-8   *Commands for Catalyst 1900 Switch Configuration (Continued)*

Command	Description
copy nvram tftp://10.1.1.1/config.cfg	Saves a configuration file to the TFTP server at IP address 10.1.1.1.
delete nvram	Removes all configuration parameters and returns the switch to factory default settings.

Summary

This chapter discussed the three functions of a switch (bridge): address learning, data forwarding/filtering, and loop avoidance. You learned about the operation of Spanning Tree and how it maintains loop-free network connections. You examined several switching technologies implemented in Catalyst switches, including switching modes and duplex modes. Finally, you learned how to use the IOS CLI to configure the Catalyst 1900 switch.

Review Questions

1   What function does the Spanning-Tree Protocol provide?

2   Which Spanning-Tree Protocol is supported by the Catalyst 1900 switch?

3   What are the different Spanning Tree port states?

4   Describe the difference between full-duplex and half-duplex operations.

5   What is the default duplex setting on the Catalyst 1900 10 Mbps port and 100 Mbps port?

6   What is the default switching mode on the Catalyst 1900?

7   What is the Catalyst 1900 CLI command to assign the IP address 192.168.1.5 with a mask of 255.255.255.0 to the switch?

8   What is the IP address used for on the Catalyst switch?

9   Which type of MAC address does not age—permanent or dynamic?

10   What is the Dynamic 1900 CLI command to display the contents of the MAC address table?

Upon completion of this chapter, you will be able to perform the following tasks:

- Identify what a VLAN is and how it operates.
- Configure a VLAN to improve network performance.
- Identify what role the switch plays in the creation of VLANs.
- Identify how network devices communicate about VLANs.
- Configure the Catalyst 1900 for VLAN operation.

CHAPTER 6

Extending Switched Networks with Virtual LANs

The nature and function of a bridged/switched network is to provide enhanced network services by segmenting the network into multiple collision domains. The fact remains, however, that without any other mechanism, the bridged/switched network is still a single broadcast domain. It is important to control broadcast propagation throughout the network. Routers, which operate at Layer 3 of the OSI model, provide broadcast domain segmentation. Switches also provide a method of broadcast domain segmentation called *virtual LANs* (VLANs). A VLAN is defined as a broadcast domain.

The benefits of VLANs include the following:

- Security
- Segmentation
- Flexibility

VLANs enable you to group users into a common broadcast domain regardless of their physical location in the internetwork. Creating VLANs improves performance and security in the switched network by controlling broadcast propagation. In a broadcast environment, a broadcast sent out by a host on a single segment would propagate to all segments, saturating the bandwidth of the entire network, as shown in Figure 6-1. Also, without forcing some method of checking at an upper layer, all devices in the broadcast domain would be able to communicate via Layer 2. This severely limits the amount of security that could be enforced on the network.

Figure 6-1 *Broadcast Propagation*

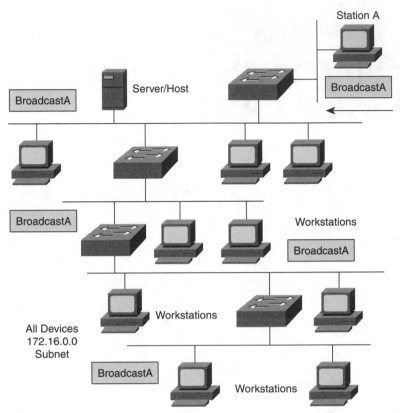

Before the introduction of switches and VLANs, networks were divided into multiple broadcast domains by connectivity through a router. Because routers do not forward broadcasts, each interface is in a different broadcast domain. Figure 6-2 shows a network broken into multiple broadcast domains using routers. Notice that each segment is an individual IP subnet and that regardless of a workstation's function, its subnet is defined by its physical location.

Figure 6-2   *Multiple Broadcast Domains Using Routers*

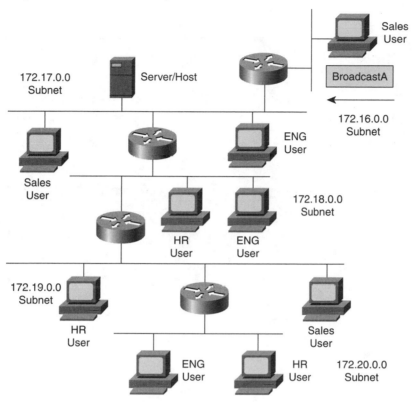

A VLAN is a logical broadcast domain that can span multiple physical LAN segments. A VLAN can be designed to provide independent broadcast domains for stations logically segmented by functions, project teams, or applications without regard to the physical location of users. Each switch port can be assigned to only one VLAN. Ports in a VLAN share broadcasts. Ports that do not belong to the same VLAN do not share broadcasts. This control of broadcast improves the network's overall performance.

VLANs enable switches to create multiple broadcast domains within a switched network, as illustrated in Figure 6-3. Notice that now all users in a given group (department in this example) are defined to be in the same VLAN. Any user in this VLAN would receive a broadcast from any other member of the VLAN, users of other VLANs would not receive these broadcasts. Each of the users in a given VLAN would also be in the same IP subnet. This is different from the broadcast domains of Figure 6-2, in which the physical location of the device determines the broadcast domain.

Figure 6-3   *VLAN Overview*

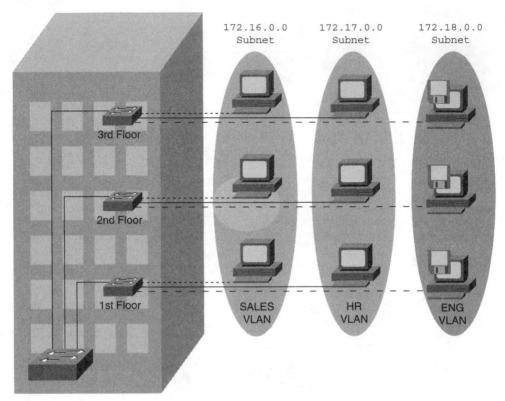

Within the switched internetwork, VLANs provide segmentation and organizational flexibility. Using VLAN technology, you can group switch ports and their connected users into logically defined communities of interest, such as coworkers in the same department, a cross-functional product team, or diverse user groups sharing the same network application.

A VLAN can exist on a single switch or span multiple switches. VLANs can include stations in a single building or multiple-building infrastructures. In rare and special cases, they can even connect across wide-area networks (WANs).

VLAN Concepts

As mentioned previously, prior to the VLAN, the only way to control broadcast traffic was through segmentation using routers. VLANs are an extension of the switched network. By having the ability to place segments (ports) in individual broadcast domains, you can control where a given broadcast will be forwarded. The following sections expand on these concepts. Basically, each switch acts independently of other switches in the network. With the concept of VLANs, a level of interdependence is built into the switch fabric. The characteristics of a typical VLAN setup are as follows:

- Each logical VLAN is like a separate physical bridge.
- VLANs can span multiple switches.
- Trunks carry traffic for multiple VLANs.

Now each switch can distinguish traffic from different broadcast domains. Each forwarding decision is based on which VLAN the packet came from; therefore, each VLAN acts like an individual bridge within a switch. In order to bridge/switch between switches, you must either connect each VLAN independently (that is, dedicate a port per VLAN) or have some method of maintaining and forwarding the VLAN information with the packets. A process called *trunking* allows this single connection. Figure 6-4 illustrates a typical VLAN setup in which multiple VLANs span two switches interconnected by a Fast Ethernet trunk.

Figure 6-4   *Multiple VLANs Can Span Multiple Switches*

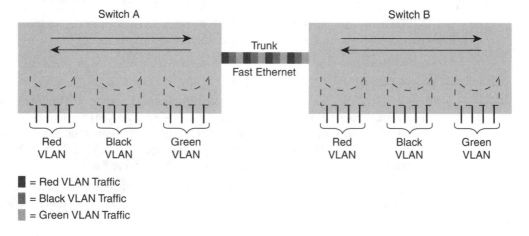

How VLANs Operate

A Catalyst switch operates in your network like a traditional bridge. Each VLAN configured on the switch implements address learning, forwarding/filtering decisions, and loop avoidance mechanisms as if it were a separate physical bridge. This VLAN might include several ports.

Internally, the Catalyst switch implements VLANs by restricting data forwarding to destination ports in the same VLAN as originating ports. In other words, when a frame arrives on a switch port, the Catalyst must retransmit the frame only to a port that belongs to the same VLAN. The implication is that a VLAN operating on a Catalyst switch limits transmission of unicast, multicast, and broadcast traffic. Flooded traffic originating from a particular VLAN floods out only other ports belonging to that VLAN. This means that each VLAN is an individual broadcast domain.

Normally, a port carries traffic only for the single VLAN it belongs to. In order for a VLAN to span multiple switches on a single connection, a trunk is required to connect two switches. A trunk carries traffic for all VLANs, as demonstrated earlier in Figure 6-4. A trunk port can only be configured on the Fast Ethernet ports on the Catalyst 1900 switches.

VLAN Membership Modes

VLANs are a Layer 2 implementation in the switch fabric of your network. Because they are implemented at the data link layer, they are protocol-independent. In order to put a given port (segment) into a VLAN, you must assign that membership on the switch. After you define a port to a given VLAN, broadcast and unicast traffic from that segment will be forwarded by the switches only to ports in the same VLAN. If you need to communicate between VLANs, you need to add a router and a Layer 3 protocol to your network.

Catalyst 1900 ports are configured with a VLAN membership mode that determines which VLAN they can belong to. The membership modes are as follows:

- **Static**—Assignment of VLAN to port is statically configured by an administrator.

- **Dynamic**—The Catalyst 1900 supports dynamic VLANs by using a VLAN Membership Policy Server (VMPS). The VMPS can be a Catalyst 5000 or an external server. The Catalyst 1900 cannot operate as the VMPS. The VMPS contains a database that maps MAC addresses to VLAN assignment. When a frame arrives on a dynamic port at the Catalyst 1900, the Catalyst 1900 queries the VMPS for the VLAN assignment based on the source MAC address of the arriving frame.

A dynamic port can belong to only one VLAN at a time. Multiple hosts can be active on a dynamic port only if they all belong to the same VLAN. Figure 6-5 demonstrates the static and dynamic VLAN membership modes.

Figure 6-5   *VLAN Membership Modes*

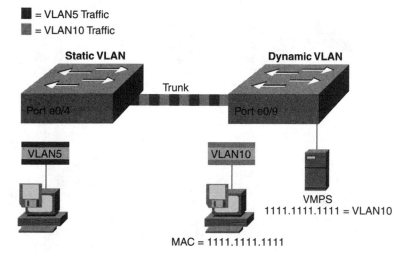

.Inter-Switch Links

This chapter discusses the functionality of Inter-Switch Link (ISL) tagging and how it is used to intercommunicate VLAN information between switches. ISL trunks enable VLANs across a switched network backbone. The fundamental characteristics of ISLs include the following:

- Performed with ASIC.
- Not intrusive to client stations; client does not see the ISL header.
- Effective between switches, routers and switches, and switches and servers with ISL network interface cards.

Figure 6-6 illustrates how an ISL functions across switches.

Figure 6-6   *ISL Tagging*

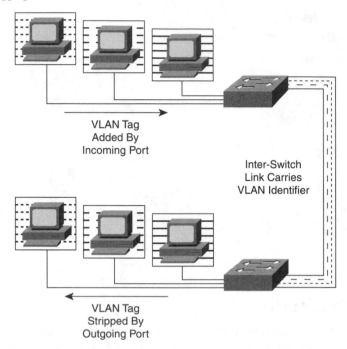

The following sections address ISL tagging and ISL encapsulation.

ISL Tagging

ISL is a Cisco proprietary protocol used to interconnect multiple switches and to maintain VLAN information as traffic goes between switches. ISL provides VLAN capabilities while maintaining full wire-speed performance over Fast Ethernet links in full- or half-duplex mode. ISL operates in a point-to-point environment. The purpose of ISL is to maintain VLAN information. This function allows a switch to forward information about which VLAN traffic originated from as it is being passed from one switch to another.

The ISL frame tagging used by the Catalyst series of switches is a low-latency mechanism for multiplexing traffic from multiple VLANs on a single physical path. It has been implemented for connections between switches, routers, and network interface cards used on nodes such as servers. To support the ISL feature, each connecting device must be ISL-capable. A router that is ISL-configured is used to allow inter-VLAN communications. This is discussed in more detail in the next chapter. A non-ISL device that receives ISL-encapsulated Ethernet frames might consider them to be protocol errors if the size of the header plus the data frame exceeds the maximum transmission unit (MTU) size

(1500 bytes) of a normal Ethernet frame. Devices that understand and can decode ISL packets do not have a problem with the size or format of these frames.

ISL Encapsulation

ISL functions at OSI Layer 2 by encapsulating a data frame with a new (ISL) header and cyclic redundancy check (CRC). ISL encapsulated frames are passed over trunk lines. ISL is protocol-independent because the data frame might carry any upper-layer protocol. Administrators use ISL to maintain redundant links and load-balance traffic between parallel links using the Spanning-Tree Protocol.

Ports configured as ISL trunks encapsulate each frame with a 26-byte ISL header and a 4-byte CRC before sending it out the trunk port. Because ISL technology is implemented in ASICs, frames are tagged at wire speed. The number of VLANs supported by a switch depends on the switch hardware. The Catalyst 1900 supports 64 VLANs with a separate Spanning Tree instance per VLAN. The ISL header supports 10 bits for ISL identification, allowing for the 1024 unique VLANs. Although a Catalyst 1900 can pass information for 1024 VLANs across a trunk line, it can support Spanning Tree for only the first 64 VLANs (1 through 64). Because there are only 27 ports on a Catalyst 1900, it could have ports in only 27 different VLANs, but it could pass traffic for any VLAN because it supports all 10 fields of the ISL header. You could create and add a port to a VLAN numbered above 65, but it would not support a Spanning Tree instance for that VLAN. This could cause bridge loops, which would cause serious network problems. It is therefore stated that the switch supports 64 active VLANs. Figure 6-7 illustrates a typical ISL encapsulated data frame.

Figure 6-7   *ISL Encapsulation*

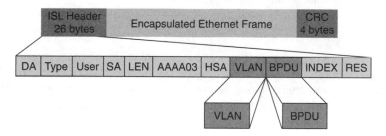

As illustrated in Figure 6-7, the ISL frame header contains the following information fields:

- **DA**—48-bit multicast destination address.

- **Type**—4-bit descriptor of the encapsulated frame types—Ethernet (0000), Token Ring (0001), FDDI (0010), and ATM (0011).

- **User**—4-bit descriptor used as the type field extension or to define Ethernet priorities. This is a binary value from 0, the lowest priority, to 3, the highest priority.

- **SA**—48-bit source MAC address of the transmitting Catalyst switch.
- **LEN**—16-bit frame-length descriptor minus DA type, user, SA, LEN, and CRC.
- **AAAA03**—Standard SNAP 802.2 LLC header.
- **HSA**—First 3 bytes of SA (manufacturer's ID or organizational unique ID).
- **VLAN**—15-bit VLAN ID. Only the lower 10 bits are used for 1024 VLANs.
- **BPDU**—1-bit descriptor identifying whether the frame is a Spanning Tree BPDU. Also set if the encapsulated frame is a CDP frame.
- **INDEX**—16-bit descriptor that identifies the transmitting port ID. Used for diagnostics.
- **RES**—16-bit reserved field used for additional information, such as FDDI frame FC field.

VLAN Trunking Protocol

In order to provide VLAN connectivity throughout the switch fabric, VLANs must be configured on each switch. Cisco's VLAN Trunking Protocol (VTP) provides an easier method for maintaining consistent VLAN configuration throughout the switched network.

NOTE	Because the focus of this book is the Catalyst 1900 Ethernet switch, we have concentrated on ISL trunking. It is important to mention, however, that there are other trunking mechanisms, such as ATM LANE and FDDI 802.10. Because VTP operates over a trunk line, it can operate on these topologies also.

VTP is a protocol used to distribute and synchronize identifying information about VLANs configured throughout a switched network. Configurations made to a single VTP server are propagated across trunk links to all connected switches in the network. VTP enables switched network solutions to scale to large sizes by reducing the network's manual configuration needs.

VTP is a Layer 2 messaging protocol that maintains VLAN configuration consistency throughout a common administration domain by managing the additions, deletions, and name changes of VLANs across networks. VTP minimizes misconfigurations and configuration inconsistencies that can cause problems, such as duplicate VLAN names or incorrect VLAN-type specifications.

A VTP domain is one switch or several interconnected switches sharing the same VTP environment. A switch is configured to be in only one VTP domain.

Figure 6-8 illustrates how VLAN configuration information is propagated from switch to switch.

Figure 6-8   *VTP Operation*

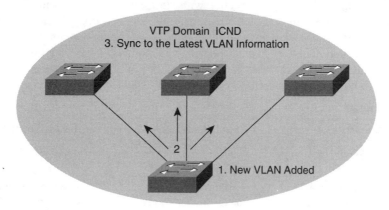

In Figure 6-8, we add a VLAN to our switched network. The steps illustrated in the figure are as follows:

Step 1   A new VLAN is added. At this point, VTP makes your job easier.

Step 2   The VTP advertisement is sent to the other switches in the VTP domain.

Step 3   The new VLAN is added to the other switch configurations. The result is consistent VLAN configuration.

By default, a Catalyst switch is in the no-management-domain state until it receives an advertisement for a domain over a trunk link, or until you configure a management domain.

VTP Modes

VTP operates in one of three modes: server mode, client mode, or transparent mode. The default VTP mode is server mode, but VLANs are not propagated over the network until a management domain name is specified or learned. A Catalyst switch operating in the VTP server mode can create, modify, and delete VLANs and other configuration parameters for the entire VTP domain. In server mode, VLAN configurations are saved in the Catalyst nonvolatile random-access memory (NVRAM). When you make a change to the VLAN configuration on a VTP server, the change is propagated to all switches in the VTP domain. VTP messages are transmitted out all trunk connections, such as ISL.

A device operating as a VTP client cannot create, change, or delete VLANs. A VTP client does not save VLAN configurations in nonvolatile memory.

In both client and server mode, the switches synchronize their VLAN configuration to that of the switch with the highest revision number in the VTP domain.

A switch operating in VTP transparent mode does not create VTP advertisements or synchronize its VLAN configuration with information received from other switches in the management domain. A switch in transparent mode forwards VTP advertisements received from other switches that are part of the same management domain. A switch configured in VTP transparent mode can create, delete, and modify VLANs, but the changes are not transmitted to other switches in the domain; they affect only the local switch. Table 6-1 offers a comparative overview of the three VTP modes.

Table 6-1   *VTP Modes*

Server Mode	Client Mode	Transparent Mode
Sends/forwards VTP advertisements.	Sends/forwards VTP advertisements.	Forwards VTP advertisements.
Synchronizes VLAN configuration information with other switches.	Synchronizes VLAN configuration information with other switches.	*Does not* synchronize VLAN configuration information with other switches.
VLAN configurations are saved in NVRAM.	VLAN configurations *are not* saved in NVRAM.	VLAN configurations are saved in NVRAM.
Catalyst switch can create VLANs.	Catalyst switch *cannot* create VLANs.	Catalyst switch can create VLANs.
Catalyst switch can modify VLANs.	Catalyst switch *cannot* modify VLANs.	Catalyst switch can modify VLANs.
Catalyst switch can delete VLANs.	Catalyst switch *cannot* delete VLANs.	Catalyst switch can delete VLANs.

When setting up VTP on a switch, it is important to choose the appropriate mode. Because VTP is a powerful tool, it can overwrite VLAN configurations on some switches and create network problems. The next section further explains this phenomenon. Nevertheless, you must be aware that the mode you choose can eliminate the chance of these problems. Server mode should be chosen for the switch that you would use to create, change, or delete VLANs. The server will propagate this information to other switches that are configured as servers or clients. Client mode should be set on any switch that is being added to a VTP domain to prevent a possible VLAN overwrite. Transparent mode should be used on a switch that needs to pass VTP advertisements to other switches but also needs the capability to have its VLANs independently administered.

How VTP Works

VTP advertisements are flooded throughout the management domain every five minutes or whenever there is a change in VLAN configurations. VTP advertisements are sent over a factory default VLAN (VLAN1) using multicast frames. Included in a VTP advertisement is a configuration revision number. A higher configuration revision number indicates that the VLAN information being advertised is more current than the stored information.

A device that receives VTP advertisements must check various parameters before incorporating the received VLAN information. First, the management domain name and the password, which can be configured to prevent unauthorized switches from altering the VTP domain, must match those configured in the local switch before information can be used. Next, if the configuration revision number indicates that the message was created after the configuration currently in use, the switch incorporates the advertised VLAN information. To reset the configuration revision number on the Catalyst 1900, use the **delete vtp** privileged EXEC command. Example 6-1 demonstrates the **delete vtp** privileged EXEC command. The **show vtp** command is executed before and after the **delete vtp** command to show the changes made by **delete vtp**.

Example 6-1 *The **delete vtp** Command Resets the Switch Configuration Revision Number*

```
Switch#sh vtp
     VTP version: 1
     Configuration revision: 53
     Maximum VLANs supported locally: 1005
     Number of existing VLANs: 5
     VTP domain name         : Wildcats
     VTP password            :
     VTP operating mode      : Server
     VTP pruning mode        : Disabled
     VTP traps generation    : Enabled
     Configuration last modified by: 172.16.100.8 at 00-00-0000 00:00:00
Switch#delete vtp
This command resets the switch with VTP parameters set to factory defaults.
All other parameters will be unchanged.

Reset system with VTP parameters set to factory defaults, [Y]es or [N]o?  Yes

Switch#sh vtp
     VTP version: 1
     Configuration revision: 0
     Maximum VLANs supported locally: 1005
     Number of existing VLANs: 5
     VTP domain name         :
     VTP password            :
     VTP operating mode      : Server
     VTP pruning mode        : Disabled
     VTP traps generation    : Enabled
     Configuration last modified by: 0.0.0.0 at 00-00-0000 00:00:00
Switch#
```

NOTE   After you answer **Yes** to reset the VTP parameters, the switch will return you to the console menu.

One of the most critical components of VTP is the configuration revision number. Each time a VTP server modifies its VLAN information, it increments the configuration revision number by one. The VTP server then sends out a VTP advertisement with the new configuration revision number. If the configuration revision number being advertised is higher than the number stored on the other switches in the VTP domain, the other switches will overwrite their VLAN configurations with the new information that is being advertised. Figure 6-9 illustrates how VTP operates in a switched network.

Figure 6-9   *VTP Operation*

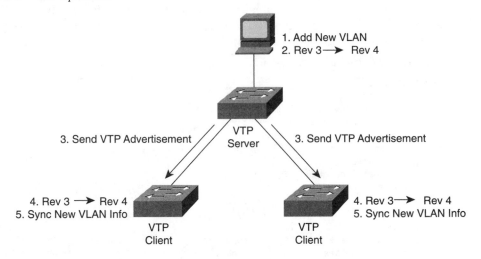

CAUTION   The overwrite process would mean that the VTP server with the highest revision number determines the overall VLAN configuration for the domain. For example, if you deleted all VLANs on a VTP server and that server had the higher revision number, the other devices in the VTP domain would also delete their VLANs. This could create a loss of connectivity.

VTP Pruning

Because ISL trunk lines carry VLAN traffic for all VLANs, some traffic might be needlessly broadcast across links that do not need to carry that traffic. VTP pruning uses VLAN advertisements to determine when a trunk connection is flooding traffic needlessly.

By default, a trunk connection carries traffic for all VLANs in the VTP management domain. Commonly, some switches in an enterprise network do not have local ports configured in each VLAN. In Figure 6-10, Switches 1 and 4 support ports statically configured in VLAN10. As illustrated, with VTP pruning enabled, when Station A sends a broadcast, the broadcast is flooded only toward any switch with ports assigned to VLAN10. As a result, broadcast traffic from Station A is not forwarded to Switches 3, 5, and 6 because traffic for VLAN10 has been pruned on the links indicated on Switches 2 and 4.

Figure 6-10 *VTP Pruning*

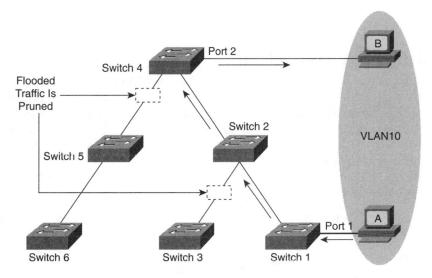

VTP pruning increases available bandwidth by restricting flooded traffic to those trunk links that the traffic must use to access the appropriate network devices.

NOTE   Because VLAN1 is the management VLAN and is used for administrative functions such as VTP advertisements, VLAN1 cannot be pruned from a trunk line.

VLAN Configuration

This chapter discusses the guidelines for configuring VLANs on the Cisco 1900 switch. You will learn the steps to configure VLANs, how to enable VTP domains, how to define a trunk, how to create a VLAN, and how to verify proper VLAN operation.

There are several facts you should remember before you begin VLAN configuration:

- The maximum number of VLANs is switch-dependent. The Catalyst 1900 supports 64 VLANs with a separate Spanning Tree per VLAN.
- VLAN1 is one of the factory default VLANs.
- CDP and VTP advertisements are sent on VLAN1.
- The Catalyst 1900 IP address is in the VLAN1 broadcast domain.
- The switch must be in VTP server mode or transparent mode to create, add, or delete VLANs.

VLAN Configuration Guidelines

A maximum of 64 VLANs can be active on most desktop Catalyst switches, such as the Catalyst 1900. The Catalyst 1900 switches have a factory default configuration in which various default VLANs are preconfigured. One of the default VLANs is VLAN1, which is used for CDP and VTP advertisements. The Catalyst 1900 IP address must also be in the VLAN1 broadcast domain. As you'll recall, the switch requires an IP address for management purposes—for example, to allow Telnet connections into the switch, or to use the Visual Switch Manager (VSM) via an HTTP browser to configure the switch.

Before you can create a VLAN, the switch must be in VTP server mode or VTP transparent mode. If you want to propagate the VLAN to other switches in the domain, use server mode. If the VLAN should only be added to the local switch, use transparent mode.

VLAN Configuration Steps

Before you create VLANs, you must decide whether to use VTP to maintain global VLAN configuration information for your network.

To allow VLANs to span multiple Catalyst 1900 switches on a single link, you must configure Fast Ethernet trunks to interconnect the switches.

By default, a switch is in VTP server mode so that VLANs can be added, changed, or deleted. If the switch is set to VTP client mode, VLANs cannot be added, changed, or deleted.

VLAN membership on the switch ports is assigned manually on a port-by-port basis. When you assign switch ports to VLANs using this method, it is known as port-based, or static, VLAN membership.

The following sections elaborate on the details of the steps to configure VLANs.

VTP Configuration Guidelines

The default VTP configuration parameters for the Catalyst 1900 switch are as follows:

- VTP domain name: None
- VTP mode: Server
- VTP password: None
- VTP pruning: Disabled
- VTP trap: Enabled

The VTP domain name can be specified by the administrator or learned across a configured trunk line from a server with a domain name configured. By default, the domain name is not set.

By default, the switch is set to the VTP server mode.

A password can be set for the VTP management domain. The password entered must be the same for all switches in the domain. If you configure a VTP password, VTP does not function properly unless you assign the same password to each switch in the domain.

VTP pruning eligibility is one VLAN parameter advertised by the VTP protocol. Enabling or disabling VTP pruning on a VTP server propagates the change throughout the management domain. Enabling or disabling VTP pruning on a VTP server affects the entire management domain.

VTP trap is enabled by default. This will cause an SNMP message to be generated every time a new VTP message is sent.

CAUTION   When adding a new switch to an existing domain, you should add the new switch in client mode to prevent the new switch from propagating incorrect VLAN information. Another method of preventing this is to use the **delete vtp** command, shown earlier in Example 6-1, to reset the VTP revision number on the new switch.

Configuring VTP

Use the **vtp** global configuration command to specify the operating mode, domain name, password, generation of traps, and pruning capabilities of VTP. The syntax for this command is as follows:

```
switch(config)# vtp {[server | transparent | client] [domain domain-name]
  [trap (enable | disable)] [password password] [pruning {enable | disable}]}
```

To verify a recent configuration change, or to just view the VTP configuration information, use the **show vtp** privileged EXEC command, as demonstrated in Example 6-2. Also displayed is the IP address of the device that last modified the configuration and a time stamp showing when the modification was made. VTP has two versions. VTP version 1 only supports Ethernet. VTP version 2 supports Ethernet and Token Ring.

Example 6-2 *show vtp Output*

```
switch# show vtp
VTP version: 1
Configuration revision: 4
Maximum VLANs supported locally: 1005
Number of existing VLANs: 6
VTP domain name:switchdomain
VTP password:
VTP operating mode: Transparent
VTP pruning mode: Enabled
VTP traps generation: Enabled
Configuration last modified by: 10.1.1.40 at 00-00-0000 00:00:00
```

Trunk Line Configuration

Use the **trunk** interface configuration command to set a Fast Ethernet port to trunk mode. On the Catalyst 1900, the two Fast Ethernet ports are interfaces fa0/26 and fa0/27. The Catalyst 1900 supports the Dynamic Inter-Switch Link (DISL) protocol. DISL manages automatic ISL trunk negotiation. The syntax for the **trunk** interface configuration command is as follows:

```
switch(config)# trunk [on | off | desirable | auto | nonnegotiate]
```

The options for the **trunk** command are as follows:

- **on**—Configures the port to permanent ISL trunk mode and negotiates with the connected device to convert the link to trunk mode.

- **off**—Disables port trunk mode and negotiates with the connected device to convert the link to nontrunk.

- **desirable**—Triggers the port to negotiate the link from nontrunk to trunk mode. The port negotiates to a trunk port if the connected device is in the **on, desirable**, or **auto** state. Otherwise, the port becomes a nontrunk port.

- **auto**—Enables the port to become a trunk only if the connected device has the state set to **on** or **desirable**.

- **nonnegotiate**—Configures the port to permanent ISL trunk mode. No negotiation takes place with the partner.

Verifying Trunk Line Configuration

To verify a trunk configuration, use the **show trunk** privileged EXEC command to display the trunk parameters, as demonstrated in Example 6-3. The syntax for the **show trunk** privileged EXEC command is as follows:

```
switch(config)# show trunk [a | b]
```

The parameters **a** and **b** represent the Fast Ethernet ports:

- Port a represents Fast Ethernet 0/26
- Port b represents Fast Ethernet 0/27

Example 6-3 *show trunk Output*

```
switch# show trunk a
DISL state: On, Trunking: On, Encapsulation type: ISL
```

Adding a VLAN

Use the **vlan** global configuration command to configure a VLAN. The syntax for the **vlan** global configuration command is as follows:

```
vlan vlan# [name vlan_name]
```

Each VLAN has a unique four-digit ID that can be a number from 0001 to 1005. To add a VLAN to the VLAN database, assign a number and name to the VLAN. VLAN1, VLAN1002, VLAN1003, VLAN1004, and VLAN1005 are the factory default VLANs. These VLANs exist on all Catalyst switches and are used as default VLANs for other topologies, such as Token Ring and FDDI. No default VLAN can be modified or deleted.

To add an Ethernet VLAN, you must specify at least a VLAN number. If no VLAN name is entered for the VLAN, the default is to append the VLAN number to the word VLAN. For example, VLAN0004 could be a default name for VLAN4 if no name is assigned.

Remember, to add, change, or delete VLANs, the switch must be in VTP server or transparent mode.

Verifying a VLAN/Modifying VLAN Parameters

When the VLAN is configured, the parameters for that VLAN should be confirmed to ensure validity. To verify the parameters of a VLAN, use the **show vlan** *vlan#* privileged EXEC command to display information about a particular VLAN. Use **show vlan** to show all configured VLANs.

The **show vlan** command output in Example 6-4 also shows which switch ports are assigned to the VLAN.

Example 6-4 *show vlan Output*

```
switch# sh vlan 9

VLAN Name              Status     Ports
-----------------------------------------------
9   switchlab2         Enabled
-----------------------------------------------
```

continues

Example 6-4 *show vlan Output (Continued)*

```
VLAN Type       SAID   MTU   Parent RingNo BridgeNo Stp  Trans1 Trans2
----------------------------------------------------------------------------
9    Ethernet   100009 1500      0    1        1   Unkn      0      0
----------------------------------------------------------------------------
```

Other VLAN parameters shown in Example 6-4 include the type (default is Ethernet), SAID (used for FDDI trunk), MTU (default is 1500 for Ethernet VLAN), Spanning-Tree Protocol (the 1900 supports only the 802.1D Spanning-Tree Protocol standard), and other parameters used for Token Ring or FDDI VLANs.

To modify an existing VLAN parameter (such as the VLAN name), use the same command syntax used to add a VLAN.

In Example 6-5, the VLAN name for VLAN9 is changed to switchlab90.

Example 6-5 *Change VLAN Name*

```
switch# conf terminal
Enter configuration commands, one per line.  End with CNTL/Z
switch(config)# vlan 9 name switchlab90
```

Use the **show vlan 9** command as demonstrated in Example 6-6 to verify the change.

Example 6-6 *Verify VLAN Change*

```
wg_sw_a# show vlan 9

VLAN Name            Status    Ports
-----------------------------------------------
9    switchlab90     Enabled
-----------------------------------------------
```

Assigning Ports to a VLAN

After creating a VLAN, you can statically assign a port or a number of ports to that VLAN. A port can belong to only one VLAN at a time.

Configure the VLAN port assignment from the interface configuration mode using the **vlan-membership** command. Here is the syntax:

```
vlan-membership {static {vlan#} | dynamic}
```

dynamic means that the Catalyst 1900 queries a VMPS for VLAN information based on a MAC address.

By default, all ports are members of the default VLAN—VLAN1.

Use the **show vlan-membership** privileged EXEC command to display the VLAN assignment and membership type for all switch ports as demonstrated in Example 6-7, where Port 1 refers to Ethernet 0/1, Port 2 refers to Ethernet 0/2, and so on.

Example 6-7 *Displaying VLAN Assignments and Membership for All Switch Ports*

```
Switch#show vlan-membership

   Port  VLAN   Membership Type      Port   VLAN   Membership Type
   ---------------------------------------------------------------------
   1      5        Static            13      1        Static
   2      1        Static            14      1        Static
   3      1        Static            15      1        Static
   4      1        Static            16      1        Static
   5      1        Static            17      1        Static
   6      1        Static            18      1        Static
   7      1        Static            19      1        Static
   8      9        Static            20      1        Static
```

Displaying Spanning-Tree Protocol Configuration Status

Use the **show spantree** privileged EXEC command to display the Spanning-Tree Protocol configuration status of the switch, as demonstrated in Example 6-8. The basic syntax for the **show spantree** privileged EXEC command is as follows:

switch# **show spantree** [*vlannumber*]

Example 6-8 *show spantree Output*

```
switch# show spantree 1
VLAN1 is executing the IEEE compatible Spanning Tree Protocol
    Bridge Identifier has priority 32768, address 0050.F037.DA00
    Configured hello time 2, max age 20, forward delay 15
    Current root has priority 0, address 00D0.588F.B600
    Root port is FastEthernet 0/26, cost of root path is 10
    Topology change flag not set, detected flag not set
    Topology changes 53, last topology change occured 0d00h17m14s ago
    Times:  hold 1, topology change 8960
            hello 2, max age 20, forward delay 15
    Timers: hello 2, topology change 35, notification 2
Port Ethernet 0/1 of VLAN1 is Forwarding
    Port path cost 100, Port priority 128
    Designated root has priority 0, address 00D0.588F.B600
    Designated bridge has priority 32768, address 0050.F037.DA00
    Designated port is Ethernet 0/1, path cost 10
    Timers: message age 20, forward delay 15, hold 1
```

Example 6-8 displays various Spanning Tree information for VLAN1, including the following:

* Port e0/1 is in the forwarding state for VLAN1.

- The root bridge for VLAN1 has a bridge priority of 0 with a MAC address of 00D0.588F.B600.
- The switch is running the IEEE 802.1d Spanning-Tree Protocol.

Recall that a Catalyst switch can support a separate Spanning Tree per VLAN. This allows for load balancing between switches. For example, one switch can be the root for VLAN1, and another switch can be the root for VLAN2. This idea is explained further in the Cisco Press title *CLSC Exam Certification Guide*.

VLAN Command Summary

Table 6-2 lists the commands covered in this chapter and briefly describes each command's function.

Table 6-2   *VLAN Command Summary*

Command	Description
delete vtp	Resets the VTP revision number and resets all VTP parameters to factory defaults.
vtp domain *name* **transparent**	Assigns a VTP domain name and sets transparent mode.
show vtp	Displays VTP status.
interface *interfacenumber* **trunk on**	Configures a trunk interface.
show trunk	Displays trunk status.
vlan *vlan# name vlanname*	Defines a VLAN and VLAN name.
show vlan	Displays VLAN information.
interface *interfacenumber* **vlan-membership static** *vlan#*	Assigns a port to a VLAN.
show vlan-membership	Displays VLAN membership.
show spantree *vlan#*	Displays Spanning Tree information for a VLAN.

Summary

This chapter discussed how VLANs operate to provide more effective networks by controlling broadcasts in your network. In order to configure VLANs on a Catalyst switch, you must first configure VTP to administer VLANs. Therefore, you learned how VTP operates and how it is configured. You also learned how to create a trunk link to carry all VLAN traffic, and how to configure a VLAN. Finally, this chapter discussed the verification of Spanning Tree operations, including the following:

- How VLANs operate
- How to configure VTP
- How to configure a trunk
- How to configure a VLAN
- How to verify Spanning Tree operations

Review Questions

1 VLANs allow for the creation of what in switched networks?

2 What are the two types of VLANs?

3 What type of port is capable of carrying all VLAN traffic?

4 What mechanism is used by switches to provide inter-switch communication between devices about which VLAN a packet originated from?

5 What is the purpose of VTP?

6 What is the default VTP mode for the Catalyst 1900?

7 Assume that a Catalyst 1900 is being added to your network. The switch needs to learn VLANs from the other switches in the network. You are not sure of the current VTP configuration and are fearful that it might overwrite your current VLAN information. How could you prevent the switch from accidentally overwriting the VLANs in your VTP domain?

8 What is the maximum number of VLANs that can be active on a Catalyst 1900?

9 List all the steps required to configure a VLAN on a Catalyst 1900 switch port.

10 Which command would you use to view the Spanning Tree configuration for VLAN9 on a Catalyst 1900 switch?

PART III

Interconnecting Cisco Routers

Upon completion of this chapter, you will be able to perform the following tasks:

- Identify the IP protocol stack, its protocol layer functions, and commonly used IP protocols.

- Identify the address classes, IP addresses, IP subnet masks, network numbers, subnet numbers, and possible host numbers, given an IP addressing scheme.

- Configure IP addresses and subnet masks on a router interface and optionally configure a host table given an IP addressing scheme.

- Interconnect VLANs with a Layer 3 device such as a router, given hosts on separate VLANs.

CHAPTER 7

Interconnecting Networks with TCP/IP

This chapter covers the Transmission Control Protocol/Internet Protocol (TCP/IP) protocol stack with an emphasis on the Layer 3 IP routed protocol and Layer 4 end-to-end functionality. This chapter also describes how to configure IP addresses on a Cisco device.

In order to understand how to configure the functions of network devices, you must have a solid understanding of the protocols and their functions. The most common protocol used in data networks today is the TCP/IP protocol stack. TCP/IP is used to interconnect devices in corporate networks as well as being the protocol of the Internet.

The TCP/IP suite of protocols was developed as part of the research done by the Defense Advanced Research Projects Agency (DARPA). Later, TCP/IP was included with the Berkeley Software Distribution of UNIX.

The Internet protocols can be used to communicate across any set of interconnected networks. They are equally well-suited for both LAN and WAN communication.

The Internet protocol suite includes not only Layers 3 and 4 specifications (such as IP and TCP), but also specifications for such common applications as e-mail, remote login, terminal emulation, and file transfer.

The TCP/IP protocol stack maps closely to the OSI reference model in the lower layers. All standard physical and data-link protocols are supported. Figure 7-1 illustrates the TCP/IP model in reference to the seven-layer OSI model.

Figure 7-1   *TCP/IP Protocol Stack*

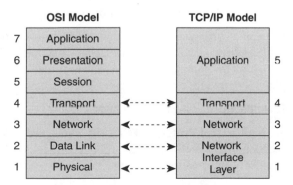

To understand the protocol stack, let's begin by looking at the upper layers and work down to the lower layers.

NOTE   The network interface layer of the TCP/IP stack shown in Figure 7-1 is sometimes separated and called the *physical* and *data link layers*.

TCP/IP Application Layer Overview

TCP/IP defines many applications used in networks today. Application protocols exist for the following operations (all items marked by an asterisk are used by the router):

- **File transfer**—For example, TFTP*, FTP, and NFS
- **E-mail**—For example, SMTP
- **Remote login**—For example, Telnet* and rlogin*
- **Network management**—For example, SNMP*
- **Name management**—For example, DNS*

Two of the common applications defined by TCP/IP that will be used when dealing with Cisco routers and switches are Telnet and TFTP. These applications are used to manage the device. If you need a refresher on device management using Telnet and TFTP, refer back to Chapter 4, "Managing Your Network Environment," which discusses how to establish a Telnet connection and complete file transfers using TFTP.

TCP/IP Transport Layer Overview

Transport services allow users to segment and reassemble several upper-layer applications onto the same transport layer data stream.

This transport layer data stream provides end-to-end transport services. The transport layer data stream constitutes a logical connection between the endpoints of the internetwork— the originating or sender host and the destination or receiving host.

The transport layer performs two functions: flow control provided by sliding windows, and reliability provided by sequence numbers and acknowledgments. Flow control is a mechanism that allows the communicating hosts to negotiate how much data is transmitted each time. Reliability provides a mechanism for guaranteeing the delivery of each packet.

Two protocols are provided at the transport layer:

- **Transmission Control Protocol (TCP)**—A connection-oriented, reliable protocol. In a connection-oriented environment, a connection is established between both ends before transfer of information can begin. TCP is responsible for breaking messages into segments, reassembling them at the destination station, resending anything that is not received, and reassembling messages from the segments. TCP supplies a virtual circuit between end-user applications.

- **User Datagram Protocol (UDP)**—A connectionless and unacknowledged protocol. Although UDP is responsible for transmitting messages, no checking for segment delivery is provided at this layer. UDP depends on upper-layer protocols for reliability.

TCP/UDP Header Format

TCP is known as a connection-oriented protocol. This means that the end stations are aware of each other and are constantly communicating about the connection. A classic example of a nontechnical connection-oriented communication would be a telephone conversation between two people. First, there is a protocol that lets the participants know that they have connected and can begin communicating. This would be an initial conversation of "Hello." UDP is known as a connectionless protocol. An example of a connectionless conversation would be the U.S. postal service. You place the letter in the mail and hope that it gets delivered. Figure 7-2 illustrates the TCP segment header format, the field definitions of which are described in Table 7-1. These fields provide the communication between end stations to control the conversation.

Figure 7-2   *TCP Header Format*

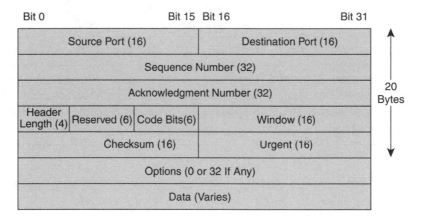

Table 7-1   *TCP Header Field Descriptions*

TCP Header Field	Description	Number of Bits
Source Port	Number of the calling port	16 bits
Destination Port	Number of the called port	16 bits
Sequence Number	Number used to ensure correct sequencing of the arriving data	32 bits
Acknowledgment Number	Next expected TCP octet	32 bits
Header Length	Number of 32-bit words in the header	4 bits
Reserved	Set to zero	6 bits
Code Bits	Control functions such as setup and termination of a session	6 bits
Window	Number of octets that the device is willing to accept	16 bits
Checksum	Calculated checksum of the header and data fields	16 bits
Urgent	Indicates the end of the urgent data	16 bits
Options	One currently defined: maximum TCP segment size	0 or 32 bits, if any
Data	Upper-layer protocol data	Varies

NOTE   The TCP header is 20 bytes. Transporting multiple packets with small data fields results in less-efficient use of available bandwidth than transporting the same amount of data with fewer, larger packets. This is like placing a small object in a large box instead of filling the box completely.

Figure 7-3 illustrates the UDP segment header format, the field definitions for which are described in Table 7-2. The UDP header length is always 64 bits.

Figure 7-3   *UDP Header*

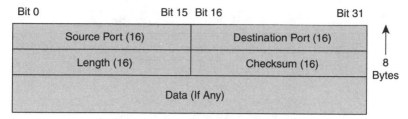

No Sequence Or Acknowledgement Fields

Table 7-2   *UDP Header Field Descriptions*

UDP Header Field	Description	Number of Bits
Source Port	Number of the calling port	16 bits
Destination Port	Number of the called port	16 bits
Length .	Length of UDP header and UDP data	16 bits
Checksum	Calculated checksum of the header and data fields	16 bits
Data	Upper-layer protocol data	Varies

Protocols that use UDP include TFTP, SNMP, Network File System (NFS), and Domain Name System (DNS).

How TCP and UDP Use Port Numbers

Both TCP and UDP use port numbers to pass information to the upper layers. Port numbers are used to keep track of different conversations crossing the network at the same time. Figure 7-4 defines some of the port numbers as used by TCP and UDP.

Figure 7-4   *Port Numbers*

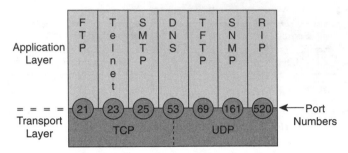

Application software developers agree to use well-known port numbers that are controlled by the Internet Assigned Numbers Authority (IANA). For example, any conversation bound for the FTP application uses the standard port number 21. Conversations that do not involve an application with a well-known port number are assigned port numbers randomly chosen from within a specific range instead. These port numbers are used as source and destination addresses in the TCP segment.

Some ports are reserved in both TCP and UDP, but applications might not be written to support them. Port numbers have the following assigned ranges:

- Numbers below 1024 are considered well-known ports.

- Numbers above 1024 are dynamically assigned ports.

- Registered ports are those registered for vendor-specific applications. Most are above 1024.

NOTE   Some applications, such as DNS, use both transport layer protocols. DNS uses UDP for name resolution and TCP for server zone transfers.

Figure 7-5 shows how well-known port numbers are used by hosts to connect to the application on the end station. The figure also illustrates the selection of a source port so that the end station knows how to communicate with the client application.

Figure 7-5 *Port Number Example*

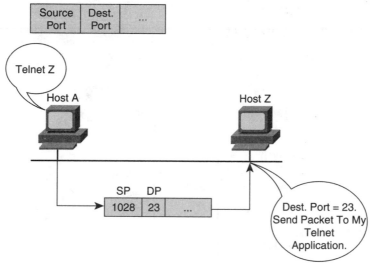

RFC 1700 defines all the well-known port numbers for TCP/IP. For a listing of current port numbers, refer to the IANA web site at www.iana.org.

End systems use port numbers to select the proper application. Originating source port numbers are dynamically assigned by the source host—some number greater than 1023.

Establishing a TCP Connection: The Three-Way Handshake

TCP is connection-oriented, so it requires connection establishment before data transfer begins. For a connection to be established or initialized, the two hosts must synchronize on each other's initial sequence numbers (ISN). Synchronization is done in an exchange of connection-establishing segments carrying a control bit called SYN (for synchronize) and the initial sequence numbers. As shorthand, segments carrying the SYN bit are also called "SYNs." Hence, the solution requires a suitable mechanism for picking an initial sequence number and a slightly involved handshake to exchange the ISNs.

The synchronization requires each side to send its own initial sequence number and to receive a confirmation of its successful transmission within the acknowledgment (ACK) from the other side. Here is the sequence of events:

Step 1   Host A → Host B SYN—My sequence number is 100, ACK number is 0, ACK bit is not set. SYN bit is set.

Step 2   Host A ← Host B ACK—I expect to see 101 next, my sequence number is 300, ACK bit is set. Host B to Host A SYN bit is set.

Step 3 Host A → Host B ACK—I expect to see 301 next, my sequence number is 101, ACK bit is set. SYN bit is set.

This exchange is called the three-way handshake and is illustrated in Figure 7-6.

Figure 7-6 *Three-Way Handshake*

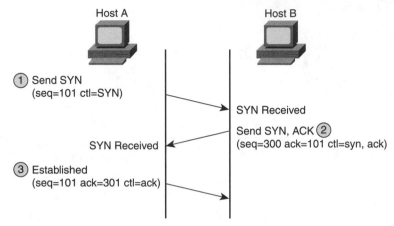

A three-way handshake is necessary because sequence numbers are not tied to a global clock in the network, and TCPs might have different mechanisms for picking the initial sequence number. Because the receiver of the first SYN has no way of knowing whether the segment was an old delayed one, unless it remembers the last sequence number used on the connection (which is not always possible), it must ask the sender to verify this SYN. Figure 7-7 illustrates the acknowledgment process.

Figure 7-7 *Simple Acknowledgment*

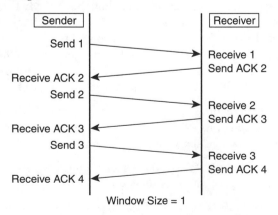

The window size determines how much data the receiving station will accept at one time before an acknowledgment will be returned. With a window size of 1 (as shown in Figure 7-7), each segment must be acknowledged before another segment is transmitted. This results in inefficient use of bandwidth by the hosts.

TCP provides sequencing of segments with a forward reference acknowledgment. Each datagram is numbered before transmission. At the receiving station, TCP reassembles the segments into a complete message. If a sequence number is missing in the series, that segment is retransmitted. Segments that are not acknowledged within a given time period result in retransmission. Figure 7-8 illustrates the role that acknowledgment numbers play when datagrams are transmitted.

Figure 7-8   *Acknowledgment Numbers*

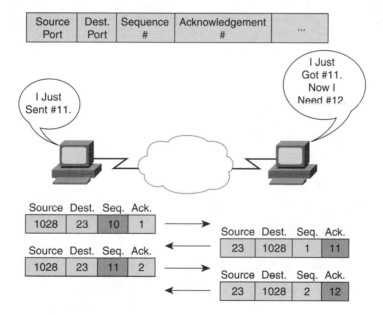

Flow Control for TCP/UDP

To govern the flow of data between devices, TCP uses a flow control mechanism. The receiving TCP reports a "window" to the sending TCP. This window specifies the number of octets, starting with the acknowledgment number, that the receiving TCP is currently prepared to receive.

TCP window sizes are variable during the lifetime of a connection. Each acknowledgment contains a window advertisement that indicates how many bytes the receiver can accept. TCP also maintains a congestion control window that is normally the same size as the receiver's window but is cut in half when a segment is lost (for example, there is congestion). This approach permits the window to be expanded or contracted as necessary to manage buffer space and processing. A larger window size allows more data to be processed.

NOTE   TCP window size is documented in RFC 793, "Transmission Control Protocol," and RFC 813, "Window and Acknowledgement Strategy in TCP," which you can find at www.isi.edu/in-notes/rfc793.txt and www.isi.edu/in-notes/rfc813.txt, respectively.

In Figure 7-9, the sender sends three packets before expecting an ACK. The receiver can only handle a window size of 2. So, it drops packet 3, specifies 3 as the next packet, and specifies a window size of 2. The sender sends the next two packets but still specifies its window size of 3 (for example, it can still accept three packets). The receiver replies by requesting packet 5 and specifying a window size of 2.

Figure 7-9   *TCP Windowing*

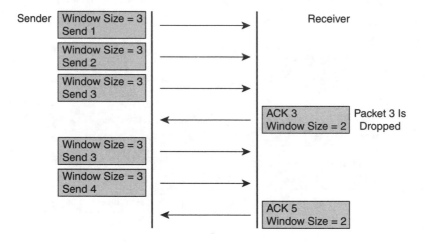

Many of the functions described in these sections, such as windowing and sequencing, have no meaning in UDP. Recall from Figure 7-3 that UDP has no fields for sequence numbers or window sizes. Application layer protocols can provide for reliability. UDP is designed for applications that provide their own error recovery process. It trades reliability for speed.

TCP/IP Internet Layer Overview

The Internet layer of the TCP/IP protocol is the part of the protocol that provides addressing and path selection. This is the layer that routers operate at in order to identify paths in the network, but there are many other functions at this layer.

Several protocols operate at the TCP/IP Internet layer, which corresponds to the OSI network layer. The following list contains some of the protocols we will discuss in this book:

- **Internet Protocol (IP)**—Provides connectionless, best-effort delivery routing of datagrams. IP is not concerned with the content of the datagrams. Instead, it looks for a way to move the datagrams to their destination.

- **Internet Control Message Protocol (ICMP)**—Provides control and messaging capabilities.

- **Address Resolution Protocol (ARP)**—Determines the data link layer address of the destination device for known destination IP addresses.

- **Reverse Address Resolution Protocol (RARP)**—Determines source network addresses when source data link layer addresses are known.

IP

Figure 7-10 shows the fields in the IP header.

Figure 7-10 *IP Header*

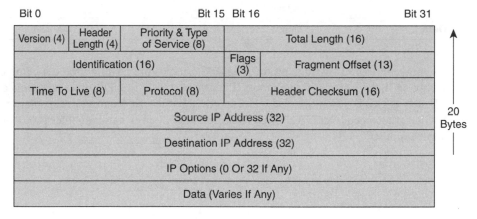

Table 7-3 documents the field definitions within the IP header illustrated in Figure 7-10.

Table 7-3   *IP Header Field Descriptions*

IP Header Field	Description	Number of Bits
Version	Version number	4 bits
Header Length	Header length in 32-bit words	4 bits
Priority & Type of Service	How the datagram should be handled. The first 3 bits are priority bits.	8 bits
Total Length	Total length (header plus data)	16 bits
Identification	Unique IP datagram value	16 bits
Flags	Specifies whether fragmenting should occur	3 bits
Fragment Offset	Provides fragmentation of datagrams to allow differing MTUs in the Internet	13 bits
TTL	Time-To-Live	8 bits
Protocol	Upper-layer (Layer 4) protocol sending the datagram	8 bits
Header Checksum	Integrity check on the header	16 bits
Source IP Address	32-bit source IP addresses	32 bits
Destination IP Addresses	32-bit destination IP addresses	32 bits
IP Options	Network testing, debugging, security, and others	0 or 32 bits if any
Data	Upper-layer protocol data	Varies

As shown in Figure 7-11, the protocol field determines the Layer 4 protocol being carried within an IP datagram. Although most IP traffic uses TCP or UDP, other protocols can use IP, such as OSPF (Open Shortest Path First), GRE (Generic Routing Encapsulation), and EIGRP (Enhanced Interior Gateway Routing Protocol). You can find other protocol numbers in RFC 1700.

Figure 7-11 *Protocol Field*

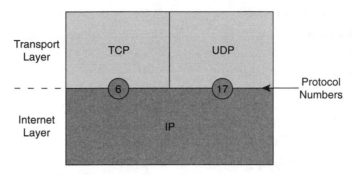

Each IP header must identify the destination Layer 4 protocol for the datagram. Transport layer protocols are numbered, similar to port numbers. IP includes the protocol number in the protocol field. Table 7-4 lists some sample protocol numbers for the transport layer protocols.

Table 7-4 *Protocol Numbers*

Protocol	Protocol Field
Internet Control Message Protocol (ICMP)	1
Interior Gateway Routing Protocol (IGRP)	9
IP version 6 (IPv6)	41
Generic Routing Encapsulation (GRE)	47
Internetwork Packet Exchange in Internet Protocol (IPX in IP)	111
Layer 2 Tunneling Protocol (L2TP)	115

There are many other Layer 4 protocols. The protocols presented here are not an exhaustive list. Refer to www.iana.org or RFC 1700 for a more complete list of all protocol field numbers.

Internet Control Message Protocol

The Internet Control Message Protocol (ICMP) is implemented by all TCP/IP hosts. ICMP messages are carried in IP datagrams and are used to send error and control messages.

ICMP uses the following types of defined messages. Other types of defined messages exist that are not included in this list:

- Destination Unreachable
- Time Exceeded

- Parameter Problem
- Subnet Mask Request
- Redirect
- Echo
- Echo Reply
- Timestamp
- Timestamp Reply
- Information Request
- Information Reply
- Address Request
- Address Reply

The most common form of these messages are pings, ICMP echo requests, and ICMP echo replies. This is not the only purpose of ICMP; it has many other functions as well. Discussions of these functions are beyond the scope of this book. Chapter 4, "Managing Your Network Environment," covers pinging in greater detail.

Address Resolution Protocol

Another IP protocol is the Address Resolution Protocol (ARP). ARP is used to resolve or map a known destination IP address to a MAC sublayer address to allow communication on a multiaccess medium such as Ethernet. To determine a destination address for a datagram, the sending station's ARP cache table is checked. If the address is not in the table, an ARP, which is a broadcast packet, is sent in an attempt to locate the destination station. Every station on the segment receives the broadcast, and the station with the IP address responds to the ARP. Figure 7-12 illustrates how ARP maps IP addresses to MAC sublayer addresses.

Figure 7-12 *ARP*

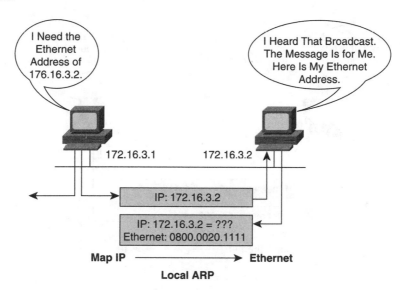

The term *local ARP* describes resolving an address when both the requesting host and the destination host share the same medium or wire, which is the case in Figure 7-12.

Reverse Address Resolution Protocol

Reverse Address Resolution Protocol (RARP) is another protocol defined at the IP layer. RARP is used for workstations that do not know their own IP address when they come up. RARP allows a station to send out a request for its own IP address by sending its own Layer 2 MAC address to a waiting RARP server. The RARP request is a broadcast packet. RARP relies on the presence of a RARP server with a table entry or other means on each subnet to respond to these requests. Figure 7-13 illustrates how RARP works so that workstations can identify their own IP addresses.

Figure 7-13 *RARP*

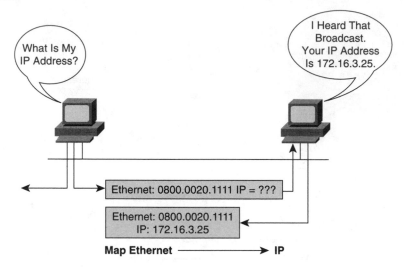

ARP and RARP are implemented directly on top of the data link layer.

NOTE   Dynamic Host Configuration Protocol (DHCP) is a modern implementation of RARP. DHCP provides a mechanism for allocating IP addresses dynamically so that addresses can be reused when hosts no longer need them. For more information on DHCP, refer to *Building Cisco Remote Access Networks*, currently available from Cisco Press.

TCP/IP Address Overview

In a TCP/IP environment, end stations communicate seamlessly with servers or other end stations. This communication occurs because each node using the TCP/IP protocol suite has a unique 32-bit logical IP address.

Each IP datagram includes a source IP address and destination IP address that identify the source and destination network and host.

Each company listed on the internetwork is seen as a single network that must be reached before an individual host within that company can be contacted. Each company network has a unique network address. The hosts that populate that network share those same bits, but each host is identified by the uniqueness of the remaining bits. Figure 7-14 illustrates a sample IP addressing scheme in a network.

Figure 7-14 *IP Addressing*

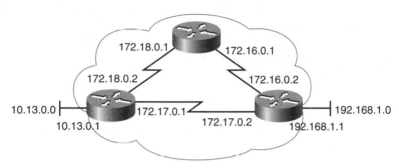

The IP address is 32 bits in length and has two parts: the *network number* and the *host number*. IP addresses are binary in nature, but are expressed in a format that can be read by the human eye. Basically, the 32 bits are broken into four sections of 8 bits each, known as *octets*. Each of these octets is then converted into decimal format and separated by dots. Figure 7-15 illustrates the format of an IP address using 172.16.122.204 as a model for explanation.

Figure 7-15 *IP Address Format*

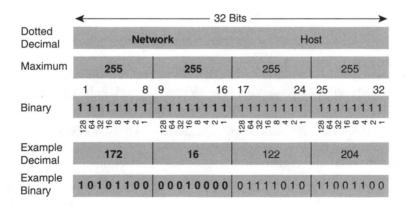

The IP address format is known as *dotted-decimal* notation. Figure 7-15 shows how the dotted-decimal address is derived from the 32-bit binary value:

- Sample address: 172.16.122.204.

- Each bit in the octet has a binary weight (such as 128, 64, 32, 16, 8, 4, 2, and 1) which sums to 255.

- The minimum value for an octet is 0; it contains all 0s.

- The maximum value for an octet is 255; it contains all 1s.

The allocation of addresses is managed by a central authority, the American Registry of Internetwork Numbers (ARIN), which you can contact at www.arin.net for more information about network numbers.

IP Address Classes

When IP was first developed, there were no classes of addresses, because it was assumed that 254 networks would be more than enough for an internet of academic and research computers. As the number of networks grew, the IP addresses were broken into classes, as illustrated in Figure 7-16.

Figure 7-16 *Address Classes*

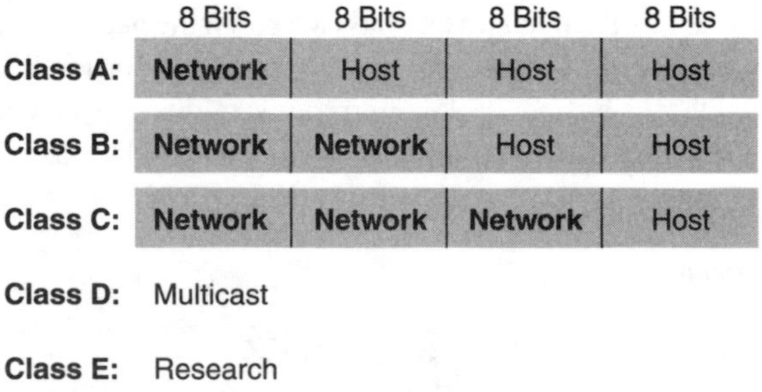

The Class A address has only 8 network bits and 24 bits in the host field. Therefore, few Class A networks, each consisting of many hosts, exist. There are more Class B and Class C networks, each with fewer hosts.

This scheme allows addresses to be assigned based on the size of the network. This address design was based on the assumption that there would be many more small networks than large networks in the world.

NOTE   Class D and E addresses are also defined. Class D addresses start at 224.0.0.0 and are used for multicast purposes. Class E addresses start at 240.0.0.0 and are used for experimental purposes.

Figure 7-17 shows how each network is classified and which bits make up the host part of the address and which make up the network portion.

Figure 7-17 *Address Classification*

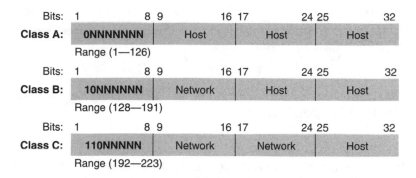

Figure 7-17 shows how the bits in the first octet identify the address class. The router uses the first bits to identify how many bits it must match to interpret the network portion of the address (based on the standard address class). Table 7-5 lists the characteristics of Class A, B, and C addresses.

Table 7-5   *IP Address Classes*

Class A Address	Class B Address	Class C Address
The first bit is 0.	The first two bits are 10.	The first three bits are 110.
Range of network numbers: 1.0.0.0 to 126.0.0.0.	Range of network numbers: 128.0.0.0 to 191.255.0.0.	Range of network numbers: 192.0.0.0 to 223.255.255.0.
Number of possible networks: 127 (1 through 126 are usable; 127 is reserved).	Number of possible networks: 16,384.	Number of possible networks: 2,097,152.
Number of possible values in the host portion: 16,777,216. (The number of usable hosts is two less than the total number possible because the host portion must be nonzero and cannot be all 1s.)	Number of possible values in the host portion: 65,536. (The number of usable hosts is two less than the total number possible because the host portion must be nonzero and cannot be all 1s.)	Number of possible values in the host portion: 256. (The number of usable hosts is two less than the total number possible because the host portion must be nonzero and cannot be all 1s.)

As illustrated in Figure 7-18, Class D addresses (multicast addresses) include the following range of network numbers: 224.0.0.0 to 239.255.255.255.

Figure 7-18 *Multicast Addresses*

Bits:	1	8	9	16	17	24	25	32
Class D:	1110MMMM		Multicast Group		Multicast Group		Multicast Group	

Range (224—239)

Class E addresses (research addresses) include the following range of network numbers: 240.0.0.0 to 247.255.255.255.

NOTE   RFC 1918 defines networks and addresses 10.0.0.0 through 10.255.255.255, 172.16.0.0 through 172.31.255.255, and 192.168.0.0 through 192.168.255.255 as reserved addresses to be used as internal private addresses and not to connect directly to the public Internet.

Host Addresses

There are specific guidelines for assigning IP addresses in a network. First of all, each device or interface must have a nonzero host number. Figure 7-19 shows devices and routers with IP addresses assigned.

Figure 7-19 *Host Addresses*

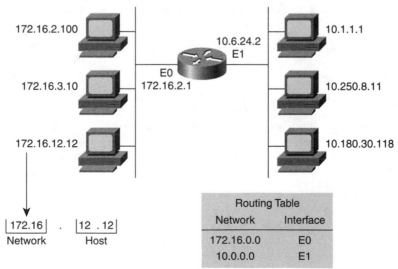

Each wire is identified as the subnet. This value is not assigned, but it is assumed. A value of 0 means "this network" or "the wire itself" (for example, 172.16.0.0). This is the information used by the router to identify each subnet. The routing table contains entries for network or wire addresses; it usually does not contain any information about hosts. Another address that exists in IP is a host address of all 1s. This address is reserved for an IP broadcast into that network—in other words, a packet that should be received by all hosts on that subnet.

As soon as the network portion is determined by the classification, you can determine the total number of hosts on the network by summing all available 1 and 0 combinations of the remaining address bits and subtracting 2. You must subtract 2 because an address consisting of all 0 bits is used to specify the network, and an address of all 1 bits is used for network broadcasts.

The same result can be derived by using the following formula:

$2^N - 2$ (where N is the number of bits in the host portion)

Figure 7-20 illustrates a Class B network, 172.16.0.0. In a Class B network, 16 bits are used for the host portion. Applying the formula $2^N - 2$ (in this case, $2^{16} - 2 = 65,534$) results in 65,534 usable host addresses.

Figure 7-20 *Determining the Available Host Addresses*

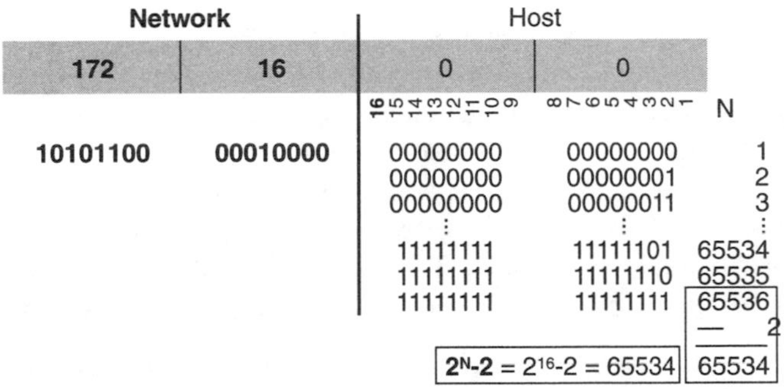

For an address with only a network portion and host portion, the outside world sees the organization as a single network, and no detailed knowledge of the internal structure is required. All datagrams addressed to network 172.16.0.0 are treated the same, regardless of the third and fourth octets of the address. A benefit of this configuration can be the relatively short routing tables that routers can use. Figure 7-21 shows an example of a network that does not use subnets.

Figure 7-21   *Addressing Without Subnets*

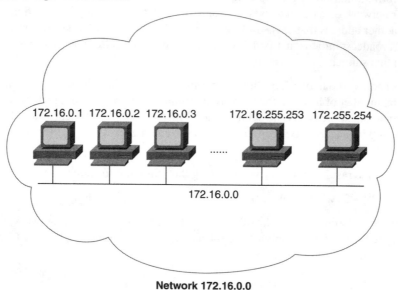

172.16.0.1 172.16.0.2 172.16.0.3   172.16.255.253 172.255.254

172.16.0.0

Network 172.16.0.0

With the addressing scheme in Figure 7-21, the network could be segmented into more granular segments using switches to increase the number of collision domains. However, there is no way of distinguishing individual segments (wires) within the network by IP addressing. A single large broadcast domain exists inside a network that has no subnetworks—all systems on the network encounter all the broadcasts on the network. Although we might have increased performance by segmenting with switches, we have no mechanism to control the broadcast. This type of configuration can result in relatively poor network performance, because a broadcast is propagated to all devices in the network.

In the extreme case, each of the 126 Class A networks would have 16,777,214 usable host addresses. The Class B address space illustrated in Figure 7-21 defines one wire with 65,534 potential workstations on it. What is needed is a way to divide this wire into segments. Subnets provide a way to address these individual segments.

Subnet Addresses

Breaking the network into smaller segments, or subnets, makes network address use more efficient. There is no change in how the outside world sees the network, but within the organization, there is additional structure.

In Figure 7-22, the network 172.16.0.0 is subdivided or broken into four subnets: 172.16.1.0, 172.16.2.0, 172.16.3.0, and 172.16.4.0. The third octet is being used as the subnet address in each of these addresses. Routers determine the destination network using the subnet address, limiting the amount of traffic on the other network segments.

Figure 7-22 *Addressing with Subnets*

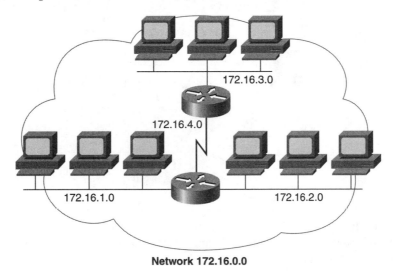

Network 172.16.0.0

Subnets are an extension of the network number. Network administrators decide the size of subnets based on organization and growth needs.

Subnet Masks

A network device uses a subnet mask to determine what part of the IP address is used for the network, the subnet, and the device (host) address, as illustrated in Figure 7-23. A *subnet mask* is a 32-bit value containing a contiguous number of 1 bits for the network and subnet ID and a contiguous number of 0 bits for the host ID. A device can also determine the class of address it has been assigned from its own IP address. The subnet mask then tells the device where the boundary is between the subnet ID and the host ID.

Figure 7-23   *Subnet Addressing on Routers*

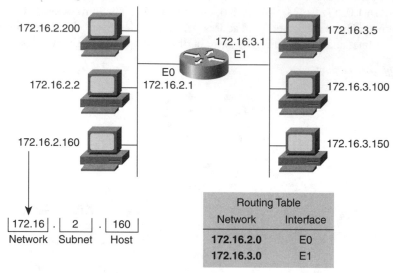

Notice that the routing table now identifies each wire by its subnet number. The router and any hosts determine what the local segment is by making a logical comparison to the subnet mask, as shown in Figure 7-24.

Figure 7-24   *Subnet Mask*

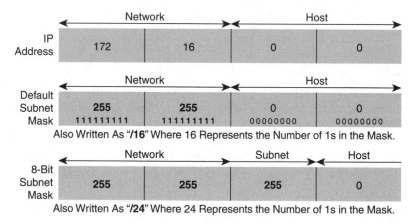

Subnet bits are taken from the host field of the address. The number of subnet bits taken from the host field is identified by a subnet mask. The subnet mask is 32 bits in size, written as four octets. Each bit in the subnet mask is used to determine how the corresponding bit in the IP address should be interpreted, as follows:

- Binary 1 for the network bits
- Binary 1 for the subnet bits
- Binary 0 for the host bits

The subnet mask for 172.16.0.0 255.255.0.0 can be denoted in the following ways:

- Dotted decimal—172.16.0.0 255.255.0.0
- Bit count—172.16.0.0/16, where 16 is the number of 1s in the subnet mask
- Hexadecimal—172.16.0.0 0xFFFF0000

Only a limited number of subnet masks can be applied to an IP address. Figure 7-25 shows what values are available in an octet for subnet addresses.

Figure 7-25 *Subnet Mask Patterns*

128	64	32	16	8	4	2	1		
↓	↓	↓	↓	↓	↓	↓	↓		
1	0	0	0	0	0	0	0	=	128
1	1	0	0	0	0	0	0	=	192
1	1	1	0	0	0	0	0	=	224
1	1	1	1	0	0	0	0	=	240
1	1	1	1	1	0	0	0	=	248
1	1	1	1	1	1	0	0	=	252
1	1	1	1	1	1	1	0	=	254
1	1	1	1	1	1	1	1	=	255

Subnet bits come from the high-order bits of the host field. To determine a subnet mask for an address, add up the decimal values of each position that has a 1 in it. For example:

$$224 = 128 + 64 + 32$$

Because the subnet mask is not defined by the octet boundary, but by bits, we need to convert dotted-decimal addresses to binary and back into dotted-decimal.

The router uses the subnet mask to determine how to route a packet. The router extracts the IP destination address from the packet and retrieves the subnet mask of the receiving interface.

The router, which sees the IP addresses in binary format, performs a logical AND operation to obtain the network number. A logical AND is a boolean algebra operation that allows for binary comparison. Table 7-6 shows the possible results for logical AND comparisons.

Table 7-6 *Logical AND*

AND	0	1
0	0	0
1	0	1

During the logical AND operation, the host portion of the destination address is removed by this process. Routing decisions are then based on network number only.

In Figure 7-26, with no subnetting, the network number "extracted" is 172.16.0.0.

Figure 7-26 *Default Subnet Mask*

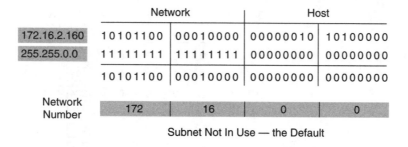

With 8 bits of subnetting, the extracted network (subnet) number is 172.16.2.0.

Figure 7-27 shows more bits turned on, extending the network portion and creating a secondary field extending from the end of the standard mask and using 8 of the host bits. This secondary field is the subnet field and is used to represent wires (or subnetworks) inside the network.

Figure 7-27 *Extending the Mask by 8 Bits*

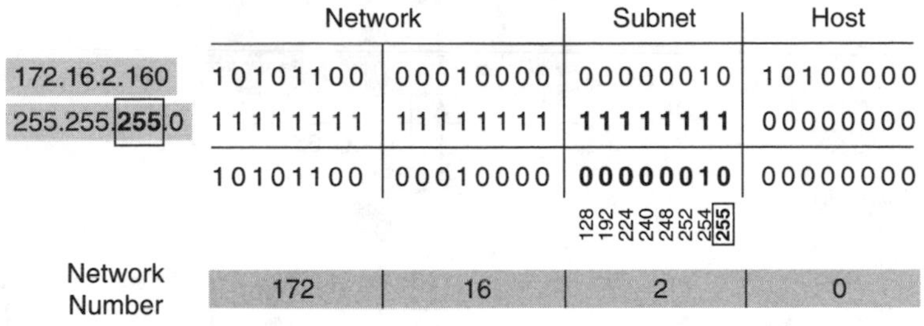

	Network		Subnet	Host
172.16.2.160	10101100	00010000	00000010	10100000
255.255.**255**.0	11111111	11111111	**11111111**	00000000
	10101100	00010000	**00000010**	00000000

128 192 224 240 248 252 254 **255**

Network Number	172	16	2	0

Subnetting does not have to occur between octets. An octet can be split into a subnet portion and a host portion. Figure 7-28 illustrates 10 bits of subnetting with 6 bits remaining for the host portion.

Figure 7-28 *Extending the Mask by 10 Bits*

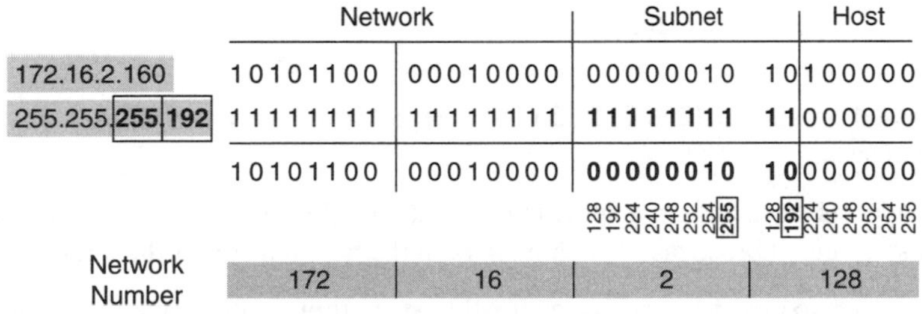

	Network		Subnet	Host
172.16.2.160	10101100	00010000	00000010	10 100000
255.255.**255**.**192**	11111111	11111111	**11111111**	**11** 000000
	10101100	00010000	**00000010**	**10** 000000

128 192 224 240 248 252 254 **255**   128 **192** 224 240 248 252 254 255

Network Number	172	16	2	128

Broadcasts

Broadcasting is supported on networks. Broadcast messages are those you want every host on the network to see. The broadcast address is formed by using all 1s within the IP address.

Cisco IOS software supports three kinds of broadcasts, as illustrated in Figure 7-29:

- Flooding
- Directed broadcasts
- All subnets broadcast

Figure 7-29 *Broadcast Addresses*

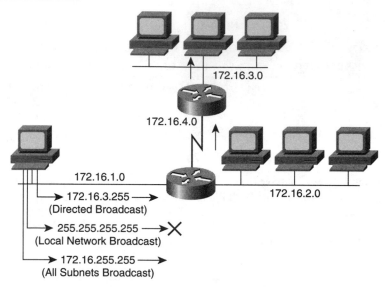

Flooded broadcasts (255.255.255.255) are not propagated, but are considered local broadcasts.

Broadcasts directed into a specific network are allowed and are forwarded by the router. These directed broadcasts contain all 1s in the host portion of the address.

You can also broadcast messages to all hosts within a subnet and to all subnets within a network. To broadcast a message to all hosts within a single subnet, the host portion of the address contains all 1s. The following example broadcasts messages to all hosts in network 172.16, subnet 3:

>   All hosts on a specific subnet = 172.16.3.255

You can also broadcast messages to all hosts on all subnets within a single network. To broadcast a message to all hosts on all subnets within a single network, the host and subnet portions of the address contain all 1s. The following example broadcasts messages to all hosts on all subnets in network 172.16:

>   All hosts on all subnets in a specific network = 172.16.255.255

NOTE   In IOS Release 12.0, routers by default will not forward all subnets or directed broadcast. Use the **ip directed-broadcast** command to enable this feature.

Identifying IP Addresses

Given an IP address and subnet mask, you can use the process illustrated in Figure 7-30 and described in the following list to identify the subnet address, the broadcast address, the first usable address, and the last usable address. (There are many ways to obtain the subnet address, the broadcast address, the first usable address, and the last usable address. This is just one method.) This method can be used to calculate the address space for your networks.

Figure 7-30 *Calculating Address Space*

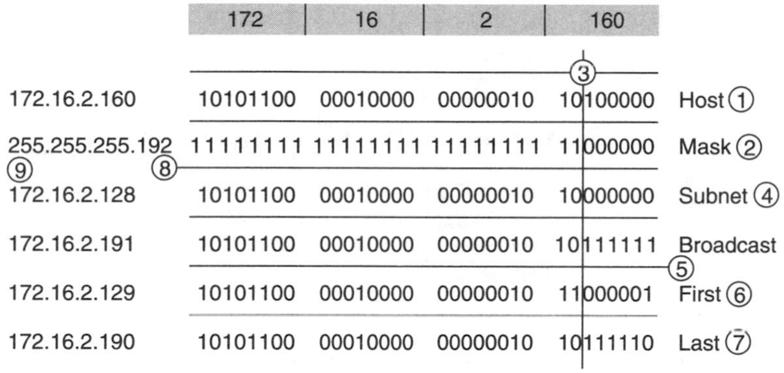

	172	16	2	160	
				③	
172.16.2.160	10101100	00010000	00000010	10100000	Host ①
255.255.255.192 ⑨ ⑧	11111111	11111111	11111111	11000000	Mask ②
172.16.2.128	10101100	00010000	00000010	10000000	Subnet ④
172.16.2.191	10101100	00010000	00000010	10111111	Broadcast ⑤
172.16.2.129	10101100	00010000	00000010	11000001	First ⑥
172.16.2.190	10101100	00010000	00000010	10111110	Last ⑦

Step 1 Write the 32-bit address in binary notation.

Step 2 Write the 32-bit subnet mask in binary just below it.

Step 3 Draw a vertical line just after the last contiguous subnet mask 1 bit.

Step 4 In a row just below, place all 0s for the remaining free spaces (to the right of the line). This will be the subnet.

Step 5 In the next row, to the right of the line, place all 1s until you reach the 32-bit boundary. This will be the broadcast address.

Step 6 On the right side of the line in the next row, place all 0s in the remaining free spaces until you reach the last free space. Place a 1 in that free space. This will be your first usable address.

Step 7 On the right side of the line in the next row, place all 1's in the remaining free spaces until you reach the last free space. Place a 0 in that free space. This will be your last usable address.

Step 8 Copy down all the bits you wrote in Step 1 for the bit fields to the left of the line for all four lines.

Step 9 Convert the bottom four rows back to dotted-decimal.

Given this method, we can determine the subnet, broadcast, first, and last addresses of the IP address 172.16.2.121 with a subnet mask of 255.255.255.0, as shown in Figure 7-31.

Figure 7-31 *Subnet Example*

IP Host Address: 172.16.2.121
Subnet Mask: 255.255.255.0

	Network	Network	Subnet	Host
172.16.2.121:	10101100	00010000	00000010	01111001
255.255.255.0:	11111111	11111111	**11111111**	00000000
Subnet:	10101100	00010000	**00000010**	00000000
Broadcast:	10101100	00010000	00000010	11111111

Subnet Address = 172.16.2.0
Host Addresses = 172.16.2.1–172.16.2.254
Broadcast Address = 172.16.2.255
Eight Bits Of Subnetting

This network has 8 bits of subnetting that provide up to 254 subnets and 254 host addresses. Table 7-7 shows how subnet masks are used to break up IP networks and the number of subnets and hosts available when you use each mask.

Table 7-7 *Class B Subnet Table*

Number of Bits	Subnet Mask	Number of Subnets	Number of Hosts
2	255.255.192.0	2	16,382
3	255.255.224.0	6	8190
4	255.255.240.0	14	4094
5	255.255.248.0	30	2046
6	255.255.252.0	62	1022
7	255.255.254.0	126	510
8	255.255.255.0	254	254
9	255.255.255.128	510	126
10	255.255.255.192	1022	62
11	255.255.255.224	2046	30
12	255.255.255.240	4094	14
13	255.255.255.248	8190	6
14	255.255.255.252	16,382	2

With subnets, you can still use the $2^N - 2$ (where N equals the number of bits) calculation to determine the number of hosts.

Subnet Planning

The sample network shown in Figure 7-32 has been assigned a Class C address of 192.168.5.0. Assume 20 subnets are needed, with 5 hosts per subnet. Subdivide the last octet into a subnet portion and a host portion and determine what the subnet mask will be.

Figure 7-32 *Subnet Planning*

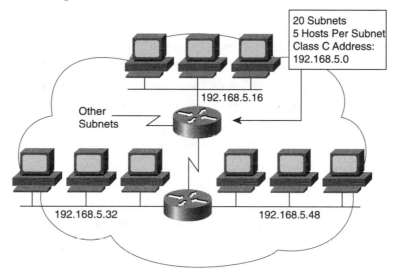

Select a subnet field size that yields enough subnetworks. In this example, choosing a 5-bit mask allows 20 subnets, each containing 32 hosts. The subnet addresses are all multiples of 8, such as 192.168.5.16, 192.168.5.32, and 192.168.5.48. This is because there are 8 addresses in each network, including the network number and broadcast address; therefore, each new subnet will be 8 greater than the previous one.

The remaining bits in the last octet are used for the host field. The 3 bits in our example allow enough hosts to cover the required five hosts per wire. The host numbers will be 1, 2, 3, 4, 5, and 6. Address 7 is the broadcast for this network, and the next subnet is the value 8.

The final host addresses are a combination of the network/subnet "wire" starting address plus each host value. The hosts on the 192.168.5.16 subnet would be addressed as 192.168.5.17, 192.168.5.18, 192.168.5.19, 192.168.5.20, 192.168.5.21, and 192.168.5.22.

A host number of 0 is reserved for the "wire" address, and a host value of all 1s is reserved because it selects all hosts—a broadcast.

Table 7-5 is used for the subnet planning example. Also, a routing sample shows the combining of an arriving IP address with the subnet mask to derive the subnet number. The extracted subnet number should be typical of the subnets generated during this planning exercise. If you look at Figure 7-33, you can see how to determine the subnet number, broadcast address, and beginning and ending ranges of the address space for the address 192.168.5.121 with the subnet 255.255.255.248.

Figure 7-33   *Subnet Planning Example*

IP Host Address: 192.168.5.121
Subnet Mask: 255.255.255.248

	Network	Network	Network	Subnet	Host
192.168.5.121:	11000000	10101000	00000101	01111	001
255.255.255.248:	11111111	11111111	11111111	11111	000
Subnet:	11000000	10101000	00000101	01111	000
Broadcast:	11000000	10101000	00000101	01111	111

Subnet Address = 192.168.5.120
Host Addresses = 192.168.5.121–192.168.5.126
Broadcast Address = 192.168.5.127
Five Bits Of Subnetting

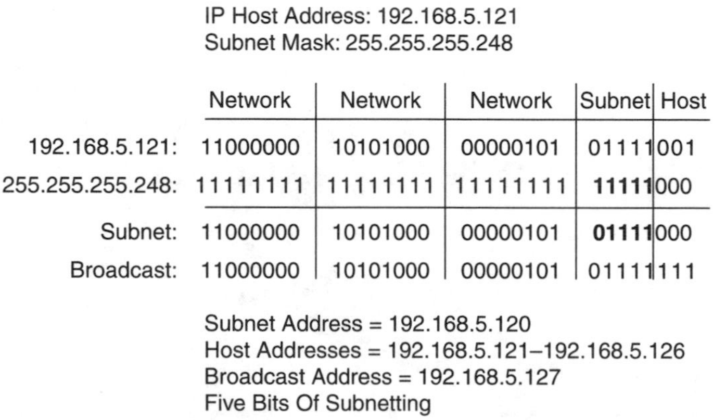

In Figure 7-33, a Class C network is subnetted to provide 6 host addresses and 30 subnets. Table 7-8 shows how subnet masks are used to divide Class C networks and the number of subnets and hosts available with each given subnet.

Table 7-8   *Class C Subnet Table*

Number of Bits	Subnet Mask	Number of Subnets	Number of Hosts
2	255.255.255.192	2	62
3	255.255.255.224	6	30
4	255.255.255.240	14	14
5	255.255.255.248	30	6
6	255.255.255.252	62	2

Configuring IP Addresses

This section explains how to configure IP addresses on a Cisco device. Specifically, it covers the following:

- How to assign the logical network address and default gateway to a switch
- How to assign the logical network address to a router interface
- How to specify the subnet mask format
- How to assign host names to IP addresses
- How to define name servers
- How to display a list of host names and addresses

Assigning Switch Logical Network Addresses and Default Gateways

Use the switch **ip address** global command to establish the logical network address on a series 1900 switch. The syntax for this command is as follows:

```
Switch(config)#ip address ip-address subnet-mask
```

Where:

- *ip-address* represents a 32-bit dotted-decimal number.
- *subnet-mask* represents a 32-bit dotted-decimal number indicating which bit positions are used to identify a network/subnet or host. 1 indicates that the bit is used to identify the network/subnet. 0 indicates that the bit is used to identify a host.

Use the **ip default-gateway** *ip-address* command to define a default gateway on a switch such as a Catalyst 1900 series. The *ip-address* argument is the gateway address (on a router, for example). The syntax for this command is as follows:

```
Switch(config)#ip default-gateway ip-address
```

Assigning Router Interface Logical Network Addresses

Use the router **ip address** interface configuration command to establish the logical network address on a router interface. The syntax for this command is as follows:

```
Router(config-if)#ip address ip-address subnet-mask
```

The *ip-address* and *subnet-mask* arguments function the same way that they do for the switch **ip address** command.

Specifying the Subnet Mask Format

As discussed earlier, IP uses a 32-bit mask, called a subnet mask or netmask, that indicates which address bits belong to the network and subnetwork fields and which bits belong to the host field. The **show** commands display an IP address and then its netmask in dotted decimal, bit count, or hexadecimal notation. By default, the netmask is displayed in dotted-decimal notation. For example, a subnet would be displayed as 172.16.11.55 255.255.255.0.

You can also display the network mask in hexadecimal format. This format is commonly used on UNIX systems. An example of this format is 172.16.11.55 0XFFFFFF00.

You can also display the netmask in bit-count format. This format appends a slash (/) and the total number of bits in the netmask to the address itself. An example of this format is 172.16.11.55/24.

Enter the **term ip netmask-format** command at the EXEC mode prompt to specify the format of network masks for the current session. The mask format will revert to the default of bit-count format when you exit the current session. The syntax for this command is as follows:

```
Router#term ip netmask-format {bitcount | decimal | hexadecimal}
```

To specify the network mask format for a specific line, enter the **ip netmask-format** command in line configuration mode. The syntax for this command is as follows:

```
Router(config-line)#ip netmask-format {bitcount | decimal | hexadecimal}
```

NOTE   When configuring the IP address and subnet mask, you must use dotted-decimal notation.

Assigning Host Names to IP Addresses

Often, traffic is forwarded through the internetwork based on a name rather than a host. If names are used instead of addresses, they must be translated to a numeric address before the traffic can be delivered. The organization's location dictates the path that the data follows through the internetwork.

Cisco IOS software maintains a table of host names and their corresponding addresses, also called *host name-to-address mapping*. Higher-layer protocols, such as Telnet, might use host names to identify network devices (hosts). The router and other network devices must be able to associate host names with IP addresses to communicate with other IP devices. Host names and IP addresses can be associated with one another through static or dynamic means.

You issue the **ip host** command from global configuration mode (as discussed in Chapter 3, "Operating and Configuring a Cisco IOS Device") to manually assign host names to addresses. The syntax for this command is as follows:

```
Router(config-line)# ip host name [tcp-port-number] address [address]
```

Where:

* *name* is any name that describes the destination.

* *tcp-port-number* is an optional number that identifies the TCP port to use when using the host name with an EXEC connect or Telnet command. The default is port 23 for Telnet.

* *address* is the IP address or addresses where the device can be reached. Each device can have up to eight different addresses to identify a host with multiple IP interfaces.

For example, entering the following command:

```
ip host Norine 172.16.3.1 192.168.3.1
```

defines two network addresses to the host **Norine**. The router will attempt the 172.16.3.1 address first when Telnetting to Norine.

As another example, entering the following command:

```
ip host Roger 172.16.4.3
```

defines Roger as a name equivalent to the address 172.16.4.3.

Each unique IP address can have a host name associated with it. Cisco IOS software maintains a cache of host name-to-address mappings for use by EXEC commands. This cache speeds the process of converting names to addresses.

Defining Name Servers

IP defines a naming scheme that allows a device to be identified by its location in IP. A name such as ftp.cisco.com identifies the domain of the File Transfer Protocol for Cisco. To keep track of domain names, IP identifies a name server that manages the name cache.

The **ip name-server** command defines which hosts can provide the name service. A maximum of six IP addresses can be specified as name servers. The syntax for this command is as follows:

```
Router(config)#ip name-server server-address1 [[server-address2]...
    [server-address6]]
```

Domain Name System (DNS) is a system used in the Internet for translating names of network nodes into addresses. Any time the operating system software receives a command or address it does not recognize, it refers to DNS for that device's IP address. Example 7-1 demonstrates the **ip domain-lookup** command, as well as the **no** form of the command.

Example 7-1   *Effects of Domain Lookup*

```
Router(config)#ip domain-lookup
Router(config)#end
Router#pat
Translating "pat"...domain server (255.255.255.255)
% Unknown command or computer name, or unable to find computer address
Router#config t
Router(config)#no ip domain-lookup
Router(config)#end
Router#pat
Translating "pat"
% Unknown command or computer name, or unable to find computer address
Router#
```

The DNS is enabled by default with a server address of 255.255.255.255, which is a local broadcast.

The **no ip domain-lookup** command turns off name-to-address translation in the router, which means that the router will not forward name system broadcast packets.

Displaying Host Names and Addresses

The **show hosts** command is used to display a cached list of host names and addresses, as demonstrated in Example 7-2.

Example 7-2   *show hosts Command Displays a Cached List of Host Names and Addresses*

```
Router#show hosts
Default domain is not set
Name/address lookup uses domain service
Name servers are 255.255.255.255

Host                     Flags       Age Type   Address(es)
Norine                   (perm, OK)  0    IP     172.16.100.100
Roger                    (perm, OK)  0    IP     172.16.100.101
Frank                    (perm, OK)  0    IP     172.16.200.200
Bob                      (perm, OK)  0    IP     172.16.200.201
```

Table 7-9 documents the significant fields generated by running the **show hosts** command.

Table 7-9   *show hosts Command Output Fields*

show hosts Command Field	Description
Host	Names of learned hosts.
Flags	Descriptions of how information was learned and its current status.
perm	Manually configured in a static host table.
temp	Acquired from DNS use. (This flag does not appear in Example 7-2.)
OK	Entry is current.
EX	Entry has aged out (expired). (This flag does not appear in Example 7-2.)
Age	Time measured in hours since software referred to the entry.
Type	Protocol field.
Address(es)	Logical addresses associated with the name of the host.

Inter-VLAN Routing

This section describes how to configure a router to interconnect networks (such as separate VLANs) with IP.

In a switched VLAN environment, packets are switched only between ports designated to be within the same "broadcast domain." VLANs perform network partitioning and traffic separation at Layer 2. So, inter-VLAN communication cannot occur without a Layer 3 device such as a router, because network layer (Layer 3) devices are responsible for communicating between multiple broadcast domains.

Figure 7-34 illustrates a router attached to a core switch. It is sometimes referred to as a "router on a stick." The router can receive packets on one VLAN and forward them to another VLAN. Note that, at Layer 2, this interface uses ISL to communicate with the switch.

Figure 7-34   *Inter-VLAN Routing Using ISL*

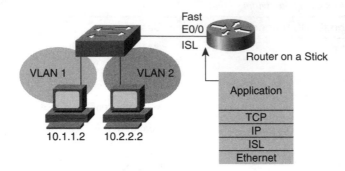

To perform inter-VLAN routing functions, the following must occur:

*   The router must know how to reach all VLANs being interconnected. To determine which end devices, including the networks, are connected in the VLAN, each end device must be addressed with a network layer address such as the IP address described in this chapter. Each router must also know the path to each destination LAN network. The router already knows about directly connected networks. It must learn routes to networks not directly connected.

*   You must have a separate physical connection on the router for each VLAN, or trunking must be enabled on a single physical connection.

NOTE   Chapter 8, "Determining IP Routes," describes how routers discover information about networks that are not directly connected to a router.

To support ISL trunking, the router's physical Fast Ethernet interface must be subdivided into multiple, logical, addressable interfaces, one per VLAN. The resulting logical interfaces are called subinterfaces.

In Figure 7-35, the Fast Ethernet 0 interface is divided into multiple subinterfaces, such as Fast Ethernet 0.1, FastEthernet 0.2, and so on.

Figure 7-35 *Physical Interfaces Can Be Divided into Multiple Subinterfaces*

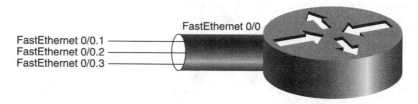

Use the **encapsulation isl** *vlan#* subinterface configuration command to enable ISL on a router's subinterface. *vlan#* is the VLAN number associated with a given subinterface. The syntax for this command is as follows:

```
Router(config-subif)#encapsulation isl vlan#
```

Example 7-3 shows how the router in Figure 7-35 would be configured for inter-VLAN communications.

Example 7-3 *ISL Router Configuration*

```
interface fastethernet 0/0
 no ip address
!
interface fastethernet 0/0.1
 ip address 10.1.1.1 255.255.255.0
 encapsulation isl 1
interface fastethernet 0/0.2
 ip address 10.2.2.1 255.255.255.0
 encapsulation isl 2
```

To configure the "router on a stick" for inter-VLAN routing, complete the following tasks:

Step 1 Enable ISL on the switch port connecting to the router.

Step 2 Enable ISL encapsulation on the router's Fast Ethernet subinterface.

Step 3 Assign a network layer address to each subinterface.

NOTE In this example, the networks are directly connected. Routing between networks not directly connected requires that the router learn the route(s) either statically or dynamically (such as through a routing protocol). Routing is discussed in Chapter 8, "Determining IP Routes."

It is possible to route across the wide-area network (WAN). ISL encapsulation is a Layer 2 implementation and has relevance only on the Fast Ethernet interface. Figure 7-36 shows how you could route across the WAN.

Figure 7-36 *Routing Across the WAN*

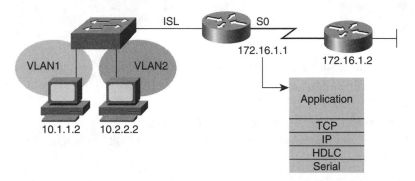

To route over other connections, such as a physical WAN serial connection, as illustrated in Figure 7-36, you must also do the following:

- Encapsulate a data link serial WAN protocol on the WAN interface.
- Assign a network layer address to each interface or subinterface. You would assign the 172.16.1.1 address to the router S0 interface in Figure 7-36 by entering the following:

```
interface Serial0
   ip address 172.16.1.1 255.255.255.0
```

NOTE   The configuration for the setup in Figure 7-36 assumes that HDLC is encapsulated on the serial interface. On Cisco devices, serial interfaces are encapsulated with HDLC by default. More information on serial WAN encapsulations can be found in Chapter 11, "Establishing Serial Point-to-Point Connections."

NOTE   In Figure 7-36, the networks are directly connected. Routing between networks not directly connected requires that the router learn the route(s) either statically or dynamically (such as through a routing protocol). Routing is discussed in Chapter 8, "Determining IP Routes."

TCP/IP Command Summary

Table 7-10 lists and briefly describes the commands covered in this chapter.

Table 7-10   *TCP/IP Command Summary*

Command	Description
ip address	Sets a switch or router interface IP host address.
ip default-gateway	Defines a default gateway at the 1900 switch.
term ip netmask-format	Changes the subnet mask output for a given session.
ip netmask-format	Changes the way that the subnet mask is displayed on a given line.
ip host	Allows the static configuration of an IP host name to an address.
ip name-server	Sets the DNS server to be used by the router to resolve IP addresses.
no ip domain-lookup	Prevents the router from doing an IP host name lookup.
encapsulation isl	Defines ISL encapsulation for an Ethernet subinterface, allowing a router to route in a switched environment.

Summary

This chapter introduced you to the IP protocol stack. You learned to configure IP addresses on a switch for management purposes and also how to configure an IP address on a router interface. You reviewed the IP address structure and learned how subnet masks extend the usefulness of IP addresses. Finally, you looked at commands associated with the IP configuration of the switch and router.

Review Questions

1 The TCP/IP protocol stack was developed as part of a project of which government agency?

2 What are the four layers of the TCP/IP protocol stack?

3 Name two TCP/IP applications used by the Cisco router.

4 Which transport layer protocol provides for reliable connection-oriented sessions with sequence and acknowledgment numbers?

5 What is the purpose of windowing?

6 What Internet layer protocol provides administrative messaging between hosts?

7 How many bits are in an IP address?

8 What class of address is the IP address of 203.133.1.34?

9 Which formula allows you to determine the number of host addresses available?

10 What is the purpose of the subnet mask?

11 Which command allows you to set an IP address on a router interface?

12 Write the following mask in bitwise notation: 255.255.255.192.

13 Which command allows you to statically enter a host name for an IP host?

14 Which subinterface command allows you to configure a "router on a stick"?

15 For the following, determine the address class, calculate the subnet of a given network address, and determine the broadcast address:

15.5.6.18 255.255.255.240

212.172.38.72 255.255.255.192

108.163.211.115 255.255.128.0

106.126.0.154 255.192.0.0

180.15.76.0 255.255.192.0

Upon completion of this chapter, you will be able to perform the following tasks:

- Identify the information needed by a router to make routing decisions.

- Identify the mechanisms for routers to obtain both dynamic and static routing information.

- Understand the process of how routers are learned by distance vector routing protocols such as RIP and IGRP.

- Enable and configure RIP and IGRP for operation on Cisco routers.

- Use the **debug** commands to see how the router exchanges routing information.

CHAPTER 8

Determining IP Routes

In order for a router to send packets to a network, it must determine which path the packet is to take. This chapter discusses path determination. Paths are determined with static routes and dynamic routing protocols such as Routing Information Protocol (RIP), Interior Gateway Routing Protocol (IGRP), Open Shortest Path First (OSPF), Enhanced Interior Gateway Routing Protocol (EIGRP), and Border Gateway Protocol (BGP). The IP routing process and dynamic routing protocols are discussed in volumes of books in the networking industry. The purpose of this chapter is to provide you with an overview of IP routing, focusing on distance vector protocols. This chapter also describes how to configure the RIP and IGRP routing protocols on a Cisco router.

Routing Overview

In order for information to travel from one network to another, some device must know how to transport that information. Routing is the process by which an item gets from one location to another. Many items get routed, such as mail, telephone calls, and trains. In networking, a router is the device used to route traffic. Figure 8-1 illustrates an example of connected routers. In order for a host on the 10.120.2.0 subnet to communicate with a host on the 172.16.1.0 subnet, the routers between them must maintain and choose the paths to be used.

Figure 8-1 *Routing Overview*

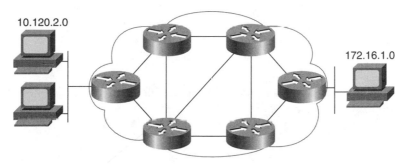

10.120.2.0

172.16.1.0

To be able to route packets of information, a router (or any other entity that performs routing, such as a UNIX workstation running the route daemon, or a Layer 3 switch) needs to know the following key information:

- **Destination address**—What is the destination (or address) of the item that needs to be routed? This is the responsibility of the host. (Network addressing was covered in Chapter 7, "Interconnecting Networks with TCP/IP.")

- **Information sources**—From which source (other routers) can the router learn the paths to given destinations?

- **Possible routes**—What are the initial possible routes, or paths, to the intended destinations?

- **Best routes**—What is the best path to the intended destination?

- **Routing information maintenance and verification**—A way of verifying that the known paths to destinations are valid and are the most current.

The routing information that a router learns from its routing sources is placed in its routing table. The router relies on this table to determine which outgoing port to use when forwarding a packet toward its destination. The routing table is how a router knows about the networks. Figure 8-2 illustrates how a router builds a routing table.

Figure 8-2 *Connected Routes*

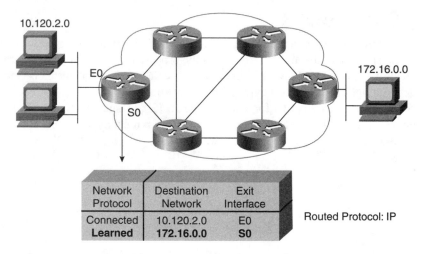

If the destination network is directly connected, the router already knows which port to use when forwarding packets.

If destination networks are not directly attached, the router must learn about and compute the best route to use when forwarding packets to these networks. The routing table is populated through one of the following methods:

- Manually by the network administrator
- Collected through dynamic processes running in the network

Here are two ways to tell the router where to forward packets that are not directly connected:

- **Static routes**—Routes learned by the router when an administrator manually establishes the route. The administrator must manually update this static route entry whenever an internetwork topology requires an update, such as during a link failure.
- **Dynamic routes**—Routes automatically learned by the router after an administrator configures a routing protocol that helps determine routes. Unlike static routes, as soon as the network administrator enables dynamic routing, route knowledge is automatically updated by a routing process whenever new topology information is received from routers within the internetwork.

Enabling Static Routes

In order for a router to route packets, it only needs to know a route to the given network.

Static routes are administratively defined routes that specify the explicit path that packets must take while moving between a source station and a destination station. These administrator-defined routes allow very precise control over the routing behavior of the IP internetwork.

Static routes can be important if the Cisco IOS software cannot build a route to a particular destination. Static routes are also useful for specifying a "gateway of last resort." The gateway of last resort is the address that a router would send a packet destined for a network not listed in the routing table.

Static routes are commonly used when routing from a network to a stub network. A stub network (sometimes called a leaf node) is a network accessed by a single route. Often, static routes are used because there is only one way on to or off of a stub network. Figure 8-3 illustrates a stub network. Because there is only one path to and from this network, static routes could be configured on each router to provide information about this path without the overhead traffic of a routing protocol.

Figure 8-3 *Static Routes*

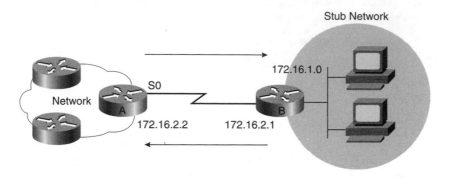

NOTE   The static route is configured for connectivity to a data link not directly connected to your router. For end-to-end connectivity, a route must be configured in both directions.

To configure a static route, enter the **ip route** command in global configuration mode. The parameters for the **ip route** command further define the static route. A static route allows manual configuration of the routing table. This table entry will remain in the routing table as long as the path is active. The only exception to this rule is the **permanent** option shown in the following example. With the **permanent** option, the route will remain in the table even if the path is not active. The syntax for the **ip route** command is as follows:

```
ip route network [mask] {address | interface} [distance] [permanent]
```

Where:

- *network* is the destination network or subnet.

- *mask* is the subnet mask.

- *address* is the IP address of the next-hop router.

- *interface* is the name of the interface to use to get to the destination network.

- *distance* is an optional parameter that defines the administrative distance. Administrative distance is covered later in this chapter.

- **permanent** is an optional parameter that specifies that the route will not be removed, even if the interface shuts down.

Consider the example shown in Figure 8-4.

Figure 8-4   *Static Route Example*

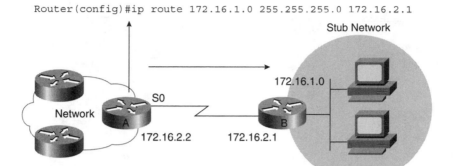

```
Router(config)#ip route 172.16.1.0 255.255.255.0 172.16.2.1
```

In Figure 8-4, the static route from Router A to the stub network is configured as follows:

Router(config)#ip route 172.16.1.0 255.255.255.0 172.16.2.1

Where:

- **ip route** identifies the static route command.
- **172.16.1.0** specifies a static route to the destination subnetwork.
- **255.255.255.0** indicates the subnet mask (8 bits of subnetting are in effect).
- **172.16.2.1** specifies the IP address of the next-hop router in the path to the destination.

The assignment of a static route to reach the stub network 172.16.1.0 is proper for Router A because there is only one way to reach that network. You must have a route configured in the opposite direction for bidirectional communication.

A default route is a special type of static route used for situations in which the route from a source to a destination is not known or when it is unfeasible for the routing table to store sufficient information about all the possible routes. The default route is also known as the gateway of last resort.

In Figure 8-5, you would need to configure Router B to forward all frames for which the destination network is not explicitly listed in its routing table to Router A. This route allows the stub network to reach all known networks beyond Router A.

Figure 8-5 *Default Route*

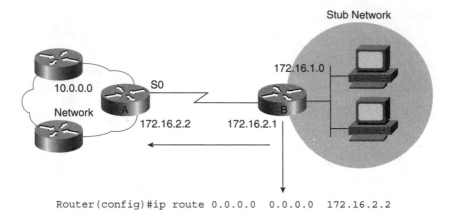

```
Router(config)#ip route 0.0.0.0  0.0.0.0  172.16.2.2
```

To configure the default route, you would enter the following command:

```
Router(config)#ip route 0.0.0.0 0.0.0.0 172.16.2.2
```

Where:

- **ip route** identifies the static route command.

- **0.0.0.0** routes to a nonexistent subnet. (With a special mask, it denotes the default network.)

- **0.0.0.0** specifies the special mask indicating the default route.

- **172.16.2.2** specifies the IP address of the next-hop router to be used as the default for packet forwarding.

Learning Routes Dynamically Using Routing Protocols

Although static routes might be useful in some situations, when the network experiences a change, the administrator must reconfigure all the routers to accommodate that change. Another method of learning about available routes and accommodating the changes is through the use of a dynamic routing protocol. Figure 8-6 illustrates that a router can populate the routing table by learning and choosing routes through dynamic routing protocols.

Figure 8-6   *Routing Protocols*

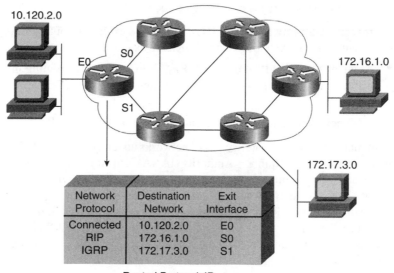

Routed Protocol: IP
Routing Protocol: RIP, IGRP

Dynamic routing relies on a routing protocol to disseminate and gather knowledge. A routing protocol defines the set of rules used by a router when it communicates with neighboring routers (that is, a routing protocol determines routing paths and maintains routing tables).

A routing protocol is a network layer protocol that intercepts packets from other participants in order to learn and maintain a routing table. In contrast, routed protocols, such as TCP/IP and IPX, define the format and use of the fields within a packet to provide a transport mechanism for user traffic. As soon as the routing protocol determines a valid path between routers, the router can route a routed protocol. Routing protocols also describe the following information:

- How updates are conveyed
- What knowledge is conveyed
- When to convey knowledge
- How to locate recipients of the updates

Two examples of routing protocols that are discussed later in this chapter are Routing Information Protocol (RIP) and Interior Gateway Routing Protocol (IGRP).

Interior Gateway Protocols Versus Exterior Gateway Protocols

Here are the two major types of routing protocols:

- **Interior Gateway Protocols (IGP)**—Used to exchange routing information within an autonomous system. RIP and IGRP are examples of IGPs.

- **Exterior Gateway Protocols (EGP)**—Used to exchange routing information between autonomous systems. Border Gateway Protocol (BGP) is an example of an EGP.

Figure 8-7 helps distinguish the difference between IGPs and EGPs.

An autonomous system is a collection of networks under a common administrative domain. The Internet Assigned Numbers Authority (IANA) is the umbrella organization responsible for allocating autonomous system numbers. Specifically, the American Registry for Internet Numbers (ARIN) has the jurisdiction for assigning numbers for the Americas, Caribbean, and Africa. Reseaux IP Europeennes-Network Information Center (RIPE-NIC) administers the numbers for Europe, and the Asia Pacific-NIC (AP-NIC) administers the autonomous system numbers for the Asia-Pacific region. This autonomous system designator is a 16-bit number.

NOTE	Using the IANA-assigned autonomous system number rather than some other number is necessary only if your organization plans to use an EGP such as BGP on a public network such as the Internet.

EGPs are not discussed further in this book. Refer to the *Advanced Cisco Router Configuration (ACRC)* coursebook, *Internet Routing Architectures,* or *Advanced IP Network Design*, all available from Cisco Press, for more information on EGPs.

Administrative Distance

Multiple routing protocols and static routes may be used at the same time. If there are several routing sources providing common routing information, an administrative distance value is used to rate the trustworthiness of each routing source. Specifying administrative distance values lets the Cisco IOS software discriminate between sources of routing information. For each network learned, the IOS selects the route from the routing source with the lowest administrative distance.

An administrative distance is an integer from 0 to 255. In general, a routing protocol with a lower administrative distance has a higher likelihood of being used. Figure 8-8 demonstrates an example of where administrative distance comes into play.

Figure 8-7   *IGPs Versus EGPs*

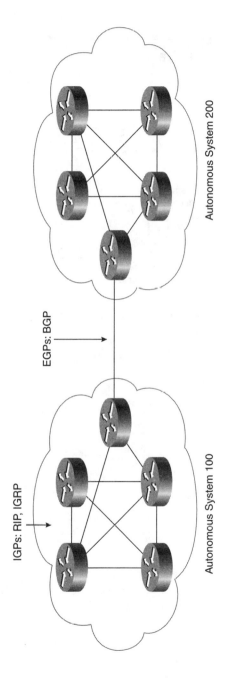

Figure 8-8 *Administrative Distance*

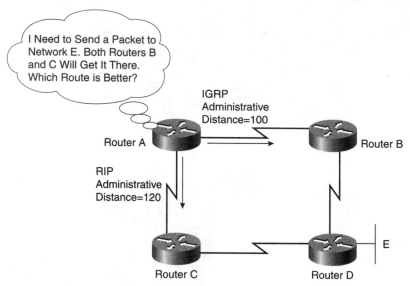

Table 8-1 shows the default administrative distance for some routing information sources.

Table 8-1 *Default Administrative Distance Values*

Route Source	Default Distance
Connected interface	0
Static route address	1
EIGRP	90
IGRP	100
OSPF	110
RIP	120
External EIGRP	170
Unknown/Unbelievable	255 (Will not be used to pass traffic)

If nondefault values are necessary, such as when you are redistributing routes, a network administrator can use the Cisco IOS to configure administrative distance values on a per-router, per-protocol, per-route basis.

NOTE   For more information on administrative distances, see the *ACRC* coursebook from Cisco Press.

Overview of Routing Protocol Classes

Although all routing protocols perform the functions highlighted in the previous sections, there are different ways to arrive at the end product. There are essentially three classes of routing protocols. Figure 8-9 shows routers exchanging information. They do this through a protocol that falls into one of these categories.

Figure 8-9   *Classes of Routing Protocols*

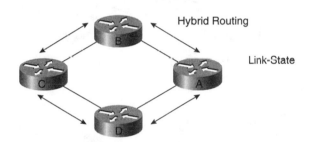

Within an autonomous system, most IGP routing algorithms can be classified as conforming to one of the following algorithms:

- **Distance vector**—The distance vector routing approach determines the direction (vector) and distance to any link in the internetwork. Examples include RIP and IGRP.

- **Link-state**—The link-state (also called shortest path first) approach recreates the exact topology of the entire internetwork for route computation (or at least the partition in which the router is situated). Examples include OSPF and NLSP.

- **Balanced hybrid**—A balanced hybrid approach combines aspects of the link-state and distance vector algorithms. An example would be EIGRP.

There is no single best routing algorithm for all internetworks. All routing protocols provide the information differently. The following sections cover the different routing protocol classes in greater detail.

Distance Vector Routing Protocols

Distance vector-based routing algorithms (also known as Bellman-Ford-Fulkerson algorithms) pass periodic copies of a routing table from router to router and accumulate distance vectors (distance means how far, and vector means in which direction). Regular updates between routers communicate topology changes.

Each router receives a routing table from its direct neighbor. For example, in Figure 8-10, Router B receives information from Router A. Router B adds a distance vector metric (such as the number of hops), increasing the distance vector. It then passes the routing table to its other neighbor, Router C. This same step-by-step process occurs in all directions between direct-neighbor routers (this is also known as "routing by rumor").

Figure 8-10 *Distance Vector Protocols*

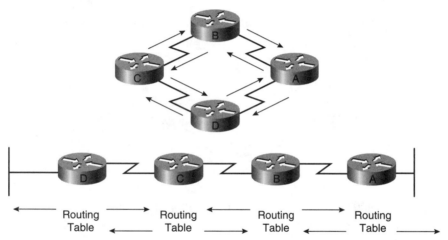

In this way, the algorithm accumulates network distances so that it can maintain a database of internetwork topology information. Distance vector algorithms do not allow a router to know the exact topology of an internetwork.

The following section explains how the distance vector routing protocols do the following:

- Identify sources of information
- Discover routes
- Select the best route
- Maintain routing information

Route Discovery, Selection, and Maintenance

In Figure 8-11, the interface to each directly connected network is shown as having a distance of 0.

Figure 8-11 *Routing Information Sources*

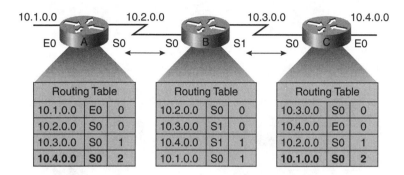

As the distance vector network discovery process proceeds, routers discover the best path to non-directly connected destination networks based on accumulated metrics from each neighbor.

For example, Router A learns about other networks based on information it receives from Router B. Each of these other network entries in the routing table has an accumulated distance vector to show how far away that network is in the given direction.

There might be multiple paths to any given destination network. When a routing protocol's algorithm updates the routing table, its primary objective is to determine the best possible route to each network. Each distance vector routing protocol uses a different routing algorithm to determine the best route. The algorithm generates a number called the metric value for each path through the network. Typically, the smaller the metric, the better the path. Figure 8-12 shows a network with multiple paths between Host A and Host B. Each routing protocol would choose the best path between these hosts by looking at the metrics. Each routing protocol uses a different value to calculate metrics.

Figure 8-12 *Routing Metrics*

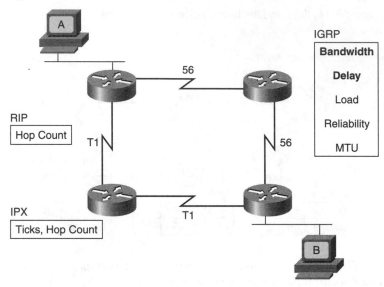

Metrics can be calculated based on either a single characteristic of a path or multiple path characteristics. Figure 8-12 lists some of the metrics that could be used by protocols. The metrics most commonly used by routers are as follows:

- **Hop count**—Number of routers through which a packet will pass.

- **Ticks**—Delay on a data link using IBM PC clock ticks (approximately 55 milliseconds).

- **Cost**—Arbitrary value, usually based on bandwidth, dollar expense, or another measurement, that may be assigned by a network administrator.

- **Bandwidth**—Data capacity of a link. For instance, normally, a 10 Mbps Ethernet link is preferable to a 64 Kbps leased line.

- **Delay**—Length of time required to move a packet from source to destination.

- **Load**—Amount of activity on a network resource, such as a router or link.

- **Reliability**—Usually refers to the bit-error rate of each network link.

- **MTU**—Maximum transmission unit. The maximum frame length in octets that is acceptable to all links on the path.

In Figure 8-12, each protocol would have chosen a route based on metrics. IGRP would have based the decision on combined characteristics, including bandwidth, delay, reliability, and MTU. Because bandwidth and delay are the most heavily weighed parts of the metric, IGRP would have chosen the route with the T1 lines. RIP, which looks only at hop counts, would say the links were equal and would have load-balanced between the paths.

When the topology in a distance vector protocol internetwork changes, routing table updates must occur. As with the network discovery process, topology change updates proceed step-by-step from router to router.

Distance vector algorithms call for each router to send its entire routing table to each of its adjacent or directly connected neighbors. Distance vector routing tables include information about the total path cost (defined by its metric) and the logical address of the first router on the path to each network it knows about.

When a router receives an update from a neighboring router, it compares the update to its own routing table. The router adds the cost of reaching the neighbor router to the path cost reported by the neighbor to establish the new metric. If the router learned about a better route (smaller total metric) to a network from its neighbor, the router updates its own routing table.

For example, if Router B in Figure 8-13 is one unit of cost from Router A, Router B would add 1 to all costs reported by Router A when Router B runs the distance vector processes to update its routing table.

Figure 8-13 *Maintaining Routes*

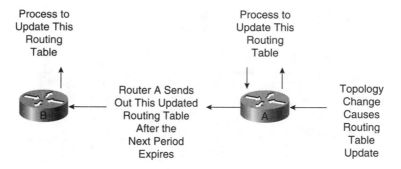

Routing Loops

When maintaining the routing information, routing loops can occur if the internetwork's slow convergence after a topology change causes inconsistent routing entries. The example presented in the next few pages uses a simple network design to convey the concepts. Later in this chapter, you will look at how routing loops occur and are corrected on more complex network designs. Figure 8-14 illustrates how each node maintains the distance from itself to each possible destination network.

Figure 8-14 *Routing Loops*

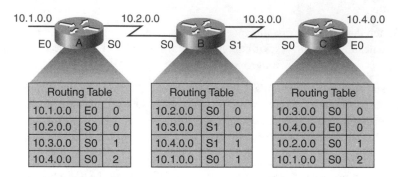

Just before the failure of network 10.4.0.0, shown in Figure 8-15, all routers have consistent knowledge and correct routing tables. The network is said to have converged. For this example, the cost function is hop count, so the cost of each link is 1. Router C is directly connected to network 10.4.0.0 with a distance of 0. Router A's path to network 10.4.0.0 is through Router B, with a hop count of 2.

Figure 8-15 *Slow Convergence Produces Inconsistent Routing*

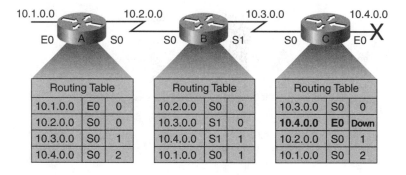

When network 10.4.0.0 fails, Router C detects the failure and stops routing packets out its E0 interface. However, Routers A and B have not yet received notification of the failure. Router A still believes it can access 10.4.0.0 through Router B. Router A's routing table still reflects a path to network 10.4.0.0 with a distance of 2.

Because Router B's routing table indicates a path to network 10.4.0.0, Router C believes it now has a viable path to network 10.4.0.0 through Router B. Router C updates its routing table to reflect a path to network 10.4.0.0 with a hop count of 2, as illustrated in Figure 8-16.

Figure 8-16 *Inconsistent Path Information Between Routers*

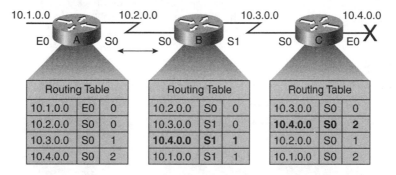

Router B receives a new update from Router C (3 hops). Router A receives the new routing table from Router B, detects the modified distance vector to network 10.4.0.0, and recalculates its own distance vector to 10.4.0.0 as 4.

Because Routers A, B, and C conclude that the best path to network 10.4.0.0 is through each other, packets destined to network 10.4.0.0 continue to bounce between the three routers, as illustrated in Figure 8-17.

Figure 8-17 *Routing Loop Exists Because of Erroneous Hop Count*

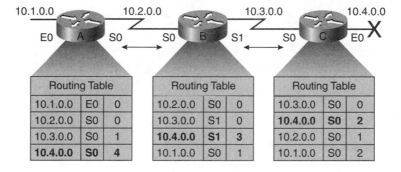

Continuing the example in Figure 8-17, the invalid updates about network 10.4.0.0 continue to loop. Until some other process can stop the looping, the routers update each other inappropriately, considering that network 10.4.0.0 is down.

This condition, called counting to infinity, continuously loops packets around the network, despite the fundamental fact that the destination network 10.4.0.0 is down. While the routers are counting to infinity, the invalid information allows a routing loop to exist, as illustrated in Figure 8-18.

Figure 8-18   *Counting to Infinity*

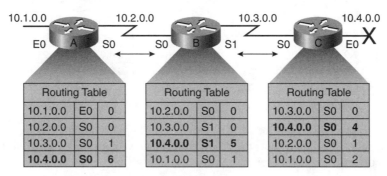

Without countermeasures to stop this process, the distance vector of hop count increments each time the packet passes through another router. These packets loop through the network because of wrong information in the routing tables. The following sections cover the countermeasures used by distance vector routing protocols to prevent routing loops from running indefinitely.

Troubleshooting Routing Loops with Maximum Metric Settings

IP distance vector routing algorithms have inherent limits via the Time To Live value in the IP header. In other words, a router must reduce the TTL field by at least 1 each time it gets the packet. If the TTL value becomes 0, the router discards that packet. However, the routing loop problem might require a count to infinity first.

To avoid this prolonged problem, distance vector protocols define infinity as some maximum number. This number refers to a routing metric, such as a hop count.

With this approach, the routing protocol permits the routing loop until the metric exceeds its maximum allowed value. Figure 8-19 shows this defined maximum as 16 hops. After the metric value exceeds the maximum, network 10.4.0.0 is considered unreachable.

Figure 8-19 *Maximum Metric*

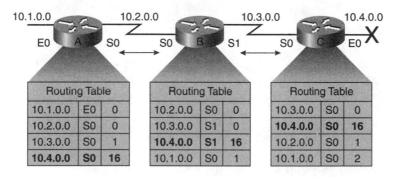

Preventing Routing Loops with Split Horizon

One way to eliminate routing loops and speed up convergence is through the technique called *split horizon*. The rule of split horizon is that it is never useful to send information about a route back in the direction from which the original update came. For example, Figure 8-20 illustrates the following:

- Router B has access to network 10.4.0.0 through Router C. It makes no sense for Router B to announce to Router C that Router B has access to network 10.4.0.0 through Router C.

- Given that Router B passed the announcement of its route to network 10.4.0.0 to Router A, it makes no sense for Router A to announce its distance from network 10.4.0.0 to Router B.

- Having no alternative path to network 10.4.0.0, Router B concludes that network 10.4.0.0 is inaccessible.

Figure 8-20 *Split Horizon*

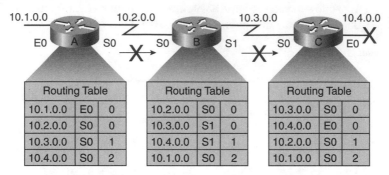

Preventing Routing Loops with Route Poisoning

Another form of split horizon employs a technique called *route poisoning*. Route poisoning attempts to eliminate routing loops caused by inconsistent updates. With this technique, the router sets a table entry that keeps the network state consistent while other routers gradually converge correctly on the topology change. Used with holddown timers (described in the following section), route poisoning is a solution to routing loops.

Figure 8-21 illustrates the following example. When network 10.4.0.0 goes down, Router C poisons its link to network 10.4.0.0 by entering a table entry for that link as having infinite cost (that is, being unreachable). By poisoning its route to network 10.4.0.0, Router C is not susceptible to other incorrect updates about network 10.4.0.0 coming from neighboring routers that might claim to have a valid alternative path.

Figure 8-21 *Route Poisoning*

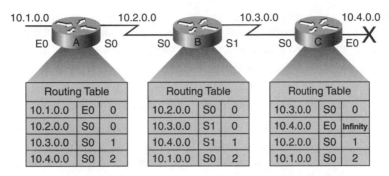

When Router B sees the metric to 10.4.0.0 jump to infinity, it sends an update called a *poison reverse* back to Router C, stating that network 10.4.0.0 is inaccessible, as illustrated in Figure 8-22. This is a specific circumstance overriding split horizon. This occurs to make sure that all routers on that segment have received information about the poisoned route.

Figure 8-22 *Poison Reverse*

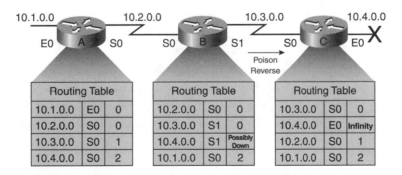

Route Maintenance Using Holddown Timers

Holddown timers are used to prevent regular update messages from inappropriately reinstating a route that might have gone bad. Holddowns tell routers to hold any changes that might affect routes for some period of time. The holddown period is usually calculated to be just greater than the period of time necessary to update the entire network with a routing change.

Holddown timers work as follows:

Step 1   When a router receives an update from a neighbor indicating that a previously accessible network is now inaccessible, the router marks the route as inaccessible and starts a holddown timer.

Step 2   If an update arrives from a neighboring router with a better metric than originally recorded for the network, the router marks the network as accessible and removes the holddown timer.

Step 3   If at any time before the holddown timer expires an update is received from a different neighboring router with a poorer metric, the update is ignored. Ignoring an update with a poorer metric when a holddown is in effect allows more time for the knowledge of the change to propagate through the entire network.

Step 4   During the holddown period, routes appear in the routing table as "possibly down."

Figure 8-23 illustrates the holddown timer process.

Figure 8-23   *Holddown Timers*

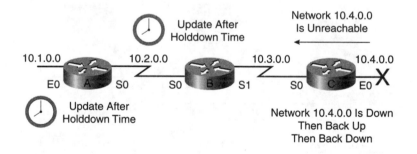

Route Maintenance Using Triggered Updates

In the previous examples, routing loops were caused by erroneous information calculated as a result of inconsistent updates, slow convergence, and timing. If routers wait for their regularly scheduled updates before notifying neighboring routers of network catastrophes, serious problems can occur, such as loops or traffic being dropped.

Normally, new routing tables are sent to neighboring routers on a regular basis. A *triggered update* is a new routing table that is sent immediately, in response to a change. The detecting router immediately sends an update message to adjacent routers, which, in turn, generate triggered updates notifying their adjacent neighbors of the change. This wave propagates throughout the portion of the network that was using the affected link. Figure 8-24 illustrates what takes place when using triggered updates.

Figure 8-24 *Triggered Updates*

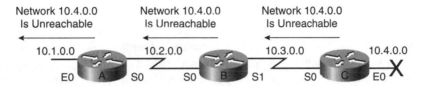

Triggered updates would be sufficient if we could guarantee that the wave of updates reached every appropriate router immediately. However, there are two problems:

- Packets containing the update message can be dropped or corrupted by some link in the network.

- The triggered updates do not happen instantaneously. It is possible that a router that has not yet received the triggered update will issue a regular update at just the wrong time, causing the bad route to be reinserted in a neighbor that had already received the triggered update.

Coupling triggered updates with holddowns is designed to get around these problems.

Route Maintenance Using Holddown Timers with Triggered Updates

Because the holddown rule says that when a route is invalid, no new route with the same or a worse metric will be accepted for the same destination for some period of time, the triggered update has time to propagate throughout the network.

The troubleshooting solutions presented in the previous sections work together to prevent routing loops in a more complex network design. As depicted in Figure 8-25, the routers have multiple routes to each other. As soon as Router B detects the failure of network 10.4.0.0, Router B removes its route to that network. Router B sends a trigger update to A and D, poisoning the route to network 10.4.0.0 by indicating an infinite metric to that network.

Figure 8-25 *Implementing Multiple Solutions*

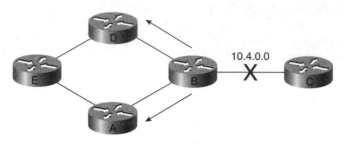

Routers D and A receive the triggered update and set their own holddown timers, noting that the 10.4.0.0 network is "possibly down." Routers D and A, in turn, send a triggered update to Router E, indicating the possible inaccessibility of network 10.4.0.0. Router E also sets the route to 10.4.0.0 in holddown. Figure 8-26 depicts how Routers A, D, and E implement holddown timers.

Figure 8-26 *Route Fails*

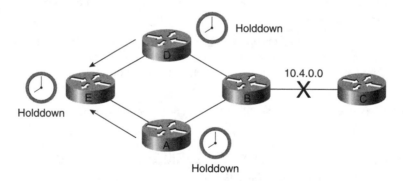

Router A and Router D send a poison reverse to Router B, stating that network 10.4.0.0 is inaccessible. Because Router E received a triggered update from A and D, it sends a poison reverse to A and D also. Figure 8-27 illustrates the sending of poison reverse updates.

Figure 8-27 *Route Holddown*

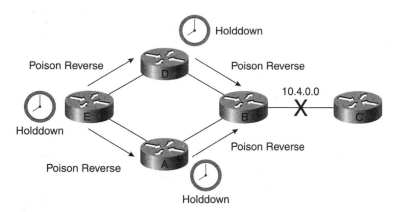

Routers A, D, and E will remain in holddown until one of the following events occurs:

- The holddown timer expires.
- Another update is received, indicating a new route with a better metric.
- A flush timer, which is the time a route would be held before being removed, removes the route from the routing table.

During the holddown period, Routers A, D, and E assume that the network status is unchanged from its original state and attempt to route packets to network 10.4.0.0. Figure 8-28 illustrates Router E attempting to forward a packet to network 10.4.0.0. This packet will reach Router B. However, because Router B has no route to network 10.4.0.0, Router B will drop the packet and send back an ICMP network unreachable message.

Figure 8-28 *Packets During Holddown*

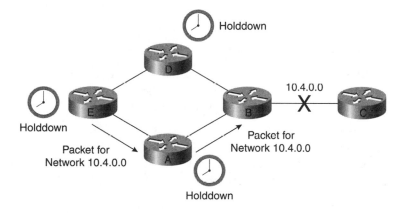

When the 10.4.0.0 network comes back up, Router B sends a trigger update to Routers A and D, notifying them that the link is active. After the holddown timer expires, Routers A and D add route 10.4.0.0 back to the routing table as accessible, as illustrated in Figure 8-29.

Figure 8-29   *Network Up*

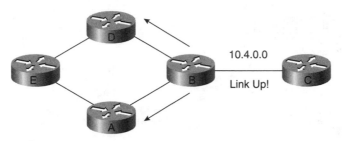

Routers A and D send Router E a routing update stating that network 10.4.0.0 is up, and Router E updates its routing table after the holddown timer expires, as illustrated in Figure 8-30.

Figure 8-30   *Network Converges*

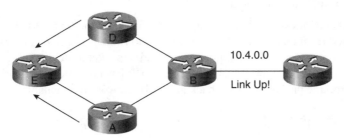

Link-State and Hybrid Routing Protocols

As mentioned earlier, volumes of information have been written about IP routing. The focus of this chapter is distance vector routing. In order to contrast the distance vector process, this section briefly describes the link-state and hybrid routing protocols.

Link-state protocols build routing tables based on a topology database. This database is built from link state packets that are passed between all the routers to describe the state of a network. The database is used by the shortest path first algorithm to build the routing table. Figure 8-31 shows the components of a link-state protocol.

Figure 8-31 *Link-State Protocols*

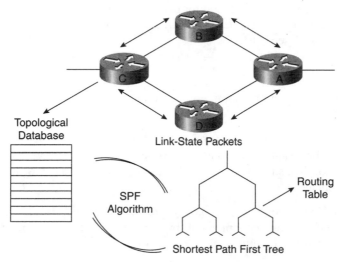

In addition to distance vector-based routing, the second basic algorithm used for routing is the link-state algorithm.

Link-state-based routing algorithms—also known as shortest path first (SPF) algorithms—maintain a complex database of topology information. Whereas the distance vector algorithm has nonspecific information about distant networks and no knowledge of distant routers, a link-state routing algorithm maintains full knowledge of distant routers and how they interconnect.

Link-state routing uses link-state packets (LSPs), a topological database, the SPF algorithm, the resulting SPF tree, and, finally, a routing table of paths and ports to each network.

As networks become larger in scale, link-state routing protocols become more attractive because of the following:

- Link-state protocols only send updates of a topology change.

- Periodic updates are more infrequent than for distance vector protocols.

- Networks running link-state routing protocols can be segmented into area hierarchies, limiting the scope of route changes.

- Networks running link-state routing protocols support classless addressing.

- Networks running link-state routing protocols support summarization.

Engineers have implemented this link-state concept in Open Shortest Path First (OSPF) routing. RFC 2328 (http://www.isi.edu/in-notes/rfc2328.txt) describes OSPF link-state concepts and operations.

NOTE   Link-state protocols are not covered further in this book. For more information regarding link-state routing protocols, refer to the *Advanced Cisco Router Configuration (ACRC)* coursebook from Cisco Press.

An emerging third type of routing protocol combines aspects of both distance vector and link-state. This third type is called *balanced hybrid* in this book.

The balanced hybrid routing protocol uses distance vectors with more accurate metrics to determine the best paths to destination networks. However, it differs from most distance vector protocols by using topology changes to trigger routing database updates as opposed to periodic updates.

The balanced hybrid routing type converges more rapidly, like the link-state protocols. However, it differs from these protocols by emphasizing economy in the use of required resources such as bandwidth, memory, and processor overhead.

An example of a balanced hybrid protocol is Cisco's Enhanced Interior Gateway Routing Protocol (EIGRP).

NOTE   Hybrid routing protocols are not covered further in this book. For more information regarding hybrid routing protocols, refer to the *Advanced Cisco Router Configuration (ACRC)* coursebook available from Cisco Press.

Configuring Dynamic Routing Protocols

Dynamic routing protocols are configured on a router to allow you to discover and dynamically manage the available paths in the network. This section describes how to configure a dynamic routing protocol on a Cisco router.

To enable a dynamic routing protocol, you must perform the following tasks:

- Select a routing protocol, such as RIP or IGRP.
- Select IP networks to be routed.

You must also assign network/subnet addresses and the appropriate subnet mask to interfaces.

Dynamic routing uses broadcasts and multicasts to communicate with other routers. As soon as a router receives information from other routers, it uses the routing metric to find the best path to each network or subnet. Figure 8-32 shows that after you select a protocol and set the networks to be advertised, the process begins.

Figure 8-32 *IP Routing Configuration Tasks*

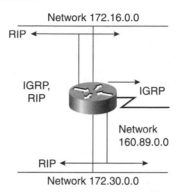

The **router** command starts the routing process. The syntax for this command is as follows:

```
router(config)#router protocol [keyword]
```

Where:

- *protocol* is either RIP, IGRP, OSPF, or EIGRP.

- *keyword* refers to an autonomous system, which is used with protocols that require an autonomous system, such as IGRP.

The **network** command is required because it allows the routing process to determine which interfaces will participate in the sending and receiving of routing updates. The **network** command starts the routing protocol on all of a router's interfaces that have IP addresses within the specified network scope. The **network** command also allows the router to advertise that network to other routers. The syntax for this command is as follows:

```
router(config-router)#network network-number
```

where the *network-number* parameter specifies a directly connected network.

The *network-number* parameter for RIP and IGRP must be based on the major-class network numbers, not subnet numbers or individual addresses. The network number also must identify a network to which the router is physically connected.

After you have enabled the protocol and chosen which networks to advertise, the router begins to dynamically learn the networks and paths available in the internetwork.

Enabling RIP

In this section, you will learn about the operation of the Routing Information Protocol (RIP) and how to configure it on a Cisco router. Figure 8-33 shows how RIP would choose a route based on the metric of hop count.

Figure 8-33 *RIP Overview*

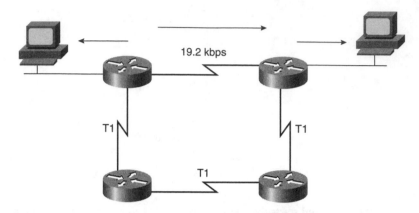

RIP version 1 (RIP-1) is described in RFC 1058 (www.isi.edu/in-notes/rfc1058.txt). An enhanced version, RIP version 2 (RIP-2), a classless routing protocol, is defined in RFC 1721 and 1722 (www.isi.edu/in-notes/rfc1721.txt and www.isi.edu/in-notes/rfc1722.txt).

Key characteristics of RIP include the following:

- It is a distance vector routing protocol.
- Hop count is used as the metric for path selection.
- The maximum allowable hop count is 15.
- Routing updates in the form of the entire routing table are broadcast every 30 seconds by default.
- RIP can load-balance over as many as six equal-cost paths (four paths is the default).
- RIP-1 requires that for each major classful network number being advertised, only one network mask can be used per network number. The mask is a fixed-length subnet mask. Standard RIP-1 does not offer triggered updates.
- RIP-2 permits variable-length subnet masks (VLSMs) on the internetwork. (Standard RIP-2 supports triggered updates, but Standard RIP-1 does not.)

Defining the maximum number of parallel paths allowed in a routing table enables RIP load balancing. With RIP, the path costs must be equal. If the **maximum-paths** command is set to 1, load balancing is disabled.

NOTE   Cisco routers support RIP-1 and RIP-2. In this book, you will only learn how to enable RIP-1.

The **router rip** command selects RIP as the routing protocol.

The **network** command assigns a major network number to which the router is directly connected. The routing process associates interface addresses with the advertised network number and begins packet processing on the specified interfaces. Figure 8-34 demonstrates how you would configure RIP on a network.

Figure 8-34   *RIP Configuration Example*

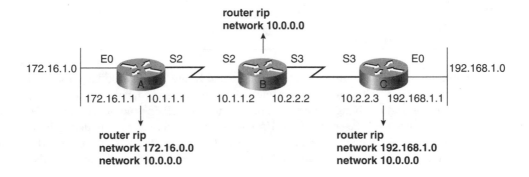

The following points are true for Router A in Figure 8-34:

- **router rip** selects RIP as the routing protocol.
- **network 172.16.0.0** specifies a directly connected network.
- **network 10.0.0.0** specifies a directly connected network.

The Router A interfaces connected to networks 172.16.0.0 and 10.0.0.0 will send and receive RIP updates. These interfaces will also be advertised to neighboring routers. These routing updates allow the router to learn the network topology.

Verifying RIP Routing Information

The **show ip protocols** command displays values associated with routing timers and network information associated with the entire router. Use this information to identify a router that is suspected of delivering bad routing information. For instance, running **show ip protocols** on Router A in Figure 8-34 results in the output shown in Example 8-1.

Example 8-1   *show ip protocols Displays Routing Timer Values and Router Network Information*

```
RouterA#sh ip protocols
Routing Protocol is "rip"
  Sending updates every 30 seconds, next due in 0 seconds
  Invalid after 180 seconds, hold down 180, flushed after 240
  Outgoing update filter list for all interfaces is
  Incoming update filter list for all interfaces is
```

continues

Example 8-1   *show ip protocols Displays Routing Timer Values and Router Network Information (Continued)*

```
Redistributing: rip
Default version control: send version 1, receive any version
  Interface        Send  Recv  Key-chain
  Ethernet0         1    1 2
  Serial2           1    1 2
Routing for Networks:
  10.0.0.0
  172.16.0.0
Routing Information Sources:
  Gateway          Distance     Last Update
  10.1.1.2            120       00:00:10
Distance: (default is 120)
```

From the output in Example 8-1, you can see that Router A sends updated routing table information every 30 seconds. (This interval can be configured, but it must be the same on the sending and receiving routers.) If a router running RIP does not receive an update from another router for 180 seconds, it marks the routes served by the nonupdating router as being invalid. As shown in Example 8-1, the holddown timer is set to 180 seconds, so an update to a route that was down and is now up will not be made until 180 seconds have passed.

If there is still no update after 240 seconds, the router removes all routing table entries from Router B. As shown in the highlighted line of Example 8-1, it has been 10 seconds since Router A received an update from Router B.

The router is advertising routes for the networks listed after the **Routing for Networks:** line.

The distance default of 120 refers to the administrative distance for a RIP route.

Displaying IP Routing Table Information in RIP Networks

The **show ip route** command displays the contents of the IP routing table for Router A in Figure 8-34, as demonstrated in Example 8-2.

Example 8-2   *show ip route Displays IP Routing Table Contents*

```
RouterA#sh ip route
Codes: C - connected, S - static, I - IGRP, R - RIP, M - mobile, B - BGP
       D - EIGRP, EX - EIGRP external, O - OSPF, IA - OSPF inter area
       N1 - OSPF NSSA external type 1, N2 - OSPF NSSA external type 2
       E1 - OSPF external type 1, E2 - OSPF external type 2, E - EGP
       i - IS-IS, L1 - IS-IS level-1, L2 - IS-IS level-2, * - candidate default
       U - per-user static route, o - ODR
       T - traffic engineered route

Gateway of last resort is not set
```

Example 8-2 *show ip route Displays IP Routing Table Contents (Continued)*

```
        172.16.0.0/24 is subnetted, 1 subnets
C           172.16.1.0 is directly connected, Ethernet0
        10.0.0.0/24 is subnetted, 2 subnets
R           10.2.2.0 [120/1] via 10.1.1.2, 00:00:07, Serial2
C           10.1.1.0 is directly connected, Serial2
R       192.168.1.0/24 [120/2] via 10.1.1.2, 00:00:07, Serial2
```

The routing table contains entries for all known networks and subnetworks. It also contains a code that indicates how that information was learned. Table 8-2 explains the output of key fields and their functions from the **show ip route** command.

Table 8-2 *show ip route Output Fields*

Output	Description
R or C	Identifies the source of the route. For example, a C indicates that the route was learned from a directly connected interface on the router. R indicates that RIP is the routing protocol that learned of the route.
192.168.1.0	Indicates the route's address of the destination network.
[120/1]	The first number in brackets is the administrative distance of the information source; the second number is the metric for the route (for example, 1 hop).
via 10.1.1.2	Specifies the address of the next hop router to reach the remote network.
00:00:07	Specifies the time since the route was updated in hours:minutes:seconds.
Serial2	Specifies the interface through which the specified network can be reached.

Examine the output to see if the routing table is populated with routing information.

If routing information is not being exchanged (that is, if the output of the **show ip route** command shows no entries that were learned from a routing protocol), use the **show running-config** or **show ip protocols** privileged EXEC commands on the router to check for a possible misconfigured routing protocol.

Displaying RIP Routing Updates

The **debug ip rip** command displays RIP routing updates as they are sent and received. Example 8-3 displays the output that results when you run **debug ip rip** on Router A in Figure 8-34.

Example 8-3 *debug ip rip Displays RIP Routing Update Information*

```
RouterA#debug ip rip
RIP protocol debugging is on
RouterA#
00:06:24: RIP: received v1 update from 10.1.1.2 on Serial2
00:06:24:       10.2.2.0 in 1 hops
00:06:24:       192.168.1.0 in 2 hops
00:06:33: RIP: sending v1 update to 255.255.255.255 via Ethernet0 (172.16.1.1)
00:06:34:       network 10.0.0.0, metric 1
00:06:34:       network 192.168.1.0, metric 3
00:06:34: RIP: sending v1 update to 255.255.255.255 via Serial2 (10.1.1.1)
00:06:34:       network 172.16.0.0, metric 1
```

The **no debug all** command turns off all debugging. Because debugging output can be overwhelming, it's often useful to turn off all debugging.

Enabling IGRP

This section provides an overview of Interior Gateway Routing Protocol (IGRP) and describes how to configure it on a Cisco router.

IGRP is an advanced distance vector routing protocol developed by Cisco in the mid-1980s. IGRP has several features that differentiate it from other distance vector routing protocols, such as RIP:

- **Increased scalability**—Improved for routing in larger networks compared to networks that use RIP. IGRP can be used to overcome RIP's 15-hop limit. IGRP has a default maximum hop count of 100 hops, which can be configured to a maximum of 255 hops.

- **Sophisticated metric**—IGRP uses a composite metric that provides significant route selection flexibility. By default, internetwork delay and bandwidth are used to arrive at a composite metric. Optionally, reliability, load, and MTU can be included in the metric computation as well.

- **Multiple path support**—IGRP can maintain up to six unequal cost paths between a network source and destination; unlike RIP, the paths do not mandate equal costs. Multiple paths can be used to increase available bandwidth or for route redundancy.

Use IGRP in IP networks that require a simple, robust, and more scalable routing protocol than RIP. IGRP also performs triggered updates, which gives it another advantage over RIP-1.

IGRP Metrics

IGRP uses a composite routing metric. This combination metric provides greater accuracy than RIP's hop-count metric when choosing a path to a destination. The path that has the smallest metric value is the best route. By default, the IGRP metrics are weighted with the constants K1 through K5. These constants convert an IGRP metric vector into a scalar quantity.

IGRP's metric includes the following components:

- **Bandwidth**—The lowest bandwidth value in the path
- **Delay**—The cumulative interface delay along the path
- **Reliability**—The reliability between source and destination, determined by the exchange of keepalives
- **Load**—The load on a link between source and destination based on bits per second
- **MTU**—The Maximum Transfer Unit value of the path

By default, only bandwidth and delay are used by the IGRP metric. Nonetheless, IGRP permits a wide range of components for its metrics. Reliability and load are unitless and can take on any value between 0 and 255. Bandwidth can take on values reflecting speeds from 1200 bps to 10 Gbps. Delay can take on any value from 1 to 2×10^{23}. Based on the composite metric, IGRP would choose the lower path in Figure 8-35 because of the high-bandwidth links.

Figure 8-35 *Composite Metric*

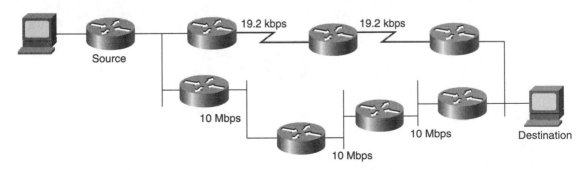

Wide metric ranges allow satisfactory metric settings in internetworks with widely varying performance characteristics. Most importantly, the metric components are combined in a user-definable algorithm.

As a result, network administrators can influence route selection in an intuitive fashion. Adjusting IGRP metric values can dramatically affect network performance. Make all metric adjustment decisions carefully.

IGRP Unequal-Cost Load Balancing

Using the IGRP composite routing metric, IGRP supports multiple paths between source and destination. For example, dual equal-bandwidth lines can run a single stream of traffic in a round-robin fashion, with automatic switchover to the second line if one line goes down.

Also, multiple paths can be used even if the metrics for the paths are different. If, for example, one path is three times better than another because its metric is three times lower, the better path will be used three times as often. Only routes with metrics that are within a certain range of the best route are used as multiple paths. Figure 8-36 illustrates that IGRP could use multiple paths between source and destination.

Figure 8-36 *IGRP Unequal Multiple Paths*

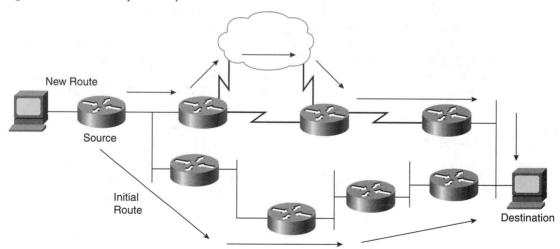

Unequal-cost load balancing allows traffic to be distributed among up to six unequal-cost paths to provide greater overall throughput and reliability.

The following general rules apply to IGRP unequal-cost load balancing:

- IGRP will accept up to six paths for a given destination network (four is the default).

- The next-hop router in any of the paths must be closer to the destination than the local router is by its best path. This ensures that a routing loop will not begin.

- The alternative path metric must be within the specified variance of the best local metric. Variance is discussed in the next section.

IGRP Routing Process

Use the **router igrp** and **network** commands to create an IGRP routing process. Note that IGRP requires an autonomous system number. The autonomous system number does not have to be registered. However, all routers within an autonomous system must use the same autonomous system number, or they will not exchange routing information. The **network** command identifies a major network number to which the router is directly connected. The routing process associates interface addresses with the advertised network number and begins packet processing on the specified interfaces. The syntax for the **router igrp** and **network** commands is as follows:

```
router(config-router)#router igrp autonomous-system
router(config-router)#network network-number
```

Figure 8-37 presents a sample IGRP configuration.

Figure 8-37 *IGRP Configuration Example*

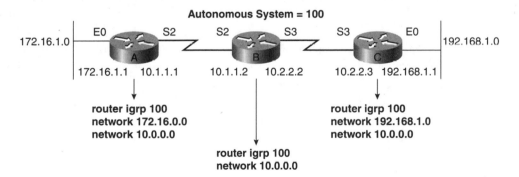

The following points are true for Router A in Figure 8-37:

- **router igrp 100** enables the IGRP routing process for autonomous system 100.

- **network 172.16.0.0** associates network 172.16.0.0 and its interfaces with the IGRP routing process.

- **network 10.0.0.0** associates network 10.0.0.0 and its interfaces with the IGRP routing process.

IGRP sends updates out interfaces in networks 10.0.0.0 and 172.16.0.0. It also advertises directly connected networks 10.0.0.0 and 172.16.0.0, as well as other networks that it learns about through IGRP (in other words, it also sends information about 198.168.1.0).

IGRP Load Balancing/Sharing

IGRP supports load balancing and load sharing. The **variance** router configuration command controls load balancing in an IGRP environment. Use the **variance** command to configure unequal-cost load balancing by defining the difference between the best metric and the worst acceptable metric. The syntax for the **variance** command is as follows:

```
router(config-router)#variance multiplier
```

where the *multiplier* parameter specifies the range of metric values that will be accepted for load balancing. This range is from the lowest (or best) metric value to the lowest metric value multiplied by the variance value. Acceptable values are nonzero, positive integers. The default value is 1, which means equal-cost load balancing.

Setting the difference between the best metric and the worst acceptable metric allows the router to determine the feasibility of a potential route. A route is feasible if the next router in the path is closer to the destination than the current router and if the metric for the entire path is within the variance. Only paths that are feasible can be used for load balancing and can be included in the routing table.

You can use the **traffic-share** {**balanced** | **min**} command to control how traffic is distributed among IGRP load sharing routes. The syntax for this command is as follows:

```
router(config-router)#traffic-share {balanced | min}
```

Using the **balanced** option with the **traffic-share** command distributes traffic proportionally to the ratios of the metrics. Using the **min** option with the **traffic-share** command specifies to use routes that have minimum costs.

Verifying IGRP Routing Information

The **show ip protocols** command displays parameters, filters, and network information about the entire router. Running the **show ip protocols** command on Router A in Figure 8-37 results in the output shown in Example 8-4.

Example 8-4   *show ip protocols Displays Router Parameters, Filters, and Network Information*

```
RouterA#sh ip protocols
Routing Protocol is "igrp 100"
  Sending updates every 90 seconds, next due in 21 seconds
  Invalid after 270 seconds, hold down 280, flushed after 630
  Outgoing update filter list for all interfaces is
  Incoming update filter list for all interfaces is
  Default networks flagged in outgoing updates
  Default networks accepted from incoming updates
  IGRP metric weight K1=1, K2=0, K3=1, K4=0, K5=0
  IGRP maximum hopcount 100
  IGRP maximum metric variance 1
  Redistributing: igrp 100
  Routing for Networks:
    10.0.0.0
    172.16.0.0
  Routing Information Sources:
    Gateway         Distance      Last Update
    10.1.1.2              100      00:01:01
  Distance: (default is 100)
```

The information from the **show ip protocols** command output includes the autonomous system, routing timers, networks, and administrative distance. Table 8-3 documents the key fields in the **show ip protocols** output in Example 8-4.

Table 8-3   *show ip protocols Output Fields*

Output	Description
Routing Protocol	Routing protocol and autonomous system.
Update	Rate at which updates are sent.
Invalid	Number of seconds after which a route is declared invalid. The default value of **Invalid** should be three times the update value.
Hold down	Number of seconds during which routing information regarding the worst path is suppressed. The value of **hold down** should be at least three times the value of **update**.
Flushed	Number of seconds that must pass before the route is removed from the routing table. The value of **flushed** should be equal to or greater than the sum of the values of **invalid** and **hold down**.

The constants used to weigh the metrics in the IGRP routing algorithm are also displayed with the **show ip protocols** command. Only the bandwidth (K1) and delay (K3) are used in the algorithm by default, because they are set to 1, as highlighted in Example 8-4.

Displaying IP Routing Table Information in IGRP Networks

The **show ip route** command displays the contents of the IP routing table. The table contains a list of all known networks and subnets associated with each entry. Running the **show ip route** command on Router A in Figure 8-37 results in the output shown in Example 8-5.

Example 8-5 *show ip route Displays IP Routing Table Contents*

```
RouterA#sh ip route
Codes: C - connected, S - static, I - IGRP, R - RIP, M - mobile, B - BGP
       D - EIGRP, EX - EIGRP external, O - OSPF, IA - OSPF inter area
       N1 - OSPF NSSA external type 1, N2 - OSPF NSSA external type 2
       E1 - OSPF external type 1, E2 - OSPF external type 2, E - EGP
       i - IS-IS, L1 - IS-IS level-1, L2 - IS-IS level-2, * - candidate default
       U - per-user static route, o - ODR
       T - traffic engineered route

Gateway of last resort is not set

     172.16.0.0/24 is subnetted, 1 subnets
C       172.16.1.0 is directly connected, Ethernet0
     10.0.0.0/24 is subnetted, 2 subnets
I       10.2.2.0 [100/90956] via 10.1.1.2, 00:00:23, Serial2
C       10.1.1.0 is directly connected, Serial2
I     192.168.1.0/24 [100/91056] via 10.1.1.2, 00:00:23, Serial2
```

Note that in Example 8-5, the information was learned from IGRP (I) or from directly connected interfaces (C). In the routing table, the highlighted **[100/90956]** output is the IGRP administrative distance and the metric.

Displaying IGRP Routing Transaction Information

The **debug ip igrp transactions** command displays transaction information between IGRP routers.

The optional parameter for the **debug ip igrp transactions** command, *ip-address*, specifies the IP address of an IGRP neighbor. Using this parameter, the resulting output includes only messages describing updates from that neighbor and updates that the router broadcasts toward that neighbor. Running the **debug ip igrp transactions** command on Router A in Figure 8-37 results in the output shown in Example 8-6.

Example 8-6 *debug ip igrp transactions Displays IGRP Routing Transaction Information*

```
RouterA#debug ip igrp transactions
IGRP protocol debugging is on
RouterA#
00:21:06: IGRP: sending update to 255.255.255.255 via Ethernet0 (172.16.1.1)
00:21:06:        network 10.0.0.0, metric=88956
00:21:06:        network 192.168.1.0, metric=91056
00:21:07: IGRP: sending update to 255.255.255.255 via Serial2 (10.1.1.1)
00:21:07:        network 172.16.0.0, metric=1100
00:21:16: IGRP: received update from 10.1.1.2 on Serial2
00:21:16:        subnet 10.2.2.0, metric 90956 (neighbor 88956)
00:21:16:        network 192.168.1.0, metric 91056 (neighbor 89056)
```

As Example 8-6 illustrates, Router A exchanges update IGRP messages with its neighbors. Use the **no debug ip igrp transactions** or **no debug all** commands to disable the debugging output.

Displaying IGRP Routing Information Summaries

When there are many networks in your routing table, displaying every update for every route can flood the console and make the router unusable. In this case, the **debug ip igrp events** command is used to display a summary of the IGRP routing information. This command indicates the source and destination of each update, as well as the number of routes in each update. Messages are not generated for each route. Running the **debug ip igrp events** command on Router A in Figure 8-37 results in the output shown in Example 8-7.

Example 8-7 *debug ip igrp events Displays IGRP Routing Information Summaries*

```
RouterA#debug ip igrp events
IGRP event debugging is on
RouterA#
00:23:44: IGRP: sending update to 255.255.255.255 via Ethernet0 (172.16.1.1)
00:23:44: IGRP: Update contains 0 interior, 2 system, and 0 exterior routes.
00:23:44: IGRP: Total routes in update: 2
00:23:44: IGRP: sending update to 255.255.255.255 via Serial2 (10.1.1.1)
00:23:45: IGRP: Update contains 0 interior, 1 system, and 0 exterior routes.
00:23:45: IGRP: Total routes in update: 1
00:23:48: IGRP: received update from 10.1.1.2 on Serial2
00:23:48: IGRP: Update contains 1 interior, 1 system, and 0 exterior routes.
00:23:48: IGRP: Total routes in update: 2
```

If the IP address of an IGRP neighbor is specified when issuing the **debug ip igrp events** command, the resulting output includes only messages describing updates from that neighbor and updates that the router broadcasts toward that neighbor. Example 8-7 illustrates updates between Router A and its neighbors.

As with the **debug ip igrp transactions** command, the optional parameter for the **debug ip igrp events** command, *ip-address*, specifies the IP address of an IGRP neighbor.

Use the **no debug ip igrp events** or **no debug all** commands to disable the debugging output.

IGRP Routing Update Example

This section runs through a routing update scenario using IGRP when an Ethernet connection fails, as illustrated in Figure 8-38.

Figure 8-38 *IGRP Routing Update with Failed Ethernet Connection*

Example 8-8 shows normal IGRP routing updates being sent and received on the router.

Example 8-8 *IGRP Debugging Example*

```
RouterA#debug ip igrp events
IGRP event debugging is on
RouterA#
00:23:44: IGRP: sending update to 255.255.255.255 via Ethernet0 (172.16.1.1)
00:23:44: IGRP: Update contains 0 interior, 2 system, and 0 exterior routes.
00:23:44: IGRP: Total routes in update: 2
00:23:44: IGRP: sending update to 255.255.255.255 via Serial2 (10.1.1.1)
00:23:45: IGRP: Update contains 0 interior, 1 system, and 0 exterior routes.
00:23:45: IGRP: Total routes in update: 1
00:23:48: IGRP: received update from 10.1.1.2 on Serial2
00:23:48: IGRP: Update contains 1 interior, 1 system, and 0 exterior routes.
00:23:48: IGRP: Total routes in update: 2
```

Next, as demonstrated by Example 8-9, the Ethernet network attached to Router A fails. Router A sends a triggered update to Router B, indicating that network 172.16.0.0 is inaccessible (with a metric of 4294967295). Router B sends back a poison reverse update.

Example 8-9 *IGRP Transaction Output*

```
RouterA# debug ip igrp trans
00:31:15: %LINEPROTO-5-UPDOWN: Line protocol on Interface Ethernet0,
  changed state to down
00:31:15: IGRP: edition is now 3
00:31:15: IGRP: sending update to 255.255.255.255 via Serial2 (10.1.1.1)
00:31:15:        network 172.16.0.0, metric=4294967295
00:31:16: IGRP: Update contains 0 interior, 1 system, and 0 exterior routes.
00:31:16: IGRP: Total routes in update: 1
00:31:16: IGRP: broadcasting request on Serial2
00:31:16: IGRP: received update from 10.1.1.2 on Serial2
00:31:16:        subnet 10.2.2.0, metric 90956 (neighbor 88956)
00:31:16:        network 172.16.0.0, metric 4294967295 (inaccessible)
00:31:16:        network 192.168.1.0, metric 91056 (neighbor 89056)
00:31:16: IGRP: Update contains 1 interior, 2 system, and 0 exterior routes.
00:31:16: IGRP: Total routes in update: 3
```

The output in Example 8-10 reveals that Router B receives the triggered update from Router A, sends a poison reverse to Router A, and then sends a triggered update to Router C, notifying both routers that network 172.16.0.0 is "possibly down."

Example 8-10 *IGRP Updates with Network Going into Holddown*

```
RouterB#debug ip igrp trans
IGRP protocol debugging is on
RouterB#
1d19h: IGRP: sending update to 255.255.255.255 via Serial2 (10.1.1.2)
1d19h:        subnet 10.2.2.0, metric=88956
1d19h:        network 192.168.1.0, metric=89056
1d19h: IGRP: sending update to 255.255.255.255 via Serial3 (10.2.2.2)
1d19h:        subnet 10.1.1.0, metric=88956
1d19h:        network 172.16.0.0, metric=89056
1d19h: IGRP: received update from 10.1.1.1 on Serial2
1d19h:        network 172.16.0.0, metric 4294967295 (inaccessible)
1d19h: IGRP: edition is now 10
1d19h: IGRP: sending update to 255.255.255.255 via Serial2 (10.1.1.2)
1d19h:        subnet 10.2.2.0, metric=88956
1d19h:        network 172.16.0.0, metric=4294967295
1d19h:        network 192.168.1.0, metric=89056
1d19h: IGRP: sending update to 255.255.255.255 via Serial3 (10.2.2.2)
1d19h:        subnet 10.1.1.0, metric=88956
1d19h:        network 172.16.0.0, metric=4294967295
```

As demonstrated by Example 8-11, Router B also places the route to network 172.16.0.0 in the holddown state for 280 seconds. During holddown state, the route to network

172.16.0.0 is marked as "possibly down" in the routing table. Router B will still try to send traffic to network 172.16.0.0 until the holddown timer expires.

Also shown in Example 8-11, an administrator attempts to **ping** network 172.16.0.0 without success.

Example 8-11 *Routing Table Shows Network in Holddown State*

```
RouterB#sh ip route
Codes: C - connected, S - static, I - IGRP, R - RIP, M - mobile, B - BGP
       D - EIGRP, EX - EIGRP external, O - OSPF, IA - OSPF inter area
       N1 - OSPF NSSA external type 1, N2 - OSPF NSSA external type 2
       E1 - OSPF external type 1, E2 - OSPF external type 2, E - EGP
       i - IS-IS, L1 - IS-IS level-1, L2 - IS-IS level-2, * - candidate default
       U - per-user static route, o - ODR
       T - traffic engineered route

Gateway of last resort is not set

I    172.16.0.0/16 is possibly down, routing via 10.1.1.1, Serial2
     10.0.0.0/24 is subnetted, 2 subnets
C       10.1.1.0 is directly connected, Serial2
C       10.2.2.0 is directly connected, Serial3
I    192.168.1.0/24 [100/89056] via 10.2.2.3, 00:00:14, Serial3
RouterB#ping 172.16.1.1

Type escape sequence to abort.
Sending 5, 100-byte ICMP Echos to 172.16.1.1, timeout is 2 seconds:
.....
Success rate is 0 percent (0/5)
RouterB#
```

If the link comes back up, Router A will send another trigger update to Router B, stating that network 172.16.0.0 is now accessible (with metric 89056). In Figure 8-39, Router B would receive the triggered update.

Figure 8-39 *Routing Update*

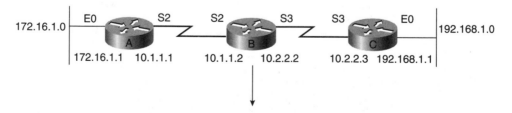

Even though Router B receives the update, Router B keeps the route in holddown state. Router B will not remove the route from holddown state and update its routing table until the holddown timer expires.

In Example 8-11, the holddown timer has not yet expired, so the route is still "possibly down." However, the administrator at Router B can now successfully **ping** network 172.16.0.0.

Assigning a Default Route to an Unknown Subnet of a Directly Attached Network

A router by default assumes that all subnets of a directly attached network should be present in the IP routing table. Should a packet be received with a destination address within an unknown subnet of a directly attached network, the router assumes the subnet does not exist and drops the packet. This behavior holds true even if the IP routing table contains a default route.

However, the administrator can change this behavior with the **ip classless** global configuration command. With **ip classless** configured, if a packet is received with a destination address within an unknown subnet of a directly attached network, the router will match it to the default route and forward it to the next hop specified by the default route. By default, the router is configured with the **no ip classless** global configuration command, so a packet with a destination address to an unknown subnet of a directly attached network will be dropped.

In Figure 8-40, the middle router will forward a packet with a 10.7.1.1 destination address out the default interface, E0, because the **ip classless** command is enabled.

Figure 8-40 *ip classless Command Forwards Packets to Unknown Subnets via a Default Route*

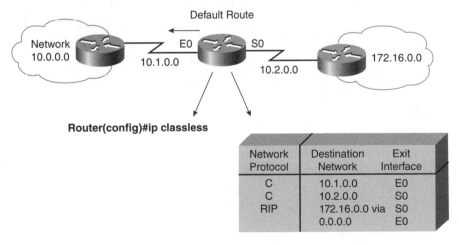

Routing Command Summary

Table 8-4 briefly describes the commands covered in this chapter.

Table 8-4 *Routing Command Summary*

Command	Description
ip route *network mask* {*address* | *interface*} [*distance*] [**permanent**]	Defines a static route.
router *protocol* [*keyword*]	Enables a dynamic routing protocol.
network *network-number*	A router subcommand. Enables a dynamic routing protocol to advertise a route and enables the protocol on the interfaces on that network.
show ip protocols	Displays information about the dynamic routing protocols configured on the router.
show ip route	Displays the IP routing table.
debug ip rip	Enables the router to display the RIP routing updates as they occur.
variance *multiplier*	Enables IGRP to do unequal path load sharing.
traffic-share {**balanced** | **min**}	Tells the router how to load-balance the traffic on the load-sharing links.
debug ip igrp transactions	Displays IGRP transaction information as transactions occur.
debug ip igrp events	Displays IGRP events as they occur.
no debug all	Turns off all debugging displays.
ip classless	Allows a routing protocol to send traffic to a less-specific route if one is available.

Summary

In this chapter, you learned the components that a router needs in order to perform routing: information sources, available routes, best routes, maintaining of routes. You learned about the different types of protocols: distance vector, link-state, and hybrid. You also learned the shortcomings and workarounds for distance vector routing protocols. Finally, you learned how to configure static and dynamic routes on a Cisco router.

Review Questions

1   Which four things does a router need in order to route?

2   What are the two types of routes?

3 Which type of route is entered by an administrator based on his or her knowledge of the network environment?

4 When is a default route used by a router?

5 Give two examples of an Interior Gateway Protocol.

6 When faced with two routes from different protocols for the same network, what does a Cisco router use to determine which route to use?

7 Which metric is used by RIP? IGRP?

8 Name one method used to eliminate routing loops.

9 What happens to traffic destined for a network that is currently in a holddown state?

10 What command is used to stop all debugging?

Upon completion of this chapter, you will be able to perform the following tasks:

- Understand the fundamentals of access lists.
- Understand access list functions and operations.
- Understand TCP/IP access lists.
- Configure standard IP access lists.
- Control vty access with access class entries.
- Understand the fundamentals of extended IP access lists.
- Verify and monitor access lists.

CHAPTER 9

Basic IP Traffic Management with Access Lists

This chapter presents coverage of standard and extended IP access lists as a means to control network traffic. When you have completed this chapter, you should be able to describe the functions and processes by which access lists filter traffic. You will learn how to configure a standard and extended access list. Also, you will learn to limit Telnet access to and from the router using a standard access list. Finally, you will learn how to verify access list configurations.

Understanding Access Lists

Networks are designed to carry user traffic from one location to another, much like roads carry vehicular traffic from one location to another. Routers are the junction points for traffic on data networks. It is sometimes necessary to control the flow of traffic on both roads and networks. There are many ways to do this on a highway, but on a network we need a way to identify and filter traffic to and from the many different data networks. *Access Control Lists (ACLs)* are used in routers to identify traffic. This identification can then be used to filter traffic to better manage the traffic in a network.

The earliest routed networks connected a modest number of LANs and hosts. As the router connections increase to legacy and outside networks, and with the increased use of the Internet, there will be new challenges to control access, as demonstrated by the sample network shown in Figure 9-1.

Figure 9-1   *Justification for Access Lists*

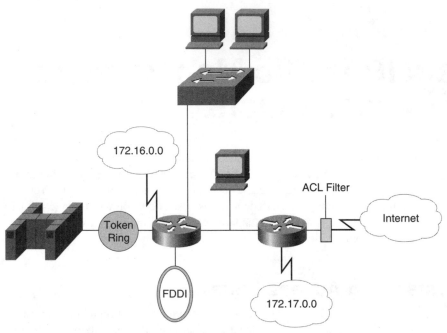

With the increase in various types of connections to the network, network administrators must decide how to deny unwanted connections while allowing appropriate access. Although tools such as passwords, callback equipment, and physical security devices are helpful, they often lack the flexible and specific controls most administrators prefer.

Access lists offer another powerful tool for network control. Access lists add the flexibility to filter the packet flow in or out of router interfaces. Such control can help limit network traffic and restrict network use by certain users or devices.

The most common use for an access list is as a packet filter. Without packet filters, all packets could be transmitted onto all parts of the network.

Packet filtering helps control packet movement through the network. Such control can help limit network traffic and restrict network use by certain users or devices. To permit or deny packets from crossing specified router interfaces, Cisco provides access lists. An IP *access list* is a sequential list of permit and deny conditions that apply to IP addresses or upper-layer IP protocols. Access lists identify traffic to be filtered in transit through the router, but they do not filter traffic that originated from the router. Because a router couldn't block a packet originating from a router, you couldn't block Telnet access from the router. Because of this, access lists can also be applied to the router's virtual terminal line (vty) ports to permit or deny Telnet traffic in or out of the router's vty ports. As shown in Figure 9-2, packets might be traveling through an interface, or they might be accessing a vty port for Telnet connectivity. Access lists allow control of this traffic.

Figure 9-2   *Access List as Packet Filter*

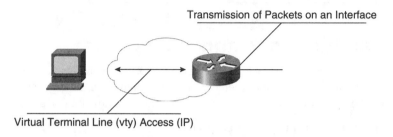

Although access lists are usually associated with packet filters, they have many other uses, as illustrated in Figure 9-3. You can use IP access lists to establish a finer granularity of control when separating traffic into priority and custom queues. An access list can also be used to identify "interesting" traffic that serves to trigger dialing in dial-on-demand routing (DDR). Access lists are also a fundamental component of route maps, which filter and, in some cases, alter the attributes within a routing protocol update.

Figure 9-3   *Other Access List Uses*

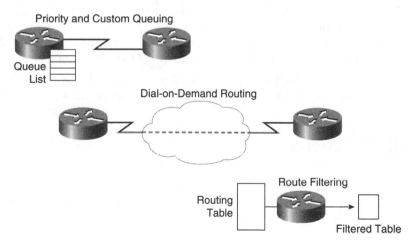

NOTE	Queuing is discussed in the *Building Cisco Remote Access Networks* coursebook, available from Cisco Press. Chapter 12, "Completing an ISDN BRI Call," discusses DDR in greater detail.

Access List Functions and Operations

Access lists are optional mechanisms in Cisco IOS software that can be configured to filter or test packets to determine whether to forward them toward their destination or to discard them. This section describes what access lists are and how they operate.

There are two general types of access lists:

- **Standard access lists**—Standard IP access lists check the source address of packets that could be routed. The result permits or denies the packet output for the entire protocol suite, based on the source network/subnet/host IP address.

- **Extended access lists**—Extended IP access lists check for both source and destination packet addresses. They can also check for specific protocols, port numbers, and other parameters, which gives administrators more flexibility in describing the packets being referenced.

Access lists can be applied as the following:

- **Inbound access lists**—Incoming packets are processed before being routed to an outbound interface. An input access list is more efficient than an output list because it saves the overhead of routing table lookups if the packet is to be discarded by the filtering tests. If the packet is permitted by the tests, it is then processed for routing.

- **Outbound access lists**—Incoming packets are routed to the outbound interface and then processed through the outbound access list before transmission.

Access List Operations

Figure 9-4 shows an overview of the access list process for a packet traveling through a router. This process is the same for an inbound packet with the exception of the routing table check. You can think of the list as a traffic cop or traffic regulation that prevents certain traffic from entering certain areas of the network.

Figure 9-4   *Access List Filter Overview*

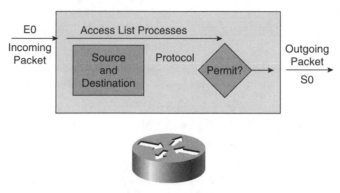

Access lists express the set of rules that give added control for packets that enter inbound interfaces, packets that relay through the router, and packets that exit the router's outbound interfaces. Access lists do not act on packets that originate from the router itself, such as routing updates or outgoing Telnet sessions. Instead, access lists are statements that specify conditions for how the router will handle the traffic flow through specified interfaces. Access lists give added control for processing the specific packets.

Figure 9-5 expands the example of an outbound access list.

Figure 9-5   *Outbound Access List Operation*

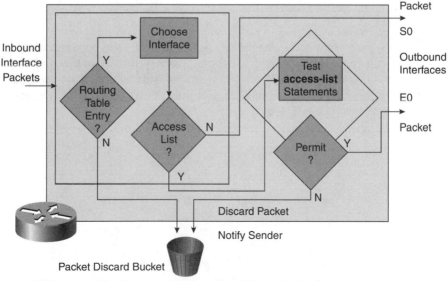

If No **access-list** Statement Matches, Then Discard the Packet.

The beginning of the process is the same regardless of whether outbound access lists are used. As a packet enters an interface, the router checks to see if the packet can be routed checking the routing table. If there is no route to the destination address, the packet is dropped.

Next, the router checks to see whether the destination interface is grouped to an access list. If not, the packet can be sent to the output buffer. For example:

- If the outbound packet is destined for Serial 0, which has not been grouped to an outbound access list, the packet is sent to Serial 0 directly.

- If the outbound packet is destined for Ethernet 0, which has been grouped to an outbound access list, before the packet can be sent out on Ethernet 0, it is tested by a combination of access list statements associated with that interface. Based on the access list tests, the packet can be permitted or denied.

For outbound lists, *permit* means send it to the output buffer, and *deny* means discard the packet. For inbound lists, *permit* means continue to process the packet after receiving it on an inbound interface, and *deny* means discard the packet. When an IP packet is discarded, ICMP returns a special packet to notify the sender that the destination is unreachable.

Access List Condition Testing

Access list statements operate in sequential, logical order. They evaluate packets from the top down, one statement at a time. If a packet header and an access list statement match, the rest of the statements in the list are skipped, and the packet is permitted or denied as specified in the matched statement. If a packet header does not match an access list statement, it is tested against the next statement in the list. This matching process continues until the end of the list is reached, at which time the packet is denied by an implicit deny.

Figure 9-6 shows the access list packet test flow. Note that, as soon as a match is made, the permit or deny option is applied, and the tests are terminated for that packet. This means that a condition that denies a packet in an earlier statement can't be overturned by a later statement. The implication of this behavior is that the order of the statements within any given access list is significant.

Figure 9-6   *Access List Condition Tests*

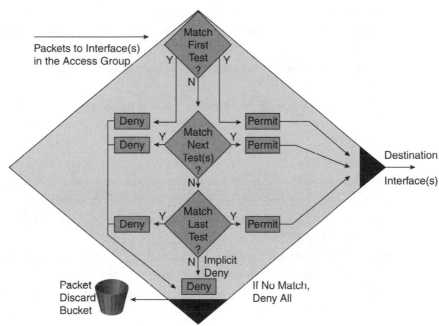

A final implied statement covers all packets for which conditions did not test true. This final test condition matches all other packets and results in a deny condition, thereby denying the packet. Instead of proceeding out an interface, all packets not matched by earlier access list statements are dropped. This final statement is often referred to as the *implicit deny any* at the end of every access list. Although this statement is not displayed in the router config, it is always active. Because of the implicit deny any, an access list should have at least one **permit** statement in it; otherwise, the access list will block all traffic.

Guidelines for Access List Implementation

An access list can be applied to multiple interfaces. However, there can be only one access list per protocol, per direction, per interface.

Following these general principles helps ensure that the access lists you create have the intended results:

- Use only the access list numbers from the Cisco-defined range for the protocol and type of list you are creating.

- Only one access list per protocol, per direction, per interface is allowed. Multiple access lists are permitted per interface, but each must be for a different protocol.

- Top-down processing:
  - Organize your access list so that more specific references in a network or subnet appear before more general ones. Place more frequently occurring conditions before less-frequent conditions.
  - Subsequent additions are always added to the end of the access list but before the implicit deny.
  - You cannot selectively add or remove access list statements when using numbered access lists, but you can do so when using named IP access lists (a Cisco IOS Release 11.2 feature).
- Implicit deny all:
  - Unless you end your access list with an explicit permit any, it will deny by default all traffic that fails to match any of the access list conditions.
  - Every access list should have at least one **permit** statement. Otherwise, all traffic will be denied.
- Create the access list before applying it to an interface. An interface with a nonexistent or undefined access list applied to it allows (permits) all traffic.
- Access lists filter only traffic going through the router. They do not filter traffic originating from the router.

Access List Command Basics

In practice, commands to configure access lists can be lengthy character strings. Access lists can be complicated to enter or interpret. However, you can better understand general access list configuration commands by reducing them to two general elements:

- The access list contains global statements to be applied for use in identifying packets. These lists are created with the global **access-list** command.
- The **ip access-group** interface configuration command activates an IP access list on an interface.

The following syntax shows the general form of the **access-list** command, which contains global statements:

```
Router(config)# access-list access-list-number {permit | deny} {test conditions}
```

This global statement identifies the access list by an access list number. This number indicates what type of access list this will be. In Cisco IOS Release 11.2 and later, access lists for IP can also use an access list name rather than a number. Named IP access lists are covered later in this chapter.

The **permit** or **deny** term in the global **access-list** statement indicates how packets that meet the test conditions will be handled by Cisco IOS software. The **permit** option means that the packet will be allowed to pass through the interfaces that you apply the list to. The **deny** option means that the router will discard the packet.

The final parameter(s) of the **access-list** statement specifies the test conditions used by this **access-list** statement. The test can be as simple as checking for a single source address. However, the access list can be expanded to include several test conditions, as you will see in the discussion of extended access lists. You will use several global **access-list** statements with the same access list number or name to stack several test conditions into a logical sequence or list of tests.

The following syntax shows the general form of the {*protocol*} **access-group** command, which is how an access list is applied to an interface:

```
Router(config-if)#{protocol} access-group access-list-number {in | out}
```

For example, applying the **ip access-group** interface configuration command activates an IP access list on an interface.

CAUTION   If you apply an access list with the **ip access-group** command to an interface before any access list lines have been created, the result will be permit any. The list is "live," so if you enter only one permit line, it goes from a "permit any" to a "deny most" (because of the implicit deny any at the end) as soon as you press Enter. For this reason, create your access list before you apply it to an interface.

Access lists can control most protocols on a Cisco router. Table 9-1 shows the protocols and number ranges of the access list types for IP and IPX. Chapter 10, "Configuring Novell IPX," covers IPX access lists in greater detail. There are other access list ranges for different protocols, such as AppleTalk and DECnet. Details on these ranges and their usage can be referenced at CCO or the Cisco Documentation CD.

Table 9-1   *Access List Numbers*

IP Access List	Number Range/Identifier
Standard	1 to 99
Extended	100 to 199
Named	Name (Cisco IOS 11.2 and later)
IPX Access List	
Standard	800 to 899
Extended	900 to 999
SAP Filters	1000 to 1099
Named	Name (Cisco IOS 11.2F and later)

An administrator enters a number in the protocol number range as the first argument of the global **access-list** statement. The router identifies which access list software to use based on this numbered entry. Access list test conditions follow as arguments. These arguments specify tests according to the rules of the given protocol suite. The test conditions for an access list vary by protocol.

Many access lists are possible for a protocol. Select a different number from the protocol number range for each new access list. The administrator can specify only one access list per protocol, per direction, per interface.

Specifying an access list number from 1 to 99 instructs the router to accept standard IP **access-list** statements. Specifying an access list number from 100 to 199 instructs the router to accept extended IP **access-list** statements.

TCP/IP Access Lists

An access list applied to an interface causes the router to look in the Layer 3 header and possibly the Layer 4 header of a network traffic packet in order to match test conditions. Standard IP access lists check only the source address in the packet (Layer 3) header. Extended IP access lists can check many options, including segment (Layer 4) header options such as port numbers. Figure 9-7 shows the breakdown of a common IP packet for access list testing.

Figure 9-7   *TCP/IP Packet Testing*

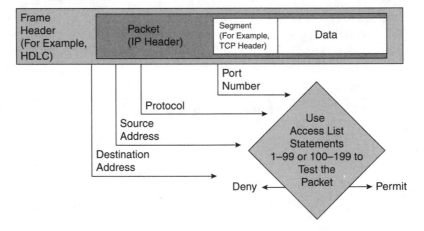

For TCP/IP packet filtering, Cisco IOS IP access lists check the packet and upper-layer headers for the following:

- Source IP addresses using standard access lists. Standard access lists are identified with a number in the range 1 to 99.

- Destination and source IP address, specific protocols, and TCP or UDP port numbers using extended access lists. Extended access lists are identified with a number in the range 100 to 199.

For all of these IP access lists, as soon as a packet is checked for a match with the **access-list** statement, it can be denied from using or permitted to use the interface for which an **access-group** statement is defined.

It might be necessary to test conditions for a group or range of IP addresses or just a single IP address. For this reason, there needs to be a method to identify which bits of a given IP address need to be checked for a match.

Address matching occurs using access list address wildcard masking to identify which bits of an IP address will require an explicit match and which bits can be ignored.

Wildcard masking for IP address bits uses the numbers 1 and 0 to indicate how to treat the corresponding IP address bits:

- A wildcard mask bit 0 means "Check the corresponding bit value."

- A wildcard mask bit 1 means "Do not check (ignore) the corresponding bit value."

By carefully setting wildcard masks, an administrator can select single or several IP addresses for permit or deny tests. Figure 9-8 shows how bits are matched against a wildcard mask.

Figure 9-8   *Wildcard Bits*

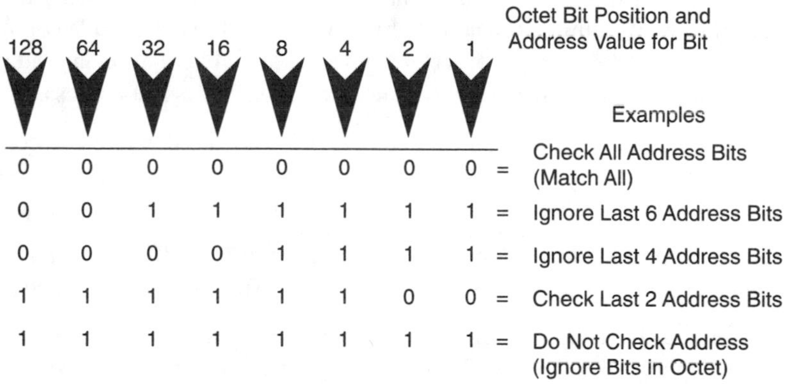

NOTE	Wildcard masking for access lists operates differently from an IP subnet mask. A 0 in a bit position of the access list mask indicates that the corresponding bit in the address must be checked; a 1 in a bit position of the access list mask indicates that the corresponding bit in the address is not "interesting" and can be ignored.

You have seen how the 0 and 1 bits in an access list wildcard mask cause the access list to either check or ignore the corresponding bit in the IP address. In Figure 9-9, this wildcard masking process is applied in an example.

Figure 9-9   *Matching a Specific IP Host*

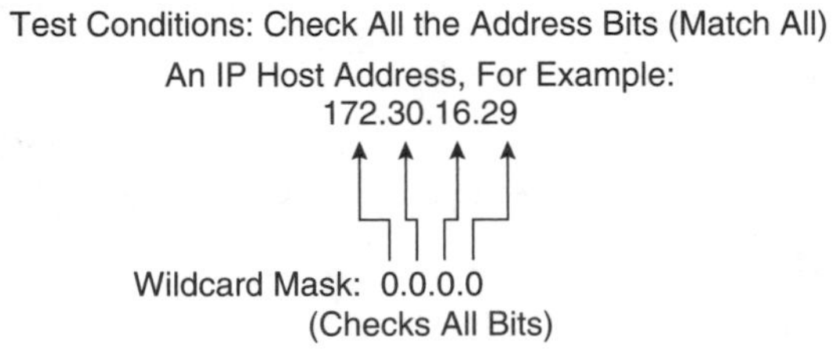

Consider a network administrator who wants to specify that a certain IP host address will be denied in an access list test. To indicate a host IP address, the administrator would enter the full address—for example, 172.30.16.29. Then, to indicate that the access list should check all the bits in the address, the corresponding wildcard mask bits for this address would be all 0s—that is, 0.0.0.0.

Working with decimal representations of binary wildcard mask bits can be tedious. For the most common uses of wildcard masking, you can use abbreviations. These abbreviations reduce how many numbers an administrator is required to enter while configuring address test conditions. One example of when you can use an abbreviation instead of a long wildcard mask string is when you want to match a specific host address.

The administrator can use the abbreviation **host** before the IP address to communicate this same test condition to Cisco IOS access list software. So, for example, instead of typing **172.30.16.29 0.0.0.0**, the administrator can use the string **host 172.30.16.29**.

A second common condition in which Cisco IOS software will permit an abbreviation term in the access list wildcard mask is when the administrator wants to match any IP address.

Consider a network administrator who wants to specify that any destination address will be permitted in an access list test. To indicate any IP address, the administrator would enter **0.0.0.0** as the IP address. Then, to indicate that the access list should ignore (allow without checking) any value, the corresponding wildcard mask bits for this address would be all 1s (**255.255.255.255**), as illustrated in Figure 9-10.

Figure 9-10 *Matching Any IP Address*

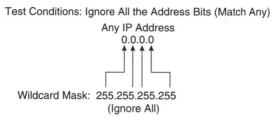

Test Conditions: Ignore All the Address Bits (Match Any)
Any IP Address
0.0.0.0

Wildcard Mask: 255.255.255.255
(Ignore All)

The administrator can use the abbreviation **any** to communicate this same test condition to Cisco IOS access list software. Instead of typing **0.0.0.0 255.255.255.255**, the administrator can use the word **any** by itself as the keyword.

Assume that an administrator wants to test a range of IP subnets that will be permitted or denied. If given a Class B IP address (the first two octets are the network number) with 8 bits of subnetting (the third octet is for subnets), the administrator might want to use the IP wildcard masking bits to match subnets 172.30.16.0/24 to 172.30.31.0/24.

Figure 9-11 shows the wildcard mask that would be used to accomplish this.

Figure 9-11 *Blocking a Range of Subnets*

Check for IP Subnets 172.30.**16**.0/24 to 172.30.**31**.0/24
Address and Wildcard Mask:
172.30.16.0   0.0.15.255

Network .Host
172.30.16.0

	0	0	0	1	0	0	0	0		
Wildcard Mask:	0	0	0	0	1	1	1	1		

|<-------- **Match** ------->|<----- Don't Care ------>|

	0	0	0	1	0	0	0	0	=	16
	0	0	0	1	0	0	0	1	=	17
	0	0	0	1	0	0	1	0	=	18
	0	0	0	1	1	1	1	1	=	31

First, the wildcard mask checks the first two octets (172.30) using corresponding 0 bits in the wildcard mask.

Because there is no interest in an individual host, you would want to set the wildcard mask to ignore all bits in the final octet. By setting all the bits in the final octet to 1s, you would ignore the host portion of the address. All 1s in an octet is a decimal value of 255.

In the third octet, where the subnet address occurs, the wildcard mask checks that the bit position for the binary 16 is on and that all the higher bits are off using corresponding 0 bits in the wildcard mask. For the final (low-end) 4 bits in this octet, the wildcard mask indicates that these bits can be ignored. In these positions, the address value can be binary 0 or binary 1, but the convention is to assign 0 to the address value being masked by an ignore wildcard mask. Thus, the wildcard mask matches subnets 16, 17, 18, and so on, up to subnet 31. The wildcard mask does not match any other subnets.

In Figure 9-11, the address 172.30.16.0 with the wildcard mask 0.0.15.255 matches subnets 172.30.16.0/24 to 172.30.31.0/24.

NOTE   Although the wildcard mask is sometimes called an *inverted subnet mask*, this is not always the case. The subnet mask in Figure 9-11 is 255.255.255.0. An inverted mask for that would be 0.0.0.255. Because we chose to match only some of the addresses in the range of subnets, our wildcard mask was 0.0.15.255.

Standard IP Access List Configuration

The first access list you will learn to configure is a standard access list. Adding an access list to a router as a packet filter is a two-step process. First, you must create the list. Then, you apply that list to any interface that you want to filter the selected traffic. The steps and commands are as follows:

Step 1   The **access-list** command creates an entry in a standard IP traffic filter list:

```
Router(config)#access-list access-list-number {permit | deny}
    source-address [wildcard mask]
```

Where:

— *access-list-number* identifies the list to which the entry belongs. It's a number from 1 to 99.

— **permit | deny** indicates whether this entry allows or blocks traffic from the specified address.

— *source-address* identifies the source IP address.

— *wildcard mask* identifies which bits in the address field are matched. The default mask is 0.0.0.0 (match all bits).

Step 2   The **ip access-group** command applies an existing access list to an interface. Only one access list per protocol, per direction, per interface is allowed:

```
Router(config)#interface serial 0

Router(config-if)#ip access-group access-list-number {in ¦ out}
```

Where:

— *access-list-number* indicates the number of the access list to be applied to this interface.

— **in** | **out** selects whether the access list is applied as an incoming or outgoing filter. If **in** or **out** is not specified, **out** is the default.

NOTE   To remove an IP access list from an interface, first enter the **no ip access-group** *access-list-number* command on the interface. Then, enter the global **no access-list** *access-list-number* command to remove the access list.

The number of the access list indicates which list you are creating. As you add statements to this list, they are added to the end of the list. Therefore, all entries in access list 1 would start with the command **access-list 1**. In the next few pages, you will see some examples of standard access lists.

Example 1: Access List Blocking Traffic from an External Network

Figure 9-12 and Example 9-1 show an access list applied to the interfaces Ethernet 0 and Ethernet 1 to prevent traffic that did not originate from the 172.16.0.0 network from being passed out those interfaces.

Figure 9-12 *Standard Access List Blocks Non-172.16.0.0 Traffic*

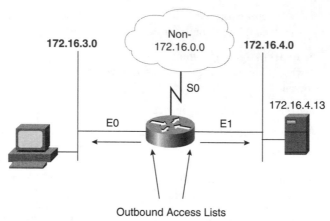

Example 9-1 *Standard Access List to Block Non-172.16.0.0 Traffic*

```
Router(config)#access-list 1 permit 172.16.0.0 0.0.255.255
Router(config)#interface ethernet 0
Router(config-if)#ip access-group 1 out
Router(config)interface ethernet 1
Router(config-if)#ip access-group 1 out
```

All access lists end with an implicit deny any statement. Traffic that does not match the first two octets of the network address 172.16.0.0, as shown in Example 9-1, moves to an unseen implicit deny any statement.

NOTE   The direction in Example 9-1 is explicitly applied as an outbound list. If you forget to specify a direction, the default is always **out**.

The following list highlights key parameters from the access list presented in Example 9-1:

- **1** is the access list number that indicates that this is a standard list.
- **permit** indicates that traffic that matches selected parameters will be forwarded.
- **172.16.0.0** is the IP address that will be used with the wildcard mask to identify the source network.
- **0.0.255.255** is the wildcard mask. 0s indicate positions that must match; 1s indicate "don't care" positions.
- **ip access-group 1 out** links the access list to the interface as an outbound filter.

Example 2: Access List Blocking Traffic from a Single Host

Using the network shown in Figure 9-12, Example 9-2 demonstrates a multiple-statement access list denying a single host. It is important to remember that when you start an access list with a **deny** statement, you must have at least one **permit** statement somewhere in the list. If you do not have a **permit** statement, the implicit deny any blocks all traffic.

Example 9-2   *Standard Access List to Block Traffic from a Single Host*

```
Router(config)#access-list 1 deny 172.16.4.13 0.0.0.0
Router(config)#access-list 1 permit 0.0.0.0 255.255.255.255
Router(config)#interface ethernet 0
Router(config-if)#ip access-group 1 out
```

The access list in Example 9-2 is designed to block traffic from a specific address, 172.16.4.13, and to allow all other traffic to be forwarded on interface Ethernet 0. The 0.0.0.0 255.255.255.255 IP address and wildcard mask combination permits traffic from any source. This combination can also be written using the keyword **any**.

The following list highlights key parameters from the access list shown in Example 9-2:

- **1** is the access list number that indicates that this is a standard list.
- **deny** indicates that traffic that matches selected parameters will not be forwarded.
- **172.16.4.13** is the IP address of the source host to be denied.
- **0.0.0.0** is the mask that requires the test to match all bits. (This is the default mask for a standard IP access list.)
- **1** is the access list number that indicates that this is a standard list.
- **permit** indicates that traffic that matches selected parameters will be forwarded.
- **0.0.0.0** is the IP address of the source host. All 0s indicates a placeholder because an address is required, and all of this address will be ignored by the mask.
- **255.255.255.255** is the wildcard mask. 0s indicate positions that must match; 1s indicate "don't care" positions. All 1s in the mask indicates that all 32 bits will not be checked in the source address.
- **ip access-group 1 out** links the access list to the interface as an outbound filter.

Example 3: Access List Blocking Traffic from a Single Subnet

Using the network shown in Figure 9-12, Example 9-3 shows a multiple statement access list denying a single subnet. This list blocks the 172.16.4.0 subnet but allows all other subnets out Ethernet 0. Notice that because the list is not applied to Ethernet 1 or Serial 0, it does not affect traffic traveling on those interfaces.

Example 9-3 *Standard Access List to Block Traffic from a Single Subnet*

```
Router(config)#access-list 1 deny 172.16.4.0 0.0.0.255
Router(config)#access-list 1 permit any
Router(config)#interface ethernet 0
Router(config-if)#ip access-group 1 out
```

The following list highlights key parameters from the access list presented in Example 9-3:

- **1** is the access list number that indicates that this is a standard list.

- **deny** indicates that traffic that matches selected parameters will not be forwarded.

- **172.16.4.0** is the IP address of the source subnet to be denied.

- **0.0.0.255** is the wildcard mask. 0s indicate positions that must match; 1s indicate "don't care" positions. The mask with 0s in the first three octets indicates that those positions must match; the 255 in the last octet indicates a "don't care" condition.

- **1** is the access list number that indicates that this is a standard list.

- **permit** indicates that traffic that matches selected parameters will be forwarded.

- **any** is the abbreviation for the source's IP address. The keyword **any** implies an IP address of all 0s (a placeholder) and a wildcard mask of 255.255.255.255. All 1s in the mask indicates that all 32 bits will not be checked in the source address.

- **ip access-group 1 out** links the access list to the interface as an outbound filter.

Controlling vty Access with Access Class Entries

Just as there are physical interfaces such as E0 and E1, there are also virtual interfaces. These virtual interfaces are called *virtual terminal lines* (*vty*). By default, there are five such virtual terminal lines, numbered vty 0 through vty 4, that are used to Telnet to the router's command-line interface. These are illustrated in Figure 9-13.

Figure 9-13 *Router Connections*

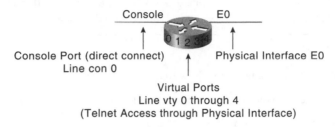

Standard and extended access lists block packets from going through the router. They are not designed to block packets that originated from the router. An outbound Telnet extended access list does not prevent router-initiated Telnet sessions.

For security purposes, users can be denied vty access to the router, or users can be permitted vty access to the router but denied access to destinations from that router. Restricting virtual terminal access is less a traffic-control mechanism than one technique for increasing network security.

When a user Telnets to a router, he or she connects on one of the vty lines, as shown in Figure 9-14.

Figure 9-14 *Telnetting to a Router*

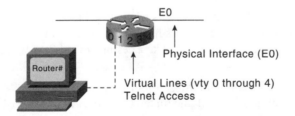

Telnet filtering is normally considered an extended IP access list function because it is filtering a higher-level protocol. However, because you know that anyone Telnetting to a router will be attaching to a virtual line (that is, vty 0 through 4), you can create a standard access list identifying the source address and apply it to the vty lines using the **access-class** command.

The **access-class** command also applies standard IP access list filtering to vty lines for outgoing Telnet sessions originating from within the router.

Normally, you set identical restrictions on all virtual terminal lines because you cannot control which vty will receive a user's Telnet connection.

NOTE	Some administrators configure one of the vty terminal lines differently from the others. This way, the administrator has a "back door" into the router.

The following commands show how to apply a standard access list to the Telnet ports.

Use the **line** command to place the router in line configuration mode:

```
Router(config)#line vty {# | vty-range}
```

Where:

- # indicates a specific vty line to be configured.
- *vty-range* indicates a range of vty lines to which the configuration will apply.

Use the **access-class** command to link an existing access list to a terminal line or range of lines:

```
Router(config-line)#access-class access-list-number {in | out}
```

Where:

- *access-list-number* indicates the number of the access list to be linked to a terminal line. This is a decimal number from 1 to 99.
- **in** prevents the router from receiving incoming Telnet connections from the source addresses in the access list.
- **out** prevents the router vty ports from initiating Telnet connections to addresses defined in the standard access list. Note that the source address specified in the standard access list is treated like a destination address when you use **access-class out**.

In Example 9-4, we are permitting any device on network 192.89.55.0 to establish a virtual terminal (Telnet) session with the router. Of course, the user must know the appropriate passwords to enter user mode and privileged mode.

Example 9-4 *Access List to Permit a Specified Network to Establish a Telnet Session*

```
Router(config)#access list 2 permit 192.168.55.0 0.0.0.255
Router(config)#line vty 0 4
Router(config-line)#access-class 2 in
```

Notice that identical restrictions have been set on all virtual terminal lines (0 to 4) because you cannot control on which virtual terminal line a user will connect.

The implicit deny any still applies to the access list when used as an access class entry.

Extended IP Access Lists

The standard access list (numbered 1 to 99) might not provide the traffic filtering control you need. Standard access lists filter based on a source address and mask. Standard access lists permit or deny the entire TCP/IP protocol suite. You might need a more precise way to filter your network traffic.

For more precise traffic-filtering control, use extended IP access lists. Extended IP access list statements test source and destination addresses. Table 9-2 compares standard and extended access lists.

Table 9-2   *Standard Versus Extended Access Lists*

Standard	Extended
Filters based on source address only.	Filters based on source and destination address and source and destination port number.
Permits or denies entire TCP/IP protocol suite.	Specifies a certain IP protocol and port number.
Range is 1 to 99.	Range is 100 to 199.

In addition, at the end of the extended **access-list** statement, you gain additional precision filtering by specifying the protocol and optional TCP or UDP port number. These port numbers can be the well-known port numbers for TCP/IP. Table 9-3 lists a few of the most common port numbers.

Table 9-3   *Well-Known Port Numbers*

Well-Known Port Number (Decimal)	IP Protocol
20	File Transfer Protocol (FTP) data
21	FTP program
23	Telnet
25	Simple Mail Transport Protocol (SMTP)
69	Trivial File Transfer Protocol (TFTP)
53	Domain Name System (DNS)

Table 9-3 is a brief listing of some well-known port numbers. For a more complete and comprehensive listing, chcck www.isi.edu/in-notes/iana/assignments/port-numbers.

By using the protocol and optional TCP or UDP port number, you can specify the logical operation that the extended access list will perform on specific protocols. IP extended access lists use a number from the range 100 to 199.

Configuring an Extended Access List

Configuring an extended access list is similar to the process for configuring a standard access list, except for the options available in the list. Adding an extended access list to a router as a packet filter is a two-step process. First you must create the access list. Then, you apply that access list to an interface. The steps and commands are as follows:

Step 1   Use the **access-list** command to create an entry to express a condition statement in a complex filter:

```
Router(config)#access-list access-list-number {permit | deny}
    protocol source-address source-wildcard [operator port]
    destination-address destination-wildcard [operator port]
    [established] [log]
```

Where:

— *access-list-number* identifies the list using a number in the range 100 to 199.

— **permit | deny** indicates whether this entry allows or blocks the specified address.

— *protocol* can be either IP, TCP, UDP, ICMP, GRE, or IGRP.

— *source* and *destination* identify source and destination IP addresses.

— *source-wildcard* and *destination-wildcard* indicate the wildcard mask. 0s indicate positions that must match; 1s indicate "don't care" positions.

— *operator port* can be lt (less than), gt (greater than), eq (equal to), or neq (not equal to) and a protocol port number.

— **established** is used for inbound TCP only. This allows TCP traffic to pass if the packet uses an established connection (for example, if it has ACK bits set).

— **log** sends a logging message to the console.

NOTE   The syntax of the **access-list** command presented here is representative of the TCP protocol form. Not all parameters and options are given. For the complete syntax of all forms of this command, refer to the appropriate Cisco IOS documentation available on CD-ROM or at the CCO web site.

Step 2   The **ip access-group** command applies an existing extended access list
to an interface. Only one access list per protocol, per direction, per
interface is allowed:

```
Router(config-if)#ip access-group access-list-number {in | out}
```

Where:

— *access-list-number* indicates the number of the access list to be
applied to an interface.

— **in | out** specifies whether the access list is applied as an input or
output filter. If **in** or **out** is not specified, **out** is the default.

Example 1: Extended Access List Blocking FTP Traffic from a Specified Subnet

Consider the network shown in Figure 9-15.

Figure 9-15   *Extended Access List to Block FTP Traffic*

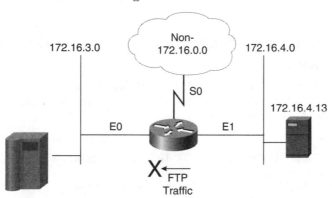

In order to block FTP traffic from subnet 172.16.4.0 to 172.16.3.0 and permit all other
traffic out interface Ethernet 0, you could create a list like the one shown in Example 9-5
and apply it as an outbound filter on Ethernet 0.

Example 9-5   *Extended Access List to Deny FTP Traffic from a Specified Subnet Out a Specified Interface*

```
Router(config)#access-list 101 deny tcp 172.16.4.0 0.0.0.255 172.16.3.0
   0.0.0.255 eq 21
Router(config)#access-list 101 deny tcp 172.16.4.0 0.0.0.255 172.16.3.0
   0.0.0.255 eq 20
Router(config)#access-list 101 permit ip any any
Router(config)#interface ethernet 0
Router(config-if)#ip access-group 101 out
```

The following list highlights key parameters from the extended access list presented in Example 9-5:

- **101** is the access list number that indicates that this is an extended IP access list.

- **deny** indicates that traffic that matches selected parameters will be blocked.

- **tcp** indicates the TCP protocol in the protocol number of the IP packet header. This is the transport protocol for FTP.

- **172.16.4.0 0.0.0.255** is the source IP address and mask. The first three octets must match, but do not care about the last octet.

- **172.16.3.0 0.0.0.255** is the destination IP address and mask. The first three octets must match, but do not care about the last octet.

- **eq 21** specifies the well-known port number for FTP control.

- **eq 20** specifies the well-known port number for FTP data.

- **ip access-group 101 out** links access list 101 to interface E0 as an output filter.

The **deny** statements deny FTP traffic from subnet 172.16.4.0 to subnet 172.16.3.0. The **permit** statement allows all other IP traffic out interface E0.

Example 2: Extended Access List Blocking Telnet Traffic from a Specified Subnet

Consider the network in Figure 9-15 again. This time your goal is to deny any Telnet traffic from the 172.16.4.0 subnet to the 172.16.3.0 subnet. This could be accomplished with the code shown in Example 9-6.

Example 9-6   *Extended Access List to Deny Telnet Traffic from a Specified Subnet Out a Specified Interface*

```
Router(config)#access-list 101 deny tcp 172.16.4.0 0.0.0.255 172.16.3.0
  0.0.0.255 eq 23
Router(config)#access-list 101 permit ip any any
Router(config)#interface ethernet 0
Router(config-if)#ip access-group 101 out
```

The following list highlights key parameters from the extended access list presented in Example 9-6:

- **101** is the access list number. It indicates that this is an extended IP access list.

- **deny** indicates that traffic that matches selected parameters will not be forwarded.

- **tcp** indicates the TCP protocol in the protocol number of the IP packet header. This is the transport protocol for Telnet.

- **172.16.4.0 0.0.0.255** indicates the source IP address and mask. The first three octets must match, but do not care about the last octet.

- **any** specifies to match any destination IP address. This keyword provides the same effect as and can be used in place of 0.0.0.0 255.255.255.255.

- **eq 23** specifies the well-known port number for Telnet.

- **permit** indicates that traffic that matches selected parameters will be forwarded.

- **ip** indicates any IP protocol. Because IP has a protocol field in the header that could be specifically chosen in an extended access list, you would need to indicate all IP packets to be permitted, or they would be denied by the implicit deny any. The parameter here specifies all IP traffic.

- **any** is the keyword that matches traffic from any source. This keyword provides the same effect as and can be used in place of 0.0.0.0 255.255.255.255.

- **any** is the keyword that matches traffic to any destination. This keyword provides the same effect as and can be used in place of 0.0.0.0 255.255.255.255.

- **ip access-group 101 out** links access list 101 to interface E0 as an output filter.

Example 9-6 denies Telnet traffic from 172.16.4.0 being sent out interface E0 to hosts in subnet 172.16.3.0. All other IP traffic from any other source to any destination is permitted out E0.

Named IP Access Lists

Announced in Cisco IOS 11.2, the named IP access list feature allows IP standard and extended access lists to be identified with an alphanumeric string (name) instead of the current numeric (1 to 199) representations.

With a numbered IP access list, an administrator who wants to alter an access list would first be required to delete the entire numbered access list and then reenter it with corrections. Individual statements within a numbered access list cannot be deleted.

Named IP access lists allow you to delete individual entries from a specific access list. Deleting individual entries allows you to modify your access lists without deleting and then reconfiguring them. Items cannot be selectively inserted into the list, however. If an item is added to the list, it is placed at the end of the list. Use named IP access lists in the following situations:

- You want to intuitively identify access lists using an alphanumeric name.

- You have more than 99 standard and 100 extended access control lists to be configured in a router for a given protocol.

Consider the following before implementing named IP access lists:

- Named IP access lists are not compatible with Cisco IOS releases prior to Release 11.2.

- You cannot use the same name for multiple access lists. In addition, access lists of different types cannot have the same name. For example, it is illegal to specify a standard access control list named "George" and an extended access control list with the same name.

Here are the steps to create and activate a named IP access list:

Step 1   Enter named access list configuration mode:

```
Router(config)#ip access-list {standard | extended} name
```

Step 2   In named access list configuration mode, type in the test conditions:

```
Router(config {std- | ext-}nacl)#{permit | deny} {test conditions}
Router(config {std- | ext-}nacl)#no {permit | deny} {test conditions}
```

Step 3   Apply the access list to an interface:

```
Router(config-if)#ip access-group name {in | out}
```

In Step 1, the name must be unique to the router (that is, no other named access list can have the name you choose). The test conditions applied in Step 2 are the same conditions applied in a numbered list (see Example 9-6 for details). To remove a single statement, precede the test condition with **no**. Example 9-7 shows a named extended access list that blocks Telnet traffic from the 172.16.4.0 subnet to the 172.16.3.0 subnet out Ethernet 0.

Example 9-7   *Named Extended Access List to Deny Telnet Traffic from a Specified Subnet Out a Specified Interface*

```
Router(config)#ip access-list extended screen
Router(config ext-nacl)# deny tcp 172.16.4.0 0.0.0.255 172.16.3.0 0.0.0.255 eq 23
Router(config ext-nacl)# permit ip any any
Router(config ext-nacl)#interface ethernet 0
Router(config-if)#ip access-group screen out
```

Example 9-7 is the same filter as the one in Example 9-6; however, this time it was accomplished using a named extended access list.

Guidelines for Standard, Extended, and Named Access List Implementation

The basic guidelines of access list configuration are as follows:

- The order of access list statements is crucial to proper filtering. Recommended practice is to create your access list on a TFTP server using a text editor and download it to the router via TFTP. Alternatively, you can use a terminal emulator or Telnet session on a PC to cut and paste the access list into the router while in configuration mode.

- Access lists are processed from the top down. If you place more specific tests and tests that will test true frequently in the beginning of the access list, you can reduce processing overhead.

- Only named access lists allow removal, but not reordering, of individual statements from a list. If you want to reorder access list statements, you must remove the whole list and re-create it in the desired order or with the desired statements.

- All access lists end with an implicit "deny any" statement.

Access lists can be used to control traffic by filtering and eliminating unwanted packets. Proper placement of an access list statement can reduce unnecessary traffic. Traffic that will be denied at a remote destination should not be allowed to use network resources along the route to that destination only to be denied upon arrival.

Consider the network shown in Figure 9-16. Suppose an enterprise's policy aims to deny Token Ring traffic on Router A to the Ethernet LAN on Router D's E1 port. At the same time, other traffic must be permitted.

Figure 9-16 *Access List Placement*

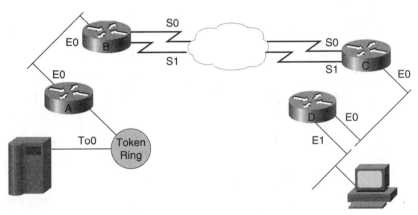

Several approaches can accomplish this policy. The recommended approach uses an extended access list because it specifies both source and destination addresses. Place this extended access list in Router A. Then, packets that will be denied do not cross Router A's Ethernet, do not cross the serial interfaces of Routers B and C, and do not enter Router D. Traffic with other source and destination addresses can still be permitted.

Extended access lists should normally be placed as close as possible to the source of the traffic to be denied.

Standard access lists do not specify destination addresses. The administrator would have to put the standard access list as close to the destination as possible. For example, you would place a standard access list on E0 of Router D to block Token Ring traffic from entering Router A.

Verifying and Monitoring Access Lists

This section introduces commands used to verify and monitor access lists.

The **show ip interface** command displays IP interface information and indicates whether any access lists are set for a specific interface. The syntax for this command is as follows:

```
Router#show ip interface interface-type interface-number
```

Example 9-8 shows the output from the **show ip interface** command. The highlighted lines indicate the status of access lists on interface Ethernet 0.

Example 9-8 *show ip interface Displays IP Interface Information and Access List Status*

```
Router#show ip int e0
Ethernet0 is up, line protocol is up
  Internet address is 10.1.1.11/24
  Broadcast address is 255.255.255.255
  Address determined by setup command
  MTU is 1500 bytes
  Helper address is not set
  Directed broadcast forwarding is disabled
  Outgoing access list is not set
  Inbound  access list is 1
  Proxy ARP is enabled
  Security level is default
  Split horizon is enabled
  ICMP redirects are always sent
  ICMP unreachables are always sent
  ICMP mask replies are never sent
  IP fast switching is enabled
  IP fast switching on the same interface is disabled
  IP Feature Fast switching turbo vector
  IP multicast fast switching is enabled
  IP multicast distributed fast switching is disabled
<text omitted>
```

The **show access-lists** command displays the contents of all access lists. The syntax for this command is as follows:

```
Router#show {protocol} access-lists {access-list-number | name}
```

By entering the access list name or number as an option for this command, you can display a specific access list. To display only the contents of all IP access lists, use the **show ip access-lists** command. To display the contents of all access lists, use the **show access-list** command.

Example 9-9 shows the output from the **show access-lists** command. The highlighted lines indicate the type of access lists that have been applied.

Example 9-9   *show access-lists Displays All Configured Access Lists*

```
Router#show access-lists
Standard IP access list 1
    permit 10.2.2.1
    permit 10.3.3.1
    permit 10.4.4.1
    permit 10.5.5.1
Extended IP access list 101
    permit tcp host 10.22.22.1 any eq telnet
    permit tcp host 10.33.33.1 any eq ftp
    permit tcp host 10.44.44.1 any eq ftp-data
```

Access List Command Summary

Table 9-4 briefly describes the commands you learned in this chapter.

Table 9-4   *Access List Command Summary*

Command	Description
access-list *access-list-number (1-99)* {**permit** I **deny**} *source-address* [wildcard mask]	Creates a standard IP access list.
access-list *access-list-number (100-199)* {**permit** I **deny**} *protocol source source-wildcard destination destination-wildcard* [*protocol-specific-option*] [**established**] [**log**]	Creates an extended access list.
ip access-group *access-list-number* {**in** I **out**}	Enables an IP access list on an interface.
line vty {**#** I vty-range}	Selects a virtual line or range of lines.
access-class *access-list-number* {**in** I **out**}	Applies an access list as a filter on a virtual terminal line.
ip access-list {**standard** I **extended**} *name*	Creates a named access list and places the router in standard or extended access list editing mode.
show ip access-lists	Displays the IP access lists.
show ip interface {*interface-type*} {*interface-number*}	Displays IP-specific information for an interface, including the access lists applied on that interface.

Summary

In this chapter, you learned how to apply IP access lists to interfaces as traffic filters. You read about how the standard access list checks against source addresses and how an extended access list checks source and destination addresses, and other options. You also learned how to determine which parts of these addresses are significant using wildcard masks. In addition, you saw how to apply a standard access list to a vty line in order to limit Telnet access to and from a router. Named access lists can also be configured to allow some flexibility in editing access lists. Finally, you learned about the guidelines for configuring these lists, placing them in your network, and verifying their configuration and application.

Review Questions

1   Access lists applied as traffic filters help do what in a network?

2   Name one other use for an access list.

3   In which direction can an access list be applied to an interface?

4   During the outbound filtering process, what must exist in the route table before the packet is checked against the filter?

5   What is the number range for IP extended access lists?

6   How many IP access lists can be applied to an interface in a given direction?

7   Every access list acting as a packet filter must have at least one what?

8   What happens if a packet does not match any of the test conditions in an access list?

9   In a wildcard mask, what value indicates to match a bit value?

10   Instead of typing 0.0.0.0 255.255.255.255, what keyword can be used in an access list?

11   Which command is used to verify that a list was applied to an interface?

12   How do you remove an access list from an interface?

13   Which command allows you to view the access lists?

14   All access lists end with what?

Upon completion of this chapter, you will be able to perform the following tasks:

- Describe basic IPX operation.

- Determine the required IPX network number and encapsulation type for a given interface.

- Enable the Novell IPX protocol.

- Verify IPX connectivity.

- Configure and monitor IPX access lists and SAP traffic filters.

CHAPTER 10

Configuring Novell IPX

This chapter presents an introduction to the Novell Internetwork Packet Exchange (IPX) protocol suite and how it operates using Cisco IOS software configurations. With the introduction of NetWare 5, Novell networks can run natively over TCP/IP, without IPX support. However, this chapter focuses on the typical IPX-based configuration of NetWare networks.

IPX Fundamentals

In today's networking environment, no single manufacturer can provide all the hardware and software required to support the computing needs of a business. As a result, most networks include a variety of vendor products, each one chosen for the powerful features it provides. For that reason, Cisco routers are often found in NetWare networks even though Novell offers routing products. As illustrated in Figure 10-1, Cisco routers provide connectivity between IPX networks.

Figure 10-1 *Cisco Routers in IPX Networks*

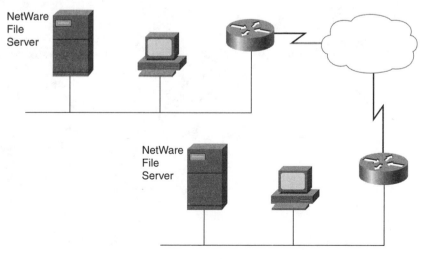

Cisco's routers offer the following features in Novell network environments:

- Support for a wide range of interfaces, including native Integrated Services Digital Network (ISDN) and Asynchronous Transfer Mode (ATM)

- Access lists and filters for IPX, Routing Information Protocol (RIP), Service Advertising Protocol (SAP), Network Control Protocol (NCP), and Network Basic Input/Output System (NetBIOS)

- Scalable routing protocols, including Enhanced Interior Gateway Routing Protocol (EIGRP) and NetWare Link Services Protocol (NLSP)

- Configurable RIP and SAP update intervals

- Serverless local-area network (LAN) support

- Dial-on-demand routing (DDR) and spoofing for IPX and Sequenced Packet Exchange (SPX)

- Rich diagnostics, management, and troubleshooting features

Novell NetWare IPX Protocol Stack

Novell IPX/SPX (Internet Packet Exchange/Sequenced Packet Exchange) is a proprietary suite of protocols derived from the Xerox Network Systems (XNS) protocol suite. Figure 10-2 shows the IPX protocol as compared to the OSI reference model.

Figure 10-2 *NetWare IPX Protocol Stack*

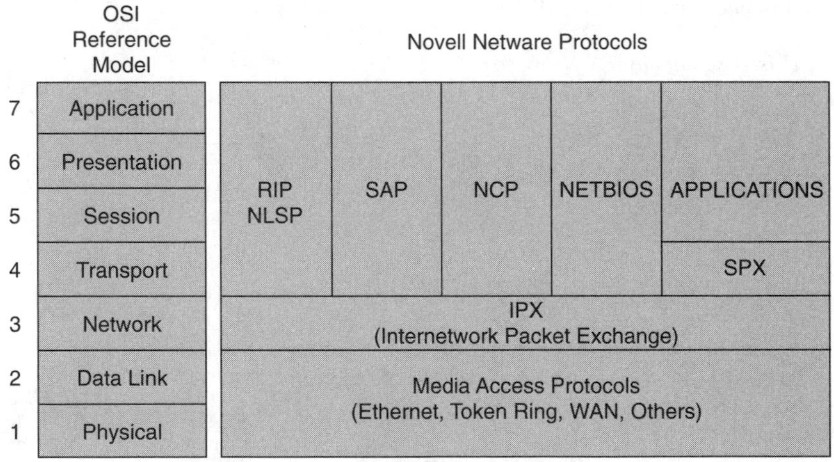

IPX is a

- Connectionless datagram protocol that does not require an acknowledgment for each packet. (It is similar to Internet Protocol [IP] and User Datagram Protocol [UDP].)
- Layer 3 protocol that defines the network layer address, which includes a network.node designator.

Novell NetWare uses its own proprietary

- Routing Information Protocol (IPX RIP) to facilitate the exchange of routing information.
- Service Advertisement Protocol (SAP) to advertise and find network services. One type of SAP broadcast is Get Nearest Server (GNS), which lets a client locate the "nearest server" for login. If two servers exist on the same network, the first server that answers is accepted as the "nearest server" even though it might not really be the nearest.
- NetWare Core Protocol (NCP) to provide client-to-server connections and application-level services.
- Sequenced Packet Exchange (SPX) service for Layer 4 connection-oriented services. (IPX and SPX together is analogous to IP and TCP.)

NOTE	Novell has developed a link-state routing protocol called NetWare Link Services Protocol (NLSP). NLSP is based on the ISO IS-IS routing protocol and is available for NetWare versions 3.11 and later. Novell also has a directory service called Novell Directory Services (NDS) that is available in versions 4.x and later. NDS is used to register and locate network services instead of SAP. NetWare 5 also supports NCP services over TCP/IP.

The NetWare protocol stack supports all common media access protocols. The data link and physical layers are accessed through the Open Data-Link Interface (ODI). ODI is a Novell specification providing a standardized interface for network interface cards (NICs) that allows multiple protocols to use a single NIC. NetWare has the following key features:

- A Novell IPX address has 80 bits—32 bits for the network number and 48 bits for the node number. It is expressed as a hexadecimal number.
- The node number contains the MAC address of an interface, or it can be administratively defined for serial interfaces.
- Novell IPX supports multiple logical networks on an individual interface. Each network requires a different encapsulation type.
- IPX RIP is the default routing protocol.

- NetWare clients locate available network services as Novell servers and routers announce those services using SAP broadcasts.

These features are discussed in detail in the following sections.

Novell IPX Addressing

Novell IPX addressing uses a two-part address—the network number (32 bits) and the node number (48 bits).

The IPX network number can be up to eight hexadecimal digits in length. Usually, only the significant digits are listed (the leading 0s are not shown). The network administrator assigns the IPX network number to the servers and routers. Clients learn the network address dynamically from the server upon startup.

Figure 10-3 shows three IPX networks — **4a1d**, **2c**, and **3f**.

Figure 10-3 *IPX Addressing*

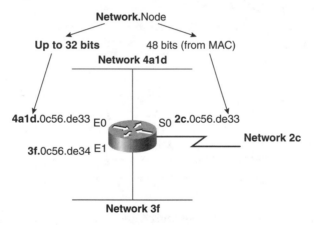

The IPX node number is 12 hexadecimal digits in length. This number is usually the MAC address obtained from a network interface that has a MAC address.

Figure 10-3 shows the IPX node address **0000.0c56.de33** on E0 and S0, and node address **0000.0c56.de34** on E1. Notice that the same node number appears for both E0 and S0. Serial interfaces do not have MAC addresses. The node number for S0 was obtained by using the MAC address from E0. Because an IPX address is a combination of the network and the node, each interface address is unique to the network. The same MAC address would be used for all serial interfaces on the device. Again, because each network number would be unique, the IPX address would also be unique for each interface. If a router does not have any LAN interfaces, an address can be defined with the **ipx routing** command.

The use of the MAC address in the logical IPX address eliminates the need for an Address Resolution Protocol (ARP). Because the MAC address is a known part of the IPX address, the workstation would use this information to build the destination address in the Layer 2 header.

Novell IPX Network Numbers

Novell file servers have one or more network interface cards (NICs). Each NIC has a physical (Layer 2) MAC address. The server is assigned an IPX network number for each interface, thereby allowing each NIC to have a unique IPX address (Layer 3) consisting of an assigned network number and the MAC address node number.

All Novell file servers also have a virtual (or logical) internal network. This internal IPX network number must be unique on the internetwork. Because there is no MAC address from which to take the node number, it will always be **.0000.0000.0001**. This can be seen in Figure 10-4 as the node of the internal network number. An internal routing process routes packets between the internal IPX network (where network services reside) and the external IPX network. This internal network number is used to advertise NetWare services on the network.

Figure 10-4 *NetWare Operation*

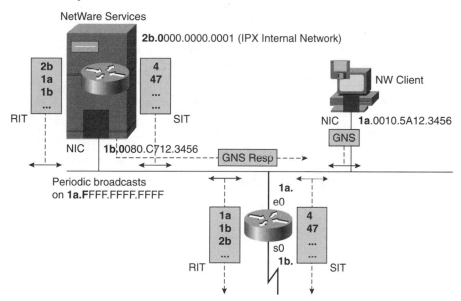

Figure 10-4 also shows how the file server keeps both a Route Information Table (RIT) and a Service Information Table (SIT). The entire contents of these tables are broadcast on directly connected IPX (1a.FFFF.FFFF.FFFF) networks every 60 seconds by default.

After the IPX process is enabled on the Cisco router, the router listens to the RIT and SIT broadcasts on the network and creates a RIT and SIT on the Cisco router as well. The router then participates in broadcasting this information every 60 seconds by default.

Figure 10-4 also illustrates how clients use GNS requests to locate and attach to servers to start the login process.

You must use a valid IPX network number when you configure the Cisco router. Because Novell NetWare networks are established by installing the server, you must determine the existing IPX network number from these established networks. The IPX network number refers to the logical "wire." All routers that provide connectivity between local devices must share the same IPX network number and encapsulation type as those local devices.

The first and recommended way to find out what IPX network number to use is to ask the NetWare administrator. Make sure that the NetWare administrator specifies the IPX network number for the same network where you want to enable IPX on your Cisco router.

If you cannot obtain an IPX network number from the NetWare administrator, you might be able to get it directly from a neighbor router. Pick the most appropriate of the several methods available to do this:

- If the neighbor router is another Cisco router, use Cisco's **show cdp neighbors detail** command to show Cisco Discovery Protocol (CDP) neighbor details. Refer to Chapter 4, "Managing Your Network Environment," for more information on using the **show cdp neighbors detail** command.

- Telnet to the neighbor router, enter the appropriate mode, and display the running configuration. Look for the IPX network number that is defined on the appropriate interface in the configuration.

- If the neighbor router is not a Cisco router (for example, a NetWare PC-based router, or a NetWare server), you might be able to run the NetWare configuration utility from the NetWare console to determine the address.

Novell IPX Packet Encapsulation

NetWare allows multiple Layer 2 frame structures for Novell IPX packets. Cisco routers support all of the framing variations.

There are four different Ethernet framing types. Each encapsulation type is appropriate in specific situations:

- **Ethernet_802.3**—Also called "raw Ethernet," Ethernet_802.3 is the default for NetWare versions 2.x through 3.11. Figure 10-5 illustrates the framing structure for the Ethernet_802.3 header.

Figure 10-5 *Ethernet_802.3 Header*

DA
SA
Length
IPX Payload
FCS

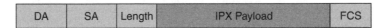

- **Ethernet_802.2**—This encapsulation type is the default for NetWare 3.12 and later versions. Figure 10-6 illustrates the framing structure for the Ethernet_802.2 header.

Figure 10-6 *Ethernet_802.2 Header*

DA
SA
Length
DSAP
SSAP
CTRL
IPX Payload
FCS

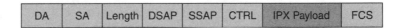

- **Ethernet_II**—This encapsulation type is also used with TCP/IP and DECnet. Figure 10-7 illustrates the framing structure for the Ethernet_II header.

Figure 10-7 *Ethernet_II Header*

DA
SA
Type
IPX Payload
FCS

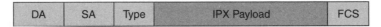

- **Ethernet_SNAP**—This encapsulation type is also used with TCP/IP and AppleTalk. Figure 10-8 illustrates the framing structure for the Ethernet_SNAP header.

Figure 10-8 *Ethernet_SNAP Header*

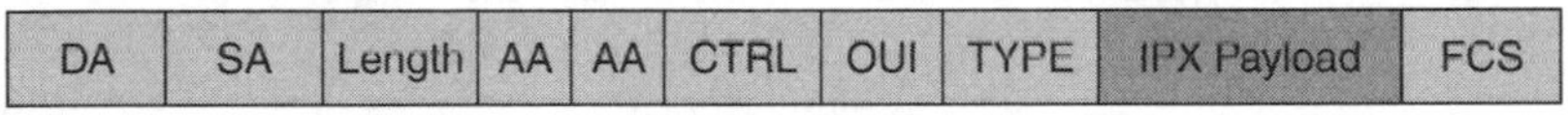

DA
SA
Length
AA
AA
CTRL
OUI
TYPE
IPX Payload
FCS

NOTE Multiple encapsulations can be specified on an interface, but only if multiple network numbers have also been assigned, where each network number belongs to only one encapsulation type and each encapsulation type has only one network number. Although several encapsulation types can share the same interface, clients and servers with different encapsulation types cannot communicate directly with each other. The default encapsulation on Cisco routers is Novell Ethernet_802.3, defined as Cisco keyword **novell-ether**.

When you configure an IPX network, you might need to specify a nondefault encapsulation type on either the Novell servers and clients or on the Cisco router. Cisco and Novell have assigned different names for the same encapsulation type. To help you specify the appropriate encapsulation type, use the information in Table 10-1, which matches the Novell term to the equivalent Cisco IOS term for the same framing types.

Table 10-1   *Novell Versus Cisco Naming for Encapsulation Types*

Media Type	Novell IPX Name	Cisco Name
Ethernet	Ethernet_802.3	**novell-ether**
	Ethernet_802.2	sap
	Ethernet_II	ARPA
	Ethernet_SNAP	snap
Token Ring	Token-Ring_SNAP	**snap**
	Token-Ring	sap
FDDI	FDDI_SNAP	**snap**
	FDDI_802.2	sap
	FDDI_Raw	novell-fddi

The bold items in the third column are the Cisco default encapsulations for that media type.

When you configure Cisco IOS software for Novell IPX, use the Cisco name for the appropriate encapsulation. Make sure that the encapsulation types match on all clients, servers, and routers that must communicate directly on the same segment.

If you do not specify an encapsulation type when you configure the router for IPX, the router will use the default encapsulation types on its interfaces.

NOTE   The default Ethernet encapsulation type on Cisco routers does not match the default Ethernet encapsulation type on Novell servers version 3.12 and later. To match the encapsulation, you would need to manually set the type using the **encapsulation** option in the **ipx network** *network* command, discussed later in this chapter.

The default encapsulation types on Cisco router interfaces and their keywords are as follows:

- Ethernet—**novell-ether**
- Token Ring—**snap**
- FDDI—**snap**
- Serial—**hdlc**

NOTE	The default IPX encapsulation type for NetWare servers 3.12 and above is Ethernet_802.2. This is what Cisco calls SAP encapsulation. Note that the default encapsulation for Cisco routers is novell_ether or what Novell calls Ethernet_802.3. If these encapsulation types do not match, you will not be able to locate services for the servers across the internetwork. To match the encapsulation, you would need to manually set the type using the **encapsulation** option in the **ipx network** *network* command, discussed later in this chapter.

NetWare Protocols

Novell RIP, also known as IPX RIP, is a distance vector routing protocol and is the default routing protocol for IPX. RIP uses two metrics to make routing decisions: ticks (a time measure ~1/18 sec) and hop count (a count of each router traversed), to a maximum of 15.

RIP checks its two distance vector metrics by first comparing the ticks for path alternatives. If two or more paths have the same tick value, RIP compares the hop count.

Each IPX router periodically broadcasts copies of its RIP routing table to its directly connected networks. The neighboring IPX routers increment the distance vector values as required before propagating their RIP tables to other networks. Figure 10-9 illustrates how tables are exchanged with neighboring routers.

Figure 10-9 *IPX Routing*

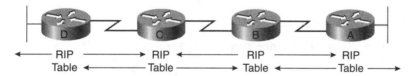

The split-horizon algorithm prevents the neighbor from broadcasting RIP tables with IPX information back to the networks from where it received that information.

RIP also uses a holddown timer to handle conditions in which an IPX router goes down without any explicit message to its neighbors. Periodic updates reset the aging timer.

Routing table updates are sent at 60-second intervals by default. The default packet size is 576 bytes and can contain up to 50 entries. This update frequency can cause excessive overhead traffic on some internetworks. Controlling this overhead through the use of access lists will be discussed later in this chapter.

All the servers on NetWare internetworks advertise their service types and service addresses. All versions of NetWare support SAP broadcasts to announce and locate registered network services. Adding, finding, and removing services on the internetwork occurs dynamically due to SAP advertisements. Figure 10-10 illustrates how SAP broadcasts internetwork services. In this figure, the servers on the Ethernet segment attached to Router A broadcast the services available. The router then "hears" these services and builds a table that it then passes on to other IPX routers to inform them of the services.

Figure 10-10 *Service Advertising Protocol*

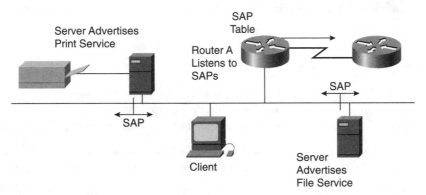

Each SAP service is an object type identified by a hexadecimal number. Table 10-2 shows a few common SAP types. You can find a more comprehensive listing of SAPs at www.novell.com.

Table 10-2   *SAP Service Type Identifiers*

SAP Type Hexadecimal Identifier	Service
4	NetWare file server
7	Print server
26B	Time synchronization (NetWare 4.x and later)
278	Directory services (NetWare 4.x and later)

All servers and routers keep a complete list of the services available throughout the network in server information tables (SITs). Like RIP, SAP uses an aging mechanism to identify and remove table entries that become invalid.

By default, service advertisements occur at 60-second intervals. The maximum packet size is 576 bytes and contains up to seven entries. Although service advertisements might work well on a LAN, broadcasting services can require too much bandwidth to be acceptable on large internetworks, or in internetworks linked through WAN serial connections. You might want to control these advertisements with access lists.

Routers do not forward SAP broadcasts. Instead, each router builds its own SAP table and forwards the SAP table to other devices on the segment. By default, this occurs every 60 seconds. The interval at which the Cisco router forwards the SAP table can be configured.

The NetWare client/server interaction begins when the client powers up and executes its client startup programs. These programs use the client's network adapter on the LAN and initiate the connection sequence to a NetWare file server.

A GNS SAP query is broadcast from the client. All local NetWare file servers respond with a SAP reply. The client attaches to the first server to respond and can then log into its target server, create a connection, negotiate packet size and other options, and proceed to use server resources.

If there is a Novell server (or any other IPX server) on the local network, the Cisco router will not respond to the GNS query. The router is aware of the local servers and knows that they should handle the GNS requests.

If there are no NetWare servers on the local network, the Cisco router will reply to the GNS query with information about a NetWare server from its SIT. Figure 10-11 illustrates the GNS SAP query process.

Figure 10-11 *Get Nearest Server*

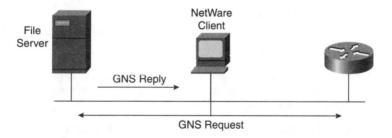

Configuring IPX Routing

To route IPX traffic, Cisco routers must be properly configured. To accomplish this, you must enable the IPX routing process and configure the network parameters on each interface. Figure 10-12 illustrates the networks and encapsulations assigned to the interface. Once routing has been enabled, each IPX configured interface begins to participate in the IPX RIP routing process.

Figure 10-12 *Basic IPX Configuration*

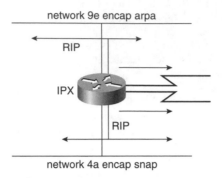

network 9e encap arpa

RIP

IPX

RIP

network 4a encap snap

Configuring Novell IPX as a routing protocol involves both global and interface parameters. They are defined as follows:

- Global tasks:

  — Start the IPX routing process.

  — Enable load sharing if appropriate for your network. Load sharing allows the router to use multiple same-cost paths to a destination. This balances the transmission of packets across multiple routers and network links.

- Interface tasks:

  — Assign unique network numbers to each interface. Multiple network numbers can be assigned to an interface, allowing support of different encapsulation types.

  — Set the optional encapsulation type if it is different from the default.

Global Tasks for IPX Routing Configuration

The **ipx routing** command enables IPX routing and SAP services. An optional node address can be specified for the serial interfaces. If no node address is specified, the Cisco router uses the MAC address of a LAN interface for the serial interfaces. The syntax for the **ipx routing** command is as follows:

```
Router(config)#ipx routing [node]
```

where the *node* option enables the IPX routing process. The node establishes a node number to be used for the serial interfaces. If none is set, the default is to use the number of a LAN interface.

CAUTION   If you choose to configure the node number manually using an administratively defined node address instead of allowing the router to use the default MAC address, you should not use the same node address on two or more devices on a shared segment. Doing so would result in an addressing conflict, effectively disabling IPX on those interfaces.

The **ipx maximum-paths** command enables load sharing. The default is 1, meaning no load sharing is enabled. The syntax for the **ipx maximum-paths** command is as follows:

```
Router(config)#ipx maximum-paths paths
```

where the *paths* option represents the maximum number of parallel paths to the destination. The default is 1, and the maximum is 512.

Interface Tasks for IPX Routing Configuration

The **ipx network** command enables IPX routing on a particular interface, assigns the IPX network number, and optionally selects an encapsulation type. The syntax for the **ipx network** command is as follows:

```
Router(config)#ipx network network [encapsulation encapsulation-type]
```

Where:

- *network* is the network number, which is an eight-digit hexadecimal number that uniquely identifies a network cable segment. The network number can be a number in the range 1 to FFFFFFFD. You do not need to specify leading 0s.

- **encapsulation** is the option that specifies that a type of encapsulation (framing) will be used on the interface.

- *encapsulation-type* specifies which of the following encapsulation types will be used: **arpa**, **novell-ether**, **novell-fddi**, **sap**, or **snap**.

Like all networks, IPX is a logical network. It is possible to assign multiple logical networks on the same physical wire. Figure 10-13 shows a wire with two logical networks.

Figure 10-13 *Multiple Logical Networks*

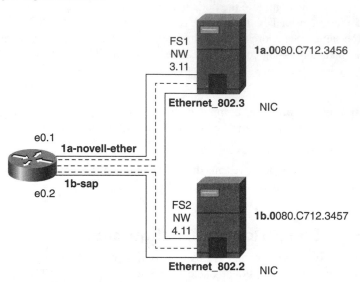

To assign network numbers to interfaces that support multiple networks, you normally use subinterfaces. A subinterface is a mechanism that allows a single physical interface to support multiple logical subinterfaces or networks. In other words, several logical subinterfaces or networks can be associated with a single physical interface.

Each subinterface uses a distinct network number and encapsulation type, and the encapsulation type must match that of the clients and servers using the same network number. To provide routing services and communication with the two servers shown in Figure 10-13, the router is configured with two subinterfaces:

- Subinterface e0.1, network 1a, encapsulation type novell-ether, to communicate with FS1

- Subinterface e0.2, network 1b, encapsulation type sap, to communicate with FS2

The two servers in Figure 10-13 cannot communicate with each other directly because they use different encapsulation types. The router can, however, provide connectivity between the two servers' networks.

The **interface** *type number.subinterface-number* command creates the logical subinterface on the physical interface. Subinterface numbers can be arbitrarily chosen and should be in the range of 1 to 4294967293. This is the preferred method of assigning multiple network numbers. You then specify the IPX network number and encapsulation type on each subinterface using the **ipx network** *network* [**encapsulation** *encapsulation-type*] command. Each subinterface must have a different encapsulation type. The syntax for each of these commands follows:

```
Router(config)#interface type number.subinterface-number
Router(config-subif)#ipx network network [encapsulation encapsulation-type]
```

When assigning network numbers to interfaces that support multiple networks, you can also configure primary and secondary networks. The **ipx network [encapsulation** *encapsulation-type*] **[secondary]** command is used to configure an additional (secondary) network number on an interface after the first network number (primary). The first logical network you configure on an interface is considered the primary network. Any additional networks are considered secondary networks. Again, each network on an interface must use a unique network number and encapsulation type, and it should match that of the clients and servers using that network number. The full syntax for the **ipx network [encapsulation** *encapsulation-type*] **[secondary]** command is as follows:

```
Router(config-if)#ipx network network [encapsulation encapsulation-type]
  [secondary]
```

NOTE	In future Cisco IOS software releases (sometime later than version 12.0), primary and secondary networks might not be supported.

IPX Routing Configuration Example

Figure 10-14 shows an example of a router connected to a wire with two logical networks out its Ethernet 0 interface.

Figure 10-14 *Physical Layout of Multiple Logical Networks*

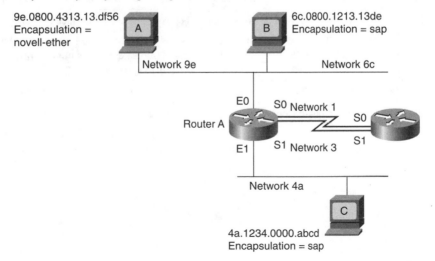

Example 10-1 shows how you would configure the router to operate in the environment depicted in Figure 10-14.

Example 10-1 *Multiple Logical IPX Networks Using Subinterfaces*

```
RouterA(config)#ipx routing
RouterA(config)#ipx maximum-paths 2
RouterA(config)#interface ethernet 0.1
RouterA(config-subif)# ipx network 9e encapsulation novell-ether
RouterA(config-subif)#interface ethernet 0.2
RouterA(config-subif)# ipx network 6c encapsulation sap
RouterA(config-if)#interface ethernet 1
RouterA(config-if)# ipx network 4a encapsulation sap
RouterA(config-if)#interface serial 0
RouterA(config-if)# ipx network 1
RouterA(config-if)#Interface serial 1
RouterA(config-if)# ipx network 3
```

Table 10-3 explains some of the key commands in Example 10-1.

Table 10-3 *Command Highlights and Explanations from Example 10-1*

Command	Description
ipx routing	Selects IPX as a routing protocol and starts the IPX routing process.
ipx maximum-paths 2	Allows load sharing over parallel equal metric paths to the destination. The number of parallel paths used is limited to two in this example for the two serial interfaces.
interface ethernet 0.1	Indicates the first subinterface on physical interface E0.
ipx network 9e encapsulation novell-ether	Network number assigned to subinterface E0.1. Specifies that Novell's unique frame format is used on this network segment. Cisco's keyword is **novell-ether**; Novell's terminology is **Ethernet_802.3**.
interface ethernet 0.2	Indicates the second subinterface on physical interface E0.
ipx network 6c encapsulation sap	Network number assigned to subinterface E0.2. Specifies that Novell's **Ethernet_802.2** frame format is used on this network segment. Cisco's keyword is **sap**.

Verifying and Monitoring IPX Routing

After IPX routing is configured, you can monitor and troubleshoot it using the commands listed in Table 10-4 and Table 10-5.

Table 10-4   *Commands for Monitoring IPX Routing*

Monitoring Command	What It Displays
show ipx interface	IPX status and parameters on all IPX interfaces.
show ipx route	IPX routing table contents.
show ipx servers	IPX server table contents.
show ipx traffic	Number and type of IPX packets being routed.

Table 10-5   *Commands for Troubleshooting IPX Routing*

Troubleshooting Command	Description
debug ipx routing activity	Displays information about RIP update packets.
debug ipx sap activity	Displays information about SAP update packets.
ping ipx	Checks IPX host reachability.

Each of the commands in Table 10-4 and Table 10-5 is discussed in detail in the following sections.

Displaying IPX Interface Status and Parameters

The **show ipx interface** command shows the status of the IPX interface and IPX parameters configured on each interface. Example 10-2 provides some sample output from the **show ipx interface** command. An explanation of key portions of the output is provided following the example.

Example 10-2 *show ipx interface Command Displays IPX Interface Status and Parameters*

```
Router#show ipx interface e0
Ethernet0 is up, line protocol is up
  IPX address is ABC.00e0.1e5d.ae2f, NOVELL-ETHER [up]
  Delay of this IPX network, in ticks is 1 throughput 0 link delay 0
  IPXWAN processing not enabled on this interface.
  IPX SAP update interval is 60 seconds
  IPX type 20 propagation packet forwarding is disabled
  Incoming access list is not set
  Outgoing access list is not set
  IPX helper access list is not set
  SAP GNS processing enabled, delay 0 ms, output filter list is not set
  SAP Input filter list is not set
```

continues

Example 10-2 *show ipx interface Command Displays IPX Interface Status and Parameters (Continued)*

```
SAP Output filter list is not set
SAP Router filter list is not set
Input filter list is not set
Output filter list is not set
Router filter list is not set
Netbios Input host access list is not set
Netbios Input bytes access list is not set
Netbios Output host access list is not set
Netbios Output bytes access list is not set
Updates each 60 seconds aging multiples RIP: 3 SAP: 3
SAP interpacket delay is 55 ms, maximum size is 480 bytes
<text omitted>
```

The first highlighted line in Example 10-2 shows the IPX address and the type of encapsulation.

The second highlighted line in Example 10-2 shows the delay on this interface. You can manually set the ticks metric. Use the command **ipx delay** *number* where the *number* option is the ticks to associate with an interface. This command manually overrides the following defaults on the Cisco router:

- For LAN interfaces, one tick
- For WAN interfaces, six ticks

Displaying IPX Routing Table Contents

The **show ipx route** command displays the contents of the IPX routing table. Example 10-3 provides some sample output from the **show ipx route** command. An explanation of key portions of the output is provided following the example.

Example 10-3 *show ipx route Command Displays IPX Routing Table Contents*

```
Router#show ipx route
Codes: C - Connected primary network,    c - Connected secondary network
       S - Static, F - Floating static, L - Local (internal), W - IPXWAN
       R - RIP, E - EIGRP, N - NLSP, X - External, A - Aggregate
       s - seconds, u - uses, U - Per-user static

2 Total IPX routes. Up to 1 parallel paths and 16 hops allowed.

No default route known.

C        ABC (NOVELL-ETHER),  Et0
R        DEF [02/01] via      ABC.00e0.1e5d.c860,   40s, Et0
```

The first highlighted line in Example 10-3 provides information about a direct connection:

- The network number is ABC.
- The encapsulation type is NOVELL-ETHER.
- The interface is Ethernet0.

The second highlighted line in Example 10-3 provides routing information for a remote network:

- The information was learned from a RIP update (denoted by code **R**).
- The network is number DEF.
- It is located two ticks or one hop away (denoted by **[02/01]**).
- The next hop in the path is a router with IPX address ABC.00e0.1e5d.c860.
- The information was updated 40 seconds ago.
- Packets destined for the remote network will be sent through interface Ethernet0.

Displaying IPX Server Information

The **show ipx servers** command lists the IPX servers discovered through SAP advertisements. Example 10-4 provides some sample output from the **show ipx servers** command. An explanation of key portions of the output is provided following the example.

Example 10-4 *show ipx servers Command Displays IPX Servers Discovered Through SAP Advertisements*

```
Router#show ipx servers
Codes: S - Static, P - Periodic, E - EIGRP, N - NLSP, H - Holddown, + - detail
U - Per-user static
2 Total IPX Servers

Table ordering is based on routing and server info

    Type Name                     Net      Address    Port   Route Hops Itf
p    4 fs1                    11.0000.0000.0001:0451    4/03    4  Et0
p    4 fs2                    21.0000.0000.0001:0451    4/03    4  Et0
```

The output in Example 10-4 provides the following information:

- The information about the server was learned from a SAP update. This is denoted by the code letter **p**, because SAP updates are periodic in nature. This is a type 4 or file server service.
- The server name (**fs1**), network address (**11**), node address (**0000.0000.0001**), and source socket number (**0451**) are shown. **0451** is the socket number for the NetWare Core Protocol (NCP).

- The ticks and hops (**4/03**) for the route (taken from the routing table).
- The number of hops (**4**) (taken from the SAP protocol).
- The interface through which to reach the server (Ethernet 0).

Displaying IPX Traffic Volume and Type Information

The **show ipx traffic** command displays information about the number and type of IPX packets received and transmitted by the router. Example 10-5 provides some sample output from the **show ipx traffic** command.

Example 10-5 *show ipx traffic Command Displays Information About the Volume and Type of IPX Traffic*

```
Router#show ipx traffic
System Traffic for 0.0000.0000.0001 System-Name: wg_ro_a
Rcvd:   15 total, 0 format errors, 0 checksum errors, 0 bad hop count,
        0 packets pitched, 15 local destination, 0 multicast
Bcast:  13 received, 6 sent
Sent:   6 generated, 0 forwarded
        0 encapsulation failed, 0 no route
SAP:    1 Total SAP requests, 0 Total SAP replies, 0 servers
        1 SAP general requests, 0 ignored, 0 replies
        0 SAP Get Nearest Server requests, 0 replies
        0 SAP Nearest Name requests, 0 replies
        0 SAP General Name requests, 0 replies
        0 SAP advertisements received, 0 sent
        0 SAP flash updates sent, 0 SAP format errors
RIP:    1 RIP requests, 0 ignored, 0 RIP replies, 2 routes
        13 RIP advertisements received, 0 sent
        0 RIP flash updates sent, 0 RIP format errors
Echo:   Rcvd 0 requests, 0 replies
        Sent 0 requests, 0 replies
        0 unknown: 0 no socket, 0 filtered, 0 no helper
        0 SAPs throttled, freed NDB len 0
Watchdog:
        0 packets received, 0 replies spoofed
<text omitted>
```

Displaying Information About RIP Update Packets

The **debug ipx routing activity** command displays information about IPX routing update packets that are transmitted to or received from other IPX routers. Example 10-6 provides some sample output from the **debug ipx routing activity** command. An explanation of key portions of the output is provided following the example.

Example 10-6 *debug ipx routing activity Command Displays Information About RIP Update Packets*

```
Router#debug ipx routing activity
IPX routing debugging is on
IPXRIP: positing full update to 3010.ffff.ffff.ffff via Ethernet0 (broadcast)
IPXRIP: positing full update to 3000.ffff.ffff.ffff via Ethernet1 (broadcast)
IPXRIP: positing full update to 3020.ffff.ffff.ffff via Serial0 (broadcast)
IPXRIP: positing full update to 3021.ffff.ffff.ffff via Serial1 (broadcast)
IPXRIP: sending update to 3020.ffff.ffff.ffff via Serial0
IPXRIP: src=3020.0000.0c03.14d8, dst=3020.ffff.ffff.ffff, packet sent
    network 3021, hops 1,  delay 6
    network 3010, hops 1,  delay 6
    network 3000, hops 1,  delay 6
IPXRIP: sending update to 3021.ffff.ffff.ffff via Serial1
IPXRIP: src=3021.0000.0c03.14d8, dst=3021.ffff.ffff.ffff, packet sent
    network 3020, hops 1,  delay 6
    network 3010, hops 1,  delay 6
    network 3000, hops 1,  delay 6
IPXRIP: sending update to 3010.ffff.ffff.ffff via Ethernet0
IPXRIP: src=3010.aa00.0400.0284, dst=3010.ffff.ffff.ffff, packet sent
    network 3030, hops 2,  delay 7
    network 3020, hops 1,  delay 1
    network 3021, hops 1,  delay 1
    network 3000, hops 1,  delay 1
IPXRIP: sending update to 3000.ffff.ffff.ffff via Ethernet1
```

A router sends an update every 60 seconds by default. Each update packet can contain up to 50 entries. If there are more than 50 entries in the routing table, the update will include more than one packet.

Displaying Information About SAP Update Packets

The **debug ipx sap activity** command displays information about IPX SAP packets that are transmitted or received. Example 10-7 provides some sample output from the **debug ipx sap activity** command. An explanation of key portions of the output is provided following the example.

Example 10-7 *debug ipx sap activity Command Displays Information About SAP Update Packets*

```
Router#debug ipx sap activity
IPX service debugging is on
Router#
05:31:18: IPXSAP: positing update to 1111.ffff.ffff.ffff via Ethernet0
  (broadcast) (full)
05:31:18: IPXSAP: Update type 0x2 len 288 src:1111.00e0.1e5d.ae2f
dest:1111.ffff.ffff.ffff(452)
05:31:18:   type 0x7, "ps21", 21.0000.0000.0001(451), 2 hops
05:31:18:   type 0x4, "fs31", 31.0000.0000.0001(451), 2 hops
05:31:18:   type 0x4, "fs41", 41.0000.0000.0001(451), 2 hops
05:31:18:   type 0x7, "ps51", 51.0000.0000.0001(451), 2 hops
Router#
```

Like RIP updates, SAP updates are sent every 60 seconds by default and might contain multiple packets. Each SAP packet appears as multiple lines in the output, as shown in Example 10-7, including a packet summary message and a service detail message.

SAP responses may be one of these types:

- **0x1**—General Service request
- **0x2**—General Service response
- **0x3**—Get Nearest Server request
- **0x4**—Get Nearest Server response

In each line, the type of service, name, address, socket, and distance of the responding or target router is listed.

Checking IPX Host Reachability

The **ping ipx** command checks IPX host reachability and network connectivity. Example 10-8 provides some sample output from the **ping ipx** command.

Example 10-8 *ping ipx Command Checks IPX Host Reachability/Network Connectivity*

```
Router# ping ipx 211.0000.0c01.f4cf

Type escape sequence to abort.
Sending 5, 100-byte IPXcisco Echoes to 211.0000.0c01.f4cf, timeout is 2 seconds.
!!!!!
Success rate is 100 percent (0/5)
```

NOTE   Cisco IPX echoes are used to ping between Cisco routers to verify connectivity and are not compatible with Novell IPX pings, which can be used to ping between servers.

IPX Access Lists

Access lists exist for IPX traffic just as they do for IP traffic. Many lists can be configured and applied to interfaces and IPX processes to control the overhead associated with IPX. Like an IP access list, the IPX access list opens the packet to test against the contents for the decision-making process.

Novell IPX access lists can test the following IPX packet header contents:

- Destination and source IPX addresses using standard access lists. Standard access lists are identified with an access list number in the range 800 to 899.
- Destination and source IPX addresses, protocols, and socket numbers using extended access lists. Extended access lists are identified with a number in the range 900 to 999.

- Service advertisement numbers, in addition to the other tests in SAP filter access lists, are identified with an access list number in the range 1000 to 1099.

For all Novell IPX access lists, after a packet is matched with the access list statement, it can be denied or permitted to use an interface in the access group. Figure 10-15 demonstrates fields in an IPX packet that could be used for testing.

Figure 10-15 *IPX Packet*

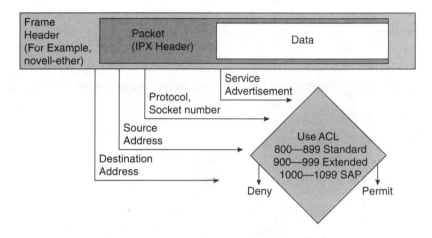

NOTE   Cisco IOS software offers several other forms of access lists for Novell IPX packets. Refer to the Cisco Documentation CD-ROM for further information.

Novell addressing is based on network.node. The network number is assigned by the administrator; the node portion is derived from the MAC address of the individual interface, or by an administrator. Serial lines adopt the MAC address of a LAN interface in the creation of their logical addresses, unless manually configured in the **ipx routing** command.

The socket number identifies a process or application (similar to the TCP/IP port number).

NetWare file servers 3.x or later have an internal IPX network number and perform IPX routing by default. External IPX networks attach to router interfaces. The IPX network number assigned on a Cisco router's interface must match the external network number on the NetWare server.

IPX standard access lists use numbers in the range 800 to 899. These access lists check for either source address or both source and destination address. To identify parts of the address to check or ignore, IPX standard access lists use a wildcard mask that operates like the mask used with IP access lists.

IPX extended access lists use numbers in the range 900 to 999. Extended access lists add checks for protocol, as well as source and destination addresses and socket numbers.

Access lists can also be used to control the traffic from SAP broadcasts. SAP filters use numbers in the range 1000 to 1099.

IPX routing and advertising processes were developed to run on LANs. As LANs interconnect with slower, more costly WAN links, there are increased concerns over the traffic that results from IPX RIP/SAP packets, thereby reducing the bandwidth available for user application traffic.

Figure 10-16 illustrates why some of the concerns about IPX RIP/SAP traffic are valid.

Figure 10-16 *IPX Overhead*

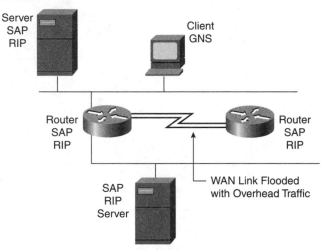

IPX servers broadcast service advertisements (SAPs) every 60 seconds by default. Likewise, routers broadcast their SAP tables every 60 seconds by default.

Routers broadcast the IPX RIP routing table to other IPX routers every 60 seconds by default.

When a client workstation starts up, it sends a GNS SAP broadcast to find a server. When a server answers, the client can then log onto a target server.

A network administrator can set up IPX access lists to control the broadcast packets from these protocols to reduce the traffic on WAN links.

Use the **access-list** command to create IPX access lists. The syntax for the **access-list** command is as follows:

```
Router(config)#access-list access-list-number {deny | permit} {test conditions}
```

Where:

- *access-list-number* is the access list number for an IPX filter.
- **deny | permit** denies or permits the IPX traffic if the IPX packet matches the **access-list** statement.
- *test conditions* can be made up of the following parameters:
  - *source-network* is the source network number, expressed as an eight-digit hexadecimal number. −1 equals any network.
  - *source-node* is the node number on the source network, represented as a 48-bit value shown in a dotted triplet of four-digit hexadecimal numbers.
  - *destination-network* is the network number to which the packet is being sent. −1 equals any network.
  - *destination-node* is the node on the destination network to which the packet is being sent.

Use the **ipx access-group** command to link an IPX access list to an interface. The syntax for the **ipx access-group** command is as follows:

```
Router(config-if)#ipx access-group access-list-number {in | out}
```

Where:

- *access-list-number* is the IPX access list number.
- **in | out** applies the access list as an input or output filter. The default is **out**.

Standard IPX Access Lists

The next few pages show how you can use access lists to control the IPX overhead in a NetWare network. Figure 10-17 shows a router connected to four IPX networks. The objective here is to permit only traffic from Network 2b to be transmitted out the Ethernet 0 interface to Network 4d.

Figure 10-17 *Standard IPX Access List*

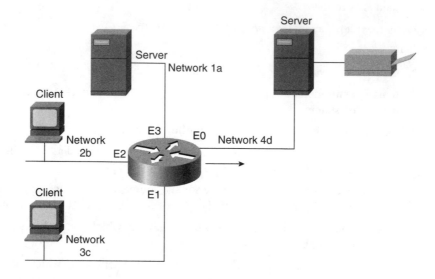

Example 10-9 provides the proper access list configuration to permit only traffic from Network 2b to be transmitted out the Ethernet 0 interface to Network 4d.

Example 10-9 *Standard IPX Access List Configuration Example*

```
Router(config)#access-list 800 permit  2b 4d
Router(config)#int e 0
Router(config-if)#ipx network 4d
Router(config-if)#ipx access-group 800 out
Router(config-if)#int e 1
Router(config-if)# ipx network 3c
Router(config-if)#int e 2
Router(config-if)# ipx network 2b
Router(config-if)#int e3
Router(config-if)# ipx network 1a
```

Table 10-6 explains some of the key commands in Example 10-9.

Table 10-6 *Command Highlights and Explanations from Example 10-9*

access-list 800 permit 2b 4d Command	Description
800	Specifies a Novell IPX standard access list.
permit	Traffic matching the selected parameters will be forwarded.
2b	Source network number.

Table 10-6   *Command Highlights and Explanations from Example 10-9 (Continued)*

access-list 800 permit 2b 4d Command	Description
4d	Destination network number.
ipx access-group 800 out	Links access list 800 to interface E0 as an output filter.

Notice that the other interfaces, E1 and E2, are not subject to the access list; they lack the **access-group** statement to link them to the access list 800.

Extended IPX Access Lists

To define an extended IPX access list, use the extended version of the **access-list** global configuration command. Extended IPX access lists filter on protocol type, with all other parameters being optional. The **ipx access-group** command links the extended IPX access list to an interface. The syntax for the extended version of the **access-list** global configuration command is as follows:

```
Router(config)# access-list access-list-number {deny | permit} protocol
[source-network][[[.source-node] | [source-network-mask.source-node-mask]]
[source-socket] [destination-network] [[[.destination-node]
destination-network-mask] |
[.destination-node destination-network-mask.destination-nodemask]]
[destination-socket] [log]
```

Where:

- *access-list-number* is the number of the extended access list. This is a decimal number from 900 to 999.

- **deny | permit** denies or permits the IPX traffic if the IPX packet matches the **access-list** statement.

- *protocol* is the name or number (decimal) of an IPX protocol type. This is sometimes referred to as the packet type.

- *source-network [.node]* and *mask* are the source network [.node] number and wildcard mask. −1 equals any network.

- *source-socket* is the source socket name or number (hexadecimal).

- *destination-network [.node]* and *mask* are the destination network [.node] number and wildcard mask. −1 equals any network.

- *destination-socket* is the destination socket name or number (hexadecimal).

- **log** logs IPX access control list violations whenever a packet matches a particular access list entry. The information logged includes source address, destination address, source socket, destination socket, protocol type, and action taken (permit | deny).

IPX Access Lists to Filter SAP Traffic

SAP broadcasts advertise the list of available services. Figure 10-18 shows how a router builds a SAP information table and passes service information throughout the network.

Figure 10-18 *SAP Operations*

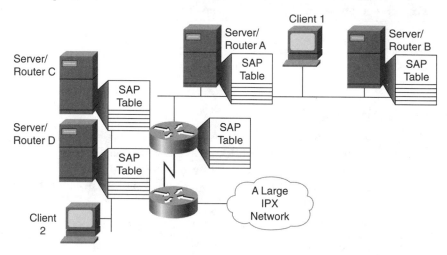

If the router forwarded a SAP broadcast over a WAN link every time it received one, the WAN link would be flooded with SAP traffic. Instead of forwarding SAP broadcasts, routers listen to SAP updates and build a SAP table. The router then advertises its SAP table every 60 seconds by default. Advertising SAP tables can still result in considerable overhead when routers send their own complete SAP table every 60 seconds.

When a SAP advertisement arrives at the router interface, the contents are placed in the SAP table portion of main memory. The contents of the table are propagated during the next SAP update.

Two types of access list filters control SAP traffic:

- **IPX input SAP filter**—When a SAP input filter is in place, the number of services entered into the SAP table is reduced. The propagated SAP updates represent the entire table, but contain only a subset of all services.

- **IPX output SAP filter**—When a SAP output filter is in place, the number of services propagated from the table is reduced. The propagated SAP updates represent a portion of the table contents and are a subset of all the known services.

You must carefully plan for SAP filtering before configuring your router. Make sure that all clients will see advertisements necessary and sufficient for their application processing. Figure 10-19 illustrates IPX input and output SAP filters.

Figure 10-19 *SAP Filters*

◦ Input Filter: Do Not Add Filtered SAPs to SAP Table

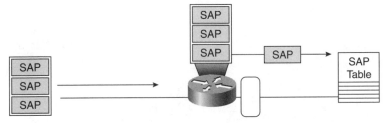

◦ Output Filter: Do Not Add Filtered SAPs to the SAP Table Sent

Place SAP filters close to the source of that SAP information. Proper placement of SAP filters conserves critical bandwidth, especially on serial links.

Use the following command to control propagation of the SAP messages:

```
Router(config)#access-list access-list-number {deny | permit} network[.node]
[network-mask.node-mask][service-type [server-name]]
```

Where:

- *access-list-number* is a number from 1000 to 1099 that indicates a SAP filter list.
- *network [.node]* is the Novell source internal network number with optional node number. −1 equals all networks.
- *network-mask.node-mask* is the mask to be applied to the network and node. Place 1s in the bit positions to be masked.
- *service-type* is the SAP service type to filter. Each SAP service type is identified by a hexadecimal number. 0 matches all services. Two examples are 4 (file server) and 7 (print server).
- *server-name* is the name of the server providing the specified service type.

The **ipx input-sap-filter** and **ipx output-sap-filter** commands place a SAP filter on an interface. The use of **input** or **output** determines whether the SAP updates are filtered before entry into the SAP table, or whether the SAP table contents are filtered before the SAP update is sent out on an interface. The syntax for these commands is as follows:

```
Router(config-if)#ipx input-sap-filter access-list-number
Router(config-if)#ipx output-sap-filter access-list-number
```

In order to help you understand the procedure for applying SAP filters, the next two sections step you through two examples of filtering SAP traffic on an IPX network.

IPX Output SAP Filter Example

In Figure 10-20, the goal is to allow only file services (SAP type 4) for FS-A and FS-B to be sent out the Serial 0 port of Router B.

Figure 10-20 *Permit File Services Only*

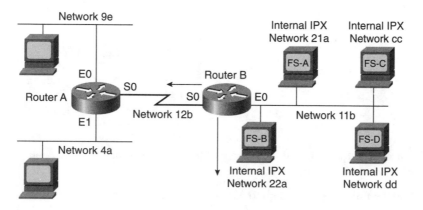

The configuration in Example 10-10 would be applied to Router B to accomplish this goal. (Assume that IPX has been properly configured on the router prior to this configuration.)

Example 10-10 *IPX Output SAP Filter*

```
Router(config)#access-list 1000 permit 21a 4
Router(config)#access-list 1000 permit 22a 4
Router(config)#interface serial 0
Router(config-if)#ipx output-sap-filter 1000
```

Table 10-7 explains some of the key command parameters in Example 10-10.

Table 10-7   *Command Highlights and Explanations from Example 10-10*

access-list 1000 permit 21a 4 Command	Description
1000	An access list number in the Novell SAP filter range.
permit	SAP services matching selected parameters will be permitted.
21a	Source network address of SAP advertisement.
4	Type of SAP service. Advertises file service.

Table 10-7   *Command Highlights and Explanations from Example 10-10 (Continued)*

access-list 1000 permit 21a 4 Command	Description
1000	Access list number.
Permit	SAP services matching parameters will be forwarded.
22a	Source network address of SAP advertisement.
4	Type of SAP service; advertises file service.
ipx output-sap-filter 1000 Command	**Description**
1000	Applies list 1000 to interface Serial 0 as an output SAP filter.

As a result of the configuration in Example 10-10, only file services from FS-A and FS-B are advertised across Router B's Serial 0 interface.

IPX Input SAP Filter Example

In Figure 10-21, the goal is to prevent all print services from the Token Ring network where file server A and B (FS-A and FS-B) reside from being added to the SIT of Router B.

Figure 10-21   *Block Print Services*

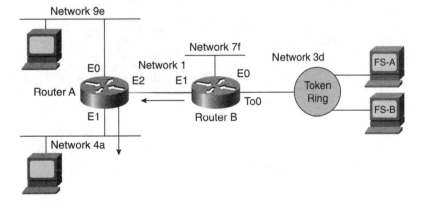

The configuration in Example 10-11 would be applied to Router B to accomplish this goal (assuming that IPX has been properly configured on the router prior to this configuration).

Example 10-11 *IPX Input SAP Filter*

```
Router(config)#access-list 1001 deny -1 7
Router(config)#access-list 1001 permit -1
Router(config)#interface Token 0
Router(config-if)#ipx input-sap-filter 1001
```

Table 10-8 explains some of the key command parameters in Example 10-11.

Table 10-8 *Command Highlights and Explanations from Example 10-11*

access-list 1001 deny -1 7 Command	Description
1001	An access list number in the Novell SAP filter range.
deny	SAP services matching selected parameters will be blocked.
-1	Any source network.
7	Type of SAP service. Advertises print service.

access-list 1001 permit -1 Command	Description
1001	Access list number.
permit	SAP services matching parameters will be forwarded.
-1	Any source network number.

ipx input-sap-filter 1001 Command	Description
1001	Places list 1001 on interface Serial 0 as an input SAP filter.

As a result of the configuration in Example 10-11, print server advertisements from file servers A and B (FS-A and FS-B) will not be entered into the SIT table of Router B and therefore will not be advertised across the Ethernet link to Router B.

Verifying/Displaying IPX Access Lists

Use the **show ipx interface** command to verify whether an IPX access list is applied to the interface. Use the **show ipx access-list** command to display the contents of the IPX access lists.

Example 10-12 demonstrates how the **show ipx interface** command verifies that an IPX access list is applied to the interface. The highlighted output from this example shows that access list 801 is applied to the Ethernet 0 interface.

Example 10-12 *show ipx interface Command Verifies That an IPX Access List Has Been Applied to an Interface*

```
Router#show ipx int e0
Ethernet0 is up, line protocol is up
  IPX address is 11.00e0.1e5d.ae2f, NOVELL-ETHER [up]
  Delay of this IPX network, in ticks is 1 throughput 0 link delay 0
  IPXWAN processing not enabled on this interface.
  IPX SAP update interval is 60 seconds
  IPX type 20 propagation packet forwarding is disabled
  Incoming access list is 801
  Outgoing access list is not set
  IPX helper access list is not set
  SAP GNS processing enabled, delay 0 ms, output filter list is not set
  SAP Input filter list is not set
  SAP Output filter list is not set
  SAP Router filter list is not set
  Input filter list is not set
  Output filter list is not set
  Router filter list is not set
  Netbios Input host access list is not set
<text omitted>
```

Example 10-13 demonstrates how the **show ipx access-list** command displays the contents of the IPX access lists.

Example 10-13 *show ipx access-list Command Displays the Contents of an IPX Access List*

```
Router#show ipx access-list
IPX standard access list 801
    permit 12 FFFFFFFF
    permit 22 FFFFFFFF
```

IPX Command Summary

Table 10-9 briefly describes the IPX-related commands covered in this chapter.

Table 10-9 *IPX-Related Commands*

Command	Description
ipx routing	Enables the IPX routing protocol globally.
ipx network *node*	Enables the IPX routing protocol on an interface.
show ipx interface	Displays the interface-specific IPX protocol information configured, including IPX network.node address and filter information.

continues

Table 10-9 *IPX-Related Commands (Continued)*

Command	Description
access-list *access-list-number*	Creates a standard or extended IPX access list or an IPX SAP filter.
ipx access-group *access-list-number*	Applies an IPX access list to an interface.
ipx input-sap-filter *access-list-number*	Applies an input SAP filter to an interface.
ipx output-sap-filter *access-list-number*	Applies an output SAP filter to an interface.
show ipx access-list	Displays configured IPX access list parameters.
show ipx route	Displays the IPX routing table.
debug ipx routing activity	Displays routing updates as they occur.
debug ipx sap activity	Displays SAP update information.

Summary

In this chapter, you learned about the operation of the IPX protocol. You saw how IPX is used to define a network and node so that each station in the internetwork can be identified. You read about how to enable the IPX routing feature on a Cisco router to interconnect these IPX networks. This chapter discussed the different types of IPX encapsulation and how to configure the router to communicate with IPX devices. Finally, you learned how to control the traffic on an IPX network with access lists.

Review Questions

1 How many bits are in an IPX address?

2 What is used as the node portion of the address?

3 Which command enables the IPX rip routing process in a Cisco router?

4 Where do IPX network numbers come from?

5 How many Layer 2 encapsulation types exist for IPX Ethernet networks?

6 What is Cisco's default encapsulation type for IPX interfaces?

7 What is the default IPX encapsulation type for NetWare 3.12 and above?

8 What type of network number is used to identify the services of an IPX server?

9 How does an IPX client find a server?

10   What does a router build in order to advertise IPX services?

11   What is the access list number range for an extended IPX access list?

12   What is the access list number range for an IPX SAP filter?

13   Which command is used to verify the application of an access list to an interface?

14   Which routing metric is used by IPX RIP?

15   How often does an IPX server send out SAP updates?

PART IV

Extending the Network to WANs

Upon completion of this chapter, you will be able to perform the following tasks:

- Configure HDLC or PPP at both ends of a connection to allow exchange of data between sites, given a leased line connecting two sites.

- Configure Password Authentication Protocol (PAP) and Challenge Handshake Authentication Protocol (CHAP) to limit access to a secure site, given a company intranet with restricted access.

- Verify proper configuration and troubleshoot an incorrect configuration so that data travels as intended across the link, given an existing network using an HDLC or PPP link.

CHAPTER 11

Establishing Serial Point-to-Point Connections

This chapter introduces the concepts, terminology, and procedures for installing and connecting to WAN service providers. It also describes Cisco's proprietary HDLC protocol and the PPP protocol.

WAN Overview

A wide-area network (WAN) differs from a local-area network (LAN). Unlike a LAN, which connects workstations, peripherals, terminals, and other devices in a single building or other small geographic area, a WAN makes data connections across a broad geographic area. Companies use a WAN to connect various company sites so that information can be exchanged between distant offices, as illustrated in Figure 11-1.

Figure 11-1 *WAN Services*

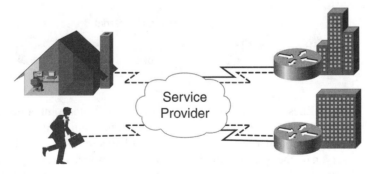

Because the cost of building out a global network to connect remote sites can be astronomical, WAN services are generally leased from service providers. You must subscribe to an outside WAN provider to use network resources that your organization does not own. Within the cloud (that is, the WAN connection that you lease), the service provider uses a portion of its network that you leased to transport the information. Connection requirements vary depending on user requirements and costs.

NOTE	The signaling in the cloud might be proprietary in nature and is not discussed in this book.

WAN Connectivity Options

Many options are available for WAN connectivity. However, not all of these services are available in all areas. Figure 11-2 illustrates three of the connection types you might select. Each is described in the following list.

Figure 11-2 *WAN Connectivity Options*

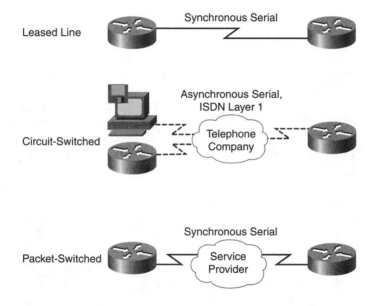

- **Leased lines**—A leased line, also known as a point-to-point or dedicated connection, provides a single preestablished WAN communications path from the customer premises through a service provider network to a remote network. This connection is reserved by the service provider for the client's private use. Leased lines eliminate the issues that arise with a shared connection, but they are costly. Leased lines are typically employed over synchronous serial connections up to T3/E3 speeds, or 45 Mbps, with guaranteed bandwidth availability.

- **Circuit switched**—Circuit switched is a WAN switching method in which a dedicated circuit path must exist between sender and receiver for the duration of the call. Circuit switching is used by the service provider network when providing basic telephone service or Integrated Services Digital Network (ISDN). Circuit-switched connections are commonly used in environments that require only sporadic WAN usage. Basic telephone service is typically employed over an asynchronous serial connection with a modem.

- **Packet switched**—Packet switched is a WAN switching method in which network devices share a single point-to-point link to transport packets from a source to a destination across a carrier network. Packet-switched networks use virtual circuits (VCs) that provide end-to-end connectivity. Physical connections are provided by programmed switching devices. Packet headers generally identify the destination. Packet switching offers services similar to those of leased lines, except the line is shared, and the cost of the service is lower. Like leased lines, packet-switched networks are often employed over serial connections with speeds ranging from 56 Kbps to T3/E3 speeds.

WAN Terminology

Many terms and concepts are associated with the WAN. Although it is not within the scope of this book to discuss operation within the WAN cloud, it is important to understand some common terminology. Figure 11-3 illustrates a typical WAN setup and highlights the WAN terminology discussed in the following list.

Figure 11-3 *WAN Terminology*

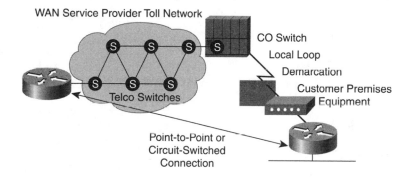

When your organization subscribes to an outside WAN provider for network resources, the provider assigns your organization the parameters for making the WAN link. Here are some commonly used terms for the main physical parts:

- **Customer premises equipment (CPE)**—Devices physically located on the subscriber's premises. The equipment includes both devices owned by the subscriber and devices leased to the subscriber by the service provider.

- **Demarcation (or demarc)**—The juncture at which the CPE ends and the local loop portion of the service begins. It often occurs at a telecommunication closet on the client's premises.

- **Local loop (or "last-mile")**—Cabling (usually copper wiring) that extends from the demarc into the WAN service provider's central office.

- **Central office (CO) switch**—A telco switching facility that provides the nearest point of presence for the provider's WAN service. Inside the long-distance toll network are several types of central offices.

- **Toll network**—The collective telco switches and facilities (called trunks) inside the WAN provider's cloud. The caller's traffic might cross a trunk to a primary center, then go to a sectional center, and then to a regional or international carrier center as the call goes the long distance to its destination. Switches operate in provider offices with toll charges based on tariffs or authorized rates.

WAN Serial Line Standards

To make a synchronous serial leased line or packet-switched WAN connection such as a Frame Relay connection, Cisco devices support the following Layer 1 serial standards:

- EIA/TIA-232
- EIA/TIA-449
- V.35
- X.21
- EIA-530

Figure 11-4 illustrates the different physical connectors for the serial interfaces.

Figure 11-4 *Layer 1 Serial Standards*

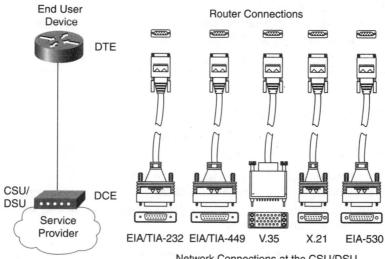

When you order the serial cable for a Cisco router, you receive a DB-60 shielded serial transition cable that has the appropriate connector for the standard you specify. The router end of the shielded serial transition cable has a DB-60 connector, which connects to the DB-60 port on a serial WAN interface card. The other end of the serial transition cable is available with the connector appropriate for the standard you specify. This depends on the connection type of your data communications equipment (DCE) device. The documentation for the device to which you want to connect should indicate the standard used for that device.

NOTE   Although many Cisco routers use the DB-60 connector, some interfaces, such as the WAN Interface Card (WIC), include a SmartSerial interface. The 4000 series routers also have an interface that uses a DB-50 connector. For more information on these interface types, check the documentation at CCO www.cisco.com.

Your customer premises equipment is the data terminal equipment (DTE), and the DCE is the device used to convert the user data from the DTE into a form acceptable to the WAN service provider (for example, channel service unit/data service unit [CSU/DSU]). The synchronous serial port is configured as DTE or DCE (except EIA/TIA-530, which is DTE only), depending on the attached cable. If the port is configured as DTE, however, it will require external clocking from the CSU/DSU or other DCE device.

NOTE	DCE cables are not typically used to connect to provider service. They are most commonly found in back-to-back laboratory router connections. In this application, one router has a DCE cable and connects to a DTE cable on another router. The DCE router must be configured to provide clocking.

WAN Layer 2 Encapsulation

As we move up the layers of the OSI model, serial devices must encapsulate data in a frame format at Layer 2. Different services can use different framing formats.

To ensure that the correct protocol is used, you need to configure the appropriate Layer 2 encapsulation type. The choice of protocol depends on the WAN technology and communicating equipment. Figure 11-5 shows the protocols that are associated with the three WAN connectivity options.

Figure 11-5 *Layer 2 WAN Encapsulation Types Based on Connection Type*

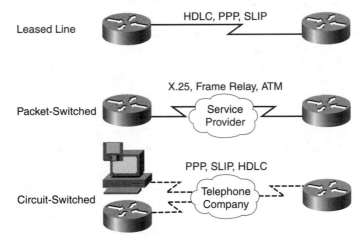

Typical WAN encapsulation types include the following:

- **Cisco High-Level Data Link Control (HDLC)**—HDLC is the default encapsulation type on point-to-point dedicated links, and circuit-switched connections. Cisco HDLC is a bit-oriented synchronous data link layer protocol typically used when communicating between two Cisco devices. HDLC is covered in more detail later in this chapter.

- **Point-to-Point Protocol (PPP)**—PPP provides router-to-router and host-to-network connections over synchronous and asynchronous circuits. PPP was designed to work with several network layer protocols, such as IP and IPX. It also has built-in security mechanisms such as Password Authentication Protocol (PAP) and Challenge Handshake Authentication Protocol (CHAP). PPP is covered in more detail later in this chapter.

- **Serial Line Internet Protocol (SLIP)**—SLIP is a standard protocol for point-to-point serial connections using TCP/IP. SLIP has been largely displaced by PPP.

- **X.25/Link Access Procedure, Balanced (LAPB)**—X.25/LAPB is an ITU-T standard that defines how connections between DTE and DCE are maintained for remote terminal access and computer communications in public data networks. X.25 specifies LAPB, a data link layer protocol. X.25 is a predecessor to Frame Relay.

- **Frame Relay**—Frame Relay is an industry-standard switched data link layer protocol that handles multiple virtual circuits. Frame Relay is a next-generation to X.25 that is streamlined to eliminate some of the time-consuming processes that were employed in X.25, such as error correction and flow control. Frame Relay is covered in more detail in Chapter 13, "Establishing a Frame Relay PVC Connection."

- **Asynchronous Transfer Mode (ATM)**—ATM is the international standard for cell relay in which multiple service types (such as voice, video, and data) are conveyed in fixed-length (53-byte) cells. Fixed-length cells allow processing to occur in hardware, thereby reducing transit delays. ATM is designed to take advantage of high-speed transmission media such as E3, Synchronous Optical Network (SONET), and T3.

NOTE   SLIP, X.25, and ATM are not covered further in this book.

NOTE   This chapter only discusses how to employ HDLC and PPP protocols on a leased line. Later in this book, you will configure a Frame Relay packet-switched connection and PPP on an ISDN BRI connection. For more information on circuit switching and ISDN, see Chapter 12, "Completing an ISDN BRI Call." For information on packet switching and Frame Relay, see Chapter 13.

The next few sections discuss the serial Layer 2 framing formats of PPP and HDLC in greater detail. The first protocol we will look at is HDLC.

Configuring HDLC Encapsulation

HDLC is often used for leased line links between Cisco routers. HDLC is an ISO standard bit-oriented data-link protocol that encapsulates data on synchronous serial data links. HDLC does not inherently support multiple protocols on a single link because it does not have a standard way to indicate which protocol it is carrying. You might recall from Ethernet frames that the type field or DSAP field indicates which Layer 3 protocol is used to transport the data. The lack of a protocol field limits standard HDLC. HDLC specifies a data encapsulation method on synchronous serial links using frame characters and checksums.

Cisco offers a proprietary version of HDLC. The Cisco HDLC frame uses a proprietary type field that acts as a protocol field, which makes it possible for multiple network-layer protocols to share the same serial link. This implementation is proprietary and can only be used between devices that can interpret the Cisco HDLC frame type. Figure 11-6 illustrates the frame formats for ISO standard HDLC and Cisco's proprietary version of HDLC.

Figure 11-6 *HDLC Frame Formats*

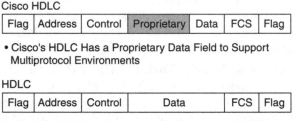

By default, synchronous serial lines use the HDLC serial encapsulation method (the term "HDLC" here refers to the Cisco-enhanced HDLC protocol). If the serial interface is configured with another encapsulation protocol, however, and you want to change the encapsulation back to HDLC, you need to enter the interface configuration mode of the interface you want to change. Enter the following interface configuration command to specify HDLC encapsulation on the interface:

```
Router(config-if)#encapsulation hdlc
```

Cisco's HDLC is a point-to-point protocol that can be used on leased lines between two devices supporting Cisco proprietary HDLC encapsulation. If communicating with a non-Cisco device, synchronous PPP is a more viable option.

PPP Encapsulation Overview

Unlike HDLC, the PPP encapsulation is not proprietary. For this reason, it is often used to connect dissimilar vendor devices. Figure 11-7 illustrates how PPP provides end-to-end connectivity for multiple protocols.

Figure 11-7 *PPP Overview*

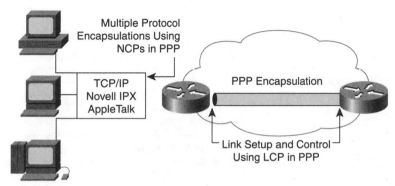

Developers of the Internet designed PPP to make the connection for point-to-point links. PPP, described in RFCs 1661 and 1332, encapsulates network-layer protocol information over point-to-point links. RFC 1661 is superseded by RFC 2153, *PPP Vendor Extensions*.

NOTE	You can find the PPP RFCs at ftp://ftpeng.cisco.com/fred/rfc-index/rfc.html.

You can configure PPP on the following types of physical interfaces:

- Asynchronous serial
- HSSI (High-Speed Serial Interface)
- ISDN
- Synchronous serial

PPP Components: NCP and LCP

Functionally, Point-to-Point Protocol (PPP) is a data link layer protocol with network layer services. As a result of this characteristic, PPP can be broken into two sublayers. These sublayers enhance PPP's functionality. Figure 11-8 shows the breakout of these layers.

Figure 11-8 *PPP Sublayers*

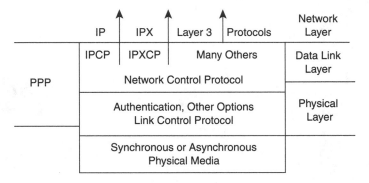

PPP uses its Network Control Program (NCP) component to encapsulate multiple protocols.

PPP uses another of its major components, the Link Control Protocol (LCP), to negotiate and set up control options on the WAN data link.

With its lower-level functions, PPP can use the following:

- Synchronous physical media
- Asynchronous physical media such as those that use basic telephone service for modem dialup connections
- ISDN

PPP offers a rich set of services that control setting up a data link. These services are options in LCP and are primarily used to negotiate and check frames to implement the point-to-point controls an administrator specifies for the call.

With its higher-level functions, PPP carries packets from several network layer protocols in NCPs. These are functional fields containing standardized codes to indicate the network layer protocol type that PPP encapsulates.

One of the major benefits of the PPP protocol is the functionality of the LCP options, as documented in Table 11-1.

Table 11-1   *LCP Options*

Feature	How It Operates	Protocol
Authentication	Requires a password.	PAP
	Performs Challenge Handshake.	CHAP
Compression	Compresses data at the source; decompress at the destination.	Stacker or Predictor
Error Detection	Monitors data dropped on link.	Magic Number
	Avoids frame looping.	Quality
Multilink	Loads balancing across multiple links.	Multilink Protocol (MP)

RFC 1548 describes PPP operation and LCP configuration options. RFC 1548 is updated by RFC 1570, PPP LCP Extensions. You can find these RFCs at ftp://ftpeng.cisco.com/fred/rfc-index/rfc.html.

Cisco routers that use PPP encapsulation might include the LCP options shown in Table 11-1:

- Authentication options require that the calling side of the link enter information to help ensure that the caller has the network administrator's permission to make the call. Peer routers exchange authentication messages. Two alternatives are

    — Password Authentication Protocol (PAP)

    — Challenge Handshake Authentication Protocol (CHAP)

- Compression options increase the effective throughput on PPP connections by reducing the amount of data in the frame that must travel across the link. The protocol decompresses the frame at its destination.

    Two compression protocols available in Cisco routers are Stacker and Predictor.

- Error-detection mechanisms with PPP allow a process to identify fault conditions. The Quality and Magic Number options help ensure a reliable, loop-free data link.

- Cisco IOS Release 11.1 and later support multilink PPP. This alternative provides load balancing over the router interfaces that PPP uses.

    Packet fragmentation and sequencing, as specified in RFC 1717, splits the load for PPP and sends fragments over parallel circuits. In some cases, this "bundle" of multilink PPP pipes functions as a single logical link, improving throughput and reducing latency between peer routers. RFC 1990, *The PPP Multilink Protocol (MP)*, makes RFC 1717 obsolete.

NOTE   This book discusses only the PAP and CHAP authentication LCP options. To learn more about other LCP options, refer to the documentation CD or Cisco's Web site at www. cisco.com.

Establishing a PPP Connection

In order for devices to communicate using PPP, the protocol must first open a session. Figure 11-9 illustrates this connection establishment.

Figure 11-9 *PPP Connection Establishment*

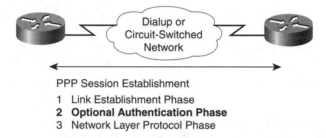

A PPP session establishment has three phases:

Step 1   **Link establishment phase**—In this phase, each PPP device sends LCP packets to configure and test the data link. LCP packets contain a Configuration Option field that allows devices to negotiate the use of options such as the maximum receive unit, compression of certain PPP fields, and the link authentication protocol. If a configuration option is not included in an LCP packet, the default value for that configuration option is assumed.

Step 2   **Authentication phase (optional)**—After the link has been established and the authentication protocol chosen, the peer can be authenticated. Authentication, if used, takes place before entering the network layer protocol phase.

PPP supports two authentication protocols: PAP and CHAP. Both of these protocols are detailed in RFC 1334, *PPP Authentication Protocols*. However, RFC 1994, *PPP Challenge Handshake Authentication Protocol*, makes RFC 1334 obsolete.

Step 3   **Network layer protocol phase**—In this phase, the PPP devices send NCP packets to choose and configure one or more network layer protocols, such as IP. As soon as each of the chosen network layer protocols has been configured, datagrams from each network layer protocol can be sent over he link.

Configuring PPP Encapsulation and PAP and CHAP Authentication

When configuring PPP authentication, you can select PAP or CHAP. As will be shown, CHAP is the preferred protocol. A brief description of each authentication method follows.

PAP Authentication

PAP provides a simple method for a remote node to establish its identity using a two-way handshake. PAP is done only upon initial link establishment. Figure 11-10 illustrates the transactions that take place during PAP authentication.

Figure 11-10 *PAP Authentication*

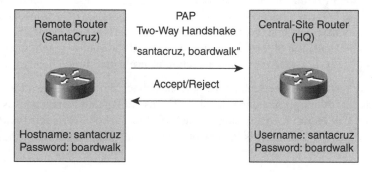

After the PPP link establishment phase is complete, a username-and-password pair is repeatedly sent by the remote node to the router until authentication is acknowledged or the connection is terminated.

PAP is not a strong authentication protocol. Passwords are sent across the link in clear text, and there is no protection from playback or repeated trial-and-error attacks. The remote node is in control of the frequency and timing of the login attempts. A clear-text password, however, may be fine in environments that use token-type passwords that change with each authentication.

CHAP Authentication

CHAP is a stronger authentication method than PAP. CHAP is used at the startup of a link, and periodically, to verify the identity of the remote node using a three-way handshake. CHAP is done upon initial link establishment and can be repeated any time after the link has been established. Figure 11-11 illustrates the transactions that take place during CHAP authentication.

Figure 11-11 *CHAP Authentication*

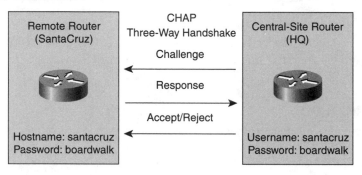

After the PPP link establishment phase is complete, the local router sends a "challenge" message to the remote node. The remote node responds with a value calculated using a one-way hash function (typically MD5). The local router checks the response against its own calculation of the expected hash value. If the values match, the authentication is acknowledged. Otherwise, the connection is terminated immediately.

CHAP provides protection against playback attack through the use of a variable challenge value that is unique and unpredictable. The use of repeated challenges is intended to limit the time of exposure to any single attack. The local router (or a third-party authentication server such as TACACS) is in control of the frequency and timing of the challenges.

Enabling PPP Encapsulation and PAP or CHAP Authentication

To enable PPP encapsulation and PAP or CHAP authentication on an interface, you need to configure the items listed in Table 11-2.

Table 11-2 *PPP Authentication Tasks*

Authenticating Router (The Router That Received the Call)	Router to Be Authenticated (The Router That Initiated the Call)
ppp encapsulation	**ppp encapsulation**
hostname	**hostname**
username	**username**
ppp authentication	**ppp authentication**
	ppp pap sent-username (PAP only)

To enable PPP encapsulation, enter interface configuration mode. Enter the **encapsulation ppp** interface configuration command to specify PPP encapsulation on the interface:

```
Router(config-if)#encapsulation ppp
```

Before you configure PPP authentication, the interface must be configured for PPP encapsulation. Enable PAP or CHAP authentication by following these steps:

Step 1 Verify that each router has a host name assigned to it. The host name will be used as a "username" to identify the router to its PPP peer. To assign a host name, enter the **hostname** *name* command in global configuration mode:

```
Router(config)#hostname name
```

The *name* option must match a user name that is configured on the peer router at the other end of the link.

Step 2 On each router, define the username and password to expect from the remote router with the **username** *name* **password** *password* global configuration command:

```
Router(config)#username name password password
```

The *name* option is the host name of the remote router. Note that it is case-sensitive.

The *password* option sets the password that will be used for the connection. On Cisco routers, the password must be the same for both routers. In pre-Release 11.2 IOS software, this password was displayed in the configuration as an encrypted, secret password. As of Release 11.2, the password is displayed as a plain-text password and is not shown encrypted. To hide the passwords from view in the configuration on your IOS router, enter the **service password-encryption** command while in global configuration mode. (This command affects only how passwords are displayed in the router configuration. CHAP passwords are still exchanged as MD5 encrypted values.)

Add a username entry for each remote system that the local router communicates with and requires authentication from. The remote device must also have a username entry for the local router. Remember that the router will match these usernames with the remote router's host name for authentication.

Step 3 Configure PPP authentication with the **ppp authentication** interface configuration command. Here is its full syntax:

```
Router(config-if)#ppp authentication {chap | chap pap | pap chap | pap}
```

NOTE   If both PAP and CHAP are enabled, the first method specified will be requested during link negotiation. If the peer suggests using the second method or simply refuses the first method, the second method will be tried.

Sample PAP/CHAP Configurations

In Figure 11-12, a two-way challenge occurs. The host name on one router must match the username that the other router has configured for it. The passwords must also match.

Figure 11-12 *Sample PAP Configuration*

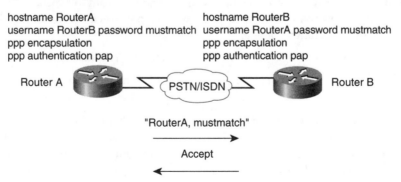

Example 11-1 demonstrates a two-way PAP authentication configuration. Both routers authenticate and are authenticated, so the PAP authentication commands mirror each other.

The PAP username and password each router sends must match those specified on the **username** *name* **password** *password* command of the other router.

Example 11-1 *PAP Authentication Configuration*

```
hostname RouterA                          hostname RouterB
username RouterB password mustmatch       username RouterA password mustmatch
interface serial 0                        interface serial 0
ip address 10.0.1.1 255.255.255.0         ip address 10.0.1.2 255.255.255.0
encapsulation ppp                         encapsulation ppp
ppp authentication pap                    ppp authentication pap
```

Verifying PPP Encapsulation Configuration

When PPP is configured, you can check its LCP and NCP states using the **show interface** command. Use the **show interface** command to verify proper configuration. Example 11-2 provides some sample output from the **show interface** command.

Example 11-2 *show interface Verifies Proper PPP Configuration*

```
Router#show interface s0
Serial0 is up, line protocol is up
  Hardware is HD64570
  Internet address is 10.140.1.2/24
  MTU 1500 bytes, BW 1544 Kbit, DLY 20000 usec, rely 255/255, load 1/255
  Encapsulation PPP, loopback not set, keepalive set (10 sec)
  LCP Open
  Open: IPCP, CDPCP
  Last input 00:00:05, output 00:00:05, output hang never
  Last clearing of "show interface" counters never
  Queueing strategy: fifo
  Output queue 0/40, 0 drops; input queue 0/75, 0 drops
  5 minute input rate 0 bits/sec, 0 packets/sec
  5 minute output rate 0 bits/sec, 0 packets/sec
     38021 packets input, 5656110 bytes, 0 no buffer
     Received 23488 broadcasts, 0 runts, 0 giants, 0 throttles
     0 input errors, 0 CRC, 0 frame, 0 overrun, 0 ignored, 0 abort
     38097 packets output, 2135697 bytes, 0 underruns
     0 output errors, 0 collisions, 6045 interface resets
     0 output buffer failures, 0 output buffers swapped out
     482 carrier transitions
     DCD=up  DSR=up  DTR=up  RTS=up  CTS=up
```

Notice in Example 11-2 that LCP is open. This means that the connection between the two PPP devices has been negotiated. This would include the authentication phase if configured. The next line indicates which NCP protocols have been opened—in this case, CDPCP (Cisco Discover Protocol Control Protocol) and IPCP (Internet Protocol Control Protocol).

Example 11-3 shows the router output for the authenticating and authenticated router when **debug ppp authentication** is enabled. Use this command to display the exchange sequence as it occurs.

Example 11-3 *Output from **debug ppp authentication** Verifying PPP Authentication*

```
Router# debug ppp authentication
4d20h: %LINK-3-UPDOWN: Interface Serial0, changed state to up
4d20h: Se0 PPP: Treating connection as a dedicated line
4d20h: Se0 PPP: Phase is AUTHENTICATING, by both
4d20h: Se0 CHAP: O CHALLENGE id 2 len 28 from "left"
4d20h: Se0 CHAP: I CHALLENGE id 3 len 28 from "right"
4d20h: Se0 CHAP: O RESPONSE id 3 len 28 from "left"
4d20h: Se0 CHAP: I RESPONSE id 2 len 28 from "right"
4d20h: Se0 CHAP: O SUCCESS id 2 len 4
4d20h: Se0 CHAP: I SUCCESS id 3 len 4
4d20h: %LINEPROTO-5-UPDOWN: Line protocol on Interface Serial0, changed state to up
```

Example 11-4 highlights one router's **debug** output for a two-way PAP authentication.

Example 11-4 *Router Output for Two-Way PAP Authentication*

```
Se0 PPP: Phase is AUTHENTICATING, by both     (Two-way authentication)
Se0 PAP: O AUTH-REQ id 4 len 18 from "left"   (Outgoing authentication request)
Se0 PAP: I AUTH-REQ id 1 len 18 from "right"  (Incoming authentication request)
Se0 PAP: Authenticating peer right            (Authenticating incoming)
Se0 PAP: O AUTH-ACK id 1 len 5                (Outgoing acknowledgment)
Se0 PAP: I AUTH-ACK id 4 len 5                (Incoming acknowledgment)
```

Serial Point-to-Point Connection Command Summary

Table 11-3 summarizes the commands relevant to point-to-point connections.

Table 11-3 *Serial Point-to-Point Connection-Related Commands*

Command	Description
encapsulation hdlc	Enables HDLC encapsulation on an interface.
encapsulation ppp	Enables PPP on a PPP interface.
ppp authentication pap	Enables PAP authentication on a PPP interface.
ppp authentication chap	Enables CHAP authentication on an interface.
username *name* **password** *password*	Establishes a username-based authentication system.
show interface	Shows the status of an interface, including encapsulation method.
debug ppp authentication	Debugs the PAP or CHAP authentication process.

Summary

In this chapter, you learned about the different Layers 1 and 2 standards involving point-to-point serial connections. You learned about Cisco's proprietary HDLC and the Internet standard PPP encapsulations. You also learned how to authenticate routers using PPP authentication such as PAP and CHAP. Finally, this chapter discussed the methods used to verify and test these configurations.

Review Questions

1 What are three connection types that can be used to connect routers over a WAN?

2 What is the default Layer 2 encapsulation type of Cisco serial interfaces?

3 Which encapsulation option discussed in this chapter would you select if you were connecting a Cisco router to a non-Cisco router?

4 How do you enable PPP encapsulation?

5 What are the two PPP authentication options?

6 Name one other PPP option.

7 How do you set the password for CHAP and PAP?

8 If both PAP and CHAP are configured, which method is tried first?

9 Which authentication option sends the password in clear text?

10 Which command is used to check the encapsulation?

Upon completion of this chapter, you will be able to perform the following tasks:

- Identify the physical components and determine how the connection operates, given a requirement to enable an ISDN BRI connection.

- Understand how to configure ISDN BRI and standard DDR on a BRI interface and complete the call, given a physical ISDN BRI connection.

- Verify proper operation with **show** and **debug** commands, given a dial-on-demand ISDN connection.

CHAPTER 12

Completing an ISDN BRI Call

This chapter describes the Integrated Services Digital Network (ISDN) Basic Rate Interface (BRI) and standard dial-on-demand routing (DDR). The purpose of this chapter is to provide a high-level overview of ISDN BRI and show you how to enable it using Cisco's DDR capabilities. This chapter also explains how to configure DDR over ISDN BRI on a Cisco router.

You read in the previous chapter that ISDN is a circuit-switched solution that allows for data transfer between data devices. ISDN is very valuable in today's networking strategy because it allows administrators to provide reliable high-speed links to remote offices without the high cost of dedicated circuits. ISDN is ideal for the telecommuter or the remote office that needs only sporadic access to the central site. In order to use these services with your Cisco router, you must first understand the ISDN technology and then learn how to configure it on your router. The next few pages provide an overview of ISDN BRI technology.

ISDN BRI Overview

ISDN stands for Integrated Services Digital Network. ISDN refers to a collection of standards that define a digital architecture that provides an integrated voice/data capability to the customer premises facility, utilizing the Public Switched Telephone Network (PSTN). The ISDN standards define the hardware and call setup schemes for end-to-end digital connectivity. Prior to ISDN, many telephone companies used digital networks within their clouds but used analog lines for the local access loop between the cloud and the actual customer site. Bringing digital connectivity via ISDN to the local site has many benefits:

- The capability to carry a variety of user-traffic feeds. ISDN provides access to all-digital facilities for video, voice, packet-switched data, and enriched telephone network services.

- Much faster call setup using out-of-band (Delta [D] channel) signaling than modem connections. For example, ISDN calls can often be set up and completed in less than one second.

- Much faster data transfer rate using Bearer (B) channel services at 64 kbps per channel as opposed to common modem alternatives of 28.8 to 56 kbps. With multiple B channels, ISDN offers users more bandwidth on wide-area networks (WANs) (for example, two B channels equal 128 kbps) than they receive with a leased line at 56 kbps in North America or 64 kbps in much of the rest of the world.

Figure 12-1 illustrates the different uses for ISDN technology.

Figure 12-1 *What Is ISDN?*

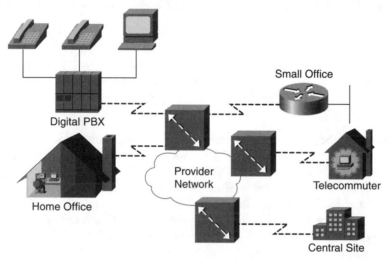

ISDN is quickly becoming the transport of choice for applications using remote connectivity, for access to the Internet, and for the World Wide Web. Before the tremendous growth of these applications, many in the United States believed ISDN was a solution looking for a problem.

Work on standards for ISDN began in the late 1960s. A comprehensive set of ISDN recommendations was published in 1984 and is continuously updated by the Consultative Committee for International Telegraph and Telephone (CCITT)—an organization that has since become the International Telecommunication Union Telecommunication Standardization Sector (ITU-T). ITU-T groups and organizes ISDN protocols according to the general topic areas outlined in Table 12-1.

Table 12-1   *ISDN Protocols Grouped by Topic Area*

Issue	Protocol	Key Examples
Telephone network and ISDN	E-Series	E.163—International telephone numbering plan
		E.164—International ISDN addressing
ISDN concepts, aspects, and interfaces	I-Series	I.100 series—Concepts, structures, and terminology
Switching and signaling	Q-Series	Q.921—LAPD (Link Access Procedure Dedicated D-channel encapsulation)
		Q.931—ISDN network layer between terminal and switch

The following list elaborates on the ISDN protocol series documented in Table 12-1.

- Protocols that begin with E recommend telephone network standards for ISDN. For example, the E.164 protocol describes international addressing for ISDN.

- Protocols that begin with I deal with concepts, terminology, and general methods. The I.100 series includes general ISDN concepts and the structure of other I-series recommendations. I.200 deals with service aspects of ISDN. I.300 describes network aspects. I.400 describes how the User-Network Interface (UNI) is provided.

- Protocols that begin with Q cover how switching and signaling should operate. The term *signaling* in this context means the process of call setup used. Q.921 describes the ISDN data link processes of LAPD, which functions like Layer 2 processes in the ISO/OSI reference model. Q.931 specifies ISO/OSI reference model Layer 3 functions.

    Q.931 recommends a network layer between the terminal endpoint and the local ISDN switch. This protocol does not impose an end-to-end recommendation. The various ISDN providers and switch types can and do use various implementations of Q.931. Other switches were developed before the standards groups finalized this standard.

Because switch types are not standardized, when configuring the router, you need to specify the type of ISDN switch to which you are connecting. In addition, Cisco routers have **debug** commands to monitor Q.931 and Q.921 processes when an ISDN call is initiated or being terminated.

ISDN Components

ISDN services are made up of many components. In order to configure and troubleshoot ISDN services, it is important to learn these components. The items described in this section define the end-to-end physical and data link layer organization of ISDN.

ISDN specifies two standard access methods, as illustrated in Figure 12-2 and documented in the following list.

Figure 12-2 *ISDN Access Methods*

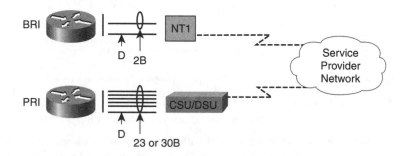

- **Basic Rate Interface (BRI)**—Consists of two 64 kbps Bearer (B) channels plus one 16 kbps Delta (D) channel service. A standard BRI interface is available on many Cisco routers. Any router with a serial interface can be connected to a BRI with a terminal adapter (discussed later in this chapter).

    — BRI is sometimes written as 2B + D. A BRI interface provides two B channels at 64 kbps and an additional 16 kbps D signaling channel.

    — The B channels can be used for digitized speech transmission or for relatively high-speed data transport. ISDN is circuit-switching–oriented. The B channel is the elemental circuit-switching unit.

    — The D channel carries signaling information (for example, call setup) to control calls on B channels at the User-Network Interface (UNI). In addition to carrying signaling information, the D channel can be used to carry subscriber low-rate packet data, such as alarm systems. Although this is a supported feature of many ISDN vendors, implementation and results vary. Traffic over the D channel employs the LAPD data link layer protocol. LAPD is based on High-Level Data Link Control (HDLC).

- **Primary Rate Interface (PRI)**—In North America and Japan, PRI offers twenty-three 64 kbps B channels and one 64 kbps D channel (a T1/DS1 facility).

    — In Europe and much of the rest of the world, PRI offers 30 B channels and a single D channel (an E1 facility).

— PRI uses a data service unit/channel service unit (DSU/CSU) for a T1/E1 connection.

NOTE   ISDN PRI is not discussed in this book. You can find more information about connecting PRI modules to a network at www.cisco.com/univercd/cc/td/doc/product/access/acs_mod/ cis2600/net_mod/conntpri.htm.

BRI Call Processing

Figure 12-3 shows the sequence of events that occurs during the establishment of a BRI call. The following list describes the event sequence in greater detail.

Figure 12-3 *RI Call Processing*

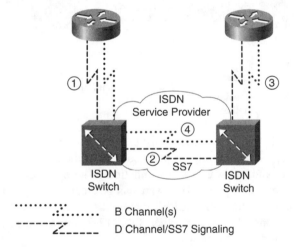

1 The D channel between the router and the ISDN switch is always up. When the call is initiated, the called number is sent to the local ISDN switch. The D channel is used for call setup, signaling, and call termination (the call control functions).

2 The local switch uses the SS7 (Signaling System 7—used by telco switches to set up calls) signaling protocols to set up a path and pass the called number to the terminating ISDN switch.

3 The far-end ISDN switch signals the destination over the D channel.

4 The B channel is then connected end-to-end. A B channel carries the conversation or data. Both B channels can be used simultaneously.

ISDN is the protocol that is used between the endpoints and the local service provider ISDN switch. Within the service provider network, the ISDN call is treated as just a 56- or 64-kbps stream of data and is handled the same as any other stream of data or voice.

ISDN CPE Equipment and Reference Points

Like many WAN protocols, ISDN has many special terms. Figure 12-4 and Table 12-2 detail the types of ISDN equipment you might encounter.

Figure 12-4 *ISDN Equipment Types and Reference Points*

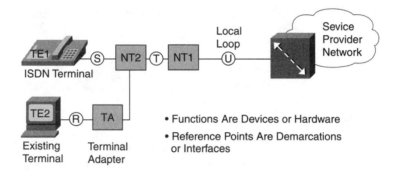

To access the ISDN network, you must use customer premises equipment (CPE) that performs specific functions to properly connect to the ISDN switch. The ISDN standards define device- and hardware-specific functions. These functions represent transitions between the reference points. Hardware can be created to support one or more of these functions. To select the correct CPE, you must be aware of what functions are available and how the functions relate to each other. Table 12-2 defines the customer premises ISDN device types and their functions.

Table 12-2   *ISDN Device Types/Functionality*

Device Type	Device Function
TE1 (Terminal Endpoint 1)	Designates a router as a device having a native ISDN interface.
NT2 (Network Termination 2)	The point at which all ISDN lines at a customer site are aggregated and switched using a customer-switching device. (Seen with an ISDN PBX.)
NT1 (Network Termination 1)	Converts BRI signals into a form used by the ISDN digital line.

Table 12-2   *ISDN Device Types/Functionality (Continued)*

Device Type	Device Function
TE2 (Terminal Endpoint 2)	Designates a router as a device requiring a TA for its BRI signals.
TA (Terminal Adapter)	Converts EIA/TIA-232, V.35, and other signals into BRI signals.

In Europe, the NT1 is CPE equipment that is owned by the Post, Telephone, and Telegraph (PTT). You must therefore buy a device that supports the appropriate connectivity.

In order to connect devices that perform specific functions, as defined in Table 12-2, the devices need to support specific reference points. Because CPEs can include one or more functions, the reference points they use to connect to other devices that support other functions can vary. As a result, the standards do not define interfaces in terms of hardware, but refer to them as *reference points*. A reference point defines a connection type between two functions. In other words, reference points are a series of specifications that define the connection between specific devices, depending on their function in the end-to-end connection.

It is important to know about these interface types because a CPE device, such as a router, can support different reference points, which could result in the need for additional equipment. Figure 12-4 shows the location of each reference point. The reference points that affect the customer side of the ISDN connection are as follows:

- **R**—References the point (connection) that is between a non-ISDN–compatible device and a terminal adapter.

- **S**—References the points that connect into the NT2, or customer-switching device. It is the interface that enables calls between the various customer premises equipment.

- **T**—Electrically identical to the S interface, it references the outbound connection from the NT2 to the ISDN network.

  The electrical similarities between the S and T references are why some interfaces are labeled S/T interface. Although they perform different functions, the port is electrically the same and can be used for either function.

- **U**—References the connection between the NT1 and the ISDN network owned by the telephone company.

Not all Cisco routers include a native ISDN terminal, nor do all of them include interfaces for the same reference point, so you must evaluate each router carefully. Figure 12-5 shows the different types of ISDN equipment and their associated reference points.

Figure 12-5 *ISDN Interfaces*

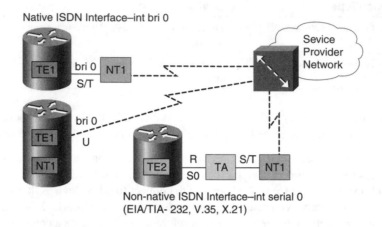

To select a Cisco router, do the following:

1 Determine whether the router supports ISDN BRI. Look on the back of your router for one of the following:

— If you see a connector labeled "BRI," you already have an ISDN interface. With a native ISDN interface already built in, your router is a TE1. Your router already contains the ISDN TA function. (Your router might also have a built-in NT1; if it has a U interface, it has a built-in NT1.)

— If you do not see a connector labeled "BRI," your router can use a serial interface. With non-native interfaces such as serial interfaces, you need to obtain an external TA device and attach it to the serial interface to provide a BRI.

2 Determine whether you or the service provider provides the NT1. An NT1 terminates the local loop of wires to the CO of your ISDN service provider. In the United States, for example, the customer is responsible for the NT1. In Europe, the NT1 is typically provided by the service provider.

If you must supply the NT1, make sure your router has a U interface, or you must purchase an external NT1.

CAUTION Never connect a router with a U interface into an NT1. It will most likely damage the interface.

ISDN Switch Types and SPIDs

ISDN service providers use a variety of switch types for their ISDN services. Services offered by the national Post, Telephone, and Telegraph (PTT) or other carriers vary considerably from nation to nation or region to region. Just like modem standards, each switch type operates slightly differently and has a specific set of call setup requirements. As a result, before you can connect your router to an ISDN service, you must be aware of the switch types used at the CO. You must specify this information during router configuration so that the router can place ISDN network-level calls and send data.

Table 12-3 is a sample of countries and ISDN switch types you are likely to encounter in your provider's ISDN cloud.

Table 12-3   *ISDN Switch Types by Locale*

Country	Switch Type
United States and Canada	AT&T 5ESS and 4ESS; Northern Telecom DMS-100
France	VN2, VN3
Japan	NTT
United Kingdom	Net3 and Net5
Europe	Net3

Some service providers program their switches to emulate another switch type. Therefore, it might be necessary to configure a router to match the emulated switch type for proper operation.

In addition to learning about which switch type your service provider is using, you might also need to know what service provider identifiers (SPIDs) are assigned to your connection. In many cases, such as when configuring the router to connect to a DMS-100 switch, you will need to input the SPIDs.

SPIDs are a series of characters (which can look like phone numbers) that identify you to the switch at the central office. When identified, the switch links the services you ordered to the connection. Remember, ISDN is typically used for dialup connectivity. The SPIDs are processed during each call setup operation.

Enabling ISDN BRI

To enable ISDN BRI, you must perform two tasks:

- Configure ISDN-specific commands
- Configure an encapsulation to use over ISDN

NOTE   The rest of this section concentrates on Task 1 for enabling ISDN BRI, configuring ISDN-specific commands. The section "Step 3: Configuring the Dialer Information" covers Task 2, configuring an encapsulation to use over ISDN.

Before using ISDN BRI, you must define the **isdn switch-type** global or interface command to specify the ISDN switch to which the router connects. The global and interface versions of the **isdn switch-type** command, respectively, are as follows:

```
Router(config)#isdn switch-type switch-type
Router(config-if)isdn switch-type switch-type
```

For ISDN BRI service, Table 12-4 documents sample *switch-type* values.

Table 12-4   *Switch Types for ISDN BRI Service*

switch-type Value	Description
basic-5ess	AT&T basic-rate switches (USA)
basic-dms100	NT (Nortel) DMS-100 (North America)
basic-ni1	National ISDN-1 (North America)
basic-ts013	Australian TS013 switches
basic-net3	Switch type for Net3 in the United Kingdom and Europe
Ntt	NTT ISDN switch (Japan)
None	No specific switch specified

NOTE   Configuring the **isdn switch-type** command globally specifies the ISDN switch type for all ISDN interfaces not explicitly assigned with their own **isdn switch-type** command.

When your ISDN service is installed, the service provider gives you information about your connection. Depending on the switch type used, you might be given two numbers, referred to as SPIDs. Depending on the switch type, you might need to add these to your configuration. For example, the National ISDN-1 and DMS-100 ISDN switches require SPIDs to be configured, but the AT&T 5ESS switch does not.

The format of the SPIDs can vary, depending on the ISDN switch type and specific provider requirements.

Use the **isdn spid1** and **isdn spid2** commands to specify the SPID required to access the ISDN network when your router makes its call to the local ISDN exchange. The syntax for these commands is as follows:

```
Router(config-if)#isdn spid1 spid-number [ldn]
Router(config-if)#isdn spid2 spid-number [ldn]
```

Where:

- *spid-number* identifies the service to which you have subscribed. This value is assigned by the ISDN service provider.

- *ldn* (optional) is the local dial number. This number must match the called-party information coming from the ISDN switch in order to use both B channels on most switches.

NOTE   SPID numbers and switch type information are available from your service provider and should be given to you after the service is set up.

Dial-on-Demand Routing Overview

ISDN services can be used for a variety of networking services. A very useful application for ISDN is dial-on-demand routing (DDR). Now that you have learned how to configure an ISDN interface, you will find out how to configure DDR to bring this interface up when there is a need to transfer traffic.

DDR refers to a collection of Cisco features that allows two or more Cisco routers to establish a dynamic connection over simple dialup facilities to route packets and exchange routing updates on an as-needed basis. DDR is used for low-volume, periodic network connections over the plain old telephone service (POTS) or an ISDN network. Figure 12-6 illustrates a typical DDR setup.

Figure 12-6 *Dial-on-Demand Routing*

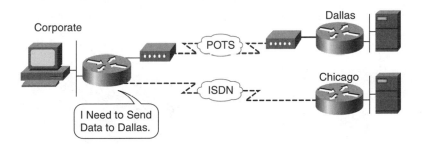

Traditionally, networks have been interconnected by dedicated WAN lines. DDR addresses the need for periodic network connections over a circuit-switched WAN service. By using WAN connections only on an as-needed basis, DDR can reduce WAN usage costs.

NOTE   More advanced features of DDR are beyond the scope of this book. Information on these options can be found on the Cisco web site, on the Documentation CD, or in Cisco Worldwide Training courses, such as Building Scalable Cisco Networks (BSCN). These advanced features include the following:

- **Dialer profiles**—The ability to configure DDR such that the physical interface configurations are separate from the logical configurations required for making a DDR call.

- **Dial backup**—The ability to enable a secondary link when the primary link fails.

- **MultiLink PPP**—The ability to aggregate traffic over multiple ISDN channels simultaneously.

More information on these and other dial subjects can be found at www.cisco.com/univercd/cc/td/doc/product/software/ios120/12cgcr/dial_c/index.htm.

DDR is the process of having the router connect to a public telephone network (or ISDN network) when there is traffic to send, and disconnect when the data transfer is complete. Not all WAN connectivity will be DDR connections. For example, you might also have DDR connections in the following situations:

- Telecommuters need to connect to the company network periodically during the day.

- As a customer, you want to order products through the automated order system that your vendor has in place.

- You have satellite offices that need to send sales transactions or order entry requests to the main computer at the central office.

- Your customers prefer that you send them reports (for example) by e-mail.

Figure 12-7 illustrates the first two uses for DDR connections cited in the preceding list.

Figure 12-7 *DDR Connections Used for Periodic Connections and Small Amounts of Data from a Vendor*

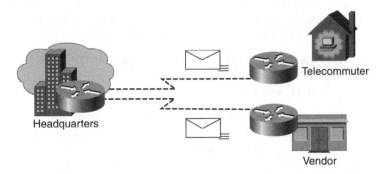

DDR is a straightforward process in which traffic that is defined as "interesting" causes the router to bring up a link to a remote site, as shown in Figure 12-8.

Figure 12-8 *DDR Operation*

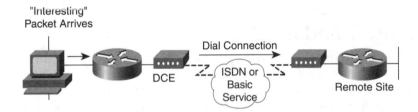

A basic description of how DDR is implemented in Cisco routers can be listed in five steps:

Step 1 The router receives traffic and does a route table lookup to determine if there is a route to the destination. If there is, the outbound interface is identified. If the outbound interface is configured for DDR, the router does a lookup to determine if the traffic is "interesting."

You, the administrator, define interesting traffic as any traffic that should trigger a call so that the traffic can be transferred.

Step 2 The router identifies the next hop router and locates the dialing instructions in what is called the dialer map.

Step 3 The router checks to see if the dialer map is in use—that is, if the interface is currently connected to the remote destination.

— If the interface is currently connected to the desired remote destination, the traffic is sent without dialing, and the idle timer is reset based on the packet's being interesting.

— If the interface is not currently connected to the remote destination, the router, which is attached to a DCE such as an ISDN TA or modem that supports V.25*bis* dialing, sends call setup information to the DCE device on the specified serial line or ISDN interface.

Step 4   After the link is enabled, the router transmits both interesting and uninteresting traffic. Uninteresting traffic can include data and routing updates. However, uninteresting traffic does not reset the idle timer.

Step 5   When no more interesting traffic is transmitted over the link, an idle timer starts. The call is disconnected after no interesting traffic is seen for the duration of the idle timeout period.

NOTE   Refer to the *Dialer Solutions Configuration Guide* on Cisco's web site at www.cisco.com/univercd/cc/td/doc/product/software/ios120/12cgcr/dial_c/index.htm or to the Cisco Documentation CD for more information on DDR implementations.

Configuring Standard DDR

There are two types of DDR routing. This book discusses the type known as standard DDR. In this section, you will learn to configure standard DDR. Figure 12-8 showed the general operation of DDR routing. The task in configuring this technology is to tell the router how to get to the remote network, what traffic brings up the link, and what number to dial to reach that network. The following steps detail this information and show you how to configure it on the router.

To configure standard DDR, follow these steps:

Step 1   **Define static routes**—What route do I take to get to the destination?

Step 2   **Specify interesting traffic**—What traffic type should enable the link?

Step 3   **Configure the dialer information**—What number do I call to get to the next hop router, and what service parameters do I use for the call?

Step 1: Defining Static Routes

Configuring standard DDR consists of telling the router how to get to the remote network. Figure 12-9 shows a sample network in which we will use DDR to reach the remote site.

Figure 12-9 *Defining Static Routes (Step 1)*

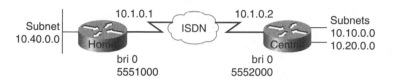

To forward traffic, routers need to know what route to use for a given destination. You wouldn't want dynamic routing protocols running across the link because they would cause the DDR interface to dial the remote sites for every periodic routing update. Instead, you can manually configure the necessary DDR routes using static routes. The static route command for IP, for example, is as follows:

```
Router(config)#ip route prefix mask {address | interface} [distance] [permanent]
```

As discussed in Chapter 8, "Determining IP Routes," when you're configuring static routes, keep in mind the following considerations:

- When using static routes, all participating routers must have static routes defined so that they can reach the remote networks. This requirement is necessary because static routes replace dynamic routing updates.

- To reduce the number of static route entries, you can define a default static route.

Step 2: Specifying Interesting Traffic

Configuring standard DDR involves identifying the protocol packets designated as interesting that will trigger a DDR call. Interesting packets are identified by you and can be identified on the basis of a variety of criteria, such as protocol type or addresses for source or destination hosts. Use the **dialer-list** global command to identify interesting traffic:

```
Router(config)#dialer-list dialer-group protocol protocol-name
   {permit | deny | list access-list-number}
```

Where:

- *dialer-group* is the number that identifies the dialer list. (**dialer-list** will be applied to an interface in steps described later in this section.)

- *protocol-name* specifies the protocol used by interesting packets. Choices include IP, IPX, AppleTalk, DECnet, and VINES.

- **permit | deny**, if used, specifically permits or denies a protocol for DDR consideration.

- **list**, if used, assigns an access list to the dialer group. The access list contains test conditions that identify the interesting traffic. Use an access list to create the interesting traffic definition if you want finer granularity of protocol choices.

Using the **dialer-list** command in conjunction with access lists gives you far greater control over what traffic you define as interesting. For example, if you wanted only Telnet or Simple Mail Transfer Protocol (SMTP) to bring up the link, you would use the configuration shown in Example 12-1.

Example 12-1 *Defining Telnet and SMTP Traffic as Interesting*

```
Router(config)#dialer-list 1 protocol ip list 101
Router(config)#access-list 101 permit tcp any any eq telnet
Router(config)#access-list 101 permit tcp any any eq smtp
```

CAUTION   If you use the **dialer-list 1 protocol ip permit** command without any further qualification, you will allow all IP traffic destined out the dial-on-demand interface to trigger a call. This might keep a DDR link up indefinitely, costing your organization a lot of money in unnecessary line charges.

Step 3: Configuring the Dialer Information

Configuring standard DDR involves configuring the physical interface to perform the dialing function, as detailed in the following list:

Step 1   Select the physical interface that you use as the dialup line.

Step 2   Configure the network address for the interface. For example:

```
Router(config-if)#ip address ip-address mask
```

Step 3   Configure the encapsulation type. For example, if configuring PPP, you would do this:

```
Router(config-if)#encapsulation ppp
```

Also, you might choose to configure PPP authentication. In this case, the **ppp authentication chap** command is used to specify CHAP authentication for this interface:

```
Router(config-if)#ppp authentication chap
```

Step 4   Bind the traffic definition to an interface by linking the interesting traffic definition you created in Step 1 to the interface:

```
Router(config-if)# dialer-group group-number
```

The *group-number* parameter specifies the number of the dialer group to which the interface belongs. The group number can be an integer from 1 to 10. This number must match the **dialer-list** *group-number*.

Each interface can have only one dialer group, but the same dialer list (using the **dialer-group** command) can be assigned to multiple interfaces.

Example: Configuring a Router for DDR Over an ISDN BRI Line

Example 12-2 is an example of the previous steps used to configure a router for DDR operation over an ISDN BRI line.

Example 12-2 *Defining Telnet and SMTP Traffic as Interesting*

```
hostname Home
username Central password cisco
!
isdn switch-type basic-5ess
!
interface BRI0
 ip address 10.1.0.1 255.255.255.0
 encapsulation ppp
 dialer idle-timeout 180
 dialer map ip 10.1.0.2 name Central 5552000
 dialer-group 1
 no fair-queue
 ppp authentication chap
!
router rip
network 10.0.0.0
!
no ip classless
ip route 10.10.0.0 255.255.0.0 10.1.0.2
ip route 10.20.0.0 255.255.0.0 10.1.0.2
!
dialer-list 1 protocol ip list 101
!
access-list 101 permit tcp any any eq telnet
access-list 101 permit tcp any any eq smtp
```

A crucial configuration parameter for the DDR interface is how to connect to the remote site. Figure 12-10 shows the remote network and its telephone number. The **dialer map** statement in Example 12-2 is used to configure the router to dial.

Figure 12-10 *Mapping a Remote Network to a Telephone Number*

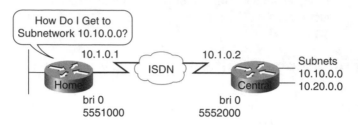

You can define one or more dial-on-demand numbers to reach one or more destinations for a particular interface with the **dialer map** command, the syntax for which is as follows:

```
Router(config-if)#dialer map protocol next-hop-address [name hostname]
   [speed 56 | 64] [broadcast] dialer-string
```

Where:

- *protocol* can be IP, IPX, AppleTalk, DECnet, VINES, and others.

- *next-hop-address* is the network address of the next hop router.

- **name** *hostname* is the host name of the remote device. This name is used for PPP authentication or ISDN calls supporting caller ID.

- **speed 56 | 64** is used for ISDN and indicates the link speed in kbps to use. The default is 64.

- **broadcast** indicates that broadcasts and multicasts are allowed to be forwarded to this destination (only when the link is enabled by interesting traffic). DDR is nonbroadcast by default, so no update traffic will cross the link unless this is set. This permits the use of dynamic routing protocols over the connection.

- *dialer-string* is the telephone number sent to the DCE device when packets with the specified next hop address are received.

The **dialer map** command must be used with the **dialer-group** command and its associated access list to initiate dialing on an interface.

The tasks to configure DDR (as shown collectively in Example 12-2) are as follows:

Step 1 **Define static routes**—What route do I take to get to the destination? The commands necessary to accomplish this step are as follows:

```
ip route 10.10.0.0 255.255.0.0 10.1.0.2
ip route 10.20.0.0 255.255.0.0 10.1.0.2
```

Step 2 **Specify interesting traffic**—What traffic type should enable the link? The commands necessary to accomplish this step are as follows:

```
dialer-list 1 protocol ip list 101
!
access-list 101 permit tcp any any eq telnet
access-list 101 permit tcp any any eq smtp
```

Step 3 **Configure the dialer information**—What number do I call to get to the next hop router, and what service parameters do I use for the call? The commands necessary to accomplish this step are as follows:

```
interface BRI0
 ip address 10.1.0.1 255.255.255.0
 encapsulation ppp
 dialer idle-timeout 180
 dialer map ip 10.1.0.2 name Central 5552000
 dialer-group 1
 no fair-queue
 ppp authentication chap
username Central password cisco
```

The optional **dialer idle-timeout** *seconds* command can be used with standard DDR to specify the number of idle seconds before a call is disconnected. The *seconds* option specifies the number of seconds until a call is disconnected after the last interesting traffic is sent. (The default is 120.)

Verifying DDR Over ISDN Configuration and Operation

To verify the configuration of ISDN and DDR configuration and operation, you can use the commands listed in Table 12-5.

Table 12-5 *Commands to Verify DDR over ISDN Configuration and Operation*

Command	Description
ping/telnet	When you ping or Telnet a remote site via DDR (assuming these are not filtered), or when other interesting traffic triggers a DDR link, the router sends a change in link status message to the console.
show dialer	Lists general diagnostic information about an interface configured for DDR, such as the number of times the dialer string has been successfully reached. Current call-specific information is also provided, such as the length of the call, and the number and name of the device to which the interface is currently connected.
show isdn active	Shows that a call is in progress and lists the number called.

continues

Table 12-5 *Commands to Verify DDR over ISDN Configuration and Operation (Continued)*

Command	Description
show isdn status	Shows the statistics of the ISDN connection.
show ip route	Displays the routes known to the router, including static and dynamically learned routes.

Troubleshooting DDR Operation

Table 12-6 includes some other useful commands that can aid in troubleshooting the operation of DDR.

Table 12-6 *Commands to Troubleshoot DDR Operation*

Command	Description
debug isdn q921	Verifies that you have a connection to the ISDN switch.
debug isdn q931	Displays call setup and teardown messages.
debug dialer	Shows information such as what number the interface is dialing.
shutdown	Administrative shutdown of the interface. Will disconnect any call in progress.

ISDN BRI Command Summary

Table 12-7 summarizes the commands you've learned in this chapter.

Table 12-7 *DDR over ISDN Command Summary*

Command	Description
isdn switch-type basic-*switch-type*	Specifies a BRI switch type.
isdn spid1 *spid-number*	Configures the service provider ID of B channel 1.
isdn spid2 *spid-number*	Configures the service provider ID of B channel 2.
dialer-list *dialer-group* **protocol** *protocol-name* {**permit** | **deny** | **list** *access-list-number* | *access group*}	Specifies interesting traffic and associates it to a dialer group.
dialer-group *group-number*	Assigns a dialer group to an interface.
dialer map ip *next-hop-address* **name** *destination-router-name phone-number*	Specifies how to call a destination.
dialer idle-timeout *seconds*	Specifies the idle time before the line is disconnected.

Table 12-7 *DDR over ISDN Command Summary (Continued)*

Command	Description
show dialer	Lists general diagnostic information about an interface configured for DDR, such as the number of times the dialer string has been successfully reached, and the idle timer and fast idle timer values for each B channel. Current call-specific information is also provided, such as the length of the call, and the number and name of the device to which the interface is currently connected.
show isdn active	Use this command when using ISDN. It shows that a call is in progress and lists the number called.
show isdn status	Shows the statistics of the ISDN connection.
show ip route	Displays the routes known to the router, including static and dynamically learned routes.
debug isdn q921	Verifies that you have a connection to the ISDN switch.
debug isdn q931	Displays call setup and teardown messages.
debug dialer	Shows information such as what number the interface is dialing.
shutdown	Administrative shutdown of the interface. Disconnects any call in progress.
no shutdown	Enables an interface.

Summary

In this chapter, you learned how to identify the physical components of an ISDN interface. In addition, you learned how to determine the type of device you need and the reference points to connect this device to an ISDN service. Also, you should now know how to configure an ISDN BRI interface to act as a DDR circuit. Finally, you should now know how to verify proper operation with **show** and **debug** commands, given a dial-on-demand ISDN connection.

Review Questions

1 What does ISDN stand for?

2 ISDN carries what type of user-traffic feeds?

3 The ISDN Q series protocol standards cover what issues?

4 The ISDN BRI consists of what services?

5 TE2 refers to what type of ISDN equipment?

6 A U interface references what connection?

7 In a location where the NT1 is furnished by the provider, what type of native ISDN reference point should be on the router?

8 Where do you obtain SPID numbers?

9 What three steps are required to configure DDR?

10 Which command specifies interesting traffic?

11 How is this command linked to a dialer interface?

12 Which command could you use to display the current status of an ISDN interface?

Upon completion of this chapter, you will be able to perform the following tasks:

- Identify the terminology and fundamental technical requirements needed to connect to a Frame Relay service provider.

- Configure a router for Frame Relay operation and verify permanent virtual circuit connectivity.

- Configure Frame Relay subinterfaces.

CHAPTER 13

Establishing a Frame Relay PVC Connection

Frame Relay is an ITU-T (CCITT) and American National Standards Institute (ANSI) standard that defines the process for sending data over a public data network (PDN). Frame Relay is a connection-oriented data link technology that is streamlined to provide high performance and efficiency. Frame Relay relies on upper-layer protocols for error correction and today's more-dependable fiber and digital networks. This chapter provides you with an overview of Frame Relay technology and shows you how to configure a router in a Frame Relay environment.

Frame Relay Overview

Frame Relay defines the interconnection process between your router and the service provider's local access switching equipment. It does not define how the data is transmitted within the service provider's Frame Relay cloud, as illustrated in Figure 13-1.

Figure 13-1 *Frame Relay Overview*

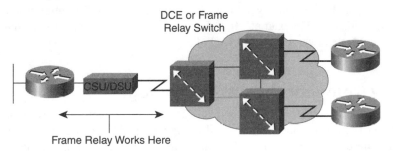

Frame Relay provides a means for statistically multiplexing many logical data conversations (referred to as *virtual circuits*) over a single physical transmission link by assigning connection identifiers to each pair of data terminal equipment (DTE). The service provider's switching equipment constructs a table that maps connection identifiers to its outbound ports. When a frame is received, the switching device analyzes the connection identifier and delivers the frame to the associated outbound port. The complete path to the destination is established prior to the sending of the first frame.

The core aspects of Frame Relay function at the lower two layers of the OSI reference model, as shown in Figure 13-2.

Figure 13-2 *Frame Relay Operates at Layer 1 and Layer 2 of the OSI Reference Model*

OSI Reference Model	Frame Relay
Application	
Presentation	
Session	
Transport	
Network	IP/IPX/AppleTalk, etc.
Data Link	Frame Relay
Physical	EIA/TIA-232, EIA/TIA-449, V.35, X.21, EIA/TIA-530

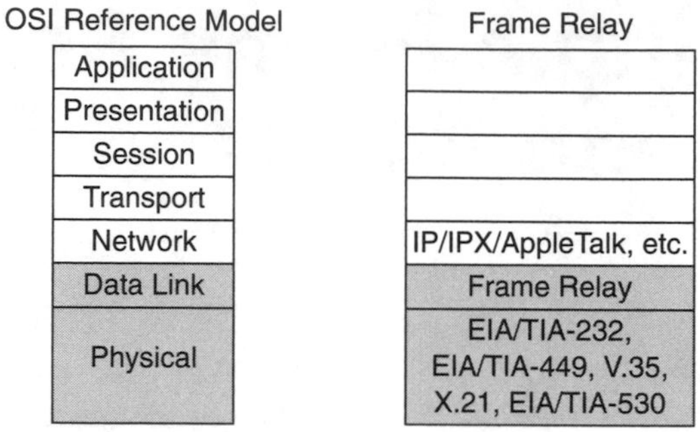

The same physical serial connections that support point-to-point environments also support the Frame Relay connection to the service provider. Cisco routers support the following serial connections:

- EIA/TIA-232
- EIA/TIA-449
- V.35
- X.21
- EIA/TIA-530

Working at the data link layer, Frame Relay encapsulates information from the upper layers of the OSI stack. For example, IP traffic would be encapsulated into a frame format that can be transmitted over a Frame Relay link.

Frame Relay Components and Terminology

Frame Relay, like most WAN services, has some unique terminology associated with it. In order to understand the operation and configuration of Frame Relay, you need to be familiar with these terms. Figure 13-3 illustrates some Frame Relay components and terminology. They are described in detail in the following list.

Figure 13-3 *Frame Relay Components*

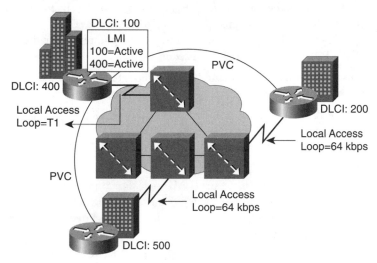

The following list defines some terms that are used frequently when discussing Frame Relay. These are generic Frame Relay terms. They might be the same as or slightly different than the terms your Frame Relay service provider uses.

- **Local access rate**—The clock speed (port speed) of the connection (local loop) to the Frame Relay cloud. This is the rate at which data travels into or out of the network, regardless of other settings.

- **Virtual circuit (VC)**—Logical circuit created to ensure communication between two network devices. A virtual circuit can be either a permanent virtual circuit (PVC) or a switched virtual circuit (SVC).

- **PVC**—Virtual circuit that is permanently established. PVCs save bandwidth associated with circuit establishment and tear down in situations where certain virtual circuits exist all the time.

- **SVC**—Virtual circuit that is dynamically established on-demand and is torn down when transmission is complete. SVCs are used in situations where data transmission is sporadic.

Note	With ANSI T1.617, ITU Q.933 (Layer 3), and Q.922 (Layer 2), Frame Relay now supports switched virtual circuits (SVCs). Cisco IOS Release 11.2 and later supports Frame Relay SVCs. Configuring Frame Relay SVCs is not covered in this book. You can find more information on SVCs at www.cisco.com/univercd/cc/td/doc/product/ software/ios120/12cgcr/wan_c/wcfrelay.htm#xtocid2427318.

- **Data-link connection identifier (DLCI)**—A number that identifies the logical circuit between the router and the Frame Relay switch. The Frame Relay switch maps the DLCIs between each pair of routers to create a PVC. DLCIs have local significance in that the identifier references the point between the local router and the Frame Relay switch to which it is connected.

- **Committed information rate (CIR)**—The rate, in bits per second, at which the service provider guarantees that data will be transferred.

- **Inverse Address Resolution Protocol (Inverse ARP)**—Method of dynamically associating a network layer address with a DLCI. It allows a router to discover the network address of a device associated with a VC. This is covered more in depth in the next section of this chapter.

- **Local Management Interface (LMI)**—A signaling standard between the router device and the Frame Relay switch that is responsible for managing the connection and maintaining status between the devices. This is covered more in depth in the next section of this chapter.

- **Forward Explicit Congestion Notification (FECN)**—When a Frame Relay switch recognizes congestion in the network, it sets the FECN bit in a Frame Relay packet traveling forward to the destination device, indicating that congestion has occurred. FECN is not covered in this book.

- **Backward Explicit Congestion Notification (BECN)**—When a Frame Relay switch recognizes congestion in the network, it sets the BECN bit in a Frame Relay packet traveling backward to the source router, instructing the router to reduce the rate at which it is sending packets. BECN is not covered in this book. More information can be found on the Frame Relay forum at www.frforum.com.

NOTE   Your Frame Relay equipment might offer flow control and traffic-shaping features that are not covered in this book. Some terms regarding Frame Relay flow control include committed burst, excess burst, forward explicit congestion notification (FECN), backward explicit congestion notification (BECN), and discard eligible.

Address Mapping and LMI Signaling for Frame Relay Connections

Frame Relay virtual circuits allow a single location to be connected to many remote locations. In order for a router to reach a remote location, it must know which IP address is associated with each VC. The DLCI identifies each VC. In order to know which IP address is associated with each VC, there must be a mapping between these components, as shown in Figure 13-4.

Figure 13-4 *Frame Relay Address Mapping*

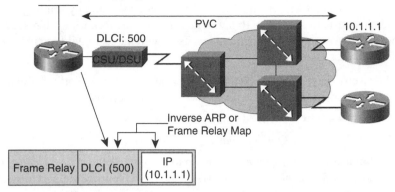

On Cisco routers, the addresses can be dynamically mapped with Inverse ARP, which associates a given DLCI to the next-hop protocol address for a specific connection. The router then updates its mapping table and uses the information in the table to route packets.

Instead of using Inverse ARP to map DLCIs to network layer addresses, you can also manually configure a static Frame Relay map in the map table.

The Local Management Interface (LMI) consists of several types of signaling standards between the router and the Frame Relay switch that are responsible for managing the connection and maintaining status between the devices. LMIs include support for a keepalive mechanism, a multicast mechanism, and a status mechanism. LMI exchange occurs over a predefined DLCI number, according to the LMI type being used. Figure 13-5 shows how LMI is used to maintain the status of the PVC between the routers. The keepalives are exchanged between the switch and the router and give the status of the PVC. Notice that the PVC for DLCI 500 is active, and the PVC for DLCI 400 is inactive.

Figure 13-5 *Frame Relay Signaling*

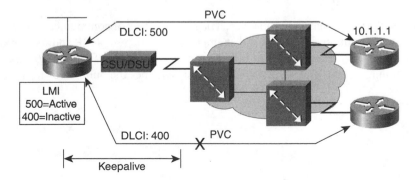

Although the LMI type is configurable, beginning in Release 11.2, the Cisco router tries to autosense which LMI type the Frame Relay switch is using by sending one or more full status requests to the Frame Relay switch. The Frame Relay switch responds with one or more LMI types. The router configures itself with the last LMI type received. Three types of LMIs are supported:

- **cisco**—LMI type defined jointly by Cisco, StrataCom, Northern Telecom, and Digital Equipment Corporation, nicknamed "the gang of four"

- **ansi**—Annex D, defined by the ANSI standard T1.617

- **q933a**—ITU-T Q.933 Annex A

An administrator setting up a connection to a Frame Relay network can choose and manually configure the appropriate LMI type from the three supported types to ensure proper Frame Relay operation.

When the router receives LMI information, it updates its VC status to one of three states:

- **Active state**—Indicates that the connection is active and that routers can exchange data.

- **Inactive state**—Indicates that the local connection to the Frame Relay switch is working, but that the remote router's connection to the Frame Relay switch is not working.

- **Deleted state**—Indicates that no LMI is being received from the Frame Relay switch, or that there is no service between the router and the Frame Relay switch.

NOTE   Although the autosensing feature of the router is useful, it should be noted that autosensing doesn't always work. When it doesn't, it is best to contact your provider to determine which type is supported and then manually set the LMI type on your router.

When the router interface initializes, it begins a process of communications with the switch in which it initializes the link and attempts to map the remote IP address through Inverse ARP. The next few pages show how an interface initializes. Figure 13-6 shows the beginning of this process. The following list describes the numbered steps shown in the figure.

Figure 13-6 *Link Initialization*

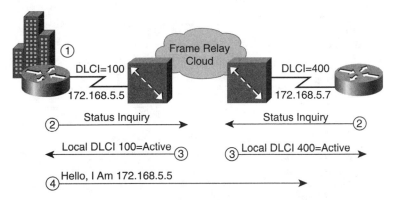

Step 1   Each router, through a channel service unit/data service unit (CSU/DSU), connects to the Frame Relay switch.

Step 2   When Frame Relay is configured on an interface, the router sends a status inquiry message to the Frame Relay switch. The message notifies the switch of the router's status and asks the switch for the connection status of the router's VCs.

Step 3   When the Frame Relay switch receives the request, it responds with a status message that includes the local DLCIs of the PVCs to the remote routers to which the local router can send data.

Step 4   For each active DLCI, each router sends an Inverse ARP packet introducing itself.

Figure 13-7 continues the process by showing how an address is mapped to a DLCI through Inverse ARP. The following list describes the numbered steps illustrated in the figure (with the exception of Step 4, which is described in the preceding list).

Figure 13-7 *Inverse ARP*

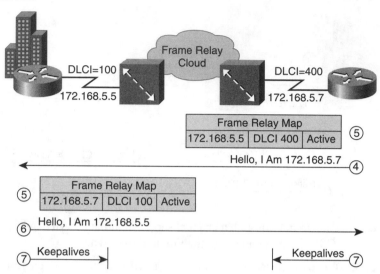

Step 5 When a router receives an Inverse ARP message, it creates a map entry in its Frame Relay map table that includes the *local* DLCI and the remote router's network layer address. Note that the DLCI is the router's local DLCI, not the DLCI that the remote router is using. Three possible connection states appear in the Frame Relay map table: active, inactive, and deleted (as described previously).

If Inverse ARP is not working, or if the remote router does not support Inverse ARP, static maps (DLCIs and IP addresses) must be configured.

Step 6 Every 60 seconds, routers send Inverse ARP messages on all active DLCIs.

Step 7 Every 10 seconds, the router exchanges LMI information with the switch (keepalives).

The router changes the status of each DLCI based on the response from the Frame Relay switch.

Configuring Frame Relay

To configure a router for operation in a Frame Relay environment, you must first enable the serial interface for Frame Relay encapsulation. Beyond that, there are several items you might or might not have to configure. In its simplest form, Frame Relay is merely the process of specifying the encapsulation, but it might be necessary to configure many options. The next few pages detail how to configure a Cisco interface for operation in a Frame Relay environment.

Example 13-1 and Example 13-2 are basic Frame Relay configurations for the routers shown in Figure 13-8.

Figure 13-8 *Basic Frame Relay Network for Configuration*

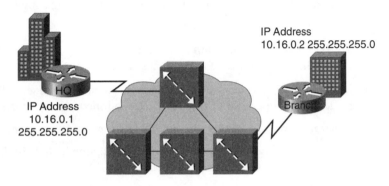

Example 13-1 *Basic Frame Relay Configuration*

```
HQ(config)#interface Serial1
HQ(config-if)#ip address 10.16.0.1 255.255.255.0
HQ(config-if)#encapsulation frame-relay
HQ(config-if)#bandwidth 64
```

Example 13-2 *Setting the LMI Type*

```
Branch(config)#interface Serial1
Branch(config-if)#ip address 10.16.0.2 255.255.255.0
Branch(config-if)#encapsulation frame-relay
Branch(config-if)#bandwidth 64
Branch(config-if)#frame-relay lmi-type ansi
```

A basic Frame Relay configuration assumes that you want to configure Frame Relay on one or more physical interfaces, and that LMI and Inverse ARP are supported by the remote router(s). In this type of environment, the LMI notifies the router of the available DLCIs. Use the following steps to configure basic Frame Relay:

Step 1 Select the interface and go into interface configuration mode.

Step 2 Configure a network layer address, such as an IP address.

Step 3 Select the Frame Relay encapsulation type used to encapsulate data traffic end-to-end. The command to accomplish this is as follows:

```
router(config-if)#encapsulation frame-relay [cisco | ietf]
```

The default encapsulation type is **cisco**. Use the **cisco** option if you're connecting to another Cisco router. Use the **ietf** option if you're connecting to a non-Cisco router.

Step 4   If you're using Cisco IOS Release 11.1 or earlier, specify the LMI type used by the Frame Relay switch, using the following command:

```
router(config-if)#frame-relay lmi-type {ansi | cisco | q933a}
```

The default LMI type is **cisco**. With IOS Release 11.2 and later, the LMI type is autosensed by default, so no configuration is needed.

Step 5   Configure the bandwidth for the link using the following command:

```
router(config-if)#bandwidth kilobits
```

The **bandwidth** command affects routing operation by protocols such as IGRP. The default for E1/T1 serial lines and below is 56.

Step 6   If Inverse ARP was disabled on the router, re-enable it. Inverse ARP is on by default. To re-enable Inverse ARP, use the following command:

```
router(config-if)#frame-relay inverse-arp [protocol] [dlci]
```

Supported protocols indicated by the *protocol* option include **ip**, **ipx**, **appletalk**, **decnet**, **vines**, and **xns.**

The *dlci* option indicates the DLCI number on the local interface that you want to use to exchange Inverse ARP messages. Acceptable numbers are integers in the range 16 through 1007.

Configuring Static Mapping for a Router

When Inverse ARP is not supported by the remote router, or when you want to control broadcast traffic when using routing, you must define the address-to-DLCI table statically. These static entries are referred to as *static maps*. Figure 13-9 illustrates a Frame Relay network candidate for static Frame Relay maps.

Figure 13-9 *Configuring a Static Frame Relay Map*

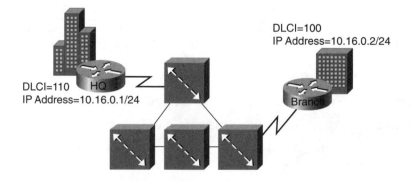

DLCI=100
IP Address=10.16.0.2/24

DLCI=110   HQ
IP Address=10.16.0.1/24

Branch

To configure a static mapping for the HQ router in Figure 13-9, you would enter the configuration shown in Example 13-3.

Example 13-3 *Configuring a Static Mapping for the HQ Router*

```
HQ(config)#interface Serial1
HQ(config-if)#ip address 10.16.0.1 255.255.255.0
HQ(config-if)#encapsulation frame-relay
HQ(config-if)#bandwidth 64
HQ(config-if)#frame-relay map ip 10.16.0.2 110 broadcast
```

The **frame-relay map** command can be used when necessary to statically map the network layer address to the DLCI. The syntax for this command is as follows:

```
router(config-if)#frame-relay map protocol protocol-address dlci [broadcast]
  [ietf | cisco] [payload-compress packet-by-packet]
```

Where:

- *protocol* defines the supported protocol, bridging, or logical link control.

- *protocol-address* defines the network layer address of the destination router interface.

- *dlci* defines the local DLCI used to connect to the remote protocol address.

- **broadcast** is an optional parameter that forwards broadcasts and multicasts over the VC. This permits the use of dynamic routing protocols over the VC.

- **ietf | cisco** enables IETF or Cisco encapsulations.

- **payload-compress packet-by-packet** is an optional parameter that enables packet-by-packet payload compression using the STAC method. This is a Cisco proprietary compression method.

Displaying Frame Relay Connection Status and Information

After you configure Frame Relay, you can verify that the connections are active using the available **show** commands. The **show interface** command displays information regarding the encapsulation and Layer 1 and Layer 2 status. It also displays information about the DLCIs used on the Frame Relay configured serial interface and the LMI DLCI used for the local management interface. Example 13-4 shows some sample output from the **show interface** command.

Example 13-4 *show interface Displays Frame Relay Connection Status and Information*

```
Router#show interface s1
Serial0 is up, line protocol is up
  Hardware is HD64570
  Internet address is 10.16.0.1/24
  MTU 1500 bytes, BW 64 Kbit, DLY 20000 usec, rely 255/255, load 1/255
  Encapsulation FRAME-RELAY, loopback not set, keepalive set (10 sec)
```

continues

Example 13-4 *show interface Displays Frame Relay Connection Status and Information (Continued)*

```
LMI enq sent  19, LMI stat recvd 20, LMI upd recvd 0, DTE LMI up
LMI enq recvd 0, LMI stat sent  0, LMI upd sent  0
LMI DLCI 1023  LMI type is CISCO  frame relay DTE
FR SVC disabled, LAPF state down
Broadcast queue 0/64, broadcasts sent/dropped 8/0, interface broadcasts 5
Last input 00:00:02, output 00:00:02, output hang never
Last clearing of "show interface" counters never
Queuing strategy: fifo
Output queue 0/40, 0 drops; input queue 0/75, 0 drops
<Output omitted>
```

The highlighted lines show the LMI type for interface Serial 1.

Displaying LMI Traffic Statistics

The **show frame-relay lmi** command displays LMI traffic statistics. For example, as highlighted in Example 13-5, **show frame-relay lmi** shows the number of status messages exchanged between the local router and the Frame Relay switch.

Example 13-5 *show frame-relay lmi Displays LMI Traffic Statistics*

```
Router#show frame-relay lmi

LMI Statistics for interface Serial0 (Frame Relay DTE) LMI TYPE = CISCO
  Invalid Unnumbered info 0 Invalid Prot Disc 0
  Invalid dummy Call Ref 0 Invalid Msg Type 0
  Invalid Status Message 0 Invalid Lock Shift 0
  Invalid Information ID 0 Invalid Report IE Len 0
  Invalid Report Request 0 Invalid Keep IE Len 0
  Num Status Enq. Sent 113100 Num Status msgs Rcvd 113100
  Num Update Status Rcvd 0 Num Status Timeouts 0
```

Displaying Frame Relay Connection and Traffic Statistics

The **show frame-relay pvc** command displays the status of each configured connection as well as traffic statistics. This command is also useful for viewing the number of backward explicit congestion notification (BECN) and forward explicit congestion notification (FECN) packets received by the router. The **PVC STATUS** can be **active**, **inactive**, or **deleted**. Example 13-6 shows some sample output from the **show frame-relay pvc** command.

Example 13-6 *show frame-relay pvc Displays Frame Relay Connection and Traffic Statistics*

```
Router#show frame-relay pvc 100

PVC Statistics for interface Serial0 (Frame Relay DTE)
```

Example 13-6 *show frame-relay pvc Displays Frame Relay Connection and Traffic Statistics (Continued)*

```
DLCI = 100, DLCI USAGE = LOCAL, PVC STATUS = ACTIVE, INTERFACE = Serial0

  input pkts 28            output pkts 10          in bytes 8398
  out bytes 1198           dropped pkts 0          in FECN pkts 0
  in BECN pkts 0           out FECN pkts 0         out BECN pkts 0
  in DE pkts 0             out DE pkts 0
  out bcast pkts 10         out bcast bytes 1198
  pvc create time 00:03:46, last time pvc status changed 00:03:47
```

If you enter **show frame-relay pvc**, you will see the status of all the PVCs configured on the router. If you enter a specific PVC, you will see the status of only that PVC. In Example 13-6, **show frame-relay pvc 100** displays the status of only PVC 100.

Displaying Frame Relay Connection Map Entry Information

To display the current map entries and information about the connections, use the **show frame-relay map** command. This command can be useful to see the static map entries configured, as well as what inverse ARP entries the router has learned. Example 13-7 shows some sample output from the **show frame-relay map** command.

Example 13-7 *show frame-relay map Displays Frame Relay Connection Map Entry Information*

```
Router#show frame-relay map
Serial0 (up): ip 10.140.1.1 dlci 100(0x64,0x1840), dynamic,
              broadcast, status defined, active
```

The following list explains the Frame Relay DLCI numbering that appears in Example 13-7:

- 100 is the decimal DLCI number.
- 0x64 is the hex conversion of this number (0x64 = 100 decimal).

Clearing Dynamically Created Frame Relay Maps

To clear dynamically created Frame Relay maps, which are created using Inverse ARP, use the **clear frame-relay-inarp** privileged EXEC command. Example 13-8 shows some sample output from the **clear frame-relay-inarp** privileged EXEC command. The **show frame-relay map** command verifies that the mappings have been cleared.

Example 13-8 *clear frame-relay-inarp Clears Dynamically Created Frame Relay Maps*

```
Router#clear frame-relay-inarp
Router#sh frame map
Router#
```

Verifying and Troubleshooting Frame Relay Connections

The **debug frame-relay lmi** command allows you to verify and troubleshoot the Frame Relay connection. Use this command to determine whether the router and the Frame Relay switch are sending and receiving LMI packets properly. Example 13-9 shows some sample output from the **debug frame-relay lmi** command.

Example 13-9 *debug frame-relay lmi Verifies and Troubleshoots Frame Relay Connections*

```
Router#debug frame-relay lmi
Frame Relay LMI debugging is on
Displaying all Frame Relay LMI data
Router#
1w2d: Serial0(out): StEnq, myseq 140, yourseen 139, DTE up
1w2d: datagramstart = 0xE008EC, datagramsize = 13
1w2d: FR encap = 0xFCF10309
1w2d: 00 75 01 01 01 03 02 8C 8B
1w2d:
1w2d: Serial0(in): Status, myseq 140
1w2d: RT IE 1, length 1, type 1
1w2d: KA IE 3, length 2, yourseq 140, myseq 140
1w2d: Serial0(out): StEnq, myseq 141, yourseen 140, DTE up
1w2d: datagramstart = 0xE008EC, datagramsize = 13
1w2d: FR encap = 0xFCF10309
1w2d: 00 75 01 01 01 03 02 8D 8C
1w2d:
1w2d: Serial0(in): Status, myseq 142
1w2d: RT IE 1, length 1, type 0
1w2d: KA IE 3, length 2, yourseq 142, myseq 142
1w2d: PVC IE 0x7 , length 0x6 , dlci 100, status 0x2 , bw 0
```

(out) is an LMI status message sent by the router. **(in)** is a message received from the Frame Relay switch.

type 0 is a full LMI status message. **type 1** is an LMI exchange.

dlci 100, status 0x2 says that the status of DLCI 100 is active. Here are the possible values of the status field:

- **0x0**—Added/inactive. Means that the switch has this DLCI programmed, but for some reason (such as the other end of this PVC is down), it is not usable.

- **0x2**—Added/active. Means that the Frame Relay switch has the DLCI, and everything is operational. You can start sending it traffic with this DLCI in the header.

- **0x4**—Deleted. Means that the Frame Relay switch does not have this DLCI programmed for the router, but it was programmed at some point in the past. This could also be caused by the DLCIs being reversed on the router, or by the PVC being deleted by the service provider in the Frame Relay cloud.

Configuring Frame Relay Subinterfaces

This section describes Frame Relay subinterfaces and shows you how to configure multiple subinterfaces on a single physical interface. Figure 13-10 illustrates the variety of Frame Relay topologies. They are described in the following list.

Figure 13-10   *Frame Relay Topologies*

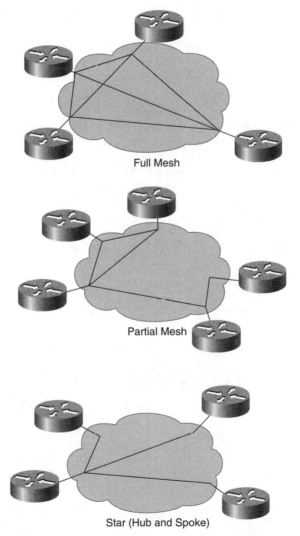

Full Mesh

Partial Mesh

Star (Hub and Spoke)

- **Star topology**—Also known as a hub-and-spoke configuration, the star topology is the most popular Frame Relay network topology. In this topology, remote sites are connected to a central site that generally provides a service or application. This is the least-expensive topology, because it requires the least number of PVCs. In this scenario, the central router provides a multipoint connection, because it typically uses a single interface to interconnect multiple PVCs.

- **Full-mesh topology**—All routers have virtual circuits to all other destinations. This topology, although costly, provides direct connections from each site to all other sites and allows for redundancy. When one link goes down, a router can reroute traffic through another site. As the number of nodes in this topology increases, a full-mesh topology can become very expensive.

- **Partial-mesh topology**—Not all sites have direct access to all other sites. Depending on the traffic patterns in your network, you might want to have additional PVCs connected to remote sites that have large data traffic requirements.

Frame Relay Nonbroadcast Multiaccess Reachability Problems

In any of the aforementioned Frame Relay topologies, when a single interface must be used to interconnect multiple sites, you might have reachability issues because of the nonbroadcast multiaccess (NBMA) nature of Frame Relay. Because a single interface connects to a cloud and can be mapped to many other sites, the cloud is said to be multiaccess. Because the Frame Relay switch doesn't replicate a broadcast packet coming from a single DLCI to all DLCIs, it is said to be nonbroadcast. With Frame Relay running multiple PVCs over a single interface, the primary issue is with split horizon. Figure 13-11 illustrates why the Frame Relay default of NBMA can be a problem.

Figure 13-11   *Frame Relay Reachability*

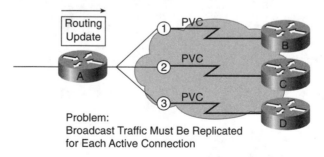

By default, a Frame Relay network provides NBMA connectivity between remote sites. In a routed network, this NBMA connectivity means that although all locations can be configured to reach each other through the cloud, routing update broadcasts received by one location might not be forwarded to all locations. This is because the Frame Relay interface uses split horizon to reduce the number of routing loops.

Split horizon reduces routing loops by not allowing a routing update received on one interface to be forwarded out the same interface. As a result, if a remote router sends an update to the headquarters router that is connecting multiple PVCs over a single physical interface, the headquarters router cannot send that broadcast through the same interface to other remote routers, even though they use separate PVCs.

Broadcasts are not a problem if there is only a single PVC on a physical interface, because this would be more of a point-to-point connection type.

Another issue with routers that support multipoint connections over a single interface is that when many DLCIs terminate in a single router, that router must replicate routing updates and service advertising updates on each DLCI to the remote routers. The updates can consume access-link bandwidth and cause significant latency variations in user traffic. The updates can also consume interface buffers and lead to higher packet rate loss for both user data and routing updates.

The amount of broadcast traffic and the number of VCs terminating at each router should be evaluated during the design phase of a Frame Relay network. Overhead traffic, such as routing updates, can affect the delivery of critical user data, especially when the delivery path contains low-bandwidth (56 kbps) links.

Resolving Frame Relay NBMA Reachability Problems with Subinterface Configuration

The simplest answer to resolving the reachability issues brought on by split horizon might seem to be to turn off split horizon. Two problems exist with this solution, however:

- Not all network layer protocols allow you to disable split horizon (however, most, such as IP and IPX, do allow this).
- Disabling split horizon increases the chances of routing loops in your network.

Disabling split horizon differs for each protocol. In order to disable split horizon, check the commands for the routing protocol you are using.

To enable the forwarding of broadcast routing updates in a Frame Relay network, you can configure the router with logically assigned interfaces called *subinterfaces*. Subinterfaces are logical subdivisions of a single physical interface. In split horizon routing environments, routing updates received on one subinterface can be sent out another subinterface. In subinterface configuration, each VC can be configured as a point-to-point connection, which allows the subinterface to act similar to a leased line. Figure 13-12 illustrates how the subinterfaces logically map to each of the virtual circuits.

Figure 13-12 *Resolving Reachability Issues*

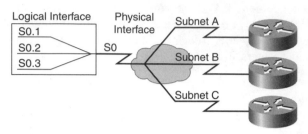

You can configure subinterfaces to support the following connection types:

- **Point-to-point**—A single subinterface is used to establish one PVC connection to another physical interface or subinterface on a remote router. In this case, the interfaces would be in the same subnet, and each interface would have a single DLCI. Each point-to-point connection is its own subnet. In this environment, broadcasts are not a problem, because the routers are point-to-point and act like a leased line.

- **Multipoint**—A single subinterface is used to establish multiple PVC connections to multiple physical interfaces or subinterfaces on remote routers. In this case, all the participating interfaces would be in the same subnet, and each interface would have its own local DLCI. In this environment, because the subinterface acts like a regular NBMA Frame Relay interface, broadcast traffic is subject to the split horizon rule.

To configure subinterfaces on a physical interface, do the following:

Step 1 Select the interface that you want to create subinterfaces on, and enter interface configuration mode.

Step 2 It is recommended that you remove any network layer address assigned to the physical interface and assign the network layer address to the subinterface.

Step 3 Configure Frame Relay encapsulation on the physical interface, as discussed in Step 3 of the six-step procedure in the "Configuring Frame Relay" section.

Step 4 Select the subinterface you want to configure, using the following command:

```
router(config)#interface serial number.subinterface-number
  {multipoint | point-to-point}
```

Where:

— *number.subinterface-number* is the subinterface number. The interface number that precedes the period (.) must match the physical interface number to which this subinterface belongs. The *subinterface-number* after the period can be arbitrarily chosen from a range of 1 to 4,294,967,293.

— **multipoint** should be selected if you're routing IP and you want all routers in the same subnet.

— **point-to-point** should be selected if you want each pair of point-to-point routers to have its own subnet.

You are required to select either the **multipoint** or **point-to-point** parameter; there is no default.

Step 5 If you configured the subinterface as point-to-point, you must configure the local DLCI for the subinterface to distinguish it from the physical interface. This is also required for multipoint subinterfaces for which Inverse ARP is enabled. This is not required for multipoint subinterfaces configured with static route maps. Here is the command to configure the local DLCI on the subinterface:

```
router(config-if)#frame-relay interface-dlci dlci-number
```

The *dlci-number* parameter defines the local DLCI number being linked to the subinterface. This is the only way to link an LMI-derived PVC to a subinterface, because LMI does not know about subinterfaces defined on the router.

NOTE   If you defined a subinterface for point-to-point communication, you cannot reassign the same subinterface number to be used for multipoint communication without first rebooting the router. Instead, you can leave the point-to-point subinterface intact but disabled and create a new multipoint subinterface with a different subinterface number. Because the subinterface numbers are arbitrarily chosen by you, the actual number or the order of subinterfaces is meaningless.

Point-to-Point Subinterface Configuration Example

Example 13-10 provides point-to-point subinterface configuration for the Frame Relay setup illustrated in Figure 13-13.

Figure 13-13 *Point-to-Point Subinterface Configuration*

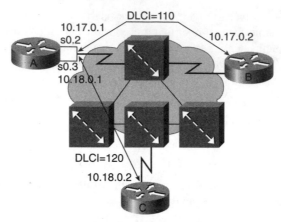

Example 13-10 *Point-to-Point Subinterface Configuration*

```
RouterA(config)#interface Serial0
RouterA(config-if)# no ip address
RouterA(config-if)# encapsulation frame-relay
RouterA(config-if)#interface Serial0.2 point-to-point
RouterA(config-subif)# ip address 10.17.0.1 255.255.255.0
RouterA(config-subif)#bandwidth 64
RouterA(config-subif)#frame-relay interface-dlci 110
RouterA(config-subif)#interface Serial0.3 point-to-point
RouterA(config-subif)# ip address 10.18.0.1 255.255.255.0
RouterA(config-subif)#bandwidth 64
RouterA(config-subif)# frame-relay interface-dlci 120
```

Example 13-10 shows you how to configure point-to-point subinterfaces. With this type of configuration, each subinterface is treated like a separate physical interface and would not be subject to split horizon.

Multipoint Subinterface Configuration Example

Example 13-11 provides multipoint subinterface configuration for RTR1, shown in Figure 13-14.

Figure 13-14   *Multipoint Subinterface Configuration*

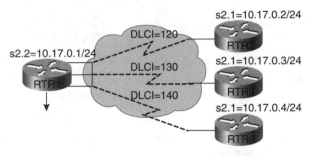

Example 13-11 *Multipoint Subinterface Configuration*

```
RTR1(config)#interface Serial2
RTR1(config-if)# no ip address
RTR1(config-if)# encapsulation frame-relay
RTR1(config-if)#interface Serial2.2 multipoint
RTR1(config-subif)#ip address 10.17.0.1 255.255.255.0
RTR1(config-subif)#bandwidth 64
RTR1(config-subif)#frame-relay map ip 10.17.0.2 120 broadcast
RTR1(config-subif)#frame-relay map ip 10.17.0.3 130 broadcast
RTR1(config-subif)#frame-relay map ip 10.17.0.4 140 broadcast
```

Example 13-11 shows you how to configure multipoint subinterfaces. With this type of configuration, the subinterface takes on the same Frame Relay characteristics as a physical interface; that is, it is NBMA and is subject to split-horizon operation. The advantage over a point-to-point interface is that you need only a single network layer address.

Frame Relay Command Summary

Table 13-1 summarizes the commands you've learned in this chapter.

Table 13-1   *Frame Relay Command Summary*

Command	Description
encapsulation frame-relay [**cisco** l **ietf**]	Sets the interface to use Frame Relay encapsulation.
frame-relay lmi-type {**ansi** l **cisco** l **q9331**}	Sets the LMI type to be used. (Don't use this command for LMI type autosensing.)
frame-relay inverse-arp [*protocol*] [*dlci*]	Used to re-enable Inverse ARP for a protocol.
frame-relay map *protocol protocol-address dlci* [**broadcast**] [**ietf** l **cisco**] [**payload-compress packet-by-packet**]	Defines a static mapping from DLCI to protocol address.

continues

Table 13-1   *Frame Relay Command Summary (Continued)*

Command	Description
show frame-relay lmi	Displays LMI information.
show frame-relay pvc	Displays PVC traffic statistics.
show frame-relay map	Displays Frame Relay DLCI-to-IP address mappings.
debug frame-relay lmi	Displays LMI debug information.
interface serial *number.subinterface-number* {**multipoint** | **point-to-point**}	Creates a serial subinterface.

Summary

This chapter discussed the Frame Relay technology and how you implement it on a serial interface on your Cisco router. You learned about the technology and terms associated with Frame Relay and the different topologies that can be used to connect your Frame Relay network devices. In addition, you learned how to set Frame Relay encapsulation and LMI types. Also, you now know how IP addresses can be mapped to DLCI numbers automatically with Inverse ARP and how to manually map these components on subinterfaces. Finally, you saw how to show vital configuration information to aid in configuration and troubleshooting of Frame Relay circuits.

Review Questions

1 Frame Relay operates at which OSI layer?

2 Name at least one physical layer standard that can be used for Frame Relay connection.

3 Which component identifies the local logical connection between the router and the switch?

4 Which method used by Frame Relay allows for the dynamic mapping of IP address to DLCI number?

5 Name the three LMI standards supported by Cisco Routers.

6 By default, how often do routers exchange LMI information with the switch?

7 What is the default encapsulation type for Frame Relay on a Cisco router?

8 Which command is used to verify the LMI type?

9 What routing issue occurs with a Frame Relay network running multiple PVCs over a single interface?

10 What is the default subinterface type: point-to-point or multipoint?

Appendixes

Upon completion of this appendix, you will be able to perform the following tasks:

- Describe basic AppleTalk routing terms and operations.
- Determine AppleTalk cable ranges and zone names.
- Enable the AppleTalk protocol and configure interfaces.
- Verify connectivity within and across AppleTalk zones.
- Discover AppleTalk addresses of remote routers.
- Monitor AppleTalk operation in the router.

Configuring AppleTalk

This appendix presents an introduction to the AppleTalk protocol suite and shows you how it operates using Cisco IOS software configurations. Specifically, this appendix addresses basic AppleTalk routing terms and operations, shows you how to determine AppleTalk cable ranges and zone names, and shows you how to enable AppleTalk protocol and configure interfaces. You will learn to verify connectivity within and across AppleTalk zones, discover the AppleTalk address of remote routers, and monitor AppleTalk operation in the router.

AppleTalk Overview

Figure A-1 illustrates how the AppleTalk protocol stack compares to the OSI reference model. Descriptions of how the AppleTalk protocol stack operates at each layer follow.

Figure A-1 *AppleTalk Protocol Stack*

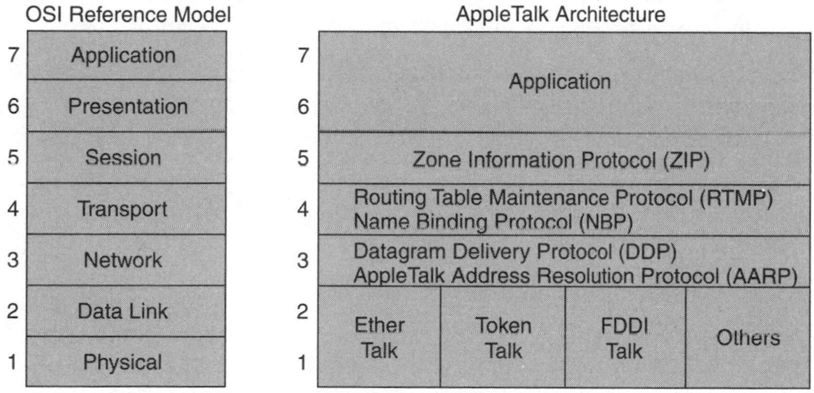

At the physical layer (Layer 1) and data link layer (Layer 2), most standard media types, such as Ethernet and Token Ring, are supported.

At Layer 3 in the AppleTalk architecture, the Datagram Delivery Protocol (DDP) provides a connectionless datagram service.

At Layer 4 in the AppleTalk architecture, the Name Binding Protocol (NBP) provides name-to-address association. Routing table updates are provided by the Routing Table Maintenance Protocol (RTMP).

At Layer 5 in the AppleTalk architecture, the Zone Information Protocol (ZIP) maps logical zones to network numbers and coordinates name lookup within zones.

Layers 6 and 7 serve as the application reference points. This is where an application programmer would link the network application into the AppleTalk architecture.

AppleTalk was designed as a client distributed network system. Users share network resources (such as files and printers) with other users. Computers supplying these network resources are called *servers*; computers using a server's network resources are called *clients*. Interaction with servers is essentially transparent to the user, because the computer itself determines the location of the requested materials and accesses them without further information from the user. Any Macintosh can be a host, a server, or both at the same time.

Clients use multicast to learn about available services. The AppleTalk environment allows propagation of lookups by the router, ensuring that all available services will be located by the user.

AppleTalk Addressing

AppleTalk addresses are composed of a 16-bit network number and an 8-bit node number.

The network portion of the address is manually configured in the router by the administrator. The node identifier portion is dynamically acquired during router startup.

The node identifier can also be manually configured on the Cisco router. This process is useful when you're configuring AppleTalk for multipoint WANs and for remote access using dialer maps.

RTMP provides routing information updates at Layer 4. RTMP is a Routing Information Protocol (RIP) derivative, using hop count as its metric for routing decisions. Hosts listen to RTMP updates to learn the router's address.

There are two versions of the AppleTalk protocol. The original mode was called Phase 1, or nonextended AppleTalk. It provided for only one network number per wire. With AppleTalk Version 2, one or more network numbers may be assigned to each wire. If more than one network number is assigned, the network is said to be *extended*. The range of logical network numbers on a single physical wire is called a *cable range* or *cable group*. The range of numbers is assigned by the administrator. Node numbers from 1 to 253 are assigned dynamically for both hosts and routers.

AppleTalk requires that a unique network.node address be applied to each router interface, as illustrated in Figure A-2.

Figure A-2 *AppleTalk Addressing*

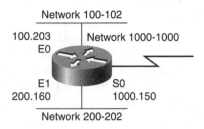

Network.Node

Extended AppleTalk Addressing

In AppleTalk's extended network addressing, the network numbers of nodes on the same wire can be different. There can be a wide network range (multiple logical networks) on a single physical network, as illustrated in Figure A-3.

Figure A-3 *Extended Addressing*

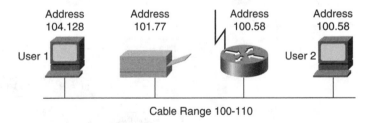

Each device in Figure A-3 has a unique address consisting of the following components:

- **Network number**—16 bits

    — A cable range states the span of network numbers available on this media.

    — Narrow-range networks (networks with a single network number) are supported.

    — A network number of 0 is reserved by the protocol for a newly attached node to use when it does not yet know the network number to use on its attached cable.

- **Node number**—8 bits

— Numbers in the range 1 to 253 represent any node (user, printer, or other device).

— The numbers 0, 254, and 255 are reserved on extended networks.

Dynamic AppleTalk Address Assignment

Node numbers are dynamically assigned. For example, in Figure A-4, when User 2's system is powered on, it has no address stored in its permanent (battery-backed) memory (P-RAM). User 2's software selects a provisional network address from the FF00-FFE0 range and a random node number. The new node sends ten AppleTalk Address Resolution Protocol (AARP) probes to verify the node ID availability. Figure A-4 shows the complete order of steps performed when a workstation powers up and configures its address.

Figure A-4 *Dynamic Address Acquisition*

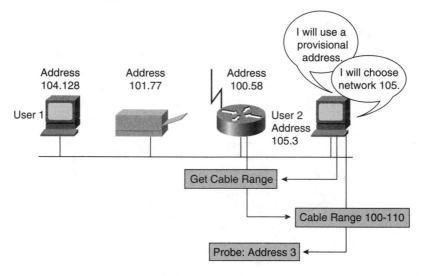

The transactions in Figure A-4 are as follows:

Step 1   A "get cable range" ZIP request is issued by User 2.

Step 2   The router's response indicates the range of network numbers available on the wire. User 2 selects a network number from the cable range.

Step 3   User 2 issues AARP probes ten times for a node ID:

— If there is a response that the node ID is in use, User 2 tries another node ID.

— If there is no response to the probe, User 2 uses this ID.

Step 4   User 2's address becomes 105.3.

After an address is acquired, it is saved in P-RAM. The stored address is probed for at the next power-up sequence. If it is in use, dynamic assignment is initiated.

AppleTalk Zones and Services

One method for controlling multicast traffic is to allocate nodes into zones. A *zone* is merely a logical group of nodes. A user node can be in only one zone. Figure A-5 demonstrates how zones help limit requests for services (control multicast traffic).

Figure A-5   *AppleTalk Zones*

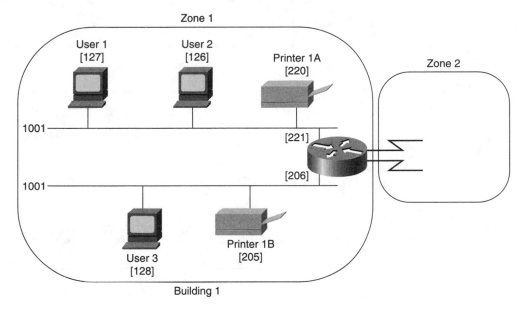

Each AppleTalk interface in the router must be assigned to a zone as part of its AppleTalk configuration.

Figure A-6 shows how AppleTalk uses zones with other AppleTalk protocols to connect clients to services.

Figure A-6   *AppleTalk Chooser*

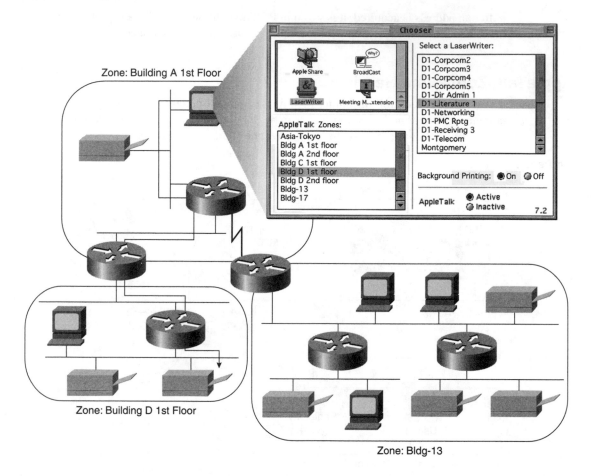

When a Macintosh user requires a service, the following transactions take place:

1 The Chooser sends a GetZoneList request to the router for a list of zones, which the routers have obtained using ZIP.

2 The NBP looks for the servers in the zone that the Macintosh user specifies.

3 The router forwards the request to each cable grouped in the selected zone.

4 A multicast (one-to-many) goes to all devices that match the device type requested.

5 Available matching services reply to the address of the Macintosh that originated the NBP process.

6 Routers in the path forward these replies until they reach the originating router.

7 The originating router sends the reply to the end user.

8 The user selects the preferred service from the list of replies.

9 A logical link for that service is retained in the Macintosh for future reference, and a list of services and zones is maintained within the router for local reference.

Users on the AppleTalk network locate specific services using NBP requests. In Figure A-7, User 2 looks for printers in the zone named Users. The router creates one request to send out cable 1001-1001 and another request to send out cable 1002-1002. Responses that the router forwards to User 2 inform User 2 about Printer 1A and Printer 1B.

Figure A-7 *Locating AppleTalk Printers*

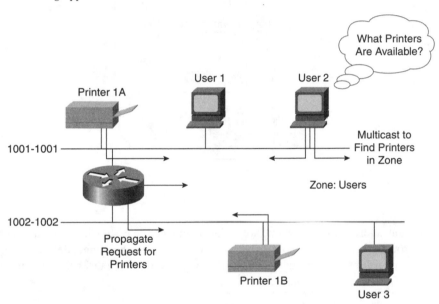

Configuring AppleTalk Routing

Configuring AppleTalk as a routing protocol requires setting both global and interface parameters as follows:

- Global task: Enable AppleTalk routing to start the routing process.
- Interface tasks:
  - Assign a range of network numbers to each interface. A narrow range can be an appropriate assignment.
  - Select a routing update protocol.
  - Assign each interface to a zone. Phase 2 allows multiple zones per segment.

After you start the process and assign the cable ranges on the interfaces, you will have enabled the RTMP routing protocol on all AppleTalk interfaces, as shown in Figure A-8.

Figure A-8   *Enabling the AppleTalk Routing Process*

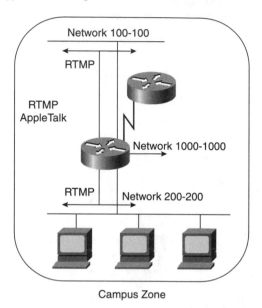

After an address and zone name are assigned, the interface is enabled for packet processing. All routers in a network or data link must agree on the cable range, default zone, and zone list. The following sections describe the global and interface tasks for configuring AppleTalk as a routing protocol.

Enabling AppleTalk and Selecting a Routing Update Protocol

The **appletalk routing** command starts the AppleTalk routing process. The syntax for this command is as follows:

```
Router(config)#appletalk routing
```

The **appletalk protocol** command selects one or more routing protocols for use on this interface. The syntax for this command is as follows:

```
Router(config-if)#appletalk protocol {rtmp | eigrp | aurp}
```

- **rtmp** specifies that the routing protocol to use is RTMP, which is the default.
- **eigrp** specifies that the routing protocol to use is Enhanced IGRP.
- **aurp** specifies that the routing protocol to use is AppleTalk Update-Based Routing Protocol (AURP). You can enable AURP only on tunnel interfaces.

If the **appletalk protocol** command is omitted in the interface specification, RTMP is selected by default.

Assigning a Range of Network Numbers to Each Interface

The **appletalk cable-range** command specifies a range of network numbers available to the interface. The syntax for this command is as follows:

```
Router(config-if)#appletalk cable-range cable-range [network.node]
```

This command has two parameters:

- *cable-range* defines the value of the cable range and specifies the start and end of the cable range, separated by a hyphen. These values are a decimal number from 1 to 65,279. The starting network number must be less than or equal to the ending network number. These ranges must not overlap with any other range in the internetwork.

- *network.node* is an optional parameter that defines the suggested AppleTalk address for the interface. The *network* parameter is the 16-bit network number, and the *node* parameter is the 8-bit node number. Both numbers are decimal. The network number must fall within the specified range of network numbers.

If the cable range value is 0-0, the interface is placed in discovery mode. This is discussed in greater detail in the "AppleTalk Discovery Mode" section later in this chapter.

The *network.node* option allows the network administrator to specify a unique address, which is useful on mapped interfaces such as Frame Relay.

Assigning Each Interface to a Zone

The **appletalk zone** command assigns the zone name to the interface. Multiple zones can be assigned to one interface in a Phase 2 installation. The first zone name is the default zone that new clients will be placed in. The syntax for this command is as follows:

```
Router(config-if)#appletalk zone zone-name
```

AppleTalk Configuration Example

Example A-1 provides AppleTalk configuration for the network shown in Figure A-9.

Figure A-9   *AppleTalk Configuration Example*

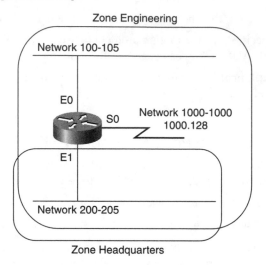

Example A-1   *AppleTalk Configuration Example*

```
Router(config)#appletalk routing

Router(config)#interface ethernet 0
Router(config-if)#appletalk cable-range 100-105
Router(config-if)#appletalk zone engineering

Router(config-if)#interface ethernet 1
Router(config-if)#appletalk cable-range 200-205
Router(config-if)#appletalk zone engineering
Router(config-if)#appletalk zone headquarters

Router(config-if)#interface serial 0
Router(config-if)#appletalk cable-range 1000-1000 1000.128
Router(config-if)#appletalk zone engineering
```

Table A-1 highlights some of the key commands from Example A-1.

Table A-1   *Command Highlights from Example A-1*

Command	Description
appletalk routing	Starts the AppleTalk routing process.
appletalk cable-range 100-105	Establishes a range of six network numbers available to devices on Ethernet 0.

Table A-1   *Command Highlights from Example A-1 (Continued)*

Command	Description
appletalk cable-range 200-205	Establishes a range of six network numbers available to devices on Ethernet 1.
appletalk zone engineering	Places interface Ethernet 0 into a zone named engineering. This is also the default zone available to client machines.
appletalk zone engineering **appletalk zone headquarters**	Places interface Ethernet 1 into two zones: engineering and headquarters.
appletalk cable-range 1000-1000 **1000.128**	Assigns a narrow cable range of 1000 to interface serial 0 and specifies the network.node address of 1000.128.

All interfaces are using RTMP as the default routing protocol because no **appletalk protocol** commands are specified.

After AppleTalk routing is enabled, interface Ethernet 0 dynamically acquires a node number on one of six available network numbers. Serial 0 has a hard-coded address of 1000.128. All interfaces in the router are part of the zone engineering, and Ethernet 1 is also part of zone headquarters.

AppleTalk Discovery Mode

Discovery mode can occur if the router is not a seed router. Seed routers seed the AppleTalk internetwork with configuration information (such as network number ranges and zones). The network administrator sets up a router as a seed router to provide configuration information to other nonseed routers. A seed router is one that has been configured with the cable range and zone names.

NOTE   AppleTalk discovery mode does not work over serial interfaces.

Placing a nonseed router interface in discovery mode allows the interface to dynamically learn its cable range and zone information from a seed router. There are two ways to place an interface into discovery mode:

- The Phase 2 method assigns the cable range as 0-0 using the following command:

```
Router(config-if)#appletalk cable-range 0-0
```

- The second alternative method involves the **appletalk discovery** command. With this option, you assign a cable range other than 0-0 to the interface using normal configuration steps which then allows dynamic learning of the actual cable range and zone names from other routers. The following syntax shows how to configure discovery mode with this method:

```
Router(config-if)#appletalk cable-range cable-range

Router(config-if)#appletalk discovery
```

Example A-2 demonstrates how to configure AppleTalk discovery mode for the network shown in Figure A-10. In this example, Routers A and B are the seed routers because they have been configured with the appropriate information. For Router C, we are unsure of the networks, so we want to use discovery mode for configuration. Here, we show each type of discovery. For Ethernet 0, we use the command **appletalk cable-range 0-0**. On interface Ethernet 1, we guess the cable range and then enable discovery mode for that interface with the command **appletalk discovery**. This allows for the discovery of the cable range and the zone name.

Figure A-10 *Discovery Mode Example*

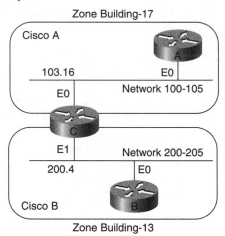

Example A-2 *AppleTalk Discovery Mode Configuration for Router C*

```
RouterC(config)#no appletalk routing
RouterC(config)#appletalk routing
RouterC(config)#interface ethernet 0
RouterC(config-if)#appletalk cable-range 0-0
RouterC(config-if)#interface ethernet 1
RouterC(config-if)#appletalk cable-range 3000-3002
RouterC(config-if)#appletalk discovery
```

Example A-2 *AppleTalk Discovery Mode Configuration for Router C (Continued)*

```
RouterC(config-if)#end
RouterC#
%SYS-5-CONFIG_I: Configured from console by console
```

Table A-2 highlights some of the key commands from Example A-2.

Table A-2 *Command Highlights from Example A-2*

Command	Description
appletalk cable-range 0-0	Places Ethernet 0 into discovery mode.
appletalk cable-range 3000-3002	Assigns a network range to Ethernet 1.
appletalk discovery	Places Ethernet 1 into discovery mode.

Both Ethernet 0 and Ethernet 1 dynamically learn their addresses and zones.

Example A-3 shows the live configuration for Ethernet 0 and Ethernet 1 after the discovery.

Example A-3 *Configuration Output After Discovery Process*

```
RouterC#show running-config
Building configuration...

Current configuration:
!
version 11.2
!
hostname RouterC
!
!
appletalk routing
!
crypto process-release 25
!
interface Ethernet0
 no ip address
 media-type 10BaseT
 appletalk cable-range 200-205 200.4
 appletalk discovery
!
interface Ethernet1
 no ip address
 media-type 10BaseT
 appletalk cable-range 100-105 103.16
 appletalk discovery
!
interface Serial0
 no ip address
!
interface Serial1
```

continues

Example A-3   *Configuration Output After Discovery Process (Continued)*

```
 no ip address
 shutdown
!
no ip classless
!
!
line con 0
 exec-timeout 0 0
 logging synchronous
line aux 0
line vty 0 4
 login
!
end

RouterC#
```

In the "live" configuration shown in Example A-3, you see that both interfaces have discovered the appropriate cable ranges and zones for the given networks. The highlighted sections show the current configuration of each interface. Notice that the interface is still in discovery mode. This means that each time the router comes up, it rediscovers the zones and cable ranges. Because these are not likely to change, you now want to disable discovery mode on each interface with the command **no appletalk discovery**. You also need to save this configuration so that it will be used when the router is reloaded. Table A-3 highlights some of the key commands from Example A-3 for interface Ethernet 0.

Table A-3   *Command Highlights from Example A-3 for Interface Ethernet 0*

Command	Description
appletalk cable-range 100-105	100-105 is the acquired network range.

Table A-4 highlights some of the key commands from Example A-3 for interface Ethernet 1.

Table A-4   *Command Highlights from Example A-3 for Interface Ethernet 1*

Command	Description
appletalk cable-range 200-205	200-205 is the acquired network range.

The AppleTalk discovery shows up on the interface after the discovery operation occurs.

Displaying AppleTalk Interface Information

Use the **show appletalk interface** command to display the status of all AppleTalk interfaces, including individual addressing, line status, timers, access lists assigned, and other details. Example A-4 provides some sample output for the **show appletalk interface** command.

Example A-4 *show appletalk interface Displays AppleTalk Interface Information*

```
RouterC#show appletalk interface ethernet 0
Ethernet0 is up, line protocol is up
  AppleTalk cable range is 200-205
  AppleTalk address is 200.4, Valid
  AppleTalk zone is "Building-13"
  AppleTalk port configuration provided by 200.234
  AppleTalk discovery mode is enabled
  AppleTalk address gleaning is disabled
  AppleTalk route cache is enabled
```

The **show appletalk interface** command is particularly useful when you first enable AppleTalk on a router interface.

The output in Example A-4 shows you the following information:

- The interface is Ethernet 0.
- The cable range contains an address value from which an address was selected. The address is marked as valid.
- The zone name is listed.
- AppleTalk address gleaning is enabled.
- AppleTalk route cache is enabled.

Displaying AppleTalk Routing Table Contents

Use the **show appletalk route** command to display the contents of the AppleTalk routing table. Example A-5 provides some sample output for the **show appletalk route** command.

Example A-5 *show appletalk route Displays AppleTalk Routing Table Contents*

```
RouterC#sh appletalk route
Codes: R - RTMP derived, E - EIGRP derived, C - connected, A - AURP
       S - static  P - proxy
3 routes in internet

The first zone listed for each entry is its default (primary) zone.

C Net 100-105 directly connected, Ethernet1, zone Building-17
C Net 200-205 directly connected, Ethernet0, zone Building-13
R Net 600-800 [1/G] via 200.234, 9 sec, Ethernet0, zone Ozone
                Additional zones: 'endzone'
```

Example A-5 shows the zones assigned to each cable range. The highlighted line shows an example of an extended cable range in the entry derived from RTMP.

Displaying AppleTalk Zone Information Table Contents

The **show appletalk zone** command displays entries in the AppleTalk zone information table. Example A-6 provides some sample output for the **show appletalk zone** command.

Example A-6 *show appletalk zone Displays AppleTalk Zone Information Table Contents*

```
RouterC#show appletalk zone
Name                                   Network(s)
Ozone                                  600-800
Building-13                            200-205
Building-17                            100-105
endzone                                600-800
```

Notice that the wide range of networks, 600-800, occurs in zone **endzone** as well as in zone **Ozone**. The NBP lookup process is limited to the zone specified by the Macintosh user's zone selection in the Chooser.

Displaying Global AppleTalk Configuration Parameters for a Router

The **show appletalk globals** command displays information and settings concerning the router's global AppleTalk configuration parameters. Example A-7 provides some sample output for the **show appletalk globals** command.

Example A-7 *show appletalk globals Displays Global AppleTalk Configuration Parameters for a Router*

```
RouterC#show appletalk globals
AppleTalk global information:
  Internet is incompatible with older, AT Phase1, routers.
  There are 3 routes in the internet.
  There are 4 zones defined.
  Logging of significant AppleTalk events is disabled.
  ZIP resends queries every 10 seconds.
  RTMP updates are sent every 10 seconds.
  RTMP entries are considered BAD after 20 seconds.
  RTMP entries are discarded after 60 seconds.
  AARP probe retransmit count: 10, interval: 200 msec.
  AARP request retransmit count: 5, interval: 1000 msec.
  DDP datagrams will be checksummed.
  RTMP datagrams will be strictly checked.
  RTMP routes may not be propagated without zones.
  Routes will not be distributed between routing protocols.
  Routing between local devices on an interface will not be performed.
  IPTalk uses the udp base port of 768 (Default).
  AppleTalk EIGRP is not enabled.
```

Example A-7 *show appletalk globals Displays Global AppleTalk Configuration Parameters for a Router (Continued)*

```
  Alternate node address format will not be displayed.
  Access control of any networks of a zone hides the zone.
RouterC#
```

The highlighted line in Example A-7 indicates incompatibility with the earliest form of AppleTalk, known as Phase I. Phase I restricted the network to the use of a single numbered cable range and a single zone per interface.

Displaying RTMP Routine Output

The **debug apple routing** command displays output from the RTMP routines. This command is used to monitor acquisition, aging, and advertisement of routes. It also reports conflicting network numbers on the same internetwork. Example A-8 provides some sample output for the **debug apple routing** command.

Example A-8 *debug apple routing Displays Output from RTMP Routines*

```
RouterC#debug apple routing
AppleTalk RTMP routing debugging is on
AppleTalk EIGRP routing debugging is on
RouterC#
AT: RTMP from 103.102 (new 0,old 0,bad 0,ign 0, dwn 0)
AT: src=Ethernet0:200.4, dst=200-205, size=16, 1 rte, RTMP pkt sent
AT: src=Ethernet1:103.16, dst=100-105, size=22, 2 rtes, RTMP pkt sent
AT: Route ager starting on Main AT RoutingTable (3 active nodes)
AT: Route ager finished on Main AT RoutingTable (3 active nodes)
AT: RTMP from 200.234 (new 0,old 1,bad 0,ign 0, dwn 0)
AT: RTMP from 103.102 (new 0,old 0,bad 0,ign 0, dwn 0)
AT: src=Ethernet0:200.4, dst=200-205, size=16, 1 rte, RTMP pkt sent
AT: src=Ethernet1:103.16, dst=100-105, size=22, 2 rtes, RTMP pkt sent
AT: Route ager starting on Main AT RoutingTable (3 active nodes)
AT: Route ager finished on Main AT RoutingTable (3 active nodes)
AT: RTMP from 200.234 (new 0,old 1,bad 0,ign 0, dwn 0)
AT: RTMP from 103.102 (new 0,old 0,bad 0,ign 0, dwn 0)
```

The output from this **debug** command shows that RTMP packets are being sent and received on the interfaces. This can be useful for troubleshooting problems.

Summary

In this appendix, you've seen how AppleTalk can be configured on your router to provide connectivity for your AppleTalk internetwork. You saw how AppleTalk defines network and node addresses and how services are divided into zones. In addition, you should now be able to enable AppleTalk routing and to configure a router to route for a specific set of cable ranges. Finally, you should now know how to verify AppleTalk configuration for the router.

AppleTalk Command Summary

Table A-5 summarizes the commands you've learned in this chapter.

Table A-5   *AppleTalk Command Summary*

Command	Description
appletalk routing	Enables the AppleTalk routing process.
appletalk protocol	Specifies the AppleTalk routing protocol to be used on a specific interface.
appletalk zone	Specifies one or more AppleTalk zones for an interface.
appletalk cable-range 0-0	Places the interface into discovery mode.
appletalk cable-range 0-0 **appletalk discovery**	Places the AppleTalk interface into discovery mode.
show appletalk interface	Shows AppleTalk interface configuration information.
show appletalk route	Displays the AppleTalk routing table.
show appletalk zone	Displays a list of all the AppleTalk zones known by the router.
show appletalk globals	Displays information and parameters concerning the router's global AppleTalk configuration parameters.
debug apple routing	Displays output from the AppleTalk routing process.

Review Questions

1 At what layer of the OSI reference model does the AppleTalk protocol operate?

2 How many bits are available for a complete AppleTalk address?

3 How do AppleTalk hosts normally get an address?

4 Zones divide networks into communities of interest in order to control what?

5 Which command enables the AppleTalk routing process?

6 Which command assigns a network to an AppleTalk interface?

7 Which command allows you to view the zones known by the switch?

Upon completion of this appendix, you will be able to perform the following task:

- Establish a HyperTerminal terminal emulation session so that you can configure your router or switch from the PC, given a PC with Windows 95 and HyperTerminal.

Establishing a HyperTerminal Session

HyperTerminal is an accessory application in Microsoft Windows 95 that allows you to create a terminal emulation session from your PC. After this terminal session is established, you can access a Cisco device through the Console port and configure the device from your PC.

Enabling the HyperTerminal terminal emulation session for a Cisco device requires the following components:

- A PC with Windows 95, HyperTerminal software, and a serial communications port (sometimes called the COM or serial port)
- A Cisco device with a console cable
- A connection cabled from the Cisco device's console port to the serial communications port on the PC

Figure B-1 illustrates all the components necessary for establishing a HyperTerminal terminal emulation session for a Cisco device.

Figure B-1   *Necessary Components for Establishing a HyperTerminal Session*

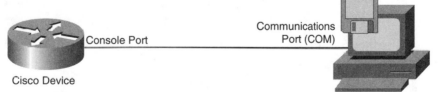

Console Port

Cisco Device

Communications Port (COM)

Windows 95 PC with HyperTerminal Terminal Emulation Software

NOTE   The cabling requirements to establish a console connection to the Cisco device are described in Chapter 2, "Assembling and Cabling Cisco Devices."

Creating a HyperTerminal Session

This section describes how to set up a HyperTerminal session so that you can access your Cisco device through the console port.

To establish a HyperTerminal session, follow these steps:

Step 1   Verify that you have a console cable attached to your Cisco device's console port. The other end of the cable should be attached to your PC's serial communications port.

Step 2   Power on the PC, and enter the Windows 95 desktop.

Step 3   Open HyperTerminal by selecting Start, Programs, Accessories, HyperTerminal. You should now be in the HyperTerminal folder, as shown in Figure B-2.

Figure B-2   *HyperTerminal Configuration Steps 3 and 4*

Step 4   Double-click the **Hypertrm.exe** icon to start a HyperTerminal session.

Step 5   Enter the Connection Description window, as shown in Figure B-3. In this window, name your connection in the Name field and select the red telephone icon. Click the OK button.

Figure B-3 *HyperTerminal Configuration Step 5*

Step 6 You enter the Connect To window, as shown in Figure B-4. In the Connect Using field of this window, select the communications serial port you will be using. (Some PCs have multiple serial communications ports.) In the figure, the port is COM1. The other fields should turn gray. Click OK.

Figure B-4 *HyperTerminal Configuration Step 6*

Step 7 You enter the serial communications port properties window (which appears as COM1 Properties in Figure B-5). Select 9600 bits per second, 8 data bits, parity None, 1 stopbit, and flow control None, as shown in the figure. Click OK.

Figure B-5 *HyperTerminal Configuration Step 7*

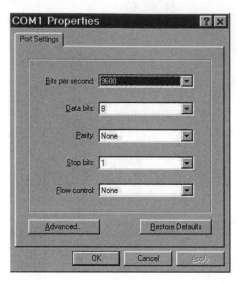

Step 8 You should now be in a HyperTerminal session. Click Return a few times, and you will see the Cisco Device prompt in the window, as shown in Figure B-6.

Figure B-6 *HyperTerminal Configuration Step 8*

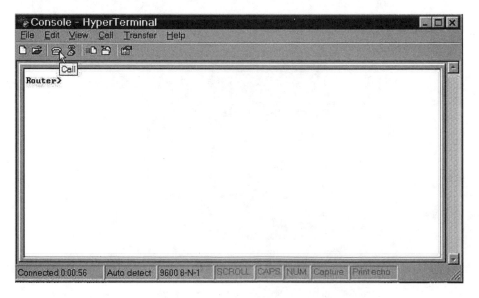

After you are in a session, you can disconnect or reconnect a session by clicking the disconnect and connect icons, shown in Figure B-6. You can also save the output from a session by selecting File, Save. The session will be saved in the hyperterm folder with the name you assigned to the session in Step 5, and you will not have to recreate a new session.

Upon completion of this appendix, you will understand the following:

- The basic features of the Cisco 700 series router.
- Basic initial configuration tasks for the Cisco 700 series router.

Cisco 700 Series Routers

This appendix contains an overview of the Cisco 700 series of small office/home office (SOHO) routers and a brief overview of basic initial configuration tasks. The Cisco 700 series of small office/home office ISDN routers provides a cost-effective solution to equipping remote offices for ISDN connectivity.

Cisco 700 Series Overview and Configuration

All the products in the Cisco 700 series product family offer maximum flexibility for remote access. The product family now includes the Cisco 761M, 762M, 765M, 766M, 771M, 772M, 775M, and 776M. These products offer two optional analog telephone interfaces to allow devices such as standard telephones, fax machines, and modems to share an ISDN BRI line, eliminating the need for multiple telephone lines or expensive ISDN telephones. Four of the Cisco 700 models (the 765M, 766M, 775M, and the 776M) offer support for two basic telephone lines as well as support for supplemental telephone services over ISDN. These telephone services include call waiting, cancel call waiting, call hold, call retrieve, three-way call conferencing, and call transfer. Figure C-1 illustrates how the 700 series router can provide network services for the SOHO.

Figure C-1   *Cisco 700 Series Router*

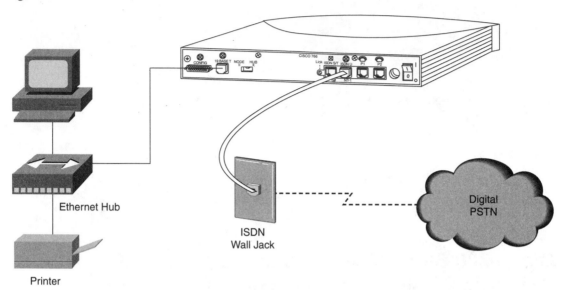

The Cisco 700 series routers all support IP and IPX routing, transparent bridging, Simple Network Management Protocol (SNMP), and multilevel authentication. All Cisco 700 series routers support the Multilink Point-to-Point Protocol (MP), providing up to 128 kbps (precompressed) of ISDN bandwidth.

All models in this family also feature ClickStart software, which allows users to configure Cisco 700 series routers using a standard World Wide Web browser, such as Netscape Navigator. ClickStart is a graphical, user-friendly configuration interface that breaks the installation process into simple steps, prompting the user for the required information, thus enabling the user to set up a new router in just a few minutes.

Cisco 700 Series Router Profiles

A *profile* is a set of configurations customized for and associated with a specific remote device. After being defined by the user, profiles are saved and stored in nonvolatile random access memory (NVRAM)—the memory used to store the router's configuration.

Instead of using one set of configurations to operate with all remote devices, you can customize your Cisco 700 series router to use individual configuration sets, or profiles, customized for each remote device.

Cisco 700 series routers are configured with three permanent profiles. These three profiles can be modified but not deleted:

- **LAN**—Determines how data is passed from the router to the LAN. It is used for routing and with the Ethernet connection.

- **Internal**—Determines how data is passed between the bridge engine and the IP/IPX router engine. It is used when routing is enabled.

- **Standard**—Used for incoming ISDN connections that do not have a profile. The Standard profile does not support routing. This profile should be used to provide the appropriate configuration and security measures for unknown callers.

When the router is turned on, the profiles are loaded. Figure C-2 illustrates the router profiles.

Figure C-2   *Cisco 700 Series Router Profiles*

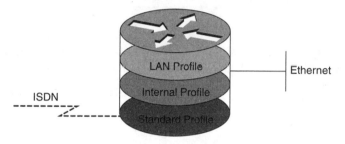

User profiles allow users to create customized sets of configuration parameters, such as filters, demand thresholds, and passwords for each remote site that is dialed. Profiles allow on-demand calls to be made to different telephone numbers based on demand filters that are tailored for each remote site.

System parameters are independent of profiles and affect the router as a system. System parameters can be changed only at the system-level prompt (**Router_name>** or **>**).

Cisco IOS-700 Commands

Because the Cisco 700 series does not use the standard Cisco IOS software, but rather the Cisco IOS-700 software, there are several commands that you must become familiar with.

Some of these commands are analogous to IOS commands, and others are unique. Table C-1 lists some of the most important IOS-700 commands.

Table C-1 *IOS-700 Command Sample*

Command	Description
set default	Reloads the router and resets the configuration to the factory default settings. The current configuration is lost.
upload	Displays the router's complete configuration, including all profiles.
cd	When this command is entered without an argument, it moves the user interface to system-level or system-profile mode. If followed by the name of an existing profile, it moves the user interface to the profile specified. Subsequent commands are entered into that profile. This command is similar to the **cd** command found in MS-DOS or UNIX.
show config	Displays the configuration of the profile from which the command is entered.

NOTE Unlike the IOS software, there is no command to save a configuration. There is no saved or current configuration. Each time you enter a command, it is saved in NVRAM.

System Profile Commands

The system profile contains parameters that affect the router as a whole and apply to all other profiles unless that profile contains a command that overrides the system parameter. Figure C-3 illustrates the system profile.

Figure C-3 *System Profile*

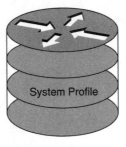

System Profile

Table C-2 lists some commonly used system profile commands (sometimes referred to as system-level commands).

Table C-2 *Cisco 700 Series Router System Profile Commands*

Command	Description
set systemname	Specifies the name of the router. This is displayed as part of the prompt and is used for authentication.
set switch *switch-type*	Configures the ISDN switch type with which the router interfaces.
set 1 spid *spid-number*	Specifies the SPID number, if required. If a second SPID is required, the **set 2 spid** *spid-number* command is used.

LAN Profile Commands

The LAN profile contains the configuration for the Ethernet interface, as illustrated in Figure C-4.

Figure C-4 *LAN Profile*

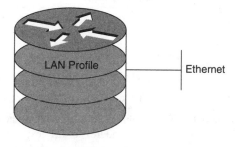

Table C-3 lists some commonly used commands for LAN profile configuration.

Table C-3 *Cisco 700 Series Router LAN Profile Commands*

Command	Description
set ip address *address*	Specifies the IP address for the 10BaseT Ethernet interface.
set ip netmask *subnet-mask*	Specifies the subnet mask for the 10BaseT Ethernet interface.
set ip routing on	Enables IP RIP routing for the 10BaseT Ethernet interface.

User Profile Commands

A user profile contains the configuration for a destination reachable through the ISDN interface, as illustrated in Figure C-5.

Figure C-5   *User Profile*

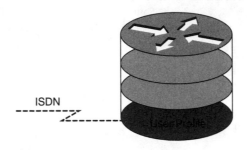

Table C-4 lists some commands used to create and configure a user profile.

Table C-4   *Cisco 700 Series Router User Profile Commands*

Command	Description
set user *profile name*	Creates a profile of the name specified and moves the user interface to that new profile.
set ip address *address*	Specifies the IP address for the ISDN interface.
set ip netmask *subnet-mask*	Specifies the subnet mask for the ISDN interface.
set ip routing on	Enables IP RIP routing over the ISDN interface.
set ip route destination 0.0.0.0/0 gateway 0.0.0.0	Establishes a static route to the destination network specified via the address of the next hop router specified. In this example, any address and any router are defined. This is the same as a default route. By specifying a specific subnet and specific router address, you can allow traffic to those destinations only. (This is a form of filtering.)
set bridging off	Turns off bridging over the ISDN interface. By default, bridging is enabled.

Cisco 700 Series Router Configuration Example

Example C-1 provides a configuration for the remote Cisco 700 router connecting to the central site router illustrated in Figure C-6.

Figure C-6   *Typical SOHO Configuration*

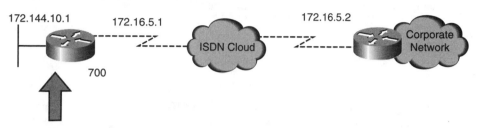

Example C-1   *Cisco 700 Series Router Configuration*

```
> set systemname 700
700> set switch 5ess
700> set 1 spid 01408555123411
700> set 1 spid 01408555432111
700> cd lan
700:LAN> set ip address 172.144.10.1
700:LAN> set ip netmask 255.255.255.0
700:LAN> set ip routing on
700:LAN> cd
700> set user Central
700:Central> set number 5554567
700:Central> set ppp secret client <password>
700:Central> set ip routing on
700:Central> set ip route destination 0.0.0.0/0 gateway 172.16.5.2
700:Central> set ip address 172.16.5.1
700:Central> set ip netmask 255.255.255.0
```

Table C-5 highlights and describes some of the key commands in Example C-1.

Table C-5   *Command Highlights from Example C-1*

Command	Description
set systemname 700	Specifies the system name as 700.
set switch 5ess	Specifies the ISDN switch type as the AT&T 5ESS.
set 1 spid 01408555123411 **set 2 spid 01408555432111**	Specifies the two SPIDs as required by the ISDN service provider.
cd lan	Moves the user interface to the LAN profile.
set ip address 172.144.10.1	Configures the Ethernet interface IP address to the value shown.

continues

Table C-5   *Command Highlights from Example C-1 (Continued)*

Command	Description
set ip netmask 255.255.255.0	Configures the Ethernet interface subnet mask to the value shown.
set ip routing on	Enables IP routing on the Ethernet interface.
cd	Moves the user interface back to the system level.
set user Central	Creates a new user profile named Central and moves to that profile.
set number 5554567	Specifies the number to dial to reach the destination.
set ppp secret client <*password*>	Specifies the PPP CHAP authentication password.
set ip routing on	Enables IP routing on the ISDN interface.
set ip route destination 0.0.0.0/0 gateway 172.16.5.2	Specifies a static route so that traffic for any destination subnet goes to the address specified.
set ip address 172.16.5.1	Configures the ISDN interface IP address to the value shown.
set ip netmask 255.255.255.0	Configures the ISDN interface subnet mask to the value shown.

Table C-6 lists some additional commands that are useful for troubleshooting and administration.

Table C-6   *Troubleshooting and Administrative Commands*

Command	Description
ping *address*	Sends ICMP echo requests to the address specified.
reboot	Reboots the router.
call *number*	Initiates a manual call to the number specified.

NOTE   For additional information on the Cisco 700 series hardware and software, refer to the *Cisco 700 Series Router Installation Guide,* the *Cisco 700 Series Command Reference,* the documentation CD-ROM, or CCO.

Upon completion of this appendix, you will be able to perform the following tasks:

- Understand the virtual configuration register.
- Perform router password recovery.

Password Recovery

This appendix contains an overview of the virtual configuration register used by the router during initialization. It supplements the material covered in Chapter 4, "Managing Your Network Environment." It also discusses how to get access to your router if you forget or lose your password. In order to understand the recovery process, you must first understand how the configuration register is used by the router during the boot process.

The Virtual Configuration Register

When a router boots, the virtual configuration register is checked to determine (among other things) what mode to enter upon booting, where to get the software image, and how to deal with the configuration file in NVRAM. This 16-bit register controls functions such as the console port baud rate, the loading operation of the software, enabling or disabling the Break key during normal operations, controlling the default broadcast address, and setting a boot source for the router. The configuration register can be displayed by typing the command **show version**.

Typically, the factory default for the configuration register is 0x2102 (a hexadecimal value). The binary form of the register value is as follows:

0010 0001 0000 0010

The bits are numbered 0 to 15, starting with the bit on the far right. Thus, bits 1, 8, and 13 would be on in this setting. All other bits would be off. Table D-1 later in this appendix lists the meaning of each virtual configuration register bit.

Changing the Virtual Configuration Register Settings

You can change the configuration register settings through the IOS software or in ROM monitor mode. Some common reasons to modify the value of the virtual configuration register are recovering a lost password, changing the console baud rate, and enabling or disabling the break function. Another reason to modify the value of the virtual configuration register might be to control the boot process.

NOTE   If the router finds no **boot system** commands, and there are no images in Flash memory, the router uses the netboot value in the configuration register to form a filename from which to netboot a default system image stored on a network server via TFTP (see Table D-3).

To change the configuration register while running the system IOS software, follow these steps:

Step 1   Enter the **enable** command and your password to enter the privileged level, as follows:

```
router> enable
    Password:
    router#
```

Step 2   At the privileged-level system prompt (**router#**), enter the **configure terminal** command. You will be prompted as follows:

```
router# configure terminal
    Enter configuration commands, one per line.
    Edit with DELETE, CTRL/W, and CTRL/U; end with CTRL/Z
Router(config)#
```

Step 3   To set the contents of the configuration register, enter the **config-register** *value* configuration command, where *value* is a hexadecimal number preceded by 0x (see Table D-1):

```
Router(config)# config-register 0x2102
```

Step 4   Exit configuration mode by pressing **Ctrl-Z**. The new value settings will be written into the virtual configuration register; however, the new settings do not take effect until the system software is reloaded when you reboot the router.

Step 5   To display the configuration register value currently in effect and the value that will be used at the next reload, enter the **show version** EXEC command. The value will be displayed on the last line of the screen display as follows:

```
Configuration register is 0x2142 (will be 0x2102 at next reload)
```

Step 6   Reboot the router. The new value takes effect. Configuration register changes take effect only when the router restarts, which occurs when you switch the power off and then on or when you issue a **reload** command from the console. It is not necessary to save the current for the register setting to be saved. When you issue the **reload** command, you will be prompted with a message asking whether you want to save your configuration before the reload. If the only thing you changed in configuration mode is the configuration register, the answer to this prompt is generally No.

NOTE   Note that although this appendix discusses the concept of the virtual configuration register, not all routers have identical settings. For example, the filenames listed in Table D-3 differ between platforms, and on some routers, an additional bit is used for console speed to allow higher speeds. For more detailed information about your specific hardware, check your Documentation CD or CCO.

Table D-1   *Common Virtual Configuration Register Bit Meaning*

Bit Number(s)	Hexadecimal Value	Meaning
00 to 03	0x0000 to 0x000F	Boot field (see Table D-2).
04	0x0010	Undefined.
05	0x0020	Undefined.
06	0x0040	Causes system software to ignore NVRAM contents.
07	0x0080	OEM bit enabled.
08	0x0100	Break disabled.
09	0x0200	Undefined.
10	0x0400	IP broadcast with all 0s if bit is on. This works with bit 14, as shown in Table D-4.
11 to 12	0x0800 to 0x1800	Console line speed (see Table D-5).
13	0x2000	Boot default ROM software if network boot fails.
14	0x4000	IP broadcasts do not have network numbers. This value works with bit 10, as shown in Table D-4.
15	0x8000	Enable diagnostic messages and ignore NVRAM contents.

CAUTION   To avoid confusion and possibly hanging the router, remember that valid configuration register settings might be combinations of settings and not just the individual settings listed in Table D-1. For example, the factory default value of 0x2102 is a combination of settings.

The lowest four bits of the virtual configuration register (bits 3, 2, 1, and 0) form the boot field. (See Table D-2.) The boot field specifies a number in binary. If you set the boot field value to 0, you must boot the operating system manually by entering the **b** command at the bootstrap prompt, as follows:

```
> b [tftp] flash filename
```

Definitions of the various **b** command options follow:

- **b**—Boots the default system software from ROM
- **b flash**—Boots the first file in Flash memory
- **b** *filename* [**host**]—Netboots using TFTP
- **b flash** [*filename*]—Boots the file (filename) from Flash memory

Table D-2   *Explanation of Boot Field (Configuration Register Bits 00 to 03)*

Boot Field	Meaning
0x0	Upon boot, this setting directs the router to enter ROM monitor mode.
0x1	Upon boot, this setting enables the router to boot from the image in ROM. This is also known as boot mode.
0x2 to 0xF	Specifies a default netboot filename. May enable boot system commands that override the default netboot filename.

If you set the boot field value to a value in the range of 0x2 through 0xF, there is a valid **system boot** command stored in the configuration file. If you set the boot field to any other bit pattern, the router uses the resulting number to form a default boot filename for netbooting (see Table D-3).

The router creates a default boot filename as part of the automatic configuration processes. To form the boot filename, the router starts with the word **Cisco** and links the octal equivalent of the boot field number, a dash, and the processor-type name. Table D-3 lists the default boot filenames or actions for the 2500 series routers.

Table D-3 *Default Boot Filenames*

Action/Filename	Bit 3	Bit 2	Bit 1	Bit 0
Bootstrap mode	0	0	0	0
ROM software	0	0	0	1
Cisco2-igs	0	0	1	0
Cisco3-igs	0	0	1	1
Cisco4-igs	0	1	0	0
Cisco5-igs	0	1	0	1
Cisco6-igs	0	1	1	0
cisco7-igs	0	1	1	1
cisco10-igs	1	0	0	0
cisco11-igs	1	0	0	1
cisco12-igs	1	0	1	0
cisco13-igs	1	0	1	1
cisco14-igs	1	1	0	0
cisco15-igs	1	1	0	1
cisco16-igs	1	1	1	0
cisco17-igs	1	1	1	1

NOTE   A valid **boot system** configuration command in the router configuration in NVRAM overrides the default netboot filename.

In Example D-1, the virtual configuration register is set to boot the router from Flash memory and to ignore Break at the next reboot of the router.

Example D-1 *Setting the Configuration Register to Boot from Flash*

```
router# configure terminal
Enter configuration commands, one per line.
Edit with DELETE, CTRL/W, and CTRL/U; end with CTRL/Z
config-register 0x2102
boot system flash [filename]
^Z
router#
```

Although the lower 4 bits of this register control the boot characteristics, other bits control other functions. Bit 8 controls the console Break key. Setting bit 8 (the factory default) causes the processor to ignore the console Break key. Clearing bit 8 causes the processor to interpret the Break key as a command to force the system into the ROM monitor, thereby halting normal operation. A break issued in the first 60 seconds while the system reboots will affect the router, regardless of the configuration settings. After the initial 60 seconds, a break will work only if bit 8 is set to 0.

Bit 10 controls the host portion of the Internet broadcast address. Setting bit 10 causes the processor to use all 0s; clearing bit 10 (the factory default) causes the processor to use all 1s. Bit 10 interacts with bit 14, which controls the network and subnet portions of the broadcast address. Table D-4 shows the combined effect of bits 10 and 14.

Table D-4   *Configuration Register Settings for IP Broadcast Address Destination*

Bit 14	Bit 10	Address (\<net\> \<host\>)
Off	Off	\<1s\> \<1s\>
Off	On	\<0s\> \<0s\>
On	On	\<net\> \<0s\>
On	Off	\<net\> \<1s\>

Bits 5, 11, and 12 in the configuration register determine the baud rate of the console terminal.

Table D-5 shows the bit settings for the four available baud rates. (The factory-set default baud rate is 9600.)

Table D-5   *System Console Terminal Baud Rate Settings*

Baud	Bit 12	Bit 11
9600	0	0
4800	0	1
1200	1	0
2400	1	1

Bit 13 determines the router response to a bootload failure. Setting bit 13 causes the router to load operating software from ROM after five unsuccessful attempts to load a boot file from the network. Clearing bit 13 causes the router to continue attempting to load a boot file from the network indefinitely. By factory default, bit 13 is set to 1.

Enabling Booting from Flash Memory

To enable booting from Flash memory, set configuration register bits 3, 2, 1, and 0 to a value between 2 and F in conjunction with the **boot system flash** [*filename*] configuration command. The actual value of 2 to F is not really relevant here. It serves only to tell the router not to boot from its ROM IOS image.

While in the system IOS software image, enter the **configure terminal** command at the privileged-level system prompt and specify a Flash filename to boot from. This is shown in Example D-2.

Example D-2 *Specifying a Flash Filename*

```
router# configure terminal
Enter configuration commands, one per line.
Edit with DELETE, CTRL/W, and CTRL/U; end with CTRL/Z
Router(config)#boot system flash [filename]
```

To disable break and enable the router to boot from Flash, enter the **config-register** command with the value shown in Example D-3.

Example D-3 *Setting the Default Configuration Register*

```
router# configure terminal
Enter configuration commands, one per line.
Edit with DELETE, CTRL/W, and CTRL/U; end with CTRL/Z
Router(config)#config-reg 0x2102
^Z
router#
```

The Password Recovery Process

Password recovery allows you to regain administrative control of your device if you have lost or forgotten the password. The basic premise is simple. You need to get access to your router without the password taking effect. Then, you need to restore the configuration and reset the password to a known value. Two password recovery procedures (discussed in the following sections) involve the following basic steps:

Step 1 Configure the router to boot up without reading the configuration memory (NVRAM). This is sometimes called the test system mode.

Step 2 Reboot the system.

Step 3   Access enable mode (which can be done without a password if you are in test system mode).

Step 4   View or change the password, or erase the configuration.

Step 5   Reconfigure the router to boot up and read the configuration in NVRAM as it normally does.

Step 6   Reboot the system.

NOTE   Some password recovery requires that a console terminal issue a Break signal, so you must be familiar with how your terminal or PC terminal emulator issues this signal. For example, ProComm uses the keys **Alt-b** by default to generate the Break signal. Windows HyperTerminal requires that you press **Ctrl-Break**.

Password Recovery Procedure 1

You use the first password recovery method to recover lost passwords on the following Cisco routers:

- Cisco 2000 series.
- Cisco 2500 series.
- Cisco 3000 series.
- Cisco 4000 series with 680x0 Motorola CPU.
- Cisco 7000 series running Cisco IOS Release 10.0 or later in ROMs installed on the RP card. The router can be booting Cisco IOS Release 10.0 software in Flash memory, but it needs the actual ROMs on the processor card too.
- IGS series running Cisco IOS Release 9.1 or later in ROMs.

To recover an enable password using Procedure 1, follow these steps:

Step 1   Attach a terminal or PC with terminal emulation software to the router's console port.

The configuration register value is on the last line of the display. Note whether the configuration register is set to enable Break or disable Break.

The factory-default configuration register value is 0x2102. Notice that the third digit from the right in this value is odd, which disables Break. If the third digit is not odd, Break is enabled.

Step 2   Turn off the router, and then turn it on.

Step 3   Press the Break key on the terminal within 60 seconds of turning on the router.

The > prompt with no router name appears. If the prompt does not appear, the terminal is not sending the correct Break signal. In that case, check the terminal or terminal emulation setup. To view the current configuration register, you can type in the value **e/s 2000002**.

Note	The number that references the location of the configuration register can change from platform to platform. Check your specific product documentation for the exact number to be used.

Step 4   Enter **o/r 0x2142** at the > prompt to boot from Flash memory or **o/r 0x2141** to boot from the boot ROMs.

Note	The first character is the letter o, not the numeral zero. If you have Flash memory and it is intact, 0x2142 is the best setting. Use 0x2141 only if Flash memory is erased or not installed.

Step 5   At the > prompt, enter the **initialize** command to initialize the router.

This causes the router to reboot but ignore its saved configuration. The system configuration display appears.

Note	If you normally use the **boot network** command, or if you have multiple images in Flash memory and you boot a non-default image, the image in Flash might be different.

Step 6   Enter **no** in response to the System Configuration dialog prompts until the following message appears:

```
Press RETURN to get started!
```

Step 7   Press Return.

The **Router>** prompt appears.

Step 8   Enter the **enable** command.

The **Router#** prompt appears.

Step 9   Choose one of the following options:

To view the password, if it is not encrypted, enter the **show startup-config** command.

To change the password (if it is encrypted, for example), enter the following commands:

```
Router # copy startup-config running-config
Router # configure terminal
Router(config)# enable secret 1234abcd
```

Step 10 Because ignoring the NVRAM and choosing to abort setup would leave all interfaces in the shutdown state, it is important to enable all interfaces with the **no shutdown** command, as demonstrated here:

```
Router(config)#interface ethernet 0
Router(config-if)#no shutdown
```

Step 11 Save your new password with the following commands:

```
Router(config-if)# ctrl-z
Router # copy running-config startup-config
```

Note   The **enable secret** command provides increased security by storing the enable secret password using a nonreversible cryptographic function; however, you cannot recover a lost password that has been encrypted.

Step 12 Enter the **configure terminal** command at the EXEC prompt to enter configuration mode.

Step 13 Enter the **config-register** command and the original value you recorded in Step 1.

Step 14 Press **Ctrl-z** to quit the configuration editor.

Step 15 Enter the **reload** command at the privileged EXEC prompt.

Password Recovery Procedure 2

Use the second password recovery method to recover lost passwords on the following Cisco routers:

- Cisco 1003
- Cisco 1600 series
- Cisco 3600 series

- Cisco 4500 series
- Cisco 7200 series
- Cisco 7500 series
- IDT Orion-based routers
- AS5200 and AS5300 platforms

To recover a password using Procedure 2, follow these steps:

Step 1 Attach a terminal or PC with terminal emulation software to the router's console port.

The configuration register value is on the last line of the display. Note whether the configuration register is set to enable Break or disable Break.

The factory-default configuration register value is 0x2102. Notice that the third digit from the left in this value is odd, which disables Break. If the third digit is not odd, Break is enabled.

Step 2 Turn off the router, and then turn it on.

Step 3 Press the Break key on the terminal within 60 seconds of turning on the router.

The **rommon>** prompt appears. If it does not appear, the terminal is not sending the correct Break signal. In that case, check the terminal or terminal emulation setup.

Step 4 Enter the **confreg** command at the **rommon>** prompt. Record the current value of the virtual configuration register as it is output from this command.

The following prompt appears:

```
Do you wish to change configuration[y/n]?
```

Step 5 Enter **yes** and press Return.

Step 6 Accept the defaults for subsequent questions until the following prompt appears:

```
ignore system config info[y/n]?
```

Step 7 Enter **yes**.

Step 8 Enter **no** to subsequent questions until the following prompt appears:

```
change boot characteristics[y/n]?
```

Step 9   Enter **yes**.

The following prompt appears:

```
enter to boot:
```

Step 10   At this prompt, enter **2** and press Return if booting from Flash memory. Or, if Flash memory is erased, enter **1**.

A configuration summary is displayed, and the following prompt appears:

```
Do you wish to change configuration[y/n]?
```

Step 11   Answer **no** and press Return.

The following prompt appears:

```
rommon>
```

Step 12   Enter the **reset** command at the privileged **rommon>** prompt, or power cycle the router.

Step 13   As the router boots, enter **no** to all the setup questions until the following prompt appears:

```
Router>
```

Step 14   Enter the **enable** command to enter enable mode.

The **Router#** prompt appears.

Step 15   Choose one of the following options:

To view the password, if it is not encrypted, enter the **show startup-config** command.

To change the password (if it is encrypted, for example), enter the following commands:

```
Router # copy startup-config running-config
Router # configure terminal
Router(config)# enable secret 1234abcd
```

Step 16   Because ignoring the NVRAM and choosing to abort setup would leave all interfaces in the shutdown state, it is important to enable all interfaces with the **no shutdown** command, as demonstrated here:

```
Router(config)#interface ethernet 0
Router(config-if)#no shutdown
```

Step 17   Save your new password with the following commands:

```
Router(config-if)# ctrl-z
Router # copy running-config startup-config
```

Note	The **enable secret** command provides increased security by storing the enable secret password using a nonreversible cryptographic function; however, you cannot recover a lost password that has been encrypted.

Step 18 Enter the **configure terminal** command at the prompt.

Step 19 Enter the **config-register** command and the original value you recorded in Step 1.

Step 20 Press **Ctrl-Z** to quit the configuration editor.

Step 21 Enter the **reload** command at the prompt.

Answers to Review Questions

Answers to Chapter 1 Review Questions

1 Which three functions are defined by the Cisco hierarchical model?

Answer: Core, distribution, and access

2 What is one advantage of the OSI reference model?

Answer: Any of the following:

— It allows for breaking down the complex operation of networking into simpler elements.

— It lets engineers specialize design and development efforts on modular functions.

— It provides the capability to define standard interfaces for "plug-and-play" compatibility and multivendor integration.

3 Describe the data encapsulation process.

Answer: Data is passed down a protocol stack. At each layer, a header is added, and the data with the header is passed down as data to the next-lower layer until it reaches the physical layer. At this point, it is converted into bits and transmitted across the wire.

4 Define a collision domain, and give an example of a device that combines all devices in a single collision domain.

Answer: A collision domain is a group of devices residing on the same physical media. It can send signals onto the media, and these signals can collide. A hub interconnects all devices into a single collision domain.

5 Define a broadcast domain, and give an example of a device that separates each segment into different broadcast domains and provides connectivity between the segments.

Answer: A broadcast domain is a group of devices that reside in a network and that all receive each others' broadcasts. A router separates each connected segment into distinct broadcast domains and provides connectivity between the segments.

6 At which layer of the OSI model does a bridge or switch operate?

Answer: Layer 2

7 How many broadcast domains are associated with a bridge or switch (assuming no VLANs)?

Answer: One. All segments connected to a switch or bridge are in the same broadcast domain.

8 Which OSI layer defines an address that consists of a network portion and a node portion?

Answer: Layer 3 addresses have a logical network portion as well as a node identifier.

9 Which OSI layer defines a flat address space?

Answer: Layer 2 addresses are flat in nature.

10 Which process establishes a connection between two end stations using a reliable TCP/IP transport layer protocol?

Answer: The three-way handshake

Answers to Chapter 2 Review Questions

1 What are the three Ethernet bandwidths?

Answer: 10 Mbps, 100 Mpbs, and 1000 Mpbs (Gigabit)

2 Which category of cable can be used for 10 Mbps and 100 Mbps Ethernet?

Answer: Category 5 Twisted Pair

3 What type of connection cable has a pinout that is identical on both ends when compared to one another?

Answer: A straight-through cable

4 Name one instance when you would use a crossover cable.

Answer: When connecting two devices with the same connection type (for example, router to router, switch to switch, hub to hub, workstation to workstation, or workstation to router).

5 Name three types of serial connectors.

Answer: (Any three) V.35, EIA/TIA-232, EIA/TIA-449, X.21, EIA-530

6 Which type of ISDN connector has an integrated NT1?

Answer: A U interface has an integrated NT1.

7 What type of cable is needed to connect to a console port?

Answer: A rollover cable

Answers to Chapter 3 Review Questions

1 What is the name of the hardware test that a switch and router runs during power up?

Answer: The POST (power-on self test)

2 What are the two default EXEC modes?

Answer: User EXEC and privileged EXEC

3 What command displays the commands in a given mode of the switch or router?

Answer: **help** or the question mark (**?**)

4 What is the command history, and how do you navigate it?

Answer: The command history is a buffer of the last 10 commands (by default) that the user has typed during a given session in a given mode. These commands can be recalled by using special keys (the up- and down-arrows or **Ctrl-u** or **Ctrl-n**) to ease the amount of typing the user must do.

5 What Ctrl key sequence moves to the beginning of a line?

Answer: If terminal editing is on (which it is by default), **Ctrl-a** moves to the beginning of a line.

6 When does a router enter setup mode automatically?

Answer: If a router does not detect any configuration file in NVRAM, it will automatically enter setup mode. It will also do this if it has been told to ignore the contents of NVRAM.

7 What mode would you use to perform advanced configuration functions not available in setup mode?

Answer: Configuring the terminal at the privileged EXEC command line enables dynamic configuration of the router, allowing access to all of the router functions.

8 Does the **bandwidth** statement affect the speed of a serial link? What is it used for?

Answer: No. The **bandwidth** statement is typically used to manipulate routing metrics.

9 How do you move back to global configuration mode from any of the specific configuration modes?

Answer: In order to move back one mode in the configuration editor, type the **exit** command.

10   What command displays the configuration file in NVRAM? When is this file used by the router?

Answer: **show startup-config** (or **show config** in Release 10.2 and earlier). The router uses this file during startup.

Answers to Chapter 4 Review Questions

1   What is the proprietary Layer 2 protocol used by all Cisco devices that provides information about those devices?

Answer: Cisco Discovery Protocol

2   What command allows you to disable CDP on a given interface?

Answer: **no cdp enable** at interface configuration mode

3   After you have discovered an IP address of a directly connected router, how could you connect to the device to manage it?

Answer: Cisco devices support the Telnet function for management purposes. It is possible to Telnet to a device in order to manage it.

4   How can you suspend an open Telnet session from a router?

Answer: The key sequence Ctrl-Shift-6 (Ctrl-^), followed by an x, suspends a Telnet session opened from the router.

5   Where is the configuration file used at startup stored in the router?

Answer: NVRAM (nonvolatile random-access memory)

6   What are the last 4 bits of the configuration register known as? And what do they do?

Answer: They are known as the boot field. They tell the microcode which mode to boot the device into.

7   What is the main purpose of Flash memory?

Answer: Flash is mainly used to store the operating system.

8   What command is used to save the current configuration to the one that will be used when the router is restarted?

Answer: **copy running-config startup-config** (or **write memory** for version 10.2 and below)

9   What command is used to save the current configuration file to a TFTP server?

Answer: **copy running-config tftp** (or **write network** for version 10.2 and earlier)

10   What commands in the startup configuration can change how the router boots?

Answer: **boot system** commands

Answers to Chapter 5 Review Questions

1 What function does the Spanning-Tree Protocol provide?

Answer: Spanning Tree prunes the bridge or switch topology to a loop-free environment by placing ports in blocking state so that there is only one path from a network to the root of Spanning Tree.

2 Which Spanning-Tree Protocol is supported by the Catalyst 1900 switch?

Answer: The Catalyst 1900 supports the IEEE 802.1d Spanning-Tree Protocol.

3 What are the different Spanning Tree port states?

Answer: Listening, learning, forwarding, blocking

4 Describe the difference between full-duplex and half-duplex operations.

Answer: Half-duplex Ethernet operation is a communications process that allows only one device to transmit at a time. This is the normal mode for Ethernet. Full-duplex Ethernet can be configured in a point-to-point Ethernet network (switch to server, switch to switch, and so on) in which there are only two devices. Full duplex allows for simultaneous communications between the devices, which doubles the effective bandwidth.

5 What is the default duplex setting on the Catalyst 1900 10 Mbps port and 100 Mbps port?

Answer: 10 Mbps: half-duplex

100 Mbps: Autoselecting duplex

6 What is the default switching mode on the Catalyst 1900?

Answer: Fragment-free

7 What is the Catalyst 1900 CLI command to assign the IP address 192.168.1.5 with a mask of 255.255.255.0 to the switch?

Answer: **ip address** 192.168.1.5 255.255.255.0

8 What is the IP address used for on the Catalyst switch?

Answer: Management. An IP address allows you to Telnet to the CLI, use the web-based management function, or use SNMP to configure and manage the switch.

9 Which type of MAC address does not age—permanent or dynamic?

Answer: Permanent. It must be removed manually.

10 What is the Dynamic 1900 CLI command to display the contents of the MAC address table?

Answer: **show mac-address-table**

Answers to Chapter 6 Review Questions

1 VLANs allow for the creation of what in switched networks?

Answer: VLANs allow for the creation of multiple broadcast domains in a switched network.

2 What are the two types of VLANs?

Answer: Static VLANs, configured and assigned by the user, and dynamic VLANs, which are assigned by end-device MAC address.

3 What type of port is capable of carrying all VLAN traffic?

Answer: A trunk port carries all VLAN traffic and is used to interconnect network devices in order to carry and communicate all VLAN packets.

4 What mechanism is used by switches to provide inter-switch communication between devices about which VLAN a packet originated from?

Answer: ISL frame tagging is used across trunk lines to communicate VLAN tagging for frames crossing from one switch to another.

5 What is the purpose of VTP?

Answer: VTP is used to allow consistent VLAN configuration across the switch fabric.

6 What is the default VTP mode for the Catalyst 1900?

Answer: Server mode

7 Assume that a Catalyst 1900 is being added to your network. The switch needs to learn VLANs from the other switches in the network. You are not sure of the current VTP configuration and are fearful that it might overwrite your current VLAN information. How could you prevent the switch from accidentally overwriting the VLANs in your VTP domain?

Answer: By placing the device in client mode before attaching it to the network, or by entering the command **delete vtp** to reset the revision number.

8 What is the maximum number of VLANs that can be active on a Catalyst 1900?

Answer: 64

9 List all the steps required to configure a VLAN on a Catalyst 1900 switch port.

Answer: Create the VTP management domain, create the VLAN, assign the port to a VLAN.

10 Which command would you use to view the Spanning Tree configuration for VLAN 9 on a Catalyst 1900 switch?

Answer: **show spantree 9**

Answers to Chapter 7 Review Questions

1 The TCP/IP protocol stack was developed as part of a project of which government agency?

Answer: DARPA (Defense Advanced Research Projects Agency)

2 What are the four layers of the TCP/IP protocol stack?

Answer: Application, Transport, Internet, Network Interface

3 Name two TCP/IP applications used by the Cisco router.

Answer: Any two: Telnet, TFTP, DNS, SNMP

4 Which transport layer protocol provides for reliable connection-oriented sessions with sequence and acknowledgment numbers?

Answer: TCP (Transmission Control Protocol)

5 What is the purpose of windowing?

Answer: Windowing provides a flow control mechanism that allows workstations to efficiently send data back and forth without overwhelming the receiver.

6 What Internet layer protocol provides administrative messaging between hosts?

Answer: ICMP (Internet Control Messaging Protocol)

7 How many bits are in an IP address?

Answer: 32

8 What class of address is the IP address of 203.133.1.34?

Answer: Class C, because 203 in binary would be 11001011. The 110 in the high-order bits defines a Class C network.

9 Which formula allows you to determine the number of host addresses available?

Answer: $2^N - 2$ (2 to the Nth power minus 2), where N is the number of bits in the host portion of the address.

10 What is the purpose of the subnet mask?

Answer: The subnet mask allows you to divide a given network into smaller networks, making more effective use of a given IP address space.

11 Which command allows you to set an IP address on a router interface?

Answer: **ip address** *ip-address subnet-mask*

12 Write the following mask in bitwise notation: 255.255.255.192

Answer: /26 (11111111.11111111.11111111.11000000—26 1s in a row)

13 Which command allows you to statically enter a host name for an IP host?

Answer: **ip host** *name* [*tcp-port-number*] *address*

14 Which subinterface command allows you to configure a "router on a stick"?

Answer: **encapsulation isl** *vlan#*

15 For the following, determine the address class, calculate the subnet of a given network address, and determine the broadcast address:

15.5.6.18 255.255.255.240

212.172.38.72 255.255.255.192

108.163.211.115 255.255.128.0

106.126.0.154 255.192.0.0

180.15.76.0 255.255.192.0

Answers:

	15	5	6	18
Address 15.5.6.18	0 0 0 0 1 1 1 1	0 0 0 0 0 1 0 1	0 0 0 0 0 1 1 0	0 0 0 1 0 0 1 0
	255	255	255	240
Subnet Mask 255.255.255.240	1 1 1 1 1 1 1 1	1 1 1 1 1 1 1 1	1 1 1 1 1 1 1 1	1 1 1 1 0 0 0 0
Network	0 0 0 0 1 1 1 1 15	0 0 0 0 0 1 0 1 5	0 0 0 0 0 1 1 0 6	0 0 0 1 0 0 0 0 16
Broadcast	0 0 0 0 1 1 1 1 15	0 0 0 0 0 1 0 1 5	0 0 0 0 0 1 1 0 6	0 0 0 1 1 1 1 1 31

	212	172	38	72
Address 212.172.38.72	1 1 0 1 0 1 0 0	1 0 1 0 1 1 0 0	0 0 1 0 0 1 1 0	0 1 0 0 1 0 0 0
Subnet Mask 255.255.255.192	255 1 1 1 1 1 1 1 1	255 1 1 1 1 1 1 1 1	255 1 1 1 1 1 1 1 1	192 1 1 0 0 0 0 0 0
Network	1 1 0 1 0 1 0 0 212	1 0 1 0 1 1 0 0 172	0 0 1 0 0 1 1 0 38	0 1 0 0 0 0 0 0 64
Broadcast	1 1 0 1 0 1 0 0 212	1 0 1 0 1 1 0 0 172	0 0 1 0 0 1 1 0 38	0 1 1 1 1 1 1 1 127

	108	163	211	115
Address 108.163.211.115	0 1 1 0 1 1 0 0	1 0 1 0 0 0 1 1	1 1 0 1 0 0 1 1	0 1 1 1 0 0 1 1
Subnet Mask 255.255.128.0	1 1 1 1 1 1 1 1	1 1 1 1 1 1 1 1	1 0 0 0 0 0 0 0	0 0 0 0 0 0 0 0
Network	0 1 0 0 0 0 0 0 108	1 0 1 0 0 0 1 1 163	1 0 0 0 0 0 0 0 128	0 0 0 0 0 0 0 0 0
Broadcast	1 1 0 1 0 1 0 0 108	1 0 1 0 1 1 0 0 163	1 1 1 1 1 1 1 1 255	1 1 1 1 1 1 1 1 255

	106	126	0	154
Address 106.126.0.154	0 1 1 0 1 0 1 0	0 1 1 1 1 1 1 0	0 0 0 0 0 0 0 0	1 0 0 1 1 0 1 1
Subnet Mask 255.255.192.0	1 1 1 1 1 1 1 1	1 1 0 0 0 0 0 0	0 0 0 0 0 0 0 0	0 0 0 0 0 0 0 0
Network	0 1 1 1 1 1 1 0 106	0 1 0 0 0 0 0 0 64	0 0 0 0 0 0 0 0 0	0 0 0 0 0 0 0 0 0
Broadcast	0 1 1 1 1 1 1 0 106	0 1 1 1 1 1 1 1 127	1 1 1 1 1 1 1 1 255	1 1 1 1 1 1 1 1 255

	180	15	75	0
Address 106.126.0.154	1 0 1 1 0 1 0 0	0 0 0 0 1 1 1 1	0 1 0 0 1 0 1 1	0 0 0 0 0 0 0 0
Subnet Mask 255.255.192.0	1 1 1 1 1 1 1 1	1 1 1 1 1 1 1 1	1 1 1 1 1 1 0 0	0 0 0 0 0 0 0 0
Network	1 0 1 1 0 1 0 0 180	0 0 0 0 1 1 1 1 15	0 1 0 0 1 0 0 0 72	0 0 0 0 0 0 0 0 0
Broadcast	1 0 1 1 0 1 0 0 180	0 0 0 0 1 1 1 1 15	0 1 0 0 1 0 1 1 75	1 1 1 1 1 1 1 1 255

Answers to Chapter 8 Review Questions

1 Which four things does a router need in order to route using a dynamic protocol?

Answer: Identify sources of routing information, discover routes, select routes, maintain routes

2 What are the two types of routes?

Answer: Static and dynamic

3 Which type of route is entered by an administrator based on his or her knowledge of the network environment?

Answer: A static route

4 When is a default route used by a router?

Answer: A default route is used for any packet destined for a network that is not in the router's routing table.

5 Give two examples of an Interior Gateway Protocol.

Answer: Any two: RIP, IGRP, OSPF, EIGRP, IS-IS

6 When faced with two routes from different protocols for the same network, what does a Cisco router use to determine which route to use?

Answer: Administrative distance

7 Which metric is used by RIP? IGRP?

Answer: RIP uses hop counts. IGRP uses a composite metric of bandwidth, delay, load, reliability, and MTU.

8 Name one method used to eliminate routing loops.

Answer: Any one: split horizon, poison reverse, defining a maximum, triggered updates, holddown timers

9 What happens to traffic destined for a network that is currently in a holddown state?

Answer: The router assumes that the network status is unchanged and forwards the packet.

10 What command is used to stop all debugging?

Answer: **no debug all** (also **undebug all**)

Answers to Chapter 9 Review Questions

1 Access lists applied as traffic filters help do what in a network?

Answer: Control network traffic.

2 Name one other use for an access list.

Answer: Any one: dial-on-demand routing, queuing, route filters, network address translations

3 In which direction can an access list be applied to an interface?

Answer: In or out

4 During the outbound filtering process, what must exist in the route table before the packet is checked against the filter?

Answer: A route to the destination

5 What is the number range for IP extended access lists?

Answer: 100 to 199

6 How many IP access lists can be applied to an interface in a given direction?

Answer: One access list, per protocol, per interface, per direction

7 Every access list acting as a packet filter must have at least one what?

Answer: One **permit** statement

8 What happens if a packet does not match any of the test conditions in an access list?

Answer: It is denied by the implicit deny any statement at the end of the access list.

9 In a wildcard mask, what value indicates to match a bit value?

Answer: 0

10 Instead of typing 0.0.0.0 255.255.255.255, what keyword can be used in an access list?

Answer: **any**

11 Which command is used to verify that a list was applied to an interface?

Answer: **show ip interface**

12 How do you remove an access list from an interface?

Answer: At the interface, type the command **no access-group** *access-list-number* {**in** | **out**}.

13 Which command allows you to view the access lists?

Answer: **show ip access-lists**

14 All access lists end with what?

Answer: An implicit "deny any" statement

Answers to Chapter 10 Review Questions

1 How many bits are in an IPX address?

Answer: 80 bits: 32 network, 48 node

2 What is used as the node portion of the address?

Answer: The MAC address of the interface. A serial port borrows a MAC address from a LAN interface.

3 Which command enables the IPX rip routing process in a Cisco router?

Answer: **ipx routing**

4 Where do IPX network numbers come from?

Answer: Network numbers are assigned by administrators when they install an IPX server.

5 How many Layer 2 encapsulation types exist for IPX Ethernet networks?

Answer: 4 (Novell-ether, SAP, ARPA, and SNAP)

6 What is Cisco's default encapsulation type for IPX interfaces?

Answer: novell-ether (Ethernet_802.3)

7 What is the default IPX encapsulation type for NetWare 3.12 and above?

Answer: Ethernet_802.2 (SAP)

8 What type of network number is used to identify the services of an IPX server?

Answer: Internal network number

9 How does an IPX client find a server?

Answer: GNS broadcast

10 What does a router build in order to advertise IPX services?

Answer: A SAP Information Table (SIT)

11 What is the access list number range for an extended IPX access list?

Answer: 900 to 999

12 What is the access list number range for an IPX SAP filter?

Answer: 1000 to 1099

13 Which command is used to verify the application of an access list to an interface?

Answer: **show ipx interface**

14 Which routing metric is used by IPX RIP?

Answer: Ticks and hops

15 How often does an IPX server send out SAP updates?

Answer: Every 60 seconds

Answers to Chapter 11 Review Questions

1 What are three connection types that can be used to connect routers over a WAN?

Answer: Leased lines, circuit-switched, and packet-switched

2 What is the default Layer 2 encapsulation type of Cisco serial interfaces?

Answer: Cisco HDLC

3 Which encapsulation option discussed in this chapter would you select if you were connecting a Cisco router to a non-Cisco router?

Answer: PPP

4 How do you enable PPP encapsulation?

Answer: With the **encapsulation ppp** interface configuration command

5 What are the two PPP authentication options?

Answer: PAP and CHAP

6 Name one other PPP option.

Answer: Any one: multilink, error correction, or compression

7 How do you set the password for CHAP and PAP?

Answer: With the **username** *name* **password** *password* command

8 If both PAP and CHAP are configured, which method is tried first?

Answer: The one that is listed first in the **ppp authentication** interface configuration command

9 Which authentication option sends the password in clear text?

Answer: PAP

10 Which command is used to check the encapsulation?

Answer: **show interface**

Answers to Chapter 12 Review Questions

1 What does ISDN stand for?

Answer: Integrated Services Digital Network

2 ISDN carries what type of user-traffic feeds?

Answer: Video, telex, data, and voice

3 The ISDN Q series protocol standards cover what issues?

Answer: Signaling and switching

4 The ISDN BRI consists of what services?

Answer: Two Bearer channels plus one Delta channel

5 TE2 refers to what type of ISDN equipment?

Answer: Terminal Endpoint 2 (TE2) designates a router as a device requiring a terminal adapter for its BRI signals. This is a nonnative ISDN device such as a router with a synchronous or asynchronous serial connection.

6 A U interface references what connection?

Answer: The connection between the NT1 and the ISDN network

7 In a location where the NT1 is furnished by the provider, what type of native ISDN reference point should be on the router?

Answer: An S/T BRI interface

8 Where do you obtain SPID numbers?

Answer: From the service provider

9 What three steps are required to configure DDR?

Answer: Define static routes, specify interesting traffic, configure dialer information

10 Which command specifies interesting traffic?

Answer: **dialer-list** *group-number* **protocol** *protocol-name*

11 How is this command linked to a dialer interface?

Answer: With the command **dialer-group** *group-number* on the interface

12 Which command could you use to display the current status of an ISDN interface?

Answer: **show isdn status**

Answers to Chapter 13 Review Questions

1 Frame Relay operates at which OSI layer?

Answer: Layer 2

2 Name at least one physical layer standard that can be used for Frame Relay connection.

Answer: Any of the following: EIA/TIA-232, EIA/TIA-449, V.35, X.21, EIA/TIA-530

3 Which component identifies the local logical connection between the router and the switch?

Answer: DLCI (Data-Link Connection Identifier)

4 Which method used by Frame Relay allows for the dynamic mapping of IP address to DLCI number?

Answer: Inverse ARP

5 Name the three LMI standards supported by Cisco Routers.

Answer: cisco, ansi (Annex D), and q933a (Annex A)

6 By default, how often do routers exchange LMI information with the switch?

Answer: Every 10 seconds

7 What is the default encapsulation type for Frame Relay on a Cisco router?

Answer: cisco

8 Which command is used to verify the LMI type?

Answer: **show interface** or **show frame-relay lmi**

9 What routing issue occurs with a Frame Relay network running multiple PVCs over a single interface?

Answer: Split horizon

10 What is the default subinterface type: point-to-point or multipoint?

Answer: There is no default. You must select a type when creating a subinterface.

Answers to Appendix A Review Questions

1 At what layer of the OSI reference model does the AppleTalk protocol operate?

Answer: Layer 3

2 How many bits are available for a complete AppleTalk address?

Answer: 24 bits (16 network, 8 node)

3 How do AppleTalk hosts normally get an address?

Answer: Through dynamic acquisition

4 Zones divide networks into communities of interest in order to control what?

Answer: Multicast traffic caused by service queries

5 Which command enables the AppleTalk routing process?

Answer: **appletalk routing**

6 Which command assigns a network to an AppleTalk interface?

Answer: **appletalk cable-range** *cable-range*

7 Which command allows you to view the zones known by the switch?

Answer: **show appletalk zone**

INDEX

Symbols

Numerics

A

D

G-H

O

P

T

VLANs
multiplexing on a single physical path,
186
VTP pruning, 192
traffic-share command, 286, 294
trailers, 12
translational bridging, 22
Transmission Control Protocol. *See* TCP
Transmission Control Protocol/Internet Protocol.
See TCP/IP
transparent bridging, 22
transparent mode (VTP), 189–190
transport layer (OSI reference model Layer 4),
28–30
triggered updates
pairing with holddown timers for route
maintenance, 271–274
route maintenance with, 270–271
troubleshooting
DDR over ISDN BRI, 406
Frame Relay connections, 424
routing loops
with maximum metric settings, 266–267
with route poisoning, 268–269
with split horizon, 267–268
trunk command, 196
trunking (VLANs), 183–184, 196–197

U

U reference point (ISDN networks), 393
UDP (User Datagram Protocol), 206
flow control, 213–214
header format, 208–209
port numbers, 209–211
unequal-cost load balancing (IGRP), 284–285
unshielded twisted pair, 47
upgrading Ethernet, 44
upload command, 466
URL prefixes (Cisco network devices), 135
user EXEC mode (IOS), 69–70, 89–90
user mode (router initialization), 84
User profile (700 series routers), 468
username command, 381, 384
usernames (routers), defining, 381
users, grouping in broadcast domains, 179

UTP (unshielded twisted pair), 47
LAN implementations, 47–52
wiring standards, 47–48

V

variance command, 294
VCs (virtual circuits), 413
design considerations, 427
IP addresses, mapping, 414
states, 416
virtual terminal lines. *See* vty
Visual Switch Manager, 194
vlan command, 197, 200
VLAN Trunking Protocol. *See* VTP
vlan-membership command, 198
VLANs (virtual LANs), 179
adding, 197
to bridged/switched networks, 189
assigning switch ports to, 198–199
benefits of, 179
broadcast domains, functionality of, 181
characteristics, 183
configuration
default requirements, 194
guidelines, 194
overwriting, 192
prerequisite steps, 194
defaults, 194
definition, 181
functionality of, 182
information
communicating with ISLs, 185–188
communicating with VTP, 188–193
forwarding, 183
inter-VLAN routing, 241–244
membership modes, 184–185
operation, 183–184
parameters
modifying, 198
verifying, 198
parameters in bridged/switched networks, 182
port switch assignments, 181
renaming, 198
switches
bridging/switching between, 183
port membership, 194

CCIE Professional Development

Cisco LAN Switching

Kennedy Clark, CCIE; Kevin Hamilton, CCIE

1-57870-094-9 • AVAILABLE NOW

This volume provides an in-depth analysis of Cisco LAN switching technologies, architectures, and deployments, including unique coverage of Catalyst network design essentials. Network designs and configuration examples are incorporated throughout to demonstrate the principles and enable easy translation of the material into practice in production networks.

Advanced IP Network Design

Alvaro Retana, CCIE; Don Slice, CCIE; and Russ White, CCIE

1-57870-097-3 • AVAILABLE NOW

Network engineers and managers can use these case studies, which highlight various network design goals, to explore issues including protocol choice, network stability, and growth. This book also includes theoretical discussion on advanced design topics.

Large-Scale IP Network Solutions

Khalid Raza, CCIE; and Mark Turner

1-57870-084-1 • AVAILABLE NOW

Network engineers can find solutions as their IP networks grow in size and complexity. Examine all the major IP protocols in-depth and learn about scalability, migration planning, network management, and security for large-scale networks.

Routing TCP/IP, Volume II

Jeff Doyle, CCIE

1-57870-089-2 • AVAILABLE NOW

Routing TCP/IP, Volume II, presents a detailed examination of exterior routing protocols (EGP and BGP) and advanced IP routing issues such as multicast routing, quality of service routing, IPv6, and router management. Readers will learn IP design and management techniques for implementing routing protocols efficiently. Network planning, design, implementation, operation, and optimization are stressed in each chapter. Cisco-specific configurations for each routing protocol are examined in detail. Plentiful review questions and configuration and troubleshooting exercises make this an excellent self-study tool for CCIE exam preparation.

Cisco Press
www.ciscopress.com

Cisco Press Solutions

Enhanced IP Services for Cisco Networks
Donald C. Lee, CCIE

1-57870-106-6 • AVAILABLE NOW

This is a guide to improving your network's capabilities by understanding the new enabling and advanced Cisco IOS services that build more scalable, intelligent, and secure networks. Learn the technical details necessary to deploy Quality of Service, VPN technologies, IPsec, the IOS firewall and IOS Intrusion Detection. These services will allow you to extend the network to new frontiers securely, protect your network from attacks, and increase the sophistication of network services.

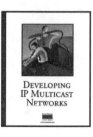

Developing IP Multicast Networks, Volume I
Beau Williamson, CCIE

1-57870-077-9 • AVAILABLE NOW

This book provides a solid foundation of IP multicast concepts and explains how to design and deploy the networks that will support appplications such as audio and video conferencing, distance-learning, and data replication. Includes an in-depth discussion of the PIM protocol used in Cisco routers and detailed coverage of the rules that control the creation and maintenance of Cisco mroute state entries.

OpenCable Architecture
Michael Adams

1-57870-135-X • AVAILABLE NOW

Whether you're a television, data communications, or telecommunications professional, or simply an interested business person, this book will help you understand the technical and business issues surrounding interactive television services. It will also provide you with an inside look at the combined efforts of the cable, data, and consumer electronics industries' efforts to develop those new services.

Designing Network Security
Merike Kaeo

1-57870-043-4 • AVAILABLE NOW

Designing Network Security is a practical guide designed to help you understand the fundamentals of securing your corporate infrastructure. This book takes a comprehensive look at underlying security technologies, the process of creating a security policy, and the practical requirements necessary to implement a corporate security policy.

Cisco Press

www.ciscopress.com

Cisco Press

ciscopress.com

Committed to being your long-term learning resource while you grow as a Cisco Networking Professional

Help Cisco Press **stay connected** to the issues and challenges you face on a daily basis by registering your product and filling out our brief survey. Complete and mail this form, or better yet ...

Register online and enter to win a **FREE** book!

Jump to **www.ciscopress.com/register** and register your product online. Each complete entry will be eligible for our monthly drawing to win a FREE book of the winner's choice from the Cisco Press library.

May we contact you via e-mail with information about **new releases, special promotions**, and **customer benefits**?

❐ Yes ❐ No

E-mail address _____

Name _____

Address _____

City _____ State/Province _____

Country _____ Zip/Post code _____

Where did you buy this product?

❐ Bookstore ❐ Computer store/Electronics store ❐ Direct from Cisco Systems
❐ Online retailer ❐ Direct from Cisco Press ❐ Office supply store
❐ Mail order ❐ Class/Seminar ❐ Discount store
❐ Other _____

When did you buy this product? _____ **Month** _____ **Year**

What price did you pay for this product?

❐ Full retail price ❐ Discounted price ❐ Gift

Was this purchase reimbursed as a company expense?

❐ Yes ❐ No

How did you learn about this product?

❐ Friend ❐ Store personnel ❐ In-store ad ❐ cisco.com
❐ Cisco Press catalog ❐ Postcard in the mail ❐ Saw it on the shelf ❐ ciscopress.com
❐ Other catalog ❐ Magazine ad ❐ Article or review
❐ School ❐ Professional organization ❐ Used other products
❐ Other _____

What will this product be used for?

❐ Business use ❐ School/Education
❐ Certification training ❐ Professional development/Career growth
❐ Other _____

How many years have you been employed in a computer-related industry?

❐ less than 2 years ❐ 2–5 years ❐ more than 5 years

Have you purchased a Cisco Press product before?

❐ Yes ❐ No

Cisco Press

c i s c o p r e s s . c o m

How many computer technology books do you own?
❏ 1 ❏ 2–7 ❏ more than 7

Which best describes your job function? (check all that apply)
❏ Corporate Management ❏ Systems Engineering ❏ IS Management ❏ Cisco Networking
❏ Network Design ❏ Network Support ❏ Webmaster Academy Program
❏ Marketing/Sales ❏ Consultant ❏ Student Instuctor
❏ Professor/Teacher ❏ Other _____

Do you hold any computer certifications? (check all that apply)
❏ MCSE ❏ CCNA ❏ CCDA
❏ CCNP ❏ CCDP ❏ CCIE ❏ Other _____

Are you currently pursuing a certification? (check all that apply)
❏ MCSE ❏ CCNA ❏ CCDA
❏ CCNP ❏ CCDP ❏ CCIE ❏ Other _____

On what topics would you like to see more coverage?

_____
_____

Do you have any additional comments or suggestions?

_____
_____

Thank you for completing this survey and registration. Please fold here, seal, and mail to Cisco Press.

Interconnecting Cisco Network Devices (1-57870-111-2)

Indianapolis, IN 46278-8046
P.O. Box #781046
Customer Registration—CP050227
Cisco Press

ciscopress.com
Indianapolis, IN 46290
201 West 103rd Street
Cisco Press

Place
Stamp
Here